Changing Course in Latin America
Party Systems in the Neoliberal Era

This book adopts a critical juncture framework to explain the impact of economic crises and free-market reforms on party systems and political representation in contemporary Latin America. It explains why some patterns of market reform align and stabilize party systems, whereas other patterns of reform leave party systems vulnerable to widespread social protest and electoral instability. In contrast to other works on the topic, this book accounts for both the institutionalization and the break-down of party systems, and it explains why Latin America turned to the Left politically in the aftermath of the market reform process. Ultimately, it explains why this "left turn" was more radical in some countries than in others and why it had such varied effects on national party systems.

Kenneth M. Roberts is Professor of Government at Cornell University. He is the author of *Deepening Democracy? The Modern Left and Social Movements in Chile and Peru* (1998). Roberts is the co-editor of *The Diffusion of Social Movements: Actors, Mechanisms, and Political Effects* (Cambridge, 2010) and *The Resurgence of the Latin American Left* (2011). His articles have appeared in the *American Political Science Review*, *World Politics*, *Comparative Political Studies*, *Comparative Politics*, *Latin American Politics and Society*, and *Studies in Comparative International Development*.

Cambridge Studies in Comparative Politics

General Editor

MARGARET LEVI University of Washington, Seattle

Assistant General Editors

KATHLEEN THELEN Massachusetts Institute of Technology
ERIK WIBBELS Duke University

Associate Editors

ROBERT H. BATES Harvard University
GARY COX Stanford University
STEPHEN HANSON The College of William and Mary
TORBEN IVERSEN Harvard University
STATHIS KALYVAS Yale University
PETER LANGE Duke University
HELEN MILNER Princeton University
FRANCES ROSENBLUTH Yale University
SUSAN STOKES Yale University
SIDNEY TARROW Cornell University

(*Continued after the Index*)

Changing Course in Latin America

Party Systems in the Neoliberal Era

KENNETH M. ROBERTS
Cornell University

CAMBRIDGE
UNIVERSITY PRESS

CAMBRIDGE
UNIVERSITY PRESS

32 Avenue of the Americas, New York, NY 10013-2473, USA

Cambridge University Press is part of the University of Cambridge.

It furthers the University's mission by disseminating knowledge in the pursuit of education, learning, and research at the highest international levels of excellence.

www.cambridge.org
Information on this title: www.cambridge.org/9780521673266

First published 2014

Printed in the United States of America

A catalog record for this publication is available from the British Library.

Library of Congress Cataloging in Publication Data
Roberts, Kenneth M., 1958–
Changing course in Latin America : party systems in the neoliberal era / Kenneth M. Roberts, Cornell University.
 pages cm
ISBN 978-0-521-85687-4 (hardback)
1. Political parties – Latin America. 2. Latin America – Politics and government – 21st century. 3. Political stability – Latin America. 4. Neoliberalism – Latin America. I. Title.
JL969.A45R628 2014
324.2098–dc23 2014011960

ISBN 978-0-521-85687-4 Hardback
ISBN 978-0-521-67326-6 Paperback

With gratitude to Guillermo O'Donnell,
whose scholarship defined my field of study

The crisis consists precisely in the fact that the old is dying and the new cannot be born; in the interregnum a great variety of morbid symptoms appears.

Antonio Gramsci, *Prison Notebooks*

Contents

Figures

Tables

Preface and Acknowledgments

This book began as a relatively straightforward attempt to understand why some party systems are more stable than others in Latin America, but it quickly evolved into a larger and more ambitious effort to identify the impact of economic crises and market reforms on democratic representation. Ultimately, it sought to explain how and why a transition from one economic era to another was also a major turning point in Latin America's political development. I began, perhaps naively, to conceive of that economic transition as a critical juncture in political development long before I was able to identify the full range of its institutional effects, much less its longer-term political legacies. To put it in Gramsci's more eloquent terms from the epigraph, I began this project in a moment of crisis in Latin America, an interregnum "when the old was dying and the new could not be born," and a great variety of "morbid" (and often fleeting) symptoms appeared. Enough time has now passed for me to hazard a claim that new political orders *were* born during this watershed period, even if some of them veered off in unexpected directions or remain institutionally fluid (as the reader will quickly discover). The purpose of this book is to trace where these new orders came from, explain why some are more stable than others, and identify what makes them different, both from each other and from the political orders that preceded them.

Any research project this long in the making is bound to incur debts to individuals and institutions that are too numerous to mention. That is surely the case with this book. Although I cannot acknowledge everyone who deserves to be thanked, I want to at least recognize a number of individuals who made especially vital contributions. From the outset of this project, Ruth Berins Collier and David Collier provided intellectual inspiration and constructive feedback. They have been remarkably generous in supporting my efforts to build upon the intellectual foundation they laid in their study of earlier critical junctures in Latin America. I also learned a great deal from intensive workshops centered on earlier drafts of my book that were organized by Erik Wibbels and Margaret Levi at the University of Washington, Jorge Lanzaro at the Universidad de la República in Uruguay, and Juan Pablo Luna at the Universidad Católica in Chile.

Jonathan Hartlyn was instrumental in pushing me to broaden my horizons by including elitist party systems in the study, while William Smith convinced me to think more dialectically about the social response to market liberalization. A grilling by Erik Wibbels, Herbert Kitschelt, and Fabrice Lehoucq during a presentation at Chapel Hill forced me to rethink the causal mechanisms embedded in the critical juncture argument, as did critical input from Vicky Murillo and Christopher Way. Steve Levitsky, Scott Mainwaring, Beatriz Magaloni, Kurt Weyland, Evelyne Huber, Wendy Hunter, Eduardo Silva, Raúl Madrid, Susan Stokes, Deborah Yashar, Richard Snyder, Noam Lupu, Karen Remmer, Carlos de la Torre, Benjamin Goldfrank, Margarita López-Maya, Steve Fish, Pierre Ostiguy, Cristóbal Rovira Kaltwasser, Anthony Pezzola, Mark Peceny, and William Stanley have all read and commented on portions of the manuscript or provided critical feedback along the way. Many of my colleagues at Cornell – including Sidney Tarrow, Ronald Herring, Valerie Bunce, Peter Katzenstein, Nic van de Walle, Gustavo Flores-Macías, Peter Enns, and Bryce Corrigan – have also shaped my thinking on this topic or provided other helpful assistance. Simon Velásquez, Don Leonard, Emma Banks, Joanna Barrett, Emma Lalley, and Natalia Cornell-Roberts offered valuable research assistance. I'm especially grateful for financial and research support from the National Science Foundation and Cornell's Institute for the Social Sciences. Finally, one could hardly ask for a more supportive editor than Lew Bateman at Cambridge, who patiently waited through several rewritings of this manuscript as the project evolved (and expanded). Some material in this book has appeared in earlier articles that I wrote, and I thank the publishers of the following articles for giving me permission to re-use material: "Social Inequalities without Class Cleavages in Latin America's Neoliberal Era," *Studies in Comparative International Development* 36, 4 (2002); "Michels and the Sociological Study of Party Organization: A Latin American Perspective," *Annali della Fondazione Liugi Einaudi* XLVI 2012 (Firenze, Italy: Leo S. Olschki Editore); "Market Reform, Programmatic (De) alignment, and Party System Stability in Latin America," *Comparative Political Studies* 46, 11 (2013); and "The Politics of Inequality and Redistribution in Latin America's Post-adjustment Era," in Giovanni Andrea Correa, ed. *Falling Inequality in Latin America: Policy Changes and Lessons* (Oxford: Oxford University Press, 2014).

My wife, Angela, and my children – Tasha, Allie, and Tristan – have had to live with this project much longer than they deserved. For their patience, good humor, and insistence that I balance work with play, I am eternally grateful.

Abbreviations

AD	Acción Democrática (Democratic Action)
ADN	Acción Democrática Nacionalista (National Democratic Action)
AL	Alianza Liberal Nicaragüense (Nicaraguan Liberal Alliance)
ALBA	Alianza Bolivariana para los Pueblos de Nuestra América (Bolivarian Alliance for the Americas)
Alianza PAIS	Alianza Patría Altiva i Soberana (Proud and Sovereign Fatherland Alliance)
ANR-PC	Asociación Nacional Republicana – Partido Colorado (National Republican Association – Colorado Party)
AP	Acción Popular (Popular Action)
APRA	Alianza Popular Revoluncionaria Americana – Partido Aprista Peruano (American Popular Revolutionary Alliance – Peruvian Aprista Party)
AR	Acción por la República (Action for the Republic)
ARENA	Aliança Renovador Nacional (National Renovating Alliance) (Brazil)
ARI	Alternativa por una República de Iguales (Alternative for a Republic of Equals)
BA	Bureaucratic-authoritarian
C90/NM	Cambio 90/Nueva Mayoria (Change 90/New Majority)
CAFTA	Central America Free Trade Agreement
CC	Coalición Cívica (Civic Coalition)
CFP	Concentración de Fuerzas Populares (Concentration of Popular Forces)
CGT	Confederación General del Trabajo (General Confederation of Labor)
CGTP	Confederación General de Trabajadores del Perú (General Confederation of Workers of Peru)

CN	Convergencia Nacional (National Convergence)
CNT	Convención Nacional de Trabajadores (National Convention of Workers)
CONAIE	Confederación de Nacionalidades Indígenas del Ecuador (Confederation of Indigenous Nationalities of Ecuador)
CONDEPA	Concencia de Patria (Conscience of the Fatherland)
COPEI	Comité de Organización Política Electoral Independiente (Political Electoral Independent Organization Committee)
CREO	Creando Oportunidades (Creating Opportunities)
CTA	Central de los Trabajadores Argentinos (Argentine Workers Central)
CTP	Confederación de Trabajadores Peruanos (Confederation of Peruvian Workers)
CTV	Confederación de Trabajadores de Venevuela (Confederation of Venezuelan Workers)
CUT	Central Única dos Trabalhadores (Unified Workers Central)
DP-UDC	Democracia Popular – Unión Demócrata Cristiana (People's Democracy – Christian Democratic Union)
FA	Frente Amplio (Broad Front)
FMLN	Frente Farabundo Martí para la Liberación Nacional (Farabundo Martí National Liberation Front)
FNRP	Frente Nacional de Resistencia Popular (National Front of Popular Resistance)
FPV	Frente para la Victoria (Front for Victory)
FREDEMO	Frente Democrático (Democratic Front)
FREPASO	Frente para un País Solidario (Front for a Country in Solidarity)
FSLN	Frente Sandinista de Liberación Nacional (Sandinista National Liberation Front)
ID	Izquierda Democrática (Democratic Left)
IMF	International Monetary Fund
ISI	Import-substitution industrialization
IU	Izquierda Unida (United Left)
LIBRE	Libertad y Refundación (Liberty and Refoundation)
LM	Labor-mobilizing
MAS	Movimiento al Socialismo (Movement toward Socialism – Bolivia and Venezuela)
MDB	Movimento Democrático Brasileiro (Brazilian Democratic Movement)
MERCOSUR	Mercado Común del Sur (Common Market of the South)
MIR	Movimiento de la Izquierda Revolucionaria (Movement of the Revolutionary Left)
MNR	Movimiento Nacionalista Revolucionario (Revolutionary Nationalist Movement)

MORENA	Movimiento de Renovación Nacional (National Renewal Movement)
MUPP-NP	Movimiento Unidad Plurinacional Pachakutik – Nuevo País (Pachakutik Plurinational Unity Movement – New Country)
MVR	Movimiento de la Quinta República (Movement of the Fifth Republic)
PAC	Partido Anticorrupción (Anti-Corruption Party) (Honduras)
PAC	Partido Acción Ciudadana (Citizen Action Party) (Costa Rica)
PALA	Partido Laborista Agrario (Labor and Agrarian Party)
PAN	Partido Acción Nacional (National Action Party)
PC	Partido Colorado (Colorado Party)
PCB	Partido Comunista Brasileiro (Brazilian Communist Party)
PCDN	Partido Conservador Demócrata (Democratic Conservative Party)
PCP	Partido Comunista Peruano (Peruvian Communist Party)
PCV	Partido Comunista de Venezuela (Communist Party of Venezuela)
PDC	Partido Demócrata Cristiano (Christian Democratic Party)
PDS/PPB	Partido Democrático Social/Partido Progressista Brasileiro (Democratic Social Party/Brazilian Progressive Party)
PDT	Partido Democrático Trabalhista (Democratic Labor Party)
PFL	Partido da Frente Liberal (Liberal Front Party)
PINU-SD	Partido Innovación Nacional y Social Demócrata (Innovation and Unity Party – social democratic)
PJ	Partido Justicialista (Justicialist Party – Argentina)
PJ	Primero Justicia (Justice First – Venezuela)
PL	Partido Laboral (Labor Party)
PL(C)	Partido Liberal Colombiano (Colombian Liberal Party)
PLD	Partido de la Liberación Dominicana (Dominican Liberation Party)
PLH	Partido Liberal de Honduras (Liberal Party of Honduras)
PLN	Partido Liberación Nacional (National Liberation Party)
PLRA	Partido Liberal Radical Auténtico (Authentic Radical Liberal Party)
PLRE	Partido Liberal Radical Ecuatoriano (Ecuadorian Radical Liberal Party)
PMDB	Partido do Movimento Democrático Brasileiro (Party of the Brazilian Democratic Movement)
PNH	Partido Nacional de Honduras (National Party of Honduras)
PN(U)	Partido Nacional de Uruguay (National Party of Uruguay)
PP	Perú Posible (Possible Peru)
PPA	Partido Panameñista Auténtico (Authentic Panameñista Party)
PPB	Partido Progressista Brasileiro (Brazilian Progressive Party)
PPC	Partido Popular Cristiano (Popular Christian Party)

PPD	Partido por la Democracia (Party for Democracy)
PPR	Partido Progressista Reformador (Reformist Progressive Party)
PR/PRSC	Partido Reformista Social Cristiano (Social Christian Reformist Party)
PRD	Partido Revoluncionario Dominicano (Dominican Revolutionary Party)
PRD	Partido de la Revolución Democrática (Party of the Democratic Revolution – Mexico)
PRE	Partido Roldosista Ecuatoriano (Ecuadorian Roldosist Party)
PRI	Partido Revolucionario Institucional (Institutional Revolutionary Party)
PRIAN	Partido Renovador Institucional de Acción Nacional (Institutional Renewal Party of National Action)
PRN	Partido Renovacão Nacional (National Reconstruction Party)
PRO	Propuesta Republicana (Republican Proposal)
PRSD	Partido Radical Socialdemócrata (Radical Social Democratic Party)
PSC	Partido Social Conservador (Social Conservative Party)
PSC	Partido Social Cristiano (Social Christian Party)
PSCh	Partido Socialista de Chile (Socialist Party of Chile)
PSD	Partido Social Democrático (Social Democratic Party)
PSDB	Partido da Social Democracia Brasileira (Brazilian Social Democracy Party)
PSP	Partido Sociedad Patriótica 21 de Enero (21st of January Patriotic Society Party)
PSUV	Partido Socialista Unida de Venezuela (United Socialist Party of Venezuela)
PT	Partido dos Trabalhadores (Workers' Party)
PTB	Partido Trabalhista Brasileiro (Brazilian Labour Party)
PU/PUSC	Partido de Unidad Social Cristiana (Social Christian Unity Party)
PUD	Partido Unificación Democrática (Democratic Unification Party)
PUM	Partido Unificado Mariateguista (Unified Mariateguista Party)
PV	Proyecto Venezuela (Project Venezuela)
RN	Renovación Nacional (National Renewal)
SP	Somos Perú (We Are Peru)
UceDé	Unión del Centro Democrático (Union of the Democratic Center)
UCR	Unión Cívica Radical (Radical Civic Union)
UCS	Unidad Cívica Solidaridad (Civic Solidarity Union)
UDI	Unión Demócrata Independiente (Independent Democratic Union)
UDN	União Democrática Nacional (National Democratic Union)

UDP/MIR	Unidad Democrática y Popular/Movimiento de la Izquierda Revolucionaria (Democratic and Popular Union/Movement of the Revolutionary Left)
UN	Unidad Nacional (National Unity)
UNT	Un Nuevo Tiempo (A New Era)

Introduction: Party System Change in the Neoliberal Era

A political earthquake struck Venezuela when Hugo Chávez was elected president in December 1998. Chávez, a former lieutenant colonel in the Venezuelan army, launched his political career in 1992 by leading a bloody military revolt against a democratic regime that had long been considered among the most stable in Latin America. The coup attempt failed, landing Chávez in prison, but it catapulted the former paratrooper instructor into the public imagination as a symbol of rebellion against the political establishment and its mismanagement of the country's oil wealth. Following a presidential pardon, Chávez founded a new political movement and launched a populist campaign for the presidency in frontal opposition to traditional parties and the free-market reforms they had supported for most of the past decade. Although Venezuela boasted one of the strongest and most highly institutionalized party systems in Latin America (Coppedge 1994; Mainwaring and Scully 1995: 17), the two dominant parties ultimately withdrew their own presidential candidates and threw their support to a less threatening independent figure in a desperate gambit to defeat Chávez's "outsider" campaign. Nevertheless, Chávez won a landslide victory that not only signaled the eclipse of traditional parties, but a collapse of the collusive, patronage-ridden political order they had anchored since the founding of the democratic regime forty years before. Within a year, Chávez had bypassed congress and convoked a series of popular referendums to elect a constituent assembly, rewrite and ratify a new constitution, and refound regime institutions. For Venezuela, a new political era had dawned.

Several years later, neighboring Brazil also elected a new leftist president, former union leader Luiz Inácio "Lula" da Silva of the Workers' Party (PT). Like Chávez, Lula had a track record of opposition to the "neoliberal" market reforms that swept across Latin America in the waning decades of the 20th century, although he had moderated his stance considerably by the time he captured the presidency in 2002 (on his fourth bid for the office). Unlike Chávez, Lula represented a party that had become a pillar of Brazil's political establishment, despite its origins in a militant labor movement that spearheaded popular protests against Brazil's military dictatorship in the late 1970s (Keck 1992; Hunter 2010). Indeed, the progressive strengthening and "mainstreaming" of the PT was integral to a broader process of institutionalization of the Brazilian party system, which had long been notorious for its weakness and instability (Mainwaring 1999a). Following a tumultuous democratic transition in the mid-1980s and a traumatizing spiral of hyperinflation and economic adjustment that lasted through the mid-1990s, Brazil also appeared to have entered a new political era – unlike Venezuela, one that was characterized by relatively stable forms of electoral competition between established parties and a consolidation of the democratic regime itself.

If Venezuela provides a paradigmatic example of party system breakdown, Brazil illustrates a pattern of at least partial party system consolidation – the institutional endpoints, respectively, on the continuum that marks the divergent fates of party systems in contemporary Latin America. Since the beginning of the region's "third wave" of democratization in the late 1970s (Huntington 1991), party systems in much of the region have been plagued by turmoil, despite the surprising durability of most of the democratic regimes in which they are embedded (Mainwaring 1999b). In many countries traditional parties have collapsed, new parties have emerged and disappeared without leaving a trace, and volatile shifts in electoral support have become commonplace. Populist "outsiders" often appeal to voters by touting their independence from traditional parties and attacking discredited political establishments. In some cases, these leaders have turned their lack of political experience – their very status as political novices, amatuers, or outsiders – into an electoral asset. Not surprisingly, many observers fear that a "crisis of representation" plagues Latin American democracies, with political parties largely failing to perform their central democratic function of representing societal interests and preferences in the formal political arena (Domínguez 1997a; Di Tella 1998; Hagopian 1998; Mainwaring, Bejarano, and Pizarro 2006).

Party system fragility and instability are hardly uniform, however. Established party systems broke down in the1990s and early 2000s in Peru, Venezuela, Colombia, Bolivia, and Ecuador, but new ones began to congeal in Brazil and El Salvador, while complex realignments occurred around both new and traditional parties in countries like Chile, Costa Rica, Mexico, and Uruguay. Indeed, elections in Colombia, Uruguay, Paraguay, and Honduras continued to be dominated through the end of the 20th century by parties with roots in 19th-century intra-oligarchic disputes that predated the onset of mass democracy. Such patterns of longevity led Charles Anderson (1967: 104) to quip that some Latin American party systems resembled "living museums" filled with historical relics. Recently, however, even these party systems have experienced major realignments or upheavals.[1] Why, then, are some party systems more stable and resilient than others, and why do seemingly entrenched party systems sometimes become dislodged? Under what conditions do traditionally weak or inchoate party systems begin to congeal? And what explains such divergent patterns of party system change and continuity in countries that share so much in common?

If Venezuela and Brazil are emblematic of the divergent fate of party systems in Latin America, so also do they illustrate the very different types of leftist alternatives that came to power in the region at the turn of the century, following a wrenching period of economic crisis and free market reform in the 1980s and 1990s. With varying degrees of enthusiasm and success, Latin American governments embraced the pro-market policies of the "Washington Consensus" in response to the 1980s debt crisis and the ensuing hyperinflationary spirals that signaled the collapse of state-led development in the region (Williamson 1990). Under the tutelage (and pressure) of international financial institutions like the International Monetary Fund (IMF) and the World Bank, technocratic policy-makers opened national economies to foreign trade and investment, privatized state-owned industries and social services, removed price controls, and liberalized capital and labor markets (Edwards 1995). With labor unions in decline and the political Left reeling from the crisis and eventual collapse of communism, every country in the region moved toward freer markets in the late 1980s and 1990s (see Morley, Machado, and Pettinato 1999; Lora 2001). Even historic labor-based populist parties implemented these neoliberal "structural adjustment" policies (Burgess 2004; Burgess and Levitsky 2003; Murillo 2001), which helped bring inflation under control and deepen Latin America's integration within global circuits of finance, production, and exchange.

By the end of the 1990s, however, the political winds had begun to shift. With inflation largely tamed but liberalized economies suffering from the spillover effects of the Asian financial crisis, popular movements that politicized inequalities and market insecurities were revived in a number of countries, and a series of mass protests toppled pro-market governments in Ecuador, Argentina, and Bolivia (Silva 2009). Although Chávez' 1998 election was initially viewed as an outlier to regional norms – an anomaly conditioned, perhaps, by the pernicious effects of oil rents on Venezuela's political culture and institutions (Romero 1997) – it gradually became apparent that *Chavismo* was the leading edge of a political countertrend against market liberalization, and a harbinger of things to come. By 2011, left-leaning presidents had been elected in ten other Latin American countries, placing two-thirds of the regional population under some form of leftist national government (Weyland, Madrid, and Hunter 2010;

---

[1] The historic two-party systems in Colombia and Uruguay – both tracing their roots to the 1840s – were overtaken by new personalistic and leftist challengers, respectively, in the early years of the 21st century. New leftist rivals have also challenged the electoral dominance of traditional oligarchic parties in Paraguay and Honduras in recent years.

Levitsky and Roberts 2011b).[2] Even where the Left did not win national elections – as in Mexico, Colombia, Honduras, and Costa Rica – leftist alternatives emerged or strengthened in the early 2000s. Following two decades of market liberalization and the collapse of the Soviet bloc, this resurgence of leftist alternatives represented a stunning turn of political events. It was also unprecedented in its scope; never before had so many countries in Latin America entrusted the affairs of state to leftist parties or political movements.

The post-1998 turn to the left had multiple and varied causes, and it was inevitably shaped by national-level political strains, opportunities, and alignments. As Remmer (2012) demonstrates, the leftward shift was not a simple protest against economic hardships; although it began during the economic downturn at the turn of the century (Queirolo 2013),[3] it gathered steam as economic performance improved after 2003 in the region. Neither was the "left turn" a simple backlash against market liberalization, as voters had a range of motives in supporting the left and did not reject all aspects of the neoliberal model (Baker and Greene 2011). As such, most of the new leftist governments were careful to modify but not reverse the market reforms they inherited. Nevertheless, as a regional phenomenon the "left turn" was clearly rooted in diverse struggles to establish or restore social and political protections against the economic insecurities of what Polanyi (1944) called "market society." Central features of the neoliberal model remained intact in most countries, but by the end of the 1990s the era of market-based structural adjustment and orthodox, technocratic policy consensus had drawn to a close. With the momentum for deepening market liberalization broken, a new, post-adjustment political era dawned – one that was marked by a broader range of policy debate and by collective struggles to craft new forms of social citizenship that would reduce inequalities, provide safeguards against market insecurities, and expand popular participation in the democratic process.

These political struggles for more inclusive forms of social citizenship were shaped and constrained by the dynamics of partisan competition, and they left indelible marks on party systems and democratic regimes in Latin America. Indeed, the left turn produced strikingly divergent national governments, leaders, and ruling parties, as the Brazilian and Venezuelan cases readily suggest. In countries like Brazil, Chile, and Uruguay, societal claims were largely channeled by established parties of the left in ways that reinforced and aligned party systems along basic programmatic or policy divides. This pattern helped to stabilize party systems and moderate the political turn to the left at the beginning

---

[2] In addition to Venezuela, these countries included Chile (2000, 2006, and 2013), Brazil (2002, 2006, and 2010), Argentina (2003, 2007, and 2011), Uruguay (2004 and 2009), Bolivia (2005 and 2009), Nicaragua (2006 and 2011), Ecuador (2006, 2009, and 2013), Paraguay (2008), El Salvador (2009) and Peru (2011).

[3] Arguably, it began much earlier at the municipal level before spreading to national-level elections starting in 1998; see Chávez and Goldfrank (2004) and Goldfrank (2011).

of the 21st century – in essence, containing the left turn within established party systems and consolidated democratic regimes. In other countries, however, societal claims were mobilized outside and against established party systems, forcing traditional parties to share the political stage with new popular contenders – or to be eclipsed by them altogether. This latter pattern was found in Venezuela, Bolivia, and Ecuador, where new populist leaders or leftist movements mobilized popular majorities through plebiscitary means that allowed them to re-found regime institutions. This pattern broke down and transformed national party systems, and it created opportunities for a more radical, extra-systemic turn to the left that included sharper breaks with the market orthodoxy of previous rulers.

What explains such diverse political trajectories in Latin America's post-adjustment era? This book explores two primary, inter-related facets of the post-adjustment political landscape: the stability of partisan and electoral competition, and the character of the leftist alternative that emerged or strengthened in the aftermath to market liberalization. The analysis suggests that variation along these two dimensions – the dependent variables, so to speak, of this study – was heavily conditioned by political alignments during the crisis-induced transition from statist to market-oriented development models in the 1980s and 1990s. Far more than a shift in economic policies, this transition was a watershed in the political and economic development of Latin American societies. The transition wreaked havoc on labor-based modes of political representation that emerged under the statist model of development known as import substitution industrialization (ISI) in the middle of the 20th century. It also de-aligned, decomposed, or realigned national party systems in ways that heavily conditioned how societal claims against market insecurities would be channeled and processed in the post-adjustment era. As such, the transition period produced a range of political outcomes that varied widely in their durability and institutional legacies.

Divergent outcomes, I argue, were shaped by three basic causal factors or independent variables: (1) the character of national party systems during the era of state-led development; (2) the depth and duration of economic crises during the transition to neoliberalism; and (3) the political orientation of leading market reformers and their opponents in each country. This third factor largely determined whether structural adjustment would align or de-align party systems along a left–right axis of programmatic competition.

In general, party systems that had been reconfigured during the statist era by the rise of a mass-based, labor-mobilizing populist or leftist party were more prone to the destabilizing effects of social dislocations and economic crises during the transition to market liberalism. By contrast, countries that retained elitist patterns of partisan competition during the statist era experienced less severe economic crises and greater electoral stability during the transition period. Even where party systems survived the transition intact, however, they varied in their ability to channel and withstand societal pressures in the post-adjustment era. Indeed, the longer-term resiliency of party systems depended heavily on political alignments during the process of structural adjustment. Market reforms that were led by conservative, pro-business parties or leaders, and consistently opposed by a major party of the left, aligned party systems programmatically. Such reform alignments channeled societal dissent against market orthodoxy toward moderate and institutionalized parties of the left, stabilizing partisan competition in the post-adjustment era. Alternatively, reforms that were imposed by labor-based populist or center-left parties de-aligned party systems programmatically, leaving opponents of the reform process without effective representation in established institutions. Such opposition was thus channeled into anti-systemic forms of social and electoral protest that spawned new populist or leftist movements, with highly destabilizing consequences for party systems in the post-adjustment era. In short, the politics of market reform aligned and stabilized some party systems, while de-aligning and de-stabilizing others, ultimately producing very different leftist alternatives in the post-adjustment era.

This study seeks to explain how Latin America's transition to neoliberalism – a regional mode of adaptation to the pressures of market globalization – dislodged traditional party systems and placed the region on a new trajectory of political development with a number of forking paths. The causal processes that produced these forking paths are analyzed through a critical juncture framework that originated in the study of institutional economics and was then adapted for the analysis of path-dependent institutional change in political science (see in particular Collier and Collier 1991; Pierson 2000; Mahoney 2001a; Capoccia and Kelemen 2007). I employ this framework cautiously, as it is designed to explain patterns of institutional change and continuity with the advantage of considerable historical hindsight. Furthermore, the framework is most directly applicable to the analysis of political changes that originate in actor decisions and crystallize in self-reinforcing institutions. The political outcomes of neoliberal transitions in Latin America do not always provide these analytical signposts; they are recent in occurrence, only loosely structured by actor decisions, and sometimes fluid (for identifiable reasons) in their institutional forms.

Nevertheless, the critical juncture framework provides a set of conceptual and analytical tools with considerable leverage for explaining why similar types of political or economic challenges produce dissimilar outcomes across a range of cases. It is especially insightful for understanding how crises or exogenous shocks can unsettle existing institutions and force actors to make contested decisions about policy or institutional innovations that have durable (though often unintended) consequences. The framework facilitates longitudinal analysis of three sequential stages of institutional development: (1) a set of "antecedent conditions" (Collier and Collier 1991: 30) that establish an institutional baseline for comparative analysis and typically influence how a crisis or challenge unfolds; (2) the critical juncture where reproduction of the institutional baseline is severely challenged (although not necessarily precluded), and where outcomes are highly contingent on the strategic choices, alignments, and interaction of leading players; and (3) an aftermath period where the political alignments and institutional outcomes of the critical juncture become crystallized through self-reinforcing feedback mechanisms (Arthur 1994; Pierson 2000), or modified through the "reactive sequences" triggered by social or political resistance (see Mahoney 2001a: 10–11). These building blocks of the critical juncture approach and their application to the study of party system change in contemporary Latin America are briefly outlined in the next section; a more complete explanatory model is developed in Chapter 3.

CRITICAL JUNCTURES AND POLITICAL CHANGE IN LATIN AMERICA

The critical juncture framework is designed to explain contingent and varied patterns of institutional change in response to similar social, political, or economic challenges. As stated by Collier and Collier (1991: 29), a critical juncture is "a period of significant change, which typically occurs in distinct ways in different countries (or in other units of analysis) and which is hypothesized to produce distinct legacies." The collapse of state-led develoment and the transition to neoliberalism, I argue, constituted such a watershed in the development of Latin American societies. The crisis-induced opening to domestic and international market forces between the mid-1970s and early 1990s did not merely reverse a half-century of inward-oriented, state-led capitalist development. More fundamentally, it altered the character and purpose of state power, the patterns of association in civil society, and the nature of state–society relations. As such, it shifted the structural moorings of national political systems and dislodged party systems that mediated between state and societal actors under the "state-centric matrix" of ISI (Cavarozzi 1994).

Institutional discontinuities were more abrupt and dramatic in some countries than others, however, depending in part on the antecedent conditions established by historical patterns of party system development following the onset of mass politics in the early 20th century. In contrast to Western Europe, where industrialization and the rise of the working class spawned class cleavages and labor-based social democratic parties that "standardized" party systems (Bartolini 2000: 10), the onset of mass politics in Latin America differentiated party systems according to alternative logics of lower-class political incorporation. In some countries, party systems were reconfigured by the rise of a mass-based, labor-mobilizing populist or leftist party with organic linkages to workers (and sometimes peasant) movements during the statist era. In others, elite-controlled parties remained electorally dominant and incorporated lower classes primarily through vertical patron–client linkages. These "elitist" and "labor-mobilizing" (LM) party systems were embedded in distinct developmental matrices or "varieties of capitalism" (Hall and Soskice 2001), with more

(Labor vs Capital)

Is there an I.E. explanation?

extensive lower-class organization and more ambitious state-led development typically being associated with the LM cases.

These characteristics created a formidable and highly destabilizing set of adjustment burdens for LM party systems during the transition to neoliberalism – in particular, the political costs of severe and often prolonged economic crises, the social dislocations attendant to market restructuring, the discrediting of statist policies and interventionist practices that historically provided parties with programmatic linkages to labor and popular constituencies, and the demise of mass-based organizational models in both civil and political society. Economic crises and market reforms weakened labor unions and created more fragmented and pluralistic civil societies that were increasingly detached from traditional party organizations (Oxhorn 1998; Roberts 2002; Collier and Chambers-Ju 2012). Not surprisingly, these adjustment burdens were associated with greater electoral volatility and major electoral realignments in the LM cases.

Antecedent structural and institutional conditions thus weighed heavily on the political dynamics of neoliberal critical junctures. The categorical distinction between elitist and LM party systems, however, provides only a blunt first cut at a theoretical explanation of party system stability and change in late 20th-century Latin America. As we will see, significant variation existed *within* each category as well, as individual party systems adapted, realigned, or decomposed in response to more contingent and short-term dynamics of national critical junctures and the reactive sequences that followed in their wake.

In particular, the resiliency of party systems in the post-adjustment era – when societal resistance to market orthodoxy often intensified – was conditioned by the leadership of the market reform process and its effects on the programmatic alignment of partisan competition. As Stokes (2001a) demonstrates, neoliberal reforms in Latin America were often adopted "by surprise" – that is, by presidents and parties that had campaigned against them or promised to protect citizens from economic hardships and insecurities. Indeed, one of the great paradoxes of the neoliberal era was that market reforms were often imposed by populist figures or labor-based and center-left parties that were historic architects of state-led development. Such "bait and switch" (Drake 1991) patterns of reform may have made structural adjustment more politically viable in the short term, but they tended to de-align party systems programmatically, weaken party "brands," and detach parties from traditional core constituencies (see Lupu 2011; Morgan 2011; Seawright 2012). They eroded business and middle-class support for conservative parties – whose platforms had been co-opted by the right-ward shift of more popular-based rivals – while weakening the programmatic linkages between these latter parties and their lower-class constituencies.

Not surprisingly, bait-and-switch reforms were tailor-made for the "out-flanking" of established party systems on the left by populist outsiders or new political movements that articulated societal dissent from neoliberal orthodoxy.

As such, de-aligned party systems were not a stable competitive equilibrium, especially in the post-adjustment period; they were susceptible to powerful reactive sequences that produced legacies of electoral volatility, realignment or even collapse. Conversely, where market reforms were adopted by conservative parties or leaders with a major party of the left in opposition, critical junctures aligned party systems programmatically and channeled societal discontent into institutionalized outlets of representation. The institutional legacies of these latter critical junctures moderated reactive sequences in the aftermath period and produced more stable patterns of partisan and electoral competition.

These divergent outcomes were an example of "structured contingency" (Karl 1997: 10), whereby political actors make meaningful choices within socio-economic and institutional constraints that delimit the range of viable options and shape the potential payoffs of strategic decisions. Economic crises and market constraints foreclosed certain policy options and undermined historic patterns of political mobilization, but leaders still made crucial strategic choices that conditioned final outcomes – for example, choices to implement or delay market reforms, and to work within or outside of established party organizations. Ultimately, however, patterns of party system change hinged on aggregate micro-level decisions by voters, who determined whether leaders' policy and institutional choices would be rewarded or punished electorally. Indeed, citizens and social actors influenced outcomes through various types of political mobilization, inside and out of the electoral arena. The complex and contingent political realignments produced by neoliberal critical junctures, then, were not straightforward crystallizations of strategic choices or institutional innovations adopted by political leaders; societal resistance and reactive sequences produced myriad unintended consequences that pushed institutional development (and sometimes decay) along unforeseen paths (Pierson 2004: 115–119).

NEOLIBERAL CRITICAL JUNCTURES IN HISTORICAL PERSPECTIVE

When viewed as a region-wide process of socioeconomic and political transformation, the neoliberal critical juncture spanned the quarter of a century that lay between the overthrow of Salvador Allende in Chile in 1973 and the election of Hugo Chávez in Venezuela in 1998. The military coup that aborted Allende's democratic transition to socialism brought into power the Pinochet dictatorship, which shortly thereafter (in 1975) launched Latin America's first great experiment in neoliberal reform. The election of Chávez, on the other hand, symbolized the shattering of the technocratic consensus for market liberalization and the intensification of the social and political resistance that would drive the reactive sequences of the post-adjustment era.

Critical junctures in individual countries, however, were compressed into shorter time periods of acute economic crisis and orthodox market reform. With the exception of Chile, where structural adjustment occurred under military rule in the second half of the 1970s (Foxley 1983; Schamis 1991; Silva

1996),[4] critical junctures began to unfold when an exogenous shock – the 1982 debt crisis – bankrupted developmentalist states and forced economic adjustment to the top of the political agenda. With heterodox adjustment measures unable to contain inflationary pressures, the stage was set for the adoption of orthodox market reforms – the truly decisive stage of the critical juncture in each country. The momentum for reform peaked in the late 1980s through the mid-1990s – the heyday of the Washington Consensus – when every country in the region liberalized markets. Critical junctures ended in each country, and the post-adjustment era began, when the major attempt(s) at market restructuring had been subjected to electoral contestation, giving voters an opportunity to ratify or reject the new economic model. In some countries, such as Argentina, Bolivia, and Peru, this electoral contestation occurred after a single administration adopted comprehensive market reforms in a context of acute economic crisis. In other countries, including Ecuador, Brazil, and Venezuela, major neoliberal reforms were gradually implemented (or attempted) by several different administrations, extending the period of electoral contestation and delaying the endpoint of the critical juncture. As such, the timing and duration of national critical junctures varied, depending in part on leadership dynamics and political agency.

In many respects, the critical junctures analyzed in this book were the obverse of those in the early 20th century studied by Collier and Collier (1991).[5] Early 20th-century critical junctures were driven by the political incorporation of labor movements as socioeconomic modernization undermined oligarchic domination and placed the "social question" on the political agenda. These critical junctures ushered in a new era of mass politics that augmented the developmental, regulatory, and social welfare roles of state institutions. States became the focal point for a diverse array of societal claims, and in some countries organized labor became a core constituency of new mass parties and a pivotal actor in governing coalitions.

Conversely, the late 20th-century critical junctures analyzed in this book revolved around the political exclusion or marginalization of labor movements, the retrenchment of states' social and economic functions, and the demise or adaptation to market principles of historic labor-based populist and leftist parties. Whereas labor-incorporating critical junctures inaugurated an era of economic nationalism in Latin America, neoliberal critical junctures were

---

[4] Argentina and Uruguay also implemented market reforms under military rule in the 1970s, but major adjustment measures were left on the agenda of their democratic successors in the 1980s. As such, their critical junctures occurred following the onset of the debt crisis – under the watch of democratic party organizations – as in the rest of Latin America outside of Chile.

[5] Ruth Berins Collier (1992) makes a similar point in other work that contrasts the politics of labor incorporation in Mexico after the revolution with the politics of market reform in the 1980s. As she states, "If the logic of the earlier critical juncture was conducive to the formation of a state–labor alliance, the logic of the potential new critical juncture points to the disarticulation of that alliance" (1992: 156).

marked by political and economic adjustments to the constraints of market globalization. The essense of neoliberal critical junctures was to dismantle the legacies of earlier labor-incorporating critical junctures.

Several of these trends have clearly been altered by the post-adjustment revival of popular mobilization and leftist politics at the turn of the century, which some have characterized as a "second" historical stage of lower-class political incorporation in Latin America (Luna and Filgueira 2009; Roberts 2008). Although it may be tempting – and more analytically analogous to the historical account of Collier and Collier (1991) – to treat re-incorporation as the new critical juncture, national patterns of re-incorporation have been heavily conditioned by the political and institutional legacies of structural adjustment during the transition from ISI to neoliberalism. For this reason, I treat the adjustment period as the critical juncture, and the post-adjustment "left turn" as part of the reactive sequences of the aftermath period.[6]

Ultimately, this book tries to locate some semblance of order in the cacophony of political and economic changes that swept across Latin America at the end of the 20th century. It explores party system change as the condensation of larger processes of socioeconomic and political transformation, since parties are uniquely positioned at the intersection of different social fields. Indeed, parties are institutional intermediaries between state authorities and societal interests that are structured (at least in part) by economic relationships. The study of party system change thus provides a lens through which to view the broader realignment of social, economic, and political fields during Latin America's turbulent transition to market globalization.

As employed here, then, the critical juncture approach makes an explicit linkage between political and economic change, and it emphasizes the structural or sociological underpinnings of partisan representation. Far from being a mere package of economic reforms, neoliberalism constituted a new social order with identifiable political correlates that diverged sharply from those of the state-centric era. In explaining why the transition to a neoliberal sociopolitical matrix was more disruptive in some countries than others, this book deviates from much of the recent work on party systems and political change, which often assumes (at least implicitly) the autonomy of the political sphere. Before proceeding, therefore, it is necessary to locate this approach more explicitly within the broader study of political change in Latin America.

RELINKING POLITICAL AND ECONOMIC CHANGE

A broad scholarly consensus recognizes that the 1980s and 1990s were a watershed in the economic history of Latin America (Williamson 1994; Edwards

---

[6] As explained in Chapter 8, these stages were compressed in Venezuela, where the critical juncture ended with the election of Hugo Chávez and the onset of the left turn. Elsewhere, left turns did not occur until several years – that is, at least one election cycle – after the end of the critical juncture.

1995). As stated by Sebastian Edwards (1995: vii) at the height of the
Washington Consensus, the "major economic reforms that have greatly changed
the region's economic landscape" have "become a sweeping movement affecting
virtually every country in the region." The political correlates of this "sweeping
movement" were more varied and opaque, however, even when it was clear that
economic crisis and market restructuring had altered the political landscape. At
the end of their landmark study of 20th-century political development, Collier
and Collier (1991: 772–774) discussed the erosion of the heritage of labor-
incorporating critical junctures, and they raised the possibility that Latin
America entered a new critical juncture in the 1980s. Along these lines, Collier
(1992: 161) treated the 1980s as a potential new critical juncture in Mexico,
arguing that "the coalitional basis of the state seems to be undergoing a profound change." Over the course of the next decade various scholars claimed that
the neoliberal era had produced a shift in "citizenship regimes" (Yashar 1999
and 2005), "a new critical juncture in Latin American politics" (Levitsky 2003:
231), and "epochal change" in the social and political order (Garretón 2003: 69;
see also Garretón et al. 2003). Not surprisingly, individual country studies
routinely proclaimed the "end of a political era" or the onset of a new one
associated with the shift in development models (Acuña 1995; Tanaka 1998).

Recognizing a political watershed, however, is different from providing a
comparative analytical framework to explain its diverse effects – to explain,
that is, how interrelated processes of socioeconomic and political change
produced divergent pathways of party system consolidation or decay. Given
the challenges of identifying different outcomes and explaining their causal
pathways, Collier and Chambers-Ju (2012: 571–572) question whether a
critical juncture approach is appropriate for analyzing the transformation of
political representation in the neoliberal era. To be sure, scholars focused
considerable attention on political change at the regime level of analysis,
where issues of democratic transition and consolidation dominated the field
for much of the 1980s and 1990s. This literature, however, often emphasized
the autonomy of the political sphere from economic influences, highlighting
such themes as the crafting of democratic pacts, elite strategic interaction, and
the design of institutional rules of the game (O'Donnell and Schmitter 1986;
Gillespie 1991; Higley and Gunther 1992; Shugart and Carey 1992; Jones
1995; Linz and Stepan 1996). In part, this theoretical orientation was a
response to the excessive economic determinism of earlier paradigms, such as
modernization theory (Lipset 1959), dependency (Cardoso and Faletto 1979),
and bureaucratic-authoritarianism (O'Donnell 1973), which linked political
outcomes to the levels, patterns, or stages of economic development. Frequent
regime changes cast doubt on such structuralist explanations of politics and left
them vulnerable to an array of criticisms (Collier 1979; Cohen 1994). The
result was a proliferation of more contingent, actor-oriented explanations of
political change and an emphasis on institutional engineering to enhance the
prospects for democratic consolidation.

By detaching politics from its socioeconomic moorings, however, institutional and actor-oriented explanations failed to identify potential linkages (or contradictions) between parallel, region-wide processes of democratization, economic crisis, and market liberalization. Such issues began to be addressed in later work that explored the political conditions for market reforms and their sustainability under democracy (Kaufman and Stallings 1989; Remmer 1990 and 1992–1993; Haggard and Kaufman 1992 and 1995; Geddes 1994; Corrales 2002; Weyland 2002; Baker 2010), as well as the role of labor-based parties in the reform process (Murillo 2001 and 2009; Levitsky 2003; Burgess and Levitsky 2003; Burgess 2004). Attention eventually shifted to post-reform political dynamics (Snyder 2001; Garretón et al. 2003; Wise and Roett 2003; Kurtz 2004b; Arce 2005), including the impact of liberalization on civil society and social protest (Eckstein and Wickham-Crowley 2003; Kurtz 2004a; Yashar 2005; Arce and Bellinger 2007; Silva 2009; Oxhorn 2011). Recent work has also analyzed the interrelationships between partisan politics and social mobilization in the post-adjustment period (Van Cott 2005; Collier and Handlin 2009; Arce 2010; Madrid 2012; Rice 2012).

Taken together, these works illustrate why so much concern has been expressed over the quality, fragility, and turbulence of democratic representation in contemporary Latin America. Given the dawning of the neoliberal era under the military dictatorships of the Southern Cone in the 1970s, scholars initially assumed that its harsh austerity and adjustment measures were incompatible with democratic representation, and thus contingent on the authoritarian exclusion of popular sectors (see Skidmore 1977; Foxley 1983; Schamis 1991). The spread of market reforms under democratic regimes in the 1980s demonstrated that the new economic model was not wedded to authoritarian repression to insulate technocratic policymakers from societal demands (Remmer 1990). But if economic liberalization was not coupled to regime type, it did have consistent effects on intermediate-level political outcomes in the domain of political representation – that is, in the "partial regimes" of party systems and popular-interest representation (Collier and Chambers-Ju 2012). In these partial or sub-regimes, neoliberalism shaped the character of democratic governance by conditioning the articulation and organization of interests in society and their relationship to state power – a relationship that is typically mediated by political parties.

The multi-field realignment of states, markets, and social actors trapped party systems in a pincer of structural changes occurring both above and below parties themselves – that is, at both state and societal levels of analysis. From above, market liberalization and globalization narrowed states' policy options and constrained their developmental and social welfare roles. These roles had long created incentives for popular mobilization, and they helped parties forge programmatic linkages to social groups and differentiate their "brands" in the eyes of voters (Lupu 2011). From below, structural adjustment fragmented labor markets and undermined lower-class collective action, thus altering the ways in which parties organized popular constituencies, processed societal demands, and mobilized voters. The conception of parties as institutional intermediaries between states and societies thus suggests that Latin America's crisis of representation was not simply a function of party system failures; it also reflected changes in social organization and state roles and capacities that made it difficult for parties to link societal interests to meaningful programmatic alternatives (see Mainwaring, Bejarano, and Pizarro 2006).

Despite Collier and Chambers-Ju's (2012) misgivings, this study suggests that a critical juncture approach is useful for explaining why some party systems confronted these challenges more effectively than others. Different partisan reform alignments during the process of market liberalization created "founding moments" that generated "stable structures" in some party systems and identifiable "patterns of change" in others (Collier and Chambers-Ju 2012: 573). Whatever their antecedent properties, party systems fared better when they were programmatically aligned during neoliberal critical junctures than when they were de-aligned, and this distinction heavily conditioned their ability to represent societal interests in the aftermath period.

This analysis, then, links underlying forces of social and economic change to a comparative historical perspective on representative institutions in Latin America. Critical junctures are decisive periods of institutional generation, transformation, or decomposition with enduring political effects. They arise when existing political institutions – such as mass-based, labor-mobilizing party systems – are dislodged or rendered ineffectual by structural changes. This structural incongruence generates intense pressures for institutional innovation, along with the threat of institutional demise. Strategic responses to these pressures produce different political alignments and outcomes, creating path-dependent institutional legacies that magnify the role of political agency during crucial "choice points" in the critical juncture (Mahoney 2001b: 113). This theoretical integration of structure, agency, and institutions – three of the basic nuclei of comparative political analysis – is a hallmark of critical juncture approaches, and the cornerstone for my analysis of party system change in contemporary Latin America.

Although authoritative voices have hailed the displacement of sociological modes of analysis in comparative politics by those drawing upon the micro-analytic logic of economics (Rogowski 1993), this book is explicit in making the structural or sociological foundations of political order the starting point (though not the end) of its analysis. The reason is straightforward. Historical patterns of dependent capitalist development have left Latin American societies with the most profound socioeconomic inequalities of any region in the world (Bulmer-Thomas 1996: 7; Karl 2000). The structural reality of social and economic exclusion is in inescapable tension with the formal institutional edifice of representative democracy, which is founded on principles of equal citizenship rights. The political manifestations of this tension vary, however, depending on historically constructed patterns of lower-class political mobilization and incorporation – something that cannot be inferred from universalistic assumptions about structurally derived individual preferences (see, for example, Boix 2003; Acemoglu and Robinson 2006). Latin American party systems have incorporated the working and lower classes in quite different ways, some of which "politicize" underlying social inequalities, and others which suppress or "depoliticize" them. The differences, I argue, have profound implications for democratic governance, as they shape the organization of civil society, the nature of political competition, and the distributive (or redistributive) impact of public policies. The fate of party systems during neoliberal critical junctures and their aftermath period can only be understood in reference to their ability to manage the politics of inequality. Consequently, the transformation of political representation in contemporary Latin America is best understood through an analytical approach that anchors party systems in their social moorings, not detaches them – an approach, in short, that searches for orderly patterns in interwoven processes of social, economic, and political change.

Such an approach is developed as follows. Chapter 2 explores the puzzle of party system instability in Latin America and its relationship to party–society linkage and cleavage structures. Chapter 3 develops the critical juncture framework for analyzing party system change during a period of economic crisis and reform. Chapter 4 explores the rise of elitist and LM party systems following the onset of mass politics in the 20th century, and explains how these party systems were embedded in distinct developmental matrices during the statist era. Chapter 5 analyzes the crisis of state-led development and the transition to market liberalism in the 1980s and 1990s, explaining why this transition was especially disruptive for countries with LM party systems. Chapter 6 examines reactive sequences in the aftermath period and explains how they were conditioned by the programmatic alignment or de-alignment of party systems during the critical juncture.

Part II of the book adopts a case-oriented comparative perspective to trace the impact of neoliberal critical junctures on national party systems. Chapter 7 compares critical junctures in four countries with elitist party systems that span the full range of potential outcomes: party system adaptation in Honduras and Costa Rica, electoral realignment in Uruguay, and decomposition in Ecuador. Chapter 8 explores the dynamics of electoral realignment or decomposition during the critical juncture in four labor-mobilizing cases: Argentina, Brazil, Chile, and Venezuela. Chapter 9 compares the aftermath period in these eight countries to trace the institutional legacies of aligning and de-aligning critical junctures. Chapter 10 concludes with an assessment of the generalizability of the findings and their implications for understanding the transformation of democratic representation in contemporary Latin America.

The analytical framework proposed here facilitates the comparative analysis of party systems across Latin America, in large countries and small, at varying levels of socioeconomic and political development. Too often, theoretical trends in Latin American scholarship are driven by the study of the region's largest and most economically advanced societies (see O'Donnell 1973; Collier 1979) – those which typically developed LM party systems following the onset of mass politics. Although these countries often serve as political and economic trendsetters, there are limits to theoretical generalization based on their rather selective attributes and experiences. Much theoretical leverage can be gained by comparing party system change in these countries with that in others which retained more elitist patterns of representation during the statist era. Similarly, most studies of the neoliberal challenge to party organizations have focused on parties with core labor constituencies (see Levitsky 2003; Burgess and Levitsky 2003; Murillo 2001; Burgess 2004). A broader comparative perspective that examines systemic challenges in diverse institutional settings should provide novel and more generalizable theoretical insights into the dynamics of political change in Latin America.

Indeed, Latin America's distinctive patterns of political change are best understood within the context of broader international trends. The transformation of parties and political representation in contemporary Latin America shares important features in common with trends in other regions that are also driven by market globalization, technological innovation, and social modernization. The impact of such global forces, however, is necessarily mediated by national and regional patterns of socioeconomic and institutional development. The analysis that follows thus dissects regional and national variants of larger international trends in political representation.

PART I

EXPLAINING REGIONAL PATTERNS

2

Partisanship and the Puzzle of Party System Stability

More than thirty years after the onset of Latin America's "third wave" of democratization, the fragility of partisanship in the region remains a major puzzle. This fragility is especially puzzling when new democratic regimes have proven to be far more durable than anyone could have imagined when the third wave began (Mainwaring and Pérez-Liñán 2005). Historically, the oscillation between democratic and authoritarian regimes interfered with the institutionalization of party systems in the region (Lupu and Stokes 2010). Authoritarian rule led to frequent proscriptions or repression of specific party organizations (especially populist or leftist parties with working-class constituencies), as well as prolonged interruptions in electoral competition that disrupted parties' efforts to recruit members, organize local branches, and construct collective identities. Consequently, as new democratic regimes demonstrated a surprising ability to withstand the region-wide economic crisis of the 1980s, scholars expressed optimism that party systems would institutionalize alongside them (Dix 1992).

In much (though not all) of the region, this institutionalization did not occur. Democratic regimes gradually consolidated and economies eventually recovered from the debt crisis and hyperinflation, but party systems, on average, did not become more electorally stable. To the contrary, they actually became progressively *less* stable during the first three decades of the third wave. Simply put, regular electoral competition did not institutionalize party systems as representative bodies or intermediaries between citizens and states.

Stable political representation – where parties reproduce most or all of their voter support from one election cycle to another – should not be equated with effective representation. Electoral stability may signify voter satisfaction with established partisan options, but it may also be attributable to the monopolization of resources by incumbents, an absence of perceived alternatives, voter dependence on patronage distributions, institutional constraints on vote choice, or unreflective habituation. Under these latter conditions, partisan representation may be stable without holding leaders accountable to their constituencies or accurately translating societal preferences into public policies. Indeed, democratic accountability is predicated on voter mobility – that is, the ability of citizens to reallocate vote shares to signal policy preferences and reward or punish incumbents for their performance in office (Fiorina 1981). Although Honduras, until recently, boasted the most electorally stable party system in Latin America during the third wave (see Chapter 5), few observers would rate the Honduran party system as providing the most effective political representation in the region. Some might even argue that greater voter mobility would be a healthy indicator of democratic accountability.

Shifts in vote shares may thus be a positive indicator of a vigilant electorate and accountable public authority. Large-scale, iterative vote shifts, however, are a sure sign of failed or ineffectual partisan representation. They suggest that voter identification with established parties is fragile or shallow, and that many voters are searching for new electoral options or punishing their old ones. Although there may be no clear threshold to distinguish healthy voter mobility from less sanguine forms of detachment or alienation, high levels of electoral volatility are a prime indicator of a crisis of political representation.

Why, then, are some party systems stable and resilient, whereas others are volatile and inchoate? This chapter suggests that stable partisanship is largely a function of two core dimensions of party–society relations: strong linkages that bind voters to parties, and sharp cleavages that differentiate rival partisan camps. Linkages are the appeals and interactive connections that parties employ to attract individual or group support, thus providing a basis for partisan identification (see Lawson 1980; Kitschelt 2000; Barr 2009).[1] Cleavages are axes of competition that divide the electorate and structure partisan rivalries. Strong linkages, therefore, create loyal adherents who are less likely to abandon their party; sharp cleavages create well-marked boundaries and deep divides that voters are unlikely to cross.

Neoliberal critical junctures were especially destabilizing where they eroded party–society linkages and blurred the distinctions between major parties. That argument is developed in subsequent chapters; the purpose of this one is to develop a set of analytical tools to frame it. This chapter identifies different types of linkages and cleavages, explores how they relate to one another as well as to partisan organizational patterns, and explains why they matter for party system stability. The analysis of linkages, cleavages, and organizational patterns provides a foundation to identify different types of political parties and different historical trajectories of party system development – the first stage in a causal explanation for the transformation of party systems in Latin America's neoliberal era.

---

[1] Barr (2009) distinguishes between rhetorical appeals and interactive connections or linkages, but for our purposes, it suffices to treat linkages more broadly as the basis by which parties appeal to voters for support.

A focus on linkages and cleavages directs attention to the social bases of partisanship and partisan competition. Linkages and cleavages heavily condition the ways in which the interests, preferences, and values of different societal constituencies are represented in – or excluded from – formal electoral and policymaking institutions. Although party systems are institutional intermediaries between citizens (or social groups) and the state, they do not directly translate majority preferences, much less the plurality of societal interests, into electoral and policymaking arenas. How societal interests "map" onto party systems is the very gist of democratic competition. Some interests may be well represented by established parties; others may be constructed by parties themselves in their strategic competition for votes; still others may mobilize outside existing partisan channels in order to be heard. Partisan competition inevitably "politicizes" some issues and interests while depoliticizing others, subject to the mobilization of societal claims outside the party system itself. In the process, partisan competition cleaves the electorate, "bundles" issue and policy stands, and defines the range of programmatic alternatives.

The social bases of partisan competition are especially important in Latin America, given the depth of social and economic inequalities in the region. Formal models of democracy often assume that distributive conflicts are the mainspring of democratic competition (Meltzer and Richard 1981; Acemoglu and Robinson 2006), and such conflicts surely help to explain the historical fragility of democracy in Latin America (O'Donnell 1973). As we will see, however, party systems in the region vary widely – both across cases and over time – in the extent to which they politicize distributive tradeoffs between the haves and have-nots. As Schattschneider famously argued, dominant economic interests prefer to privatize distributive conflicts, whereas the weak try to socialize them and broaden their scope. Democratic government "is the single greatest instrument" for this socialization (Schattschneider 1975: 12), but the level of socialization is contingent on the ability of subaltern groups to engage in collective action and political mobilization. Some types of partisan competition, therefore, mobilize lower classes around redistributive claims that challenge elite interests, whereas others suppress such claims and diffuse (or privatize) distributive conflicts. The anchoring of partisan competition in socioeconomic inequalities and distributive conflicts is thus a variable rather than a constant in Latin American democracies; party systems are historical and political constructs that do not map automatically onto any given set of societal divisions, no matter how gaping they might be.

This variation in the politicization of inequalities differentiates national party systems, and it has played a central role in the critical junctures that marked the transitions from one political era to another. The transition from import substitution industrialization (ISI) to neoliberalism disarticulated forms of labor-based political representation that thrived – in some countries – during the era of state-led industrialization. By contrast, the transition was less disruptive in the short term for elitist party systems that historically depoliticized inequalities. These latter party systems, however, were not well suited to withstand the revival of societal redistributive pressures in the post-adjustment period. Party systems were more likely to withstand this critical juncture and its reactive sequences where they were configured by relatively institutionalized programmatic contestation of the neoliberal model and its distributive effects. To explain why this was so, however, requires a deeper theoretical exploration of the social bases of partisanship.

THE DUAL FUNCTIONS OF PARTISANSHIP

By definition, a political party represents a portion or "part" of the body politic. Parties are, therefore, Janus-faced institutions; as "expressions of sociability" (Rosenblum 2008: 69), they appeal to and aggregate some societal interests, but in the process they also divide them from others. Indeed, the etymological origins of the term "party" are found in the Latin verb which means "to divide" (see Sartori 1976: 3–4, 64–65). These dual functions of linkage and cleavage are closely intertwined, as appeals made to some constituencies may exclude or antagonize others, creating an axis of partisan competition. From political theorists such as Hume and Madison to modern populist outsiders like Alberto Fujimori and Hugo Chávez, this functional dualism has led parties to be associated with "factions" and "special interests." As such, it has nourished anti-party sentiments among those claiming to be concerned with the larger public interest – or in some cases, those adhering to a more holistic or organic conception of the body politic (see Rosenblum 2008). These dual functions, however, are inescapable where social and political pluralism are managed through democratic representation, and their interaction is the starting point for explaining stable and unstable forms of partisan competition.

Theoretically, a party system can be electorally stable in the aggregate (that is, at the macro level) even in a context of widespread individual-level vote shifts. Such stability requires that citizens continue to vote for established parties rather than new ones, and that micro-level vote shifts offset each other in the aggregate (i.e., the number of voters who withdraw support from any given party roughly matches the number of voters who switch their vote to that party). But if micro-level stability cannot be inferred from macro-level stability, the former clearly contributes to the latter. Party systems are more stable where large numbers of citizens routinely vote for the same party in all or most elections – in short, where large numbers of citizens vote on the basis of durable (if not necessarily fixed) partisan loyalties and identities, as opposed to more contingent and conditional preferences. Likewise, stability is enhanced when individual voter mobility is limited by deep social or political cleavages that separate different parties and place some out of bounds for certain types of voters.

Much of the classical work on political representation sees stable partisanship as a natural by-product of institutionalized democratic competition. Although rationalist and social-psychological approaches have quite different theoretical underpinnings – the former is focused on interests, instrumentality, and choice, whereas the latter emphasizes cultural identities, affect, and conformity – both provide compelling explanations for stable partisanship. For some social-psychological approaches, partisanship is more of a social identity, like religion, than a political choice, and can thus withstand even major disruptions associated with crises or historical processes of economic and political change. Green, Palmquist, and Schickler (2002), for example, find that citizens "update" political beliefs in response to major events, but generally hold fast to the images they have about specific parties and the social constituencies they represent. These images – formed early in life and rarely altered past early adulthood – provide a basis for the deep affective bonds of stable partisanship. Voters do not choose a party because they agree with its stands on the issues, but rather internalize the positions of the party with which they identify (Green, Palmquist, and Schickler (2002: 3–4). Indeed, the construction of partisan identities is often seen as a process of social conformity, with adolescents and young adults being socialized by families, peer groups, and other primary social networks characterized by trust and frequent interaction (Zuckerman, Dasović, and Fitzgerald 2007). Partisan identities may also be forged by distinctive generational or cohort experiences, then transmitted from one generation to the next through the socializing effects of primary networks (Campbell, Converse, Miller, and Stokes 1960; Nie, Verba, and Petrocik 1976). Over time, party systems are expected to stabilize as identities congeal and voting behavior becomes habituated (Converse 1969).

Rationalist accounts strip partisanship of these deep affective dimensions, but they reach many of the same conclusions regarding its durability. In the seminal work of Aldrich (2011), stable partisanship is in the self-interest of both voters and political elites. For voters, partisanship is an information shortcut that provides cues about the principles and policy orientations of candidates running for public office. Partisanship allows citizens to minimize the information costs of voting decisions by supporting candidates who are sponsored by a familiar and trusted party. As Dalton (2006: 185) states, "Once voters decide which party generally represents their interests, this single piece of information can act as a perceptual screen – guiding how they view events, issues, and candidates." Similarly, political elites (or "entrepreneurs") have powerful incentives to create, join, and remain in parties that cultivate "name-brand loyalties" in the electorate. As Aldrich (2011) argues, such parties help elites regulate access to public office, minimize collective action problems in the mobilization of electoral support, and resolve coordination problems in legislative and policymaking arenas. Where name-brand loyalties bind voters to established parties, political entrepreneurs do not have to mobilize voters from scratch in every election cycle. In Hirschman's (1970) terms, "loyalty" to a party is more effective than "exit" if the latter cuts off a political entrepreneur from preexisting voting blocs.

Spatial and game theoretic variants of rational choice models suggest that political elites will adapt party platforms in response to changing currents in public opinion in order to remain electorally competitive (Downs 1957: 114–41;

Hug 2001). This programmatic flexibility contributes to stability by helping established parties absorb new societal demands and preempt the formation of new parties. In Hug's game theoretic model, changes in the composition of party systems are rooted in the emergence of new programmatic interests or issues; when established parties cannot respond to emerging societal demands, new parties are formed.

Research on "critical elections" and party system realignment suggests that new parties may arise, or large vote shifts among established parties will occur, in response to major socioeconomic changes or political crises that redraw the lines of political cleavage. Once realigned, however, partisan competition is expected to stabilize around a new equilibrium with only minor deviations (Key 1955; Burnham 1970: 4). This suggests a model of punctuated equilibrium, whereby stable competition is the norm, punctuated by brief moments of dis-continuous change or re-equilibration.[2] Outside these "flash points" (Burnham 1970: 10) – that is, in normal times – mechanisms for the reproduction of partisan attachments are expected to prevail over the corrosive effects of social, political, and economic change. Partisanship, in short, is presumed to be "sticky"; it anchors voters or constrains their electoral mobility by creating durable loyalties in place of contingent preferences.

Finally, structural or sociological approaches argue that this stickiness is attrib-utable not only to strong identities or linkages between parties and voters, but also to their roots in social conflicts or cleavages that shape collective interests, induce political mobilization, and cause competitive alignments to crystallize around rival party organizations and their programmatic positions (Lipset and Rokkan 1967). In this tradition, parties are seen not as aggregates of individual voters or instruments of political entrepreneurs, but rather as the organizational expression of social blocs with shared interests and identities – for example, a social class, a distinctive regional population, or a racial, ethnic, or religious group. Party system stability, then, is a product of deep sociopolitical cleavages that are clearly defined, well organized, and difficult to cross – that is, cleavages that sharply differentiate competing social blocs and accentuate their internal political cohesion. The organization of these social blocs reinforces collective identities, encapsulates voters, and limits their electoral mobility (Bartolini and Mair 1990), such that voting becomes less a matter of individual choice than an expression of group membership and solidarity. Cleavage enclosure may even "freeze" partisan align-ments once universal suffrage is in place and the electorate is fully mobilized (Lipset and Rokkan 1967).

Even where social cleavages are not well defined and densely organized, this emphasis on differentiation – and not just linkages or shared identities – is

---

[2] Work in this tradition conceptualizes realignment in electoral terms – that is, as a basic shift in the distribution of vote shares among contending parties. I will refer to such vote shifts as "electoral realignments," which may or may not be associated with "programmatic realignments," which entail a shift in the policy or programmatic basis of partisan competition.

instructive for understanding the strength and durability of partisanship. Recent scholarship on the United States, for example, has argued that partisanship strengthened in the late 20th century as party elites and activists in both the Republican and Democratic camps became more ideologically cohesive in their programmatic stands, differentiating the parties themselves. Polarization at the elite level then induced voters to sort into rival partisan camps according to their programmatic preferences (see Aldrich 2011, Part 3; Hetherington 2011; Sniderman and Stiglitz 2012). In short, clear boundaries or lines of demarcation help to solidify party–voter linkages and anchor voters in their respective partisan camps.

If partisanship involves the dual functions of linkage and cleavage, it must be recognized that different types of parties and party systems perform these functions in distinct ways. Variation exists across cases as well as over time, with linkage and cleavage patterns often evolving in response to socioeconomic and technological changes. As explained below, this variation has important implications for the strength of partisanship, the nature of lower-class political incorporation, and the politicization of social and economic inequalities.

LINKAGES, CLEAVAGES, AND PARTY ORGANIZATION IN LATIN AMERICA

As Kitschelt (2000) suggests, partisanship can be grounded in programmatic, clientelistic, or charismatic linkages. Since parties cleave the electorate as they mobilize support, these linkages shape the social and/or political cleavages that structure partisan competition, including their degree and type of sociological differentiation and the extent to which they politicize inequalities. The density and forms of partisan and party-affiliated civic organization are correlated as well with different linkage and cleavage patterns; some of these foster mass-based organizational models, whereas others encourage cadre-based party organizations that are built along narrower leadership networks (Duverger 1964). These qualitative distinctions can produce quite disparate modes of political representation, even where party systems have similar scores on conventional indicators like the number of parties or electoral volatility.

Where partisan rivalries are rooted in social group distinctions such as class, religion, ethnicity, or region, social cleavages are formed (Lipset and Rokkan 1967). Although some scholars limit the cleavage concept to competitive alignments that are anchored in such sociological distinctions (see, for example, Bartolini and Mair 1990), all party systems, by definition, divide or "cleave" the electorate, whether or not partisan constituencies are sociologically differentiated. Consequently, political cleavages based on organizational loyalties with little or no grounding in sociological differences are sometimes found (Aldrich 2011: 191–195) and are, in fact, quite common historically in Latin America. Given their lack of sociological grounding, strictly political cleavages are necessarily "segmented" in character; that is, they cut vertically across class distinctions, with all major parties drawing support from heterogeneous, multi-class constituencies. Social cleavages, on the other hand, may be either segmented (i.e., when they differentiate religious, ethnic, or other sociocultural groups that are not concentrated in particular class positions) or "stratified" (i.e., when they cut horizontally across society, establishing an axis of competition between different social classes or, more loosely, "elite" and "popular" sectors). Whether segmented or stratified, the group-based logic of social cleavages is conducive to – and in turn reinforced by – forms of civic associationism that enhance organizational density in both civil society and the partisan arena.

These distinctions have important implications for the articulation of popular demands on the state, particularly those related to the redress of social and economic inequalities. Inequalities are most likely to be politicized when parties establish programmatic linkages to social groups, when they cleave the electorate along stratified axes of competition, and when popular sectors are incorporated through mass-based civic and party organizations. Programmatic linkages exist when parties appeal for support on the basis of ideological platforms or policy packages "that they promise to pursue if elected into office" (Kitschelt 2000: 850). Such linkages require that rival parties pursue different policy objectives, or at least propose distinct policy measures to achieve objectives that are widely shared among the electorate. They also require that citizens form prospective policy preferences on the basis of their interests or values, rather than simply vote retrospectively to cast judgment on incumbents' performance in office (Kinder and Kiewiet 1979; Kiewiet 1983). Programmatic linkages are invariably weakened when party platforms are indistinguishable from one other, when they lack internal coherence and consistency, or when they provide little guidance as to what parties are likely to do in public office (see Lupu 2011).

Programmatic linkages are conducive to social cleavages in general, and stratified cleavages in particular. Although religious beliefs, cultural values, and other political differences can generate programmatic linkages, Kitschelt et al. (2009) convincingly demonstrate that economic issues and material interests are the primary basis of programmatic linkages in Latin America. In short, parties forge programmatic linkages by advocating policy bundles with distributive consequences that favor some societal interests over others, even where such policies are framed in terms of larger public goods such as economic growth or efficiency.[3] Parties may, for example, articulate workers' demands for higher wages and collective bargaining rights, peasant claims for land redistribution,

---

[3] Ideological appeals are often couched in terms of universal values and interests rather than those of more narrowly defined social groups. Nevertheless, historically dominant ideological expressions like liberalism and socialism were closely tied to the class interests, respectively, of capitalists and workers; in Gramscian terms, the struggle for ideological hegemony involves the attempt to convince society at large that the particular interests of a given class are synonymous with the public good.

pensioners' claims for expanded social security, or capitalists' interests in low taxes, secure property rights, and flexible labor and capital markets. The distributive (and often redistributive) consequences of such policies provide a potential basis for collective (rather than individualized) partisan loyalties, and for cleavage structures that align different social groups in competition with one another. Cleavages are stratified – and inequalities politicized – when these groups occupy different stations on the social hierarchy.

Since programmatic linkages and stratified cleavages are forged around policy alternatives that affect group interests, they stimulate collective action and diverse forms of social and political organization. Potential stakeholders mobilize and counter-mobilize to advance or defend their interests in civic arenas, creating forms of associational power that enhance their leverage when pressing claims on the state. Civic associations, in turn, may develop organizational ties to the parties that channel their claims into formal political arenas. Labor unions, peasant associations, and other popular organizations often mobilize resources and activists for affiliated parties, swelling their ranks and creating sociopolitical identities that help to secure partisan loyalties (Bartolini and Mair 1990). Indeed, parties may penetrate or form civic associations to increase their programmatic leverage and encapsulate potential voting blocs within participatory networks. Such parties are not simply electoral vehicles for political elites (Downs 1959); they are agents of social integration that perform a wide variety of social functions (Kirchheimer 1966). They may form study groups, establish their own media, and create auxiliary branches for women and students, along with sports and cultural clubs. Some go so far as to provide a broad range of social services for their members, including medical and dental care, scholarships, and child care centers. These social functions require strong local branches that transform party supporters into activists or *militantes* who do much more than vote in elections; they are permanently engaged in partisan political work.

Programmatic linkages to densely organized social blocs thus foster the development of mass party organizations with extensive local branches, strong grassroots participation, and permanent forms of political activation (Duverger 1964). This set of traits is characteristic of *mass programmatic parties*, one of the ideal-type party organizations analyzed in this book. These parties often generate stratified cleavage structures that are based on distributive conflicts, and they augment the associational power of social groups in ways that politicize inequalities.

Other types of parties and competitive alignments, however, tend to diffuse both the associational power of popular sectors and the political expression of social inequalities. As such, they encourage patterns of "classless inequality," where deep social and economic inequalities do not give rise to class-based political organization, representation, or competition (Ossowski 1963). These alternatives appeal to individual voters through patron–clientelism, personalistic leadership, or short-term image marketing rather than group-based programmatic linkages. They also generate segmented cleavages that cut vertically across social strata, forming competitive alignments in the political arena with little grounding in class distinctions. Finally, they do little to foster horizontal forms of association in either civic or partisan arenas. Labor unions and other popular associations are unlikely to be densely organized, and parties have limited bureaucratic or grassroots organization beyond their leadership cadres (Duverger 1964). With weak or nonexistent local branches, parties have little capacity to penetrate or mobilize civil society, and their organizational reach does not extend far beyond their clientele networks. They may appeal to mass electorates, but they are not structured as mass party organizations.[4]

The first of these alternatives, what I call *machine parties*, are decentralized networks of leaders and local or regional power brokers who dispense patronage to loyal constituents. Linkages based on patron–clientelism entail an exchange of political loyalty for selective material benefits, such as employment in the public sector, preferential access to government programs and services, or contacts that help to expedite a claim through the public bureaucracy (Valenzuela 1977; Auyero 2000; Kitschelt 2000; Brusco, Nazareno, and Stokes 2004; Calvo and Murillo 2004). In contrast to the collective policy benefits of programmatic linkages, clientelist linkages offer rewards that are particularistic and discretionary – in essence, selective incentives for organizational loyalty that are detached from the programmatic concerns of larger social blocs. As stated by Kitschelt et al. (1999: 48), "voters give up control over the politicians' pursuit of public policies and content themselves with the immediate tangible benefits derived from surrendering their vote." Likewise, patron–clientelism does not require horizontal organization and collective action in civil society; clientelist networks are loosely and vertically organized across class distinctions, and individuals access rewards through personal or community contacts rather than broad-based associational power.

Clientelist exchanges are thus widely recognized to be "mechanisms of class control" (Kitschelt et al. 1999: 49) that depoliticize social inequalities. They allow elite-dominated parties to attract lower-class support, creating segmented political cleavages between rival patronage machines that draw support from heterogeneous and relatively undifferentiated social constituencies, save for their political loyalties. Local party brokers cultivate personal relationships within informal social networks to broker and monitor the exchange of benefits for votes (Stokes 2005), but clients are not necessarily organized in dense, participatory local branches; little is expected from clients other than their vote.

Machine parties, therefore, have weak programmatic linkages, cadre-based party organizations with shallow grassroots structures, and sociologically diffuse cleavage patterns, but they are not necessarily fragile political formations. Indeed, as rival machines compete for access to state resources, they can translate economic dependency and exclusive clientele networks into formidable partisan

---

[4] In other words, mass parties are defined by the depth and breadth of their organization rather than the scope of their electoral appeal.

sub-cultures with durable loyalties, as in the historic party systems of Colombia and Uruguay (Payne 1968; Hartlyn 1988: 16–27; Gillespie 1991). In so doing, they may entrench segmented organizational cleavages as a functional alternative to the stratified social cleavages spawned by mass programmatic parties.

According to Kitschelt et al. (1999: 47), parties may also attract popular support through charismatic linkages, or appeals based on the "exceptional capabilities and personality traits" of a given leader. Charismatic bonds have been integral to Latin America's storied populist tradition (Madsen and Snow 1991; Conniff 1999; de la Torre 2010). Populist figures generate fervent devotion and, in many cases, equally fervent opposition, sharply cleaving the electorate along a personality-based axis of competition. Some populist figures, such as Juan Perón in Argentina, Lázaro Cárdenas in Mexico, Victor Raúl Haya de la Torre in Peru, and Hugo Chávez in Venezuela, mobilized working and lower class groups behind reformist or redistributive programs that politicized inequalities and at least partially stratified partisan cleavages. Often, however, charismatic authority seeks to avoid divisive forms of ideological definition and "promise all things to all people" (Kitschelt 2000: 849) so that it can mobilize support across class lines. Populist leaders such as José María Velasco Ibarra in Ecuador and Alberto Fujimori in Peru thus appealed directly to multi-class constituencies, but did little to organize popular sectors or politicize inequalities. Typically, such leaders generate support through "outsider" attacks on the political establishment rather than programmatic commitments to social reform or redistributive policies (Roberts 1995; Weyland 1996).

The charismatic linkages of populism are a subset of personality-based political competition, as non-charismatic forms of personal authority exist as well (Ansell and Fish 1999). Patrimonialism is the most common of these alternatives. Although Weber's concept of patrimonialism is generally used to describe authority relations at the regime level of analysis (see Hartlyn 1998: 14–17; Van de Walle 2001), its basic attributes are readily identifiable in the partisan sphere as well: electoral vehicles that are instruments of personalistic authority, the blurring of distinctions between personal and collective interests, and support that is generated by "ties of loyalty and dependence" (Hartlyn 1998: 14). Followers identify with a party founder or elder statesman who has become synonymous with the party itself and dispenses favors to loyal subjects. Patrimonial linkages thus tend to be paternalistic rather than charismatic, and they uphold tradition and conserve the status quo rather than politicize inequalities or mobilize forces for change. These linkages cut across class distinctions, and they do little to foster programmatic competition or mass organization in either civic or partisan arenas.

It makes sense, then, to conceptualize the third type of party as *personalist*, recognizing the possibility of patrimonial and charismatic (or populist) subtypes of the category. Under both subtypes, parties are personal vehicles of dominant leaders who eschew ideological definition in order to "avoid constituency divisions" (Kitschelt et al. 1999: 47) and appeal to a broad range of societal interests. Indeed, these leaders "disarticulate political programs that would distract from their personality," and they try to "maintain maximum personal discretion over the strategy of the party vehicle" (Kitschelt 2000: 849). The subtypes differ primarily in their sponsorship of lower-class associational power and their potential for politicizing inequalities.

Differences aside, mass programmatic, machine, and personalist parties are all capable of forging strong, durable political loyalties that outlive any particular cycle of electoral mobilization. In short, their diverse linkage and cleavage patterns are mechanisms for generating stable partisanship. The socioeconomic and political conditions under which they are able to form such partisanship vary, however. Machine parties and patrimonial variants of personalism may thrive when lower classes are politically disorganized – that is, when they have a limited capacity for autonomous collective action in both partisan and civic arenas. These parties are highly vulnerable, however, to forms of lower-class mobilization that politicize inequalities. Conversely, mass programmatic parties are hard-pressed to respond to the claims of popular constituencies when economic or market constraints sharply limit states' developmental and social welfare roles. These conditions weighed heavily on the fate of parties during neoliberal critical junctures and their aftermath period.

Indeed, as discussed below, relatively few Latin American citizens have formed durable attachments to any of these different types of party organizations in recent decades. Many individuals vote without the benefit of name-brand loyalties, forcing parties to compete in an electoral marketplace that contains a large number of mobile, unattached voters. Their votes are, so to speak, up for grabs, and they treat each election as a discrete event. Parties must find ways to appeal or market themselves to these uncommitted voters, since the mobilization of partisans is rarely sufficient to win national elections.

Marketing appeals aimed at mobile voters create contingent preferences rather than linkages, as the latter imply a brand-name identity that outlives a particular election cycle. Contingent preferences are fluid and conjunctural in nature, and they are typically generated by some combination of performance, candidate, and image marketing. Voters, for example, may treat an election as a referendum on incumbent performance, punishing parties that mismanage the economy or get embroiled in corruption scandals, and rewarding those that govern during periods of economic well-being and political tranquility. Retrospective economic voters fit this pattern, as they extend and withdraw contingent support in response to economic performance, rather than forging name-brand loyalties based on programmatic, clientelist, or personalist linkages (Kiewiet 1983; Lewis-Beck 1988). And without durable linkages, stable cleavages can hardly be formed, as the axes of competition are fluid and subject to perpetual realignment.

Obviously, parties compete to frame issues in ways that allow them to claim responsibility for good economic times and blame opponents for hardship. Parties thus try to market themselves by crafting attractive public images or reputations on "valence issues," or those "on which all parties declare to pursue the same objective but dispute each other's competence" in achieving the desired outcome (Kitschelt et al. 1999: 137). Parties do not adopt countervailing positions on issues like economic growth, clean government, or public safety, as these objectives are favored by a broad societal consensus. Parties may craft distinct programmatic alternatives for pursuing such objectives, but they often campaign to convince voters that they are more competent or reliable to address such problems than their opponents.

Such image marketing on valence issues is designed to generate contingent support within a broad cross-section of societal interests. Programmatic linkages that politicize inequality, on the other hand, are forged around "positional" issues – such as land reform, taxation, or income redistribution – where stratified constituencies manifest rival preferences. Whereas mass programmatic parties prioritize positional issues, *professional electoral parties* emphasize valence issues that allow them to evade divisive programmatic commitments, maximize policy flexibility, and market themselves to a heterogeneous mix of electorally mobile, unattached voters (Panebianco 1988: 262–267). Candidates are surrounded by teams of professional pollsters, fundraisers, media consultants, and campaign handlers, chosen as much for their expertise as for their political loyalty. These professionalized cadres – backed by modern survey and communications technologies – help parties gauge voter sentiments, raise campaign funds, and shape public perceptions of issues and candidates without building mass membership organizations. Parties neither organize civil society nor perform significant social functions outside the electoral arena to encapsulate voters. Instead, they organize cyclically from the top down to compete in the electoral marketplace, waging capital-intensive campaigns that are quite different from the labor-intensive campaigns of mass party organizations.

The four types of political parties outlined above and their corresponding linkage, cleavage, and organizational patterns are depicted in Table 2.1. In the real world of politics, the boundaries between these ideal–typical categories may be blurred by hybrid forms of representation. Linkage patterns, for example, are not mutually exclusive, as a given party may rely on different types of linkage to appeal to distinct social constituencies. This was the strategy of classical Peronism, for example, which combined charismatic bonds with programmatic linkages to organized labor and clientelist linkages to the unorganized rural and urban poor (see Gibson 1997) – in the process, spawning what is arguably Latin America's most durable and adaptable mass party organization. Any type of party that commands state resources can cultivate clientelist linkages, and in an era of mass communications technology and mobile voters, virtually all parties adopt elements of professional electoralism to attract contingent support.

Nevertheless, tradeoffs are likely to exist, as linkage strategies are nested in different political and organizational logics, and efforts to maximize one type of appeal may partially nullify others (Kitschelt 2000: 853–855). No party can be all things to all people. These ideal types thus help to identify the range of logical

TABLE 2.1. *Typology of Political Parties*

	Mass Programmatic	Machine	Personalist	Professional Electoral
Societal Linkages	Ideology or Programmatic Appeals	Patron–Clientelism	Charisma, Personal Loyalty	Contingent Preferences, Political Marketing
Cleavage Structures	Potentially Stratified Social Cleavages	Segmented Political and Organizational Cleavages	Leadership-Based Political Cleavage	Fluid Political Divides
Organizational Models	Mass Organization, Strong Local Branches	Cadre Organization, Clientelist Networks with Local Brokers	Cadre (patrimonial) or potentially Mass (populist)	Professional Teams

possibilities and the largely unexplored interrelationships among the linkage, cleavage, and organizational dimensions of party–society relations. In so doing, they shed light on the distinct patterns by which parties incorporate lower-class citizens into the political arena and either augment or diffuse their associational power. Where mass programmatic parties are formed, popular sectors are incorporated through large-scale, horizontally organized secondary associations in civil and political society that are potentially autonomous of traditional elites and often in direct conflict with them. In contrast, popular sectors are politically incorporated as individual voters or dependent clients where machine, patrimonial-personalist, or professional-electoral parties predominate. Such parties provide little autonomous collective voice to subaltern groups, and they typically reinforce traditions of elite political domination and unorganized, "classless" inequality.

But if parties can appeal to voters and align electoral competition in such diverse ways, why is partisanship so fragile in Latin America, and why does it vary so starkly across countries? The following section returns to these questions and lays the foundation for a historical institutionalist perspective on party-system development in the region.

THE PUZZLE OF STABLE PARTISANSHIP

Although stable partisanship is hardly absent from Latin America, in many countries it is clearly not the norm. The fragility of partisanship can be seen in a number of different indicators. A major survey conducted in 2010 by Vanderbilt University's Latin American Public Opinion Project (LAPOP), for

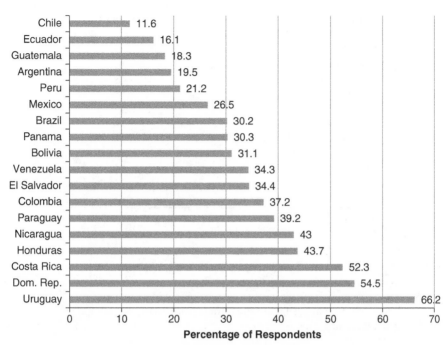

FIGURE 2.1. Party Identification in Latin America, 2010
Source: AmericasBarometer, Latin American Public Opinion Project (Díaz-Domínguez 2010: 1). Data points report the percentage of survey respondents who answered "Yes" to the question "Do you currently identify with a political party?"

example, found a regional average of only 33.8 percent of citizens who claimed to identify with a political party (see Figure 2.1). Relatively high levels of party identification were found in Uruguay, the Dominican Republic, and Costa Rica, where over 50 percent of survey respondents claimed to identify with a party. In Peru, Argentina, Guatemala, Ecuador, and (more surprisingly) Chile, however, the percentage of party identifiers was under 22 percent, indicating that a substantial majority of the electorate was mobile and unattached.

If relatively few citizens identify with political parties, even fewer appear to have confidence or trust in them. In Latinobarómetro's 2010 region-wide survey, only 23 percent of respondents claimed to have trust in parties, even though a majority – 59 percent – said there can be no democracy without political parties (Latinobarómetro 2010: 28, 72). Indeed, parties finished last in the survey's ranking of trust in governmental and societal institutions, behind municipal governments, the military, national legislative, judicial, and executive branches, and non-governmental institutions like banks, private firms, the mass media, and the church (see Table 2.2). A mere 15 percent of survey respondents said that the most effective way to influence government decisions was to work

TABLE 2.2. *Trust in Institutions of Democracy and Society*

Church	67
Television	55
Armed Forces	45
National Government	45
Banks	44
Private Companies	42
Local Government	40
Police	35
Congress	34
Judiciary	32
Political Parties	23

Source: Latinobarómetro (2010: 72). Percentage of survey respondents who report trust in specified institutions.

TABLE 2.3. *Most Effective Way to Influence Government Decisions*

Attract people with the same interest in the subject and form a group	32
Work through personal or family connections with government employees	27
Write to government employees explaining your point of view	22
Organize a protest	19
Work through your political party	15

Source: Latinobarómetro (2010: 61). Percentage of survey responses to the question "Here is a list of things one can do in order to influence a government decision. Which one do you think is the more effective?" Respondents were allowed to identify more than one effective strategy, yielding a total greater than 100 percent.

through a party organization, less than the percentage who said it was most effective to organize a social protest, write to a government official, use personal or family connections, or form an interest group (see Table 2.3). A majority of respondents – 54 percent – said that if they had to vote this week, they would prefer not to vote for a political party (Latinobarómetro 2010: 59).

Given the weakness of partisan identities to guide vote choices, it is hardly surprising that voting behavior is highly unstable in much of the region. This can be seen in Figure 2.2, which compares average electoral volatility in Latin America to that in the United States and Europe. Using the most common indicator of party system stability, the Pedersen index of electoral volatility,[5] the figure shows that nineteen West European democracies had an average net vote shift

[5] The Pedersen index is calculated by summing the vote (or legislative seat) gains and losses of individual parties from one election to the next and then dividing by two. The index provides a measure of net aggregate vote shifts, with a score of zero indicating that no party lost or gained votes (or seats), and a score of 100 signifying that all the votes (or seats) were captured by a new set of parties.

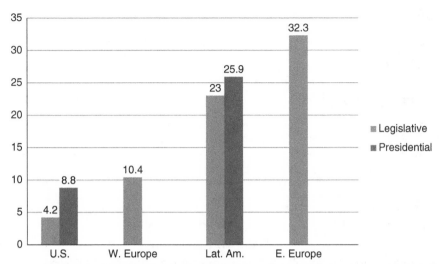

FIGURE 2.2. Electoral Volatility in Comparative Perspective (Pedersen index of volatility)
Sources: For the United States and Latin America, calculated from Nohlen (2005) and
Georgetown University's *Political Database of the Americas* (http://pdba.georgetown.edu).
Legislative volatility for these countries is calculated on the basis of seat shares. For Western
Europe, scores were taken from Gallagher, Laver and Mair (2011: 10), and reflect changes
in parliamentary vote shares. East European scores are taken from Tavits (2008: 551), and
are also based on parliamentary vote shares. For the United States, Western Europe, and
Latin America, volatility scores cover the period from 1980 to 2010; for Eastern Europe,
from 1991 to 2004.

of 10.5 percent in parliamentary elections from 1980 to 2010.[6] Although
the European literature has been rife with discussions of electoral de-
alignment and instability (Dalton, Flanagan and Beck 1984; Franklin
et al. 1992), the mean regional volatility score has changed little over
time, averaging 9.4 percent in the 1980s, 11.3 percent in the 1990s, and
10.5 percent in the first decade of the 21st century. Electoral volatility in
the United States is even lower, averaging 4.2 percent in congressional
elections and 8.8 percent in presidential elections between 1980 and 2010.
By contrast, mean volatility in Latin American countries during this period
was 23 percent in legislative elections and 25.9 percent in presidential
elections. Although volatility was even higher (32.3 percent) in
Central and Eastern Europe following the demise of communism, it must

---

[6] In Figure 2.2, the scores for Western Europe taken from Gallagher, Laver, and Mair (2011: 310) do
not include votes received by new parties that split off from established parties in the calculation of
volatility. In Latin America, however, such splits are often an important indicator of the erosion of
support for traditional parties, as seen, for example, in the division of Mexico's ruling party that led
to the formation of a new leftist rival in the late 1980s. Since failure to count such changes would
seriously underestimate electoral volatility in the region, my calculations include such splits in the
measure of aggregate volatility in Latin America.

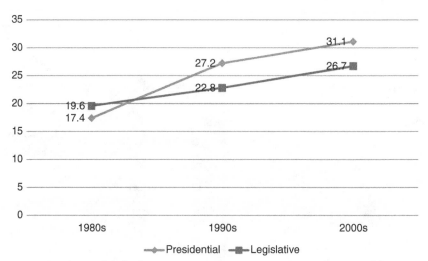

FIGURE 2.3. Electoral Volatility in Latin America, 1980–2010 (Pedersen index)
Sources: Calculated by the author from electoral data provided by Nohlen (2005) and
Georgetown University's *Political Database of the Americas* (http://pdba.georgetown.edu/).

be noted that competitive party systems in that region were still in gestation after more than forty years of single-party rule; other than communist successor parties, elections were contested by parties that had been
newly formed during post-communist regime transitions. By contrast, most
new democratic regimes in Latin America in the 1980s inherited party
systems – many of them quite longstanding – from previous periods of
democratic contestation.

Furthermore, in contrast to Eastern Europe – where volatility declined over
time after regime transitions (see Powell and Tucker 2009) – volatility progressively increased in Latin America after 1980. As Figure 2.3 shows, volatility
scores in legislative elections increased from 19.6 in the 1980s to 22.8 in the
1990s and 26.7 in the first decade of the 21st century; the corresponding scores
for presidential elections were 17.4 in the 1980s, 27.2 in the 1990s, and 31.1
after 2000. Rising volatility challenged claims that party systems were becoming
institutionalized (Dix 1992), and it demonstrated that instability was not just a
function of short-term perturbations associated with authoritarian interludes,
regime transitions, or the debt crisis of the 1980s. Despite progress toward
democratic consolidation and economic stabilization after the 1980s, electoral
volatility increased, indicative of more deeply rooted processes of voter detachment from party organizations.

In short, a large and growing number of Latin American voters are electorally
mobile, making vote choices on the basis of contingent and conjunctural preferences rather than name-brand loyalties. In such contexts, political elites have
weak incentives to rely on parties to resolve collective action problems in the
mobilization of electoral support. Rather than investing in the time and

resource-intensive tasks of organization building – and accepting the constraints on their strategic autonomy that party organizations inevitably impose – political entrepreneurs may opt to appeal to a mobile electorate through some combination of the mass media, non-partisan civic networks, and teams of professionalized, for-hire campaign managers. In contexts of economic crises that call into question the competence of established parties, name brands may even become an electoral liability rather than an asset.

Not surprisingly, then, Latin American democracies are rife with aspiring political entrepreneurs who abandon or avoid established parties and opt to form new parties or campaign as independent outsiders to the partisan establishment. The region's populist tradition has taken a number of different social and economic forms, but anti-establishment politics has been a constant feature (Weyland 2001; Barr 2009; de la Torre 2010). Populist figures often eschew party organization, as they thrive on direct and unmediated relationships to mass constituencies who can be mobilized in opposition to established parties and political elites. Where they do form party organizations, these are kept strictly subordinate to the political authority and interests of the populist leader. As a form of anti-elite and anti-establishment politics, populism flourishes where large numbers of citizens are excluded or alienated from traditional parties – that is, where partisanship is fragile, fluid, or fleeting.

Limited partisanship, of course, is hardly exclusive to Latin American democracies. As Philippe Schmitter (2001) observed, political parties "are not what they once were," even in the European democracies that spawned most of our theoretical models about them. Socioeconomic and technological modernization can detach parties from social constituencies in a number of ways. The religious and class cleavages that built party systems in the industrial era may erode in more secularized, post-industrial societies with larger middle classes, weaker labor unions, universal welfare states, and post-materialist values (Dalton, Flanagan and Beck 1984; Inglehart 1984; Clark and Lipset 1991; Franklin et al. 1992; Pakulski and Waters 1996). Technological changes that professionalize election campaigns – including television advertising, public opinion surveys, and direct mail or internet campaigns – diminish the role of encapsulating mass party organizations in the process of electoral mobilization (see Epstein 1980; Swanson and Mancini 1996). Well-educated citizens have less need for partisan cues to provide information shortcuts in their voting decisions, and a variety of media outlets, interest groups, and social movements now perform some of the interest articulation and socialization functions that parties once monopolized. It's no wonder, then, that scholars detect a generalized detachment of parties from voters (Katz and Mair 1995), a phenomenon that Dalton and Wattenberg (2000) characterize as "parties without partisans."

Building on such insights, Mainwaring and Zoco (2007) provocatively suggest that party systems in "third wave" democracies are naturally less institutionalized than those founded during earlier periods of democracy that were more conducive to the development of mass party organizations with deep roots in social cleavages. Such period and sequencing effects may distinguish Latin American from West European party systems, but they do not readily explain much of the cross-national variation found within the Latin American region. Indeed, Latin America includes relatively new party systems that were founded in the third wave and progressively institutionalized (such as those in Brazil and El Salvador), as well as much older party systems that have suddenly broken down (as in Colombia and Venezuela). Similarly, this cross-national variation isn't explained by Samuels and Shugart's (2010) institutionalist account of party organization, which persuasively argues that presidential systems with separate executive and legislative branches produce party organizations that are prone to internal conflict, personalistic leadership, programmatic ambiguity, and diffuse electorates. "Presidentialized" parties may well differ from those in parliamentary systems, but variation in the strength of partisanship among Latin American cases that are uniformly presidentialist remains a major puzzle.

The organizational properties and adaptive capabilities of individual parties may provide some clues to this puzzle, but they also fall short of a complete explanation. Organizational institutionalization is generally associated with routinization and stability (see Huntington 1968: 12–24; March and Olsen 1989), but it can also produce bureaucratic rigidities that make parties vulnerable to exogenous shocks. Informally organized parties, on the other hand, may be more nimble in adapting to environmental challenges with changes in their program, leadership, or core constituencies (Panebianco 1988; Kitschelt 1994; Roberts 1998; Burgess and Levitsky 2003). Organizational informality, therefore, may be a source of adaptive stability rather than an indicator of fragility. Explanations at the level of individual parties, however, do not account for system-level patterns of stability and change. Systemic patterns are more than the sum of the adaptive capabilities of individual parties, and they possess their own dynamic properties.

This does not mean that systemic properties are fixed in stone. The categorizations of national party systems as institutionalized or inchoate in the seminal study by Mainwaring and Scully (1995) do not necessarily remain valid in the contemporary period. Longstanding party systems have since broken down in Venezuela and Colombia (Pizarro Leongómez 2006), whereas Brazil's notoriously inchoate system gradually solidified, even if it remained fragmented (Hagopian, Gervasoni, and Moraes 2009). Institutionalization, then, is a dynamic rather than a static property, and it is hardly a teleological process; it can vary longitudinally, in either positive or negative directions, within national party systems. Such change over time clearly exists in the absence of changes in electoral rules that might affect the competitive balance or the barriers to the entry of new parties. Explaining variation over time, therefore, can be as daunting as explaining variation across cases, as contemporary patterns cannot be identified simply by extrapolating from the historical record. Where dynamic processes are at work, essentialist characterizations or single-shot measurements of individual party systems can easily become dated, placing a premium on efforts to explain longitudinal patterns of institutional development and decay.

Similar challenges beset efforts to explain the programmatic structuring (or non-structuring) of party systems. The path-breaking study by Kitschelt et al. (2009) marshals a wealth of survey data to demonstrate that some Latin American party systems in the 1990s offered voters reasonably coherent and differentiated programmatic alternatives, whereas others did not. These varying levels of programmatic alignment – which were structured largely but not exclusively by rival preferences toward economic and redistributive policies – were then traced to historical patterns of political and economic development, including a relatively early process of industrialization, extended periods of democratic competition, and more inclusive social welfare policies during the ISI era. Countries that lacked these favorable historical conditions were less likely to structure partisan competition along programmatic lines, making the latter a durable and path-dependent legacy of early 20th-century development experiences.

Kitschelt et al. should be applauded for demonstrating that history matters and that economic structures condition political competition, but the possibility clearly exists that programmatic alignments – like party system institutionalization – can vary over time within a national party system. Such variation can be seen, for example, in the polarization of once-overlapping partisan platforms in the United States (Hacker and Pierson 2005; Hetherington 2011; Aldrich 2011). In Latin America, the collapse of ISI and the onset of market liberalization at the end of the 20th century diffused programmatic competition in many party systems, while the post-adjustment turn to the left restructured it in much of the region; national dynamics depended largely on what types of political actors led and opposed the process of market reform, as explained in subsequent chapters. These shifts hardly deny the significance of the long-term inducements to programmatic structuration identified by Kitschelt et al., but they suggest nevertheless that programmatic alignments are dynamic properties that are susceptible to short-term perturbations, as well as long-term corrosive forces.

CONCLUSION

To understand both longitudinal and cross-national variation in the stability and programmatic alignment of Latin American party systems, it is essential to look at national and regional patterns of change that are located analytically in between the particularism of individual parties and the sweeping universalism of explanations based on societal modernization and the changing functional roles of parties. The starting point is to recognize that party system change in contemporary Latin America is a subset of a larger and vastly more complicated process of societal transformation; namely, the region-wide political adjustment to market globalization in the 1980s and 1990s, and the factors that caused this adjustment to be more traumatic and politically disruptive in some countries than others.

The adjustment to market globalization posed special challenges to mass programmatic parties and the labor-mobilizing party systems they had reconfigured in the middle of the 20th century. The programmatic linkages, stratified sociopolitical cleavages, and encapsulating organizational forms of these party systems were all threatened by the collapse of ISI and the transition to market liberalism. Destabilizing effects were hardly limited to these party systems, however, as those formed around machine, personalist, and professional-electoral parties were also buffeted by economic crises and the erosion of clientelist linkages to popular sectors. Although general trend lines pointed to an expansion of the latter two types of parties – that is, toward the personalization and professionalization of political representation – neither necessarily led to greater institutionalization of political representation.

The longer-term destabilizing effects of this economic transition could be mitigated, however, by certain types of competitive alignments during the process of market reform. Although market liberalization encountered social and political resistance everywhere in Latin America, this resistance was not always channeled by party organizations. Where this resistance cleaved party systems – that is, where clearly-differentiated partisan alternatives existed in support and opposition to the neoliberal model – electoral competition was more stable and institutionalized in the post-adjustment era, moderating the eventual turn to the left. Where this resistance was left largely outside party systems, and partisan competition was not clearly structured by programmatic distinctions, post-adjustment reactive sequences destabilized party systems and outflanked them with new and more radical leftist alternatives.

This variation demonstrates the limits of purely structural explanations of political outcomes, and it suggests that we need an analytical approach that is sensitive to political agency and contingency as well as to structure, and to political continuity in addition to change. It calls, in short, for a critical juncture approach to the study of institutional development, disruption, and transformation. Chapter 3 develops such an approach, and applies it to Latin America's interwoven patterns of political and economic change in the waning decades of the 20th century.

3

Critical Junctures and Party System Change

The process of market globalization – understood as the transnational integration of markets for goods, services, and capital – is inevitably shaped by the particularities of world regions (Katzenstein 2005; Stallings 1995), including their distinctive patterns of political development and their modes of insertion in the global economy. The realignment of states, markets, and social actors associated with globalization and market liberalization in late 20th-century Latin America occurred in a context of redemocratization that inevitably imposed major adjustment burdens on political parties. Although democratization restored parties to political prominence after extended periods of military rule, the "dual transitions" to democracy and economic liberalism were deeply unsettling to party systems in much of the region.

The economic crises of the early 1980s undermined military governments and helped trigger democratic transitions (see Remmer 1992–1993), but they also imposed political costs on incumbent parties after democracy had been installed. Although the ensuing process of market liberalization may have contributed to the stabilization of new democratic regimes by defeating hyperinflation and forging a technocratic consensus in key areas of public policy, it also eroded many of the social and programmatic linkages that bound parties to popular constituencies. Indeed, market liberalization inevitably clashed with modes of political representation that had been forged during a half-century of state-led capitalist development.

The critical juncture framework developed in this chapter seeks to explain why this period of transition aligned and stabilized some party systems, while dealigning and destabilizing others. For most party systems, the political stakes of structural change could not have been higher; they could adapt, realign, or decompose in response to the economic transition, but they could not run in place. The stakes were high, however, precisely because political outcomes were not predetermined by structural change. The collapse of ISI and the transition to neoliberalism generated pressures for political change throughout the region, but the level of "shock" was greater in some countries than in others, and partisan alignments around strategic choices to support or oppose market reforms produced widely varying effects. Institutional effects were thus contingent, and political agency weighed heavily on final outcomes.

The critical juncture approach suggests that party system change in response to exogenous shocks is varied but not random. Variation exists because shocks differ in magnitude or form, and because their effects are mediated by antecedent party system attributes and the strategic choices or alignments of sociopolitical actors. The challenge, then, is to identify the conditional relationships that track countries onto different trajectories of crisis-induced, path-dependent institutional change.

CRITICAL JUNCTURE APPROACHES TO INSTITUTIONAL CHANGE

As a mode of historical institutional analysis, critical juncture approaches allow for the comparison of cross-national, path-dependent political changes that unfold "through a series of sequential stages" (Mahoney 2001b: 112). Although the approach has been widely used, explicitly or implicitly, to study the historical development of both party systems (Lipset and Rokkan 1967) and political regimes (Collier and Collier 1991; Luebbert 1991; Yashar 1995; Mahoney 2001a), it is sometimes criticized for conceptual imprecision, particularly in the identification of what constitutes a critical juncture.[1] Clearly, all countries experience political moments when institutions change, actors rise or fall, or electoral and policy shifts occur. If change is ubiquitous in political affairs, then not all changes can be considered critical junctures, as these (by definition) have lasting effects; critical junctures produce institutional outcomes that condition what follows in their wake, even if they do not lock such outcomes into place. A shift in a party's electoral fortunes, for example, may simply reflect cyclical fluctuations in voting behavior, a partial increment in a cumulative process of electoral change, or a temporary deviation from established voting patterns that reassert themselves in subsequent electoral cycles. None of these changes have the durable consequences that are the hallmark of critical junctures. The same can be said about the "serial replacement" of institutional arrangements analyzed by Levitsky and Murillo (forthcoming), whereby one set of temporary and contingent institutions is routinely displaced by others, without leaving behind any durable legacies.

Furthermore, as Thelen (2004: 35–36) suggests, cumulative processes of political change often come nested within broader patterns of institutional continuity. Change, therefore, may occur incrementally through "periodic political realignment and renegotiation," with institutions adapting to pressures for

[1] See, for example, the reviews by Paul W. Drake in the *American Political Science Review* 86, 3 (September): 823–824 and Domínguez (1992: 327).

change through processes of "layering" (grafting new elements onto old) or "conversion" (altering political roles in response to new goals or coalition members). Established parties, for example, may remain electorally dominant while adapting to societal change by altering their linkage patterns, coalitional bases, organizational forms, or policy orientations. Basic changes in political representation can thus occur within an overarching process of electoral continuity and institutional adaptation.

The obverse is also possible, whereby institutions are fluid, but underlying patterns of representation are quite stable. This can sometimes be seen when weakly institutionalized "flash" parties come and go, creating high levels of electoral volatility (Sanchez 2009). Voters, however, may simply be cycling among a fluid set of personalistic vehicles, in which case there is little change in the logic of political (dis)organization or the character of partisan appeals based on personalistic linkages. Whether a scholar highlights patterns of change or continuity in any context thus depends on the political phenomenon under investigation and the level of analysis that is chosen (see Capoccia and Kelemen 2007: 349).

Given these complexities, what are the identifying markers of a critical juncture, and how can one be distinguished from the more gradual, cumulative patterns of institutional evolution analyzed by Thelen (2004; see also Mahoney and Thelen 2010), or the fluid serial replacement analyzed by Levitsky and Murillo? Clearly, critical junctures are not periods of "normal politics" when institutional continuity or incremental change can be taken for granted. They are periods of crisis or strain that existing policies and institutions are ill-suited to resolve. As such, they challenge the reproduction of existing institutions and generate powerful pressures for policy and/or institutional changes that are (a) abrupt; (b) discontinuous; and (c) path dependent. Changes are abrupt because critical junctures contain decisive "choice points" when major reforms are debated, policy choices are made, and institutions are created, reconfigured, or displaced. They are discontinuous because they diverge sharply from baseline trajectories of institutional continuity or incremental adaptation; in short, they represent a significant break with established patterns. Finally, change is path dependent because it creates new political alignments and institutional legacies that shape and constrain subsequent political development.

Critical junctures are characterized by high levels of uncertainty and political contingency. As Capoccia and Kelemen (2007: 343) state, "the range of plausible choices available to powerful political actors expands substantially" during a critical juncture, while "the consequences of their decisions . . . are potentially much more momentous." Given the centrality of strategic choice, political outcomes are indeterminate and varied; they are not structurally determined by the crises or strains that precipitate the critical juncture (Collier and Collier 1991: 29). As such, there is a limited basis for claims that a major change in a single unit of analysis constitutes a critical juncture, in isolation from patterns observed elsewhere. A counterfactual thought experiment might explain potential variance in hypothesized outcomes in a single case (Capoccia and Kelemen 2007: 355–357), but a critical juncture approach has more analytical leverage when controlled comparisons are used to identify the causal processes that produce divergent outcomes across a range of cases that are subjected to similar pressures for change.

Indeed, systematic comparison across a range of cases may provide evidence of significant variation in how abrupt, discontinuous, and path dependent institutional change actually is within a shared critical juncture. Political actors can adopt bold policy or institutional innovations in response to a crisis – for example, the comprehensive neoliberal "shock treatments" applied to contain hyperinflationary spirals in Bolivia, Peru, and Argentina – but they may also try to "muddle through" a crisis with only minor or piecemeal adjustments. Some leaders, constrained by interest group pressures, internal party opposition, or ideological predispositions, may even postpone reforms altogether in hopes that a crisis will pass or be handed down to political successors to manage. Such paralysis, however, runs the risk that a crisis will deepen or spread, possibly leading to more dramatic disruptions down the road – as Alan García and APRA painfully learned in Peru.

Likewise, critical junctures create major institutional discontinuities in many cases, but such change is not imperative for *every* case in a shared critical juncture. Some cases may weather the storm with less disruption than others; indeed, taken on their own, they may not appear to have passed through a critical juncture at all. Such cases of relative institutional continuity at the "low end" of the spectrum of change, however – such as the Honduran party system in this study – can be highly instructive from a comparative perspective for understanding causal mechanisms and conditional effects during a shared critical juncture. To exclude such cases would truncate the dependent variable, introducing a form of selection bias that could skew causal inferences (Collier and Mahoney 1996). Unbiased causal inference, therefore, requires a full range of variation on the dependent variable of change and continuity in party systems that experienced the transition to market liberalism at the end of the 20th century.

Finally, if critical junctures produce sharper discontinuities in some cases than others, so also do their political legacies vary in their durability or level of institutionalization. Critical juncture arguments conventionally posit a punctuated equilibrium model of institutional change, whereby an institutional equilibrium is disrupted by a shock, eliciting a discontinuous shift to a new equilibrium state that is reproduced through positive feedback or increasing returns processes (Pierson 2000). When viewed across a range of cases, however, it is possible to see that critical junctures may spawn durable legacies of new, self-reinforcing institutional equilibria in some cases, but equilibria that are prone to "negative feedback" or "undermining" processes in others (and, consequently, susceptible to endogenous processes of change; see Grief and Laitin 2004). Indeed, some cases may experience an institutional breakdown or exit a critical juncture with the forms of institutional disequilibria captured by Levitsky and Murillo's notion of serial replacement. To paraphrase Schumpeter (1950), critical junctures are periods of creative destruction; they typically dislodge or de-align institutions, but they need not re-align or re-equilibrate them in every case, much less generate durable new ones to take the place of the old.

This does not mean that critical junctures do not produce path-dependent legacies. Rather, it suggests that the institutional "lock in" produced by increasing returns is not the only possible type of legacy, for two principal reasons. First, as Levitsky and Murillo argue (forthcoming), de-institutionalization can also follow a self-reinforcing, path-dependent logic, with initial institutional failures "in historically contingent circumstances" fostering expectations and strategic behavior that make institutional fluidity a durable condition. Political actors may adopt short time horizons, hedge their bets, and invest resources in extra-institutional arenas that do little to stabilize – and may even undermine – more formal types of institutions (such as party organizations). The Peruvian case – which has essentially functioned without a party "system" since the early 1990s (Sanchez 2009) – demonstrates that de-institutionalized, personalistic forms of electoral competition may well be a self-reinforcing equilibrium under certain conditions. A broad comparative perspective thus suggests that a critical juncture, in some cases, might produce a durable legacy of de-institutionalization rather than institutional lock-in. This study provides evidence of both types of legacies.

Second, as Grief and Laitin (2004: 649) argue, the behavior of rational actors in equilibrium is self-reinforcing for institutions "in larger or smaller sets of situations," beyond which it may undermine said institutions. Consequently, institutional equilibria are "more or less sensitive to exogenous shocks" and "environmental changes." This insight has important implications for understanding the varying durability of political outcomes produced by a shared critical juncture. As we will see, the social and political "environment" during the critical juncture of structural adjustment was quite different from that of the post-adjustment or aftermath period; some market reform alignments were highly sensitive to the social pressures and reactive sequences of the post-adjustment environment, whereas others were resilient or even self-reinforcing. Indeed, partisan reform alignments *conditioned*, in a path-dependent manner, the types and intensity of reactive sequences that they would encounter in aftermath periods, with some types – namely, mass social protest – being far more disruptive than others. The policy and institutional outcomes of any critical juncture may be contested in reactive sequences (Mahoney 2001a), but these sequences are not random; they are patterned events and processes that often follow a path-dependent logic. Reactive sequences may reinforce some outcomes, producing linear legacies of institutional continuity, but they may corrode or destabilize others and generate a legacy of ongoing institutional change or fluidity.

These different types of institutional legacies are readily apparent in the aftermath of Latin America's neoliberal critical junctures, and they drive home the importance of a broad comparative perspective in the study of institutional change and continuity. Such a perspective suggests that the incremental patterns of institutional change identified by Thelen and the serial replacement analyzed by Levitsky and Murillo are not necessarily antithetical to a critical juncture approach. They may, in fact, represent alternative institutional legacies of a critical juncture that also produces patterns of discontinuous but self-reinforcing institutional change – that is, the conventional punctuated equilibrium model – in a specified set of cases.

With respect to party systems, cross-national pressures for change are likely to have powerful structural determinants. This reflects both the common political strains associated with particular stages of socioeconomic development and the shared vulnerability to international disturbances of dependent, globally integrated national economies. Severe, region-wide economic crises related to international shocks and domestic developmental bottlenecks have been integral features of critical junctures in Latin America; they signal the exhaustion of a given development model, and they generate pressures for a shift in the mode of capital accumulation. Critical junctures, then, have been periods when states significantly augment or scale back their developmental and social welfare responsibilities, the range of societal outcomes determined by market exchanges sharply contracts or expands, and the social landscape is transformed by new patterns of collective action or the demise of old ones. These realignments of multiple social fields alter the ways in which party systems mediate between citizens and states, producing fundamental changes in the social bases and programmatic structuring of partisan competition.

So conceived, cross-national critical junctures in party system development correspond to major turning points in the stages or patterns of capitalist development. Such turning points are rare in occurrence, broad in their scope, and profound in their institutional effects. They are not simply periods of political or institutional change, but of multidimensional realignment of economic, social, and political fields. Two such periods are identifiable in the modern Latin American experience. The first was associated with the onset of mass politics in the early 20th century as the commodity-export model of development entered into crisis and incipient industrialization transformed the social landscape. The political mobilization of the working class challenged oligarchic political domination and transformed national party systems, while states sharply expanded their developmental and social welfare roles as the ISI model got underway during the Great Depression. The second period corresponded to the demise of the ISI model and the realignment of states and markets around global circuits of production, finance, and exchange, especially in the aftermath of the debt crisis of the early 1980s. This second critical juncture undermined the labor-based modes of political representation that thrived during the ISI era, thus altering parties' societal linkages, cleavage structures, and organizational patterns. Party systems varied widely in their ability to respond to these exogenous shocks.

For a critical juncture approach to explain such variation, it is essential to identify three distinct stages of institutional development. The first stage corresponds to the antecedent conditions, which establish the institutional baseline for the critical juncture and at least some of the political actors and power relations that will shape its dynamics. The second stage is the critical juncture itself, when an exogenous shock or endogenous strains challenge the institutional baseline and force political actors to make decisive choices about policy or institutional reform. The third stage is the aftermath period, when the outcomes of the critical juncture are challenged by reactive sequences that can lock in or reconfigure its institutional legacies. These three stages, and their relationship to party system change, are examined below.

ANTECEDENT CONDITIONS, INSTITUTIONAL BASELINES, AND CONDITIONING CAUSES

Antecedent conditions, or the prevailing political and socioeconomic conditions prior to the onset of a critical juncture, are much more than the "start of the story." More fundamentally, they perform three important theoretical roles in a critical juncture account. First, they establish a policy and/or institutional baseline against which to assess political change and continuity during a critical juncture. Without the specification of such a baseline, it is not possible to measure the degree of change or to assess its varied dimensions. For our purposes, the most basic dimensions along which to assess institutional change and continuity are (1) the organizational composition of a party system; (2) the competitive balance between its constituent units; and (3) the programmatic structuring of partisan competition. Organizational composition refers to the major party units in any given system, while the competitive balance refers to their relative electoral strength (i.e., the allocation of vote shares among them). Programmatic structuring is the extent to which major parties compete on the basis of policy or ideological distinctions; it is heavily conditioned by parties' societal linkages and cleavage patterns.

Second, although critical junctures are often triggered by exogenous shocks, they may have roots as well in endogenous societal strains or pressures that are embedded in antecedent conditions. Antecedent conditions are thus important for contextualizing a critical juncture and explaining its origins (Falleti and Lynch 2008), as well as the social and political actors who will adopt – or contest – potential policy or institutional reforms. For example, neoliberal critical junctures began in most Latin American countries with an exogenous shock – the onset of the debt crisis in 1982. In much of the region, however, the ISI model had already run out of steam when the debt crisis hit, creating endogenous political and economic pressures for policy reform. This was especially true in the early-industrializing Southern Cone countries of Argentina, Chile, and Uruguay, where prolonged economic stagnation and military coups in the mid-1970s led to initial attempts at market liberalization well in advance of the region-wide debt crisis. Indeed, the heavy reliance on external debt that culminated in the region-wide crisis of the 1980s was itself related to the developmental bottlenecks that threatened to "exhaust" the ISI model in the 1960s and 1970s. Clearly, then, endogenous strains both contextualized and interacted with pressures for change emanating from an exogenous shock.

Third, and most important for our purposes, antecedent conditions may be part of the causal chain in a theoretical explanation of institutional change when they differentiate units undergoing similar critical junctures. They may, in short, possess "conditioning causes" that "vary before a critical juncture, and that predispose cases to diverge as they ultimately do" (Slater and Simmons 2008: 8). Consequently, similar strains or exogenous shocks may produce critical junctures in multiple units that have distinct baselines, and thus experience the critical juncture in different ways. Conditioning causes do not generate the critical juncture itself, but they weigh directly on its dynamics and shape its divergent outcomes.

Such conditioning causes were clearly present in Latin America's transition from ISI to neoliberalism. Three types of conditioning causes differentiated countries as they entered the critical juncture: (1) the nature of party systems as they developed over the course of the ISI era; (2) the depth of the ISI experience and state-led development; and (3) the balance between conservative and populist or leftist forces. The first two conditioning causes shaped the depth and duration of economic crises during the critical juncture, as well as their levels of political disruption. Simply put, countries that developed labor-mobilizing (LM) party systems and pursued aggressive state-led development models during the ISI era were prone to more severe economic crises and more disruptive patterns of institutional change (see Chapters 4 and 5). The third conditioning cause was important because it shaped the partisan alignments of market reform; programmatically aligning patterns of reform were more likely where conservative forces were dominant yet contested, whereas de-aligning reforms were common where conservative forces were too weak to impose structural adjustment (see Chapter 6). For this reason, the military dictatorships of the 1970s and the democratic transitions of the 1980s were major components of the antecedent conditions, as they bequeathed very different partisan balances that weighed heavily on reform alignments during the process of market liberalization.

Variation in these three conditioning causes ensured that Latin American countries would not enter neoliberal critical junctures on equal footing. Those with LM party systems and deeper ISI experiences required more traumatic adjustments to align their political economy with the globalized market logic of the neoliberal era. Those with conservative forces that were too weak to lead the process of market reform, or leftist forces that were too weak to contest it, developed reform alignments that were poorly suited to withstand the reactive sequences of the aftermath period. Although antecedent conditions did not dictate the outcomes of critical junctures, they had a major impact on the dynamic properties that differentiated national experiences.

In short, LM party systems were an unstable equilibrium during neoliberal critical junctures, and de-aligned party systems were an unstable equilibrium in the very different setting of the aftermath period. No specific pattern of change was pre-determined by antecedent institutional or structural conditions, however. Had outcomes been pre-determined, the critical juncture itself would have no effect, and causal attribution would have to be sought in more distant historical conjunctures – what Mahoney (2001b: 113) refers to as "the problem of infinite explanatory regress into the past." What makes a juncture truly "critical" is the realistic possibility of divergent outcomes – or, put another way, the contingency of outcomes, based on the dynamic properties of the critical juncture itself.

DYNAMICS OF CHANGE DURING CRITICAL JUNCTURES

In their most elemental form, critical junctures in party system development are periods of crisis, choice, and change. They emerge when structural dislocations or crises generate pressures for fundamental policy or institutional reform that threaten to dislodge party systems or otherwise alter the ways in which they mediate between states and societies. The causal relationships between crisis, choice and change are best understood by first identifying different patterns of party system transformation – adaptation, electoral realignment, decomposition, and reconstitution – and then explaining how these patterns are shaped by crises and policy choices.

Patterns of Party System Transformation

From any given institutional baseline, the starting points for measuring party system change and continuity are (1) the organizational composition of the party system (i.e., the party units that comprise the system), and (2) the competitive balance between these parties (i.e., the allocation of vote shares among them). Together, these make up a party system's *electoral alignment*; the notion of *programmatic alignment*, which refers to policy and ideological differentiation among competing parties, will be addressed below. Continuity in organizational composition means that the same major parties remain electorally dominant from the antecedent period through the critical juncture. A change in organizational composition occurs when major parties disappear, split, or merge, and/or when new parties emerge as major power contenders. For example, let party system P_i at time period t be composed of major parties A, B, and C, such that $P_{it} = A + B + C$. A change in organizational composition would occur if A, B, or C were to disappear or merge in time period $t + 1$, or if they were joined by a new major party, D.

Continuity in the competitive balance signifies that there are no significant, durable vote shifts among the major party units, even if there are short-term fluctuations from one election cycle to another. Change in the competitive balance, on the other hand, means that there has been a durable reallocation of vote shares (for example, a vote shift in P_i from party A and/or B to party C that persists over time). Major vote shifts can alter the competitive balance of a party system with or without changes in its organizational composition.

Combining these two dimensions, it is possible to identify four ideal–typical patterns of change and continuity in the electoral alignment of national party systems during a critical juncture. First, party system *adaptation* signifies that there is little or no change in either the organizational composition or the competitive balance of a given party system; established parties weather destabilizing pressures without experiencing durable vote shifts, adapting their programmatic positions and societal linkages to the demands of a new period. In Honduras, for example, the two traditional parties – the Nationals (PNH) and Liberals (PLH) – remained electorally dominant and alternated in office throughout the critical juncture and well into the aftermath period, without experiencing durable shifts in vote shares. In this case, $P_{it} = (A + B) \rightarrow P_{it+1} = (A + B)$, with no major change in the competitive equilibrium between A and B.

Second, *electoral realignment* occurs when there is little or no change in the organizational composition of a party system, but major vote shifts alter the competitive balance between these parties. Realignment, in short, is a shift from one competitive equilibrium to another among the same set of party organizations. Uruguay provides a good example; the same three major parties composed the system from the antecedent period through the critical juncture, but the two traditional conservative parties progressively lost vote shares to a strengthening leftist alternative, the *Frente Amplio* (FA, or Broad Front). In short, $P_{it} = (A + B + C) \rightarrow P_{it+1} = (A' + B' + C')$, with C' gaining votes at the expense of A' and B'.

Third, party system *decomposition* occurs when established parties lose control over electoral outcomes and are largely or entirely displaced by new political movements, short-lived "flash parties," or independent personalities. Decomposition produces an organizationally fluid competitive dynamic, as the electoral arena does not have a stable set of contending parties. Peru, following the demise of traditional parties in the early 1990s, is a paradigmatic case.[2]

Finally, where durable new party organizations displace the old ones, party system *reconstitution* occurs. Reconstitution essentially entails a shift from one party system to another, such that $P_{it} = (A + B + C) \rightarrow P_{it+1} = (D + E + F)$. Clearly, decomposition could be merely a preliminary stage in the construction of a reconstituted party system; Venezuela, Bolivia, and Ecuador provide partial examples, as dominant new leftist parties have largely displaced traditional parties. Opposition forces struggled to institutionalize partisan alternatives, however, delaying a full-fledged process of party system reconstitution. Indeed, as the Peruvian case demonstrates, reconstitution is far from automatic, given the prevalence and electoral viability of loosely organized personalist

---

[2] APRA survived the meltdown of the early 1990s in gravely weakened form, and thereafter was electorally competitive only when Alan García was running for office.

movements and short-lived electoral coalitions (Hale 2006). In short, party systems that break down or decompose do not necessarily re-compose; as noted above, party system de-institutionalization may well create its own competitive equilibrium.

Party systems that are relatively stable during a critical juncture may re-align or even decompose in the aftermath period if they are susceptible to disruptive reactive sequences. Furthermore, national party systems can experience complex, hybrid mixes of these different patterns of change, with some parties adapting or re-aligning, and others decomposing or reconstituting. In Argentina, for example, the Peronist party continually adapted, while the anti-Peronist side of the party system decomposed in the aftermath period (and has not, to date, been reconstituted). The ideal–typical patterns outlined above, however, outline the range of logical possibilities of party system change and continuity during a critical juncture and its aftermath.

Crises and Party System Change

The structural dislocations and crises that transform party systems during critical junctures can take a number of different forms. Even before the exogenous shock of the Great Depression, early 20th-century critical junctures were shaped by a crisis of political incorporation – that is, the need for oligarchic political orders to incorporate the rising urban working and middle classes (Collier and Collier 1991). In some countries, like Uruguay and Colombia, party system adaptation occurred when traditional oligarchic parties built linkages to working- and lower-class voters and remained electorally dominant. In much of the region, however, party systems were at least partially reconstituted by the rise of new populist or leftist parties that mobilized previously excluded groups.

The crisis associated with the late 20th-century transition from ISI to market liberalism, however, created a very different type of critical juncture for party systems – one driven by the need to reproduce their electoral support during a period of acute economic crisis, social dislocation, and demobilization. In many respects these critical junctures were exclusionary rather than incorporating, especially in the Southern Cone countries of Chile, Argentina, and Uruguay, where market reforms began under military dictatorships that brutally repressed unions and labor-based parties. Even where market liberalization occurred under democratic auspices, economic crises and structural adjustment undermined the organizational and political weight of labor and popular movements (Roberts 2002). Indeed, market liberalization often followed a technocratic political logic that helped to insulate policymakers from societal pressures and democratic contestation (Centeno 1994; Haggard and Kaufman 1995; Domínguez 1997b; Teichman 2001), effectively depoliticizing much of the policymaking process (Roberts 2008). While not formally excluded from political participation, popular sectors were surely weakened as collective political subjects for most of the critical juncture.

Although some party systems adapted (in the short term) to this context of economic crisis and social dislocation, most experienced major electoral realignments or patterns of decomposition. As shown in Chapter 5, the path of adaptation was restricted to a small number of countries with elitist party systems in the antecedent period; countries that entered the critical juncture with LM party systems experienced the more significant discontinuities associated with electoral realignment or organizational decomposition. This variation was attributable, in part, to the greater disruption of party system linkage and cleavage patterns in the LM cases.

Discontinuity in the LM cases, however, also reflected the political turmoil caused by especially severe economic crises during the critical juncture. The management of crisis, stabilization, and reform was fraught with both peril and opportunities for parties, producing highly variable allocations of political costs and benefits among established parties and outsiders. As Remmer (1991) has shown, incumbent parties that became mired in economic crises – even crises that were partially attributable to exogenous international shocks – tended to face large anti-incumbent vote shifts. Conversely, parties that inherited a severe crisis, especially hyperinflation, and then managed stabilization and recovery could reap electoral dividends in the form of pro-incumbent vote swings (Roberts and Wibbels 1999). Consequently, the highest levels of institutional continuity – namely, those associated with party system adaptation – should be found in countries that experienced relatively mild economic crises and thus generated only moderate pressures for retrospective, performance-based vote shifts, whether pro- or anti-incumbent. Rival parties might alternate in office, but no durable realignment is likely to be produced by the crisis itself. Honduras provides the best example of this dynamic.

Electoral re-alignment, on the other hand, is likely when a serious crisis produces uneven political effects that reallocate vote shares, altering the competitive balance of a party system. A crisis may, for example, shift votes from an incumbent party deemed responsible for a crisis to a successor party that reaps electoral rewards from stabilization and recovery. Such vote shifts can endure if they reflect changing partisan reputations for effective economic governance. Argentina's economic crisis at the end of the 1980s produced such a re-alignment, with hyperinflation draining support from the incumbent Radical Party, and subsequent stabilization helping to strengthen the Peronists after the imposition of market reforms.[3]

---

[3] This dynamic was repeated in 2001–2002 when a severe financial crisis erupted under a Radical Party-led coalition government, and the Peronists managed a vibrant recovery. The anti-Peronist side of the party system largely decomposed after this second major crisis, leaving Peronist dominance largely uncontested.

Whereas electoral re-alignment suggests that the political costs of economic crisis and/or reform are concentrated on a portion of the party system, decomposition implies that these costs are widely diffused among the major established parties. In short, costs are systemic in their form and effects, as votes are eventually transferred from established parties to extra-systemic outsiders, independents, or political movements. This is most likely where economic crises are prolonged or recurring, spreading the costs of crisis management among the major power contenders. Established parties may take turns in office through a process of iterative anti-incumbent vote swings, producing decomposition as a cumulative effect of retrospective verdicts. Unless one of the established parties can convince the electorate that a new set of leaders or policies will turn things around, voters may shift *en masse* to a political outsider who is untainted by an association with a failed status quo. Party system decomposition in Ecuador, Peru, and Venezuela manifested elements of this pattern.

The different causal logics underpinning electoral realignment and decomposition suggest that crisis severity – a factor that is often stressed in studies of the political conditions for market reform (Nelson 1990; O'Donnell 1994b; Weyland 2002) – may be less important than crisis duration in explaining party system breakdowns. A severe crisis of short duration may damage a ruling party and realign a party system electorally, but it need not bring down the entire system if a rival party can reap the dividends from economic stabilization. Prolonged or recurrent crises that diffuse political costs widely, however, are more likely to spawn populist outsiders who mobilize support by attacking the partisan establishment.

Ultimately, however, the destabilizing effects of neoliberal critical junctures were not simply a function of the depth or duration of economic crises and performance-induced shifts in vote shares. Crisis management was high-stakes politics, and it accentuated the importance of political agency and policy choices. The demise of ISI and the transition to market liberalism may have been rooted in deep structural bottlenecks and global market pressures, but their political effects were far more contingent. Although every country in the region liberalized, the pace, depth, timing, and political alignments of the liberalization process differentiated national experiences. The implications of these differences for party systems are analyzed in the next section.

Policy Choice and the Programmatic (De-)Alignment of Party Systems

The structural dislocations and crises that trigger critical junctures inevitably force political actors to make difficult policy choices – often ones with high risks and uncertain payoffs. In neoliberal critical junctures, the central policy choice faced by political elites was whether or not to adopt orthodox austerity and structural adjustment measures in response to mounting inflationary pressures generated by fiscal and foreign exchange deficits. Political leaders who rejected the orthodox recipe – and the potential for international financial relief it provided – typically relied on more heterodox measures, such as wage and price controls, to tame inflationary pressures. The basic choice between orthodox and heterodox stabilization strategies had several features that were characteristic of "choice points" in critical junctures.

First, although acute fiscal and foreign exchange constraints foreclosed some statist policy alternatives of the past, they created openings for a multi-faceted, orthodox policy shift that was scarcely imaginable beforehand. Conservative political and business elites in Latin America had long advocated more liberal development policies, but the comprehensive market orthodoxy that spread across the region during the critical juncture was nowhere on the agenda until Chile's Chicago School technocrats were plucked from academic obscurity by the country's military rulers in the mid-1970s (see Silva 1996). Even then, the new economic model was so thoroughly intertwined with the military dictatorships of the Southern Cone (Foxley 1983), and so clearly threatening to a broad array of societal interests, that it seemed inconceivable for it to be introduced by democratic regimes that lacked a Pinochet's license for coercion. Only under the grave circumstances of the debt and inflationary crises of the 1980s did the policy shift become a plausible alternative for elected rulers who were accountable to popular preferences.

Second, policy choices during the critical juncture were uncertain in their political payoffs and their impact on economic performance. Governing parties that resisted market reforms and clung to heterodox policies in the midst of deepening inflationary crises typically paid a steep price at the ballot box; such was the fate, for example, of the Bolivian left in the early 1980s, the Peruvian APRA, and Argentina's Radical Party. Conversely, leaders who adopted structural adjustment policies in hyperinflationary contexts that contributed to stabilization and recovery – such as Fujimori in Peru, Menem in Argentina, and Cardoso in Brazil – could reap electoral rewards for "swallowing the bitter pill" of market orthodoxy (Weyland 1998). As Remmer (2003: 51) argued, electoral competition "exercised a disciplining impact on economic policy, generating political incentives for government leaders to introduce and sustain reforms in order to maintain macroeconomic stability and restore growth."

Orthodox adjustment, however, provided no guarantee against voter backlash. As the Venezuelan and Ecuadorean cases demonstrate (see Part II), the social costs of market reforms – real or perceived – carried their own political risks, including the threat of explosive social protest. Given short-term hardships and uncertain secular economic improvements, societal resistance to market reforms – especially comprehensive shock treatment – could be pronounced where they weren't adopted in a context of hyperinflationary spirals that thoroughly discredited the status quo (Weyland 2002). Even more gradual reforms sometimes drained support from incumbent parties and strengthened their opponents, thus realigning electoral competition; the progressive strengthening of the Uruguayan left during the critical juncture is a case in point. Consequently, electoral realignment signifies that a durable, directional vote shift has occurred, but such vote shifts may be either toward or away from market reformers.

In short, the effects of market liberalization on party systems and voting behavior could not be mechanically inferred from the performance of the economy or the content of specific policies, and the political costs of miscalculation by reformers rivaled those associated with heterodox mismanagement or non-reform. Political effects could vary with the timing of reforms in a crisis cycle and the packaging of different reform measures. Such conditional effects indicate that neoliberal critical junctures were characterized by causal complexity (Ragin 1987), whereby the impact of a variable depended on the presence or absence of other variables.

This causal complexity is especially apparent when considering a third key attribute of policy choices during neoliberal critical junctures – their contested character, and how this contestation mapped onto partisan alignments. Structural adjustment was controversial everywhere, as it affected a wide range of societal interests and created both winners and losers. Societal interests and preferences, however, mapped imperfectly onto the partisan logic of market liberalization, as reforms were adopted by a remarkably diverse set of parties and political actors. In some cases, market reforms reinforced traditional alignments between societal preferences and party organizations; in others, they diffused or reshuffled those alignments. Consequently, beyond their effects on the *electoral* alignment of party systems – that is, their impact on the allocation of vote shares – neoliberal critical junctures also influenced the *programmatic* alignment of party systems, or the extent to which partisan competition cleaved the electorate around alternative policy preferences and programmatic linkages. Critical junctures aligned some party systems programmatically, but de-aligned others, with fateful consequences for the stability of party systems in the aftermath period.

To understand these consequences, it is important to clarify three basic requirements for the programmatic structuring of party systems (see Kitschelt et al. 2009; Lupu 2011). First, parties must adopt relatively coherent stands on salient issues that divide the body politic, allowing them to construct programmatic linkages to voters with policy preferences. Programmatic linkages are diffused when different sub-units or factions of a party adopt disparate positions on major issues, rendering the party's programmatic stance incoherent. Likewise, programmatic structuring is weakened when parties compete on the basis of non-programmatic distinctions, such as personalistic appeals, the distribution of clientelist rewards, or their relative capacity to achieve "valence" goals about which everyone agrees.

Second, the policies adopted by a party in public office must have some meaningful resemblance to the platform on which it ran, and to the principles or policy commitments that it has historically championed. No governing party fully implements its campaign platform, given the emergence of unforeseen circumstances and the inevitable compromises and modifications that arise during legislative and policymaking processes. Nevertheless, for programmatic linkages to be sustained, voters need to be confident that platforms provide at least a basic policy or philosophical orientation to guide a party's response to changing conditions. Programmatic inconsistency or "bait and switch" tactics – when parties win an electoral mandate by advocating policies that they quickly jettison after taking office – sever the relationships between election campaigns, voter preferences, and the content of public policy. Such inconsistency prevents voters from forming reasonable expectations about party behavior in public office.

Third, meaningful differences must exist in the programmatic alternatives offered by major parties. Even if parties adopt clear policy stands, programmatic competition will be undermined if they overlap or position themselves so close together on major policy issues that voters cannot easily tell them apart, or cannot identify tangible differences in the likely outcomes associated with partisan choices. In the absence of programmatic differentiation, voters have little reason to expect one party to favor their interests more than others, and thus little rationale to form partisan loyalties around programmatic commitments.

In much of Latin America, the politics of market reform undermined all three of these preconditions for programmatic structuration. Policy switching was widespread (Stokes 2001a), as a diverse range of populist and center-left parties often took the lead in the market reform process, despite its incongruence with their established programmatic commitments. Bait-and-switch reforms were not a simple function of political opportunism or deception, as they were often a response to the tightening of global market constraints and the need to signal credibility to international lenders who conditioned financial relief on market orthodoxy. Whatever their policy preferences, rulers' options were limited by yawning fiscal deficits, balance-of-payments crises, acute inflationary pressures, and the policy conditionality of external lenders.

Nevertheless, policy switches generated internal dissent and factionalism that undermined the programmatic coherence of governing parties. Voters questioned who spoke for a party and what it really stood for, making it difficult to sustain programmatic linkages. Furthermore, policy switches produced a de facto technocratic convergence that largely dissolved traditional programmatic differences between conservative and populist parties. The Washington Consensus may have faced significant (though politically fragmented) opposition at the grassroots level, but it was hegemonic within policymaking circles by the late 1980s, when the heterodox experiments in Argentina, Brazil, and Peru had been thoroughly discredited by hyperinflationary spirals. For the next decade, even governing parties and political leaders who did not embrace neoliberal orthodoxy in the normative sense accepted some variant of market liberalism as "the only game in town." Although the specific content of market reforms adopted by populist parties differed from those of more conservative rivals (see Murillo 2009), the overarching technocratic consensus weakened the programmatic structuring of partisan competition. This consensus – while it lasted – may have diminished ideological conflict in Latin America (Colburn 2002), but it also made it difficult for parties to construct collective identities and societal linkages on the basis of meaningful programmatic distinctions (Lupu 2011; Morgan 2011). In such a context, electoral competition increasingly turned on non-programmatic distinctions such as personality, clientelist networks, or valence and performance reputations.

Programmatic de-structuring, however, was not inevitable in neoliberal critical junctures, as market reforms led by conservative, business-allied political actors were largely compatible with existing programmatic alignments. Indeed, neoliberal critical junctures could actually *enhance* programmatic structuration under two critical conditions: that conservative political actors (whether parties or military rulers) take the lead in the adoption of market reforms, and that a major party of the left remain in opposition during the period of adjustment, allowing societal dissent from market orthodoxy to be channeled into the party system. Where this occurred, electoral competition could pivot on an axis that consistently divided supporters and critics of the neoliberal model, or at least provided voters with a relatively coherent choice between pro-market orthodoxy and alternatives that favored a stronger role for the state – even if global market constraints compressed the policy space between these programmatic alternatives.

The programmatic structuring of partisan competition around the process of market liberalization was thus heavily contingent on the leadership of the reform process and the presence of a major leftist party in opposition. These variables make it possible to distinguish among three basic types of critical junctures: those that structured or aligned party systems programmatically, those that de-aligned them, and those that were neutral in their effects. Programmatic alignment occurred where conservative actors took the lead in the adoption of market reforms and a major party of the left expressed consistent opposition. De-alignment occurred where populist or center-left parties and leaders played a major role in the implementation of market reforms. Neutral critical junctures occurred where conservative actors led the process of market reform, but no major party of the left was present to offer consistent programmatic opposition. Under these latter two types of critical junctures, all the major political contenders supported or participated in the process of market liberalization. Alternatives to neoliberal orthodoxy were thus poorly defined or electorally insignificant, and no consistent programmatic divide structured electoral competition.

Ultimately, then, neoliberal critical junctures could transform both the electoral and programmatic alignments of partisan competition, leaving behind party systems that were differentiated along two primary dimensions: their level of institutionalization and their degree of programmatic structuration. Institutionalized party systems were relatively stable in their organizational composition during the critical juncture; in short, they experienced adaptation or electoral realignment among established parties, rather than decomposition.

Programmatic Structuring of Political Competition	Institutionalized Party System	Non-Institutionalized Party System
High	Contested Liberalism	Polarized Populism/Political Movements
Low	Neoliberal Convergence	Serial Populism

FIGURE 3.1. Institutional Outcomes of Neoliberal Critical Junctures

Party systems were structured programmatically where electoral competition was grounded in a central cleavage between supporters and critics of the neoliberal model. This outcome depended on the aligning or de-aligning character of the market-reform process, and the level of contestation it faced.

Variation along these two dimensions can be depicted in a two-by-two table that identifies four different institutional outcomes of the region-wide critical juncture – in essence, the new institutional baselines for political competition in the aftermath period that began in the late 1990s (see Figure 3.1). In the top left cell, an outcome that I label *contested liberalism*, party systems were both institutionalized and programmatically aligned, as major conservative and leftist parties provided voters with well-established alternatives that defended and challenged market orthodoxy, respectively. In the lower left cell, labeled *neoliberal convergence*, party systems were relatively institutionalized in their organizational composition, but not clearly aligned by a programmatic axis of competition. Two or more established parties competed for office, but none consistently challenged the neoliberal model, as all the major parties had supported or participated in the market-reform process. In the lower right cell labeled *serial populism*, political competition was neither institutionalized nor programmatically aligned, as traditional parties had decomposed and been replaced by independent personalities who largely adhered to the neoliberal model. Finally, in the upper right cell labeled *polarized populism/political movements*, electoral competition was programmatically aligned but not institutionalized. This outcome emerged where party systems decomposed and the electoral arena was cleaved by a dominant populist figure or a new sociopolitical movement that vigorously contested neoliberal orthodoxy.

In short, countries exited the critical juncture with different institutional baselines for confronting the political challenges of the aftermath period, when societal resistance to market liberalization often intensified. The political expression of such resistance was heavily conditioned by these new institutional baselines, which channeled dissent into or outside of (and against) established party systems, spawning very different types of reactive sequences. Reactive sequences either reinforced and stabilized the partisan alignments bequeathed by the critical juncture – in the cases of contested liberalism – or broke them down and generated new pressures for party system change, in the cases of neoliberal convergence and serial populism. In so doing, reactive sequences generated very different types of "left turns" in the aftermath period. Neoliberal critical junctures, therefore, produced divergent institutional outcomes that weighed heavily on the stability of party systems and post-adjustment political shifts to the left.

THE AFTERMATH PERIOD: SOCIAL RESISTANCE, REACTIVE SEQUENCES, AND INSTITUTIONAL LEGACIES

Critical junctures are expected to produce path-dependent trajectories of institutional change that reproduce themselves through a variety of positive feedback mechanisms (Pierson 2000). The mechanisms identified by Pierson help to explain why party system alignments produced by a critical juncture might create such a stable equilibrium; the "sunk costs" represented by investments in party organization, the "adaptive expectations" of voters and political entrepreneurs who benefit from an association with established parties, and the coordination advantages of such parties in electoral and legislative arenas may all contribute to durable partisanship. Such mechanisms produce long-term institutional legacies that can be traced back to formative experiences during the critical juncture itself.

As explained above, however, aftermath periods do not always reproduce the institutional outcomes of a critical juncture. Both policy and institutional outcomes are invariably contested by social and political actors, and some outcomes may be more resilient in the face of such challenges than others. Indeed, different outcomes may well generate distinct types of challenges or strategies for responding to them. Aftermath periods, therefore, generate reactive sequences in which the political outcomes of critical junctures are contested and defended. Where these outcomes are a stable equilibrium, reactive sequences should reinforce and reproduce them under a wide range of circumstances, creating legacies of institutional continuity. Where outcomes are not a stable equilibrium, or are stable only under a restrictive set of conditions, reactive sequences are likely to be corrosive or transformative, creating legacies of de-institutionalization or a susceptibility to new forms of institutional change.

The institutional outcomes of neoliberal critical junctures varied widely in their durability and resiliency. Whereas some outcomes – namely, contested liberalism – proved to be highly resilient in the aftermath period, the outcomes of neoliberal convergence and serial populism were more tenuous, largely because they were the product of critical junctures that failed to align partisan competition programmatically. To reproduce such de-alignment in the aftermath period required the continued technocratic depoliticization of market liberalism and the de-mobilization of popular sectors who opposed it. Consequently, neoliberal convergence and serial populism were not stable equilibriums where societal resistance to market orthodoxy intensified and found political expression; indeed, they were highly vulnerable to the destabilizing effects of reactive sequences that were driven by the mobilization of such resistance.

Clearly, societal resistance to market liberalization did not begin in the aftermath period. As Polanyi (1944) argued, the expansion of markets into new spheres of social relations creates economic insecurity for diverse social groups, fostering a "double movement" of societal pressures to defend, restore, or construct protective measures (see also Smith and Korzeniewicz 1997). In some countries, austerity and adjustment measures during the critical juncture triggered an immediate social backlash in the form of urban protests, strikes, or riots (Walton and Seddon 1994). At times these "IMF riots" succeeded in delaying or watering down subsequent reforms. In countries like Ecuador and Venezuela, social protest helped shape political dynamics during the critical juncture by blocking the full implementation of the neoliberal model and undermining the parties that initiated reforms.

In most of the region, however, early cycles of social protest were too short-lived and narrowly based to block structural adjustment or threaten the political viability of market reformers. They were not, in other words, decisive factors in determining the outcomes of critical junctures in most of the region. Indeed, scholars often noted that societal resistance to market liberalization, especially among organized labor, was significantly less than what had been expected at the dawning of the neoliberal era (see Geddes 1995). As discussed in Chapter 5, economic crises and market reforms eroded the structural conditions for class-based collective action in both industrial and agrarian sectors of the workforce (Kurtz 2004a, 2004b). Traditional labor and peasant movements thus entered into decline in most of the region, helping to insulate technocratic reformers from societal pressures as they focused on the urgent tasks of stabilization and structural adjustment. The decline of class-based actors, therefore, was both a prerequisite for, and a consequence of, aggressive market liberalization.

This logic of demobilization predominated in much of the region so long as inflationary pressures placed structural adjustment at the forefront of the political agenda, while keeping labor and popular movements on the political defensive. Nevertheless, as explained in Chapter 6, mass publics never fully embraced the Washington Consensus that was hegemonic in technocratic policymaking circles. Many citizens supported liberalizing measures that promised to control inflation and improve access to imported goods (Armijo and Faucher 2002; Baker 2003), but privatization policies faced greater opposition (Baker 2009), and sizable majorities supported an active state role in the provision of social welfare. Once stabilization had been achieved – Brazil was the last country in the region to defeat hyperinflation in 1994 – structural adjustment had accomplished the most essential part of its historical mission, and the political agenda shifted to focus on issues of economic growth and social welfare where the performance of liberalized economies was more suspect (see Huber and Solt 2004).

Consequently, Latin America's "Polanyian backlash" – muted during the crisis-plagued period of economic adjustment – intensified in the post-adjustment era as social mobilization and democratic competition politicized the social deficits of the neoliberal model. Market reforms left a sequel of unmet social needs and insecurities, including stagnant wages, unstable and informalized employment, higher prices for once-subsidized consumer goods and public utilities, the loss of community control over land, water, and resources, and access to public services that had been cut or privatized (Eckstein 2001; Eckstein and Wickham-Crowley 2003). The social claims that stemmed from these problems did not generate a centralized collective actor like the labor movements of the past, but they encouraged mobilization by a diverse array of popular subjects in different structural and territorial locations, some of them defined by class positions, and others shaped by common interests as consumers, users of public services, or members of local communities. The decline of organized labor, then, was sometimes offset by the rise of other collective actors, including pensioners, the unemployed, indigenous communities, students, neighborhood groups, and women's organizations. The net result was a decentralized and pluralistic civil society that was largely shorn of corporatist control by states and parties (Oxhorn 1998; Collier and Handlin 2009), but amenable to political mobilization against market orthodoxy – the point of intersection for their otherwise disparate grievances (Silva 2009).

An extensive body of literature has chronicled the rise of social protest movements in Latin America since the late 1990s (Arce and Bellinger 2007; Auyero 2007; Lucero 2008; Rice 2012). Some of the best research, recognizing that generalized mass protest was hardly a universal response to market reforms, has sought to explain why levels of protest were substantially higher in some countries than others (Yashar 2005; Silva 2009). What remains poorly understood is why societal opposition to market liberalization – Polanyi's "double movement" – has been expressed in widely-varying political forms.

Polanyi (1944) provided little systematic guidance for addressing this question, but he recognized that societal resistance could be channeled into institutional political forms and not merely into social protest. That clearly was the case in post-adjustment Latin America, where societal resistance found three quite different types of political expression: (1) social protest movements, including strikes, riots, demonstrations, highway blockages, and occupations of land or public buildings; (2) electoral protest movements, consisting of mass electoral support for anti-neoliberal populist figures or political movements from outside the established party system; and (3) institutionalized partisan competition, which involved growing electoral support for established parties of the left that challenged neoliberal orthodoxy. The first two forms of expression were clearly compatible with each other; indeed, mass social protest often (though not always) preceded the rise of powerful electoral protest movements. These two forms of protest, however, were inversely related to the third type of societal resistance, as established, electorally competitive parties of the left – where they existed – provided institutionalized outlets for social grievances that otherwise might have been channeled into anti-systemic forms of protest.

As explained in Chapter 6, these diverse forms of resistance were conditioned by the political alignments and institutional outcomes of neoliberal critical junctures. The countries with the most explosive patterns of social protest – Venezuela and Ecuador during the critical juncture, and Argentina, Bolivia, and Ecuador in the aftermath period (see Silva 2009) – were all cases of bait-and-switch market reform that programmatically de-aligned party systems and fostered powerful reactive sequences, including partial or complete party system decomposition and the rise of new and more polarizing electoral protest movements with populist or leftist tendencies.[4] Electoral protest movements also emerged in the aftermath period in other countries like Paraguay, Peru, and Costa Rica, where social protest was less extensive, but critical junctures left behind de-aligned or decomposed party systems – that is, forms of neoliberal convergence or serial populism that were vulnerable to electoral "outflanking" on the left.

The political expression of societal resistance was quite different where conservatives imposed market reforms over staunch leftist opposition and critical junctures left in place party systems that were both institutionalized and programmatically aligned – the outcome of contested liberalism. Under contested liberalism, societal resistance could be channeled toward established parties of the left, thus weakening anti-systemic forms of social or electoral protest. This outcome moderated the reactive sequences of the aftermath period, which largely consisted of the progressive electoral strengthening of these institutionalized leftist or center-left parties, including the PT in Brazil, the Socialist/PPD bloc in Chile, the Broad Front in Uruguay, the PRD in Mexico, and the FMLN in El Salvador. In short, reactive sequences produced moderate electoral shifts that reinforced and reproduced the institutional underpinnings of contested liberalism.

As such, contested liberalism spawned a legacy of programmatic and institutionalized competition that was a relatively stable equilibrium, even in a context of shifting societal preferences in the aftermath period. Parties aggregated societal interests and preferences into reasonably coherent and differentiated policy bundles that provided a basis for the reproduction of name-brand loyalties around a programmatic axis of competition. Neoliberal convergence and serial populism, on the other hand, were unstable equilibriums, as their reproduction was contingent on maintaining low levels of social mobilization and preventing democratic competition from politicizing social needs. When mobilization occurred and needs were politicized in the aftermath period, reactive sequences tended to be de-institutionalizing and polarizing – trend lines that pointed in the direction of polarized populism.

Neoliberal critical junctures, then, were not the end of the story, and the political orders they bequeathed were hardly static end-points. Critical junctures were major turning points that heavily conditioned what followed in their wake, and they left behind institutional legacies that varied widely in their durability and susceptibility to reactive sequences. The different stages and elements of the critical juncture argument are summarized in the diagram below (see Figure 3.2).

---

[4] The electoral response in Argentina was different from that in the other three cases, as it involved a shift toward the left within Peronism rather than the rise of an anti-systemic electoral protest movement.

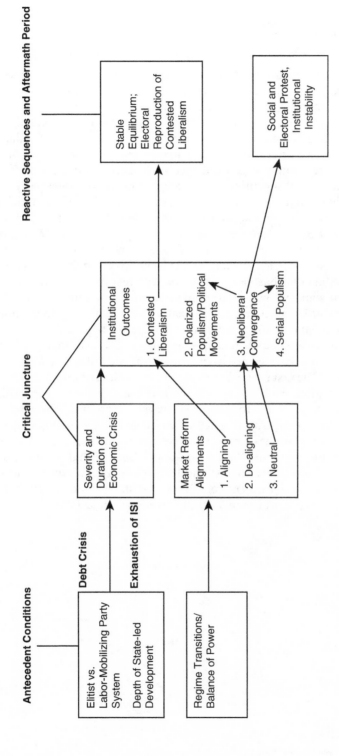

FIGURE 3.2. Outline of the Critical Juncture Model

CONCLUSION

Critical junctures are watershed periods when social and economic strains dislodge and reconfigure political institutions. As major turning points in the turbulent transitions from one political and economic era to another, they realign states, markets, and social actors. In the process, they transform parties' intermediary roles and produce widely varying patterns of change and continuity in party systems. Patterns of party system adaptation, electoral realignment, decomposition, and reconstitution are shaped both by antecedent conditions and by the more contingent political effects of the critical juncture itself.

Neoliberal critical junctures were more disruptive for some party systems than others in Latin America, in part due to variation in the severity and duration of the economic crises that accompanied them, but also because the politics of market liberalization could be programmatically aligning or de-aligning for party systems. Patterns of alignment and de-alignment heavily conditioned the channeling of societal dissent from market orthodoxy and the stability of partisan competition in the post-adjustment era. Different types of critical junctures, therefore, left some party systems more susceptible than others to destabilizing reactive sequences associated with social and/or electoral protest, and they produced different types of "left turns" in the aftermath period.

As conceived here, critical junctures are rare and transformative events that reconfigured party systems during two major periods of societal transition in Latin America. The first ushered in an era of mass politics during the early stages of industrialization, while the second marked a shift from the nationalist and state-centered logic of ISI to globalized market liberalism. The institutional legacies of the earlier critical juncture weighed heavily on Latin American societies during the transition from ISI to neoliberalism at the end of the century. The next chapter explores these institutional legacies and shows how they differentiated countries with elitist and labor-mobilizing party systems during the ISI era, creating antecedent conditions that shaped and constrained more recent patterns of political change during neoliberal critical junctures.

4

Antecedent Conditions: Party System Differentiation in 20th-Century Latin America

Party system change during the transition from ISI to neoliberalism cannot be understood merely by analyzing political alignments and events during the critical juncture itself. Neither can it be understood by examining national cases in isolation from others. A comparative perspective suggests that different countries entered the transition period with distinct antecedent conditions that shaped their respective critical junctures. As such, the causal chains that produced the divergent political outcomes of neoliberal critical junctures can be traced back to development patterns during the ISI era – that is, to the institutional legacies of the earlier, labor – incorporating critical junctures that ushered in the era of mass politics in Latin America.

This chapter and the next explore the party system effects of these two critical junctures. They trace the development of elitist and labor-mobilizing (LM) party systems following the first critical juncture, locate them within their different political economies, and explain why the LM cases were susceptible to more severe political and economic crises during the transition to market liberalism. These two critical junctures demarcate three distinct eras of socioeconomic and political development in Latin America, each of which possessed an alignment of states, markets, and societal actors that shaped national party systems. The first of these alignments, the *oligarchic order*, was characterized by elite political domination, commodity-export development models, and exclusive, oligarchic party systems. This order prevailed from independence in the early 19th century until the early decades of the 20th century, when industrialization, labor mobilization, and eventually the Great Depression undermined oligarchic rule and launched a new era of mass politics. This critical juncture led to the emergence of what Cavarozzi (1994) calls the *state-centric matrix*, which was characterized by state-led industrialization, corporatist patterns of interest intermediation, and the formation – in part of the region – of mass parties with programmatic linkages to organized labor.

This state-centric matrix collapsed in the 1970s and 1980s under the pressures of political polarization, an authoritarian backlash, and the debt crisis, triggering the second critical juncture and the emergence of a more liberal development matrix. Although the origins of this new order were located in the authoritarian regimes of the Southern Cone, its political dynamics were marked by the dual transitions to democracy and market liberalism in the 1980s and 1990s. The hallmarks of this order were global market integration and technocratic state retrenchment, with labor-based forms of social and political representation giving way to heterogeneous popular coalitions – under quite varied forms of partisan expression and political institutionalization – that contested social exclusion under liberalized political economies.

To unravel the complex causal chains underlying these shifts in developmental matrices, I start with a historical overview of party system differentiation during the transition from oligarchic to mass politics. The onset of mass politics diversified parties and party systems, as elitist and LM party systems had quite different societal linkages, cleavage patterns, and organizational models. This political differentiation and its socioeconomic correlates largely defined the antecedent conditions for the critical junctures of the neoliberal era.

PARTY SYSTEMS UNDER OLIGARCHIC RULE

The party systems that emerged in early post-independence Latin America were heavily conditioned by prevailing structures of socioeconomic and political domination. The most distinctive features of the post-independence century of oligarchic rule were exclusivity and elitism. The public sphere was exclusive because only small minorities were granted rights to political participation or representation; it was elitist because these minorities were drawn from elite social circles. These patterns reflected the concentration of economic and political power in pre-industrial societies that specialized in the export of primary commodities and relied on coercive, semi-feudal forms of labor control (see Huber and Safford 1995). With a miniscule proletariat, a small and unorganized middle class, and a large peasantry or rural labor force under the social and political control of landlord *patrones*, the commercial and landed oligarchy was a largely uncontested (though often highly fractious) dominant class in the post-independence period. Oligarchs shared the political stage with military (or militia) forces, which typically allied with one or another elite faction.

Peasants, workers, and the middle classes were excluded from the political arena by a combination of structural and institutional constraints on participation and collective action. On the structural side, economic liberalism and the commodity export model of development predominated into the 1930s. Delayed industrialization stunted the growth of urban middle and working classes, preventing organized labor from emerging as a significant political force until the early decades of the 20th century. The peasantry, although far more numerous, was inhibited from organizing collectively by the web of clientelistic and coercive controls exercised by landlords and local authorities. The slow pace of industrialization and the prevalence of semi-feudal labor practices in the countryside thus inhibited autonomous social mobilization among the lower classes.

Institutional constraints included the presence of authoritarian regimes, which suppressed political participation in many countries. Even where competitive elections were held, property and literacy restrictions on suffrage ensured that the political arena was the exclusive preserve of elite groups. The poor were at times mobilized from above as foot soldiers in the militias that waged the factional struggles of elites (de la Fuente 2000), but this generally did not translate into democratic citizenship rights. Under the control of export-oriented elites or their military allies, states preserved the social hierarchy by enforcing political exclusion and supporting the free-trade principles of economic liberalism.

Latin America's first political parties, therefore, were unabashedly elitist, as they were organized by competing factions of the landed and commercial oligarchies that dominated export-based economies. Although significant variation existed in the strength, durability, and competitiveness of oligarchic party systems, there was relatively little variation in their representational models. In the absence of social mobilization from below, competitive alignments were necessarily rooted in intra-elite divisions rather than conflict between classes. In some cases partisan cleavages were shaped by the competing interests of the landed and commercial oligarchy, and regional distinctions were also common. These structural underpinnings, however, were often loosened by the intermingling of landed and commercial interests through economic diversification, marriage and family ties, and business or financial partnerships (Graham 1990: 177; Zeitlin and Ratcliff 1988). Consequently, intra-oligarchic cleavages were heavily conditioned by political differences, reflecting elite conflicts over ideology (the social and political role of the Catholic Church), patronage distributions (i.e., partisan control over state resources), or personality (the leadership role of political and military strongmen known as *caudillos* in an era of exceptionally weak public institutions).

Given the power struggles between *caudillos* that marked the early decades after independence, competition based on leadership schisms undergirded by regional loyalties was prevalent. *Caudillos* were often landowners who commanded regional militia forces that doubled as political movements. Patrimonial ties to peasants, *gauchos*, and the rural poor enabled *caudillos* to build a base of support by dispensing patronage to their followers (de la Fuente 2000). In an era when both state and representative institutions were still in gestation, political competition was often structured by the polarities of support and opposition aroused by such patrimonial figures. As Graham notes (1990: 148), in 19th century Brazil "citizens divided politically not because of party loyalties, much less ideological considerations, but because of personal ties, making party labels seriously misleading at both the local and the national level."

In some countries, such as Venezuela, rivalries between *caudillos* failed to generate an organized, competitive party system during the 19th century. In countries like Colombia and Uruguay, however, *caudillista* movements born in factional civil wars and regional conflicts congealed as early as the 1840s, giving birth to oligarchic parties that dominated national political systems even after the advent of mass politics in the 20th century. Competition between rival parties led to the development of deeply ingrained clientelist linkages between local party notables and their followers. Personalistic movements thus evolved into rival party machines that were built around vertically organized patron–client networks. These parties competed for access to state power and patronage resources (Payne 1968; Hartlyn 1988; Gillespie 1991), or they simply used such resources to solidify single-party hegemony – a pattern found in Argentina, Mexico, Peru, Paraguay, and most Brazilian states (Mainwaring 1999a: 65).

Organizational rivalries were sometimes reinforced by ideological divisions between liberal and conservative factions of the oligarchy. In countries like Chile, Mexico, Colombia, and Uruguay, liberals and conservatives clashed over church–state relations (see Scully 1992). These conflicts did not pit rival religious communities against each other, but rather expressed a divide between staunch Catholics, who defended the traditional roles and privileges of the church, and elites who preferred a more secular state. Issues related to federalism, free trade, and agricultural commercialization also contributed to the ideological divide between liberals and conservatives (Mahoney 2001a). Liberal–conservative conflict waned, however, as mass politics arose, presenting new popular challenges to all factions of the traditional elite.

Political parties during the oligarchic era appealed to individuals through informal social networks in kinship groups or local communities. Those spawned by military conflicts sometimes garnered broad-based support (Coppedge 1998b: 179), but they did not form mass party organizations or extensively mobilize popular sectors, who generally lacked suffrage rights until the early decades of the 20th century. Indeed, parties were loosely and informally organized groups of notables who controlled local or regional patronage networks, but did not construct permanent, centralized bureaucratic structures. Mainwaring's (1999a: 66) depiction of the Brazilian case was typical:

> Brazilian politics was restricted to a narrow elite group, and the franchise remained extremely restricted until the 1930s. Indeed, there was a consensus among political elites that the masses should deliberately be excluded from politics. The other main defining feature of modern parties, permanent organization, was also absent. Even though parties were important stepping stones to power and resources, they themselves were bereft of resources, institutionalized structures, and party professionals.

Across the region, then, party systems during the oligarchic era varied in their competitiveness and institutionalization, but they were strikingly similar in the elitist character of their leadership, social foundations, and organizational patterns. This mode of political representation, however, was rooted in structural and institutional conditions that were gradually overtaken by economic modernization and the rise of new social and political actors. The diverse ways in which popular sectors were mobilized and politically incorporated (or excluded) during the critical junctures that launched the era of mass politics produced much greater cross-national variation in party systems. The relative homogeneity of elitist organizational forms dissolved, creating divergent, path-dependent development trajectories that shaped national political systems through the remainder of the 20th century.

FORKING PATHS: MASS POLITICS AND PARTY SYSTEM
DIFFERENTIATION

The early decades of the 20th century were marked by struggles – some relatively successful, others not – to make oligarchic political orders more popular and inclusive. These struggles politicized Latin America's egregious inequalities and placed the "social question" front and center on the political agenda of democratic regimes. Thereafter democratic rulers would be forced to manage the tensions between social inequalities and political institutions that provided new channels for lower-class participation and demand articulation.

These struggles, and the critical junctures they produced, were shaped by underlying structural and institutional changes – the social and economic development generated by the export boom of the late 19th and early 20th centuries, along with a series of suffrage reforms that gradually extended voting rights to the middle and working classes. Economic diversification and incipient industrialization created more complex social structures, with the growth of urban middle and working classes that were not bound by traditional rural social controls and were thus better positioned to mobilize pressure for social and political reform. Workers concentrated in factory settings, transportation hubs, and mining enclaves shared common material and political interests, facilitating class-based collective action that broke with vertical linkage patterns based on patrimonialism and clientelism (Bergquist 1986). Newly armed with the right to vote, workers and other low-income groups could translate their strength in numbers and organization into formidable political influence in democratic settings. The rise of the industrial proletariat and the organization of labor unions thus signaled the dawning of a new era of mass politics; although oligarchic rule proved to be remarkably resilient in a number of countries, the political arena had ceased to be the exclusive domain of traditional elites and their military allies.

Labor movements began to emerge as significant social actors during the turn-of-the-century export boom, but their size and political leverage swelled as ISI policies were adopted during and after the Great Depression of the 1930s. The depression demonstrated the extreme vulnerabilities of export-dependent economies, and it spurred domestic manufacturing, as local industries emerged to supply consumer needs that could no longer be satisfied by imports, given declining export revenues. A new mode of capital accumulation was in gestation, one which shifted the emphasis from agriculture to industry and from export to domestic markets. It also elicited a major expansion of state responsibilities for economic development and social integration (Díaz Alejandro 2000). Developmentalist states invested in public enterprises, protected and subsidized domestic industries, and regulated labor markets in the name of social peace and (sometimes) workers' rights. Likewise, as social mobilization raised the costs of political exclusion, states extended suffrage and organizational rights to workers, and forged corporatist ties to unions that allowed for an exchange of material benefits for political control (Schmitter 1971; Malloy 1977).

Although socioeconomic modernization was uneven, in most (though not all) of the region the realignment of states, markets, and social actors under ISI entailed a shift from the political logic of popular exclusion to one of social mobilization and political incorporation (Collier and Collier 1991).[1] Parties played a critical role in mediating this political incorporation. From below, they encouraged workers (and sometimes peasants) to unionize, articulated their claims, and formed organic linkages to national labor confederations – what Collier and Hadlin (2009) call "union-party hubs." From above, they crafted policy reforms and provided states with an instrument to penetrate the largest popular organizations in civil society – an instrument that could exert a measure of control over labor mobilization, demand articulation, and leadership selection (see, for example, Collier and Collier 1979; Middlebrook 1995).

The nature of this mediation depended on which party (if any) took the lead in labor mobilization, as incorporation varied with parties' ideological and strategic orientations as well as their status in government or opposition. In the critical junctures triggered by the onset of mass politics, a basic fork in the road differentiated party systems that were reconfigured by the rise of a new, labor-mobilizing mass party (or parties) from those where elitist parties remained electorally dominant. In the LM cases, the onset of mass politics engendered at least a partial reconstitution of national party systems.[2] New populist or leftist parties displaced the traditional parties of the oligarchy or forced them to share the political stage, and a central cleavage between reformist, LM parties and more conservative, elite-based opponents aligned competition during the ISI era.

---

[1] In a number of countries – particularly Guatemala, El Salvador, Honduras, Nicaragua, and Paraguay – authoritarian rule maintained working-class exclusion throughout most of the ISI era.

[2] Clearly, in labeling a party system labor-mobilizing I do not mean to suggest that every party in the system sought to mobilize the working class. The concept implies, however, that the rise of LM parties produced systemic effects by creating a new axis of competition between popular and elitist forces. It should also be recognized that LM parties – especially when they achieved sustained access to state power, as in Mexico and Venezuela – could at some point shift their emphasis from labor mobilization to cooptation or control (Ellner 1995; Middlebrook 1995). Nevertheless, the genetic imprint of early labor mobilization left an indelible mark on party organizations and the competitive alignments of party systems.

Elsewhere, elitist party systems held fast following the onset of mass politics, through one of two basic models. Under the first model, traditional oligarchic parties broadened their appeal by incorporating labor and popular sectors into their electoral constituencies, thus maintaining their electoral dominance and containing the process of labor mobilization. Alternatively, traditional oligarchic parties were displaced by new elite and middle-class-based parties or personalistic leaders who provided little impetus for labor mobilization.

In short, socioeconomic modernization and suffrage reform introduced mass politics, but in contrast to Western Europe (Bartolini 2000), they did not spawn labor-based mass parties throughout the region. As "union-party hubs" were far stronger in some countries than others, mass politics diversified rather than standardized party systems in Latin America's ISI era. Parties were forced to broaden their electoral appeal to remain competitive, but mass programmatic parties committed to redistributive policies were not a prerequisite for this task; in much of the region elite-based party machines were able to attract multi-class support, predominantly by means of clientelist linkages.

These divergent paths of party system development are outlined in the following section. The assignment of cases to the elitist or LM category is determined by both party system and labor movement attributes, according to two basic criteria. The first criterion for assignment to the LM category was the emergence in the ISI era of a new, mass-based populist or leftist party (or parties, in the Chilean case) that was strong enough to exercise political leadership of the trade union movement and to be a serious contender for national political power through electoral means. Operationally, this meant that a new populist or leftist party became allied to, and provided political direction for, the largest national labor confederation, while also developing into the first or second largest electoral force in the country during the ISI era. Indeed, in all the LM cases the primary labor-based party or coalition either captured executive office at some point prior to the 1980s debt crisis or, in the Peruvian case, was prevented from doing so only through repeated military interventions and electoral proscription or manipulation. A party system is categorized as elitist if the largest union confederation was affiliated primarily with traditional oligarchic parties, or with leftist parties that remained electorally marginal during the ISI era.

The second criterion was the density of trade unionization in the ISI era, since a party system can hardly be considered labor-mobilizing if it does not achieve a critical mass in trade union development. The available data on unionization levels in Latin America are inconsistent and not fully reliable, so they should be treated with caution.[3] Nevertheless, they help to differentiate our cases. As

---

[3] No single source provides reliable time series data on either trade union density or union concentration in Latin America. My estimates for these indicators of union strength rely heavily on membership data for the 1980s and 1990s reported by the International Labour Organization (1997b: 235). This ILO data was used to calculate peak union density scores in Colombia, Costa Rica, the Dominican Republic, Mexico, Paraguay, and Venezuela. Where the ILO's data did not

TABLE 4.1. *Indicators of Union Strength in Elitist and Labor-Mobilizing Party Systems*

Elitist Party Systems	Peak Trade Union Density	Union Concentration	Labor-Mobilizing Party Systems	Peak Trade Union Density	Union Concentration
Colombia	9.2	Low	Argentina	50.1	High
Costa Rica	15.4	Low	Bolivia	24.8	High
Dominican Republic	17.0	Low	Brazil	24.3	Low
Ecuador	13.5	Medium	Chile	35.0	Medium
Honduras	8.5	Low	Mexico	32.1	High
Panama	17.0	Low	Nicaragua	37.3	Medium
Paraguay	9.9	Low	Peru	25.0	High
Uruguay	20.9	High	Venezuela	26.4	High
Mean	13.9		Mean	31.9	

Source: See Footnote 3.

shown in Table 4.1, all the countries with LM party systems organized nearly a quarter of their workforce or more during their peak periods of labor mobilization in the 1970s or 1980s, prior to the onset of structural adjustment. Peak union density in the LM cases ranged from 24.3 percent in Brazil to 50.1 percent in Argentina, with an average of 31.9 percent. This was below the West European average of 41.4 percent reported by Cameron (1984: 165), a level achieved only by Argentina in Latin America, but it was more than double the level in Latin American countries that retained elitist party systems. Union density in these latter countries averaged only 13.9 percent, ranging from 8.5 percent in Honduras to 20.9 percent in Uruguay. Clearly, union density was higher where a major new populist or leftist party mobilized labor as a core constituency.

In most cases, the combination of strong unions and a major LM party spawned greater organizational concentration of the labor movement as well. Simply put, labor movements in the LM cases tended to be more politically

cover periods of peak unionization, data was drawn from the following authoritative sources: for Argentina, Godio, Palomino, and Wachendorfer (1988: 87–88); for Bolivia, Harper (1987: 52); for Brazil, *Anuário Estatístico do Brasil* (1993: 2–250); for Chile, Barrera and Valenzuela (1986: 234); for Ecuador and Panama, the *Foreign Labor Trends* series of the U.S. Department of Labor; for Honduras and Peru, Kurian (1982); for Nicaragua, Upham (1996) and Centro Nicaraguense de Derechos Humanos (1995: 35–42); and for Uruguay, Gargiulo (1989: 231). Union concentration scores were also calculated from data provided by the ILO (1997b: 235), Harper (1987), and Upham (1996). Additionally, I drew information from Greenfield and Maram (1987). Trade union density scores reported by the Inter-American Development Bank (2004: 233) are consistently higher than those shown in Table 4.1, and are unreliable for several cases (most notably Peru and Honduras).

cohesive and centrally organized, as shown in Table 4.1. The table ranks countries by their level of union concentration in the 1980s, with a low ranking indicating that less than 40 percent of unionized workers belonged to the largest labor confederation, a medium ranking indicating that between 40 and 70 percent of union members belonged to the largest confederation, and a high ranking indicating that greater than 70 percent of unionized workers belonged to the largest confederation.[4] Five of the eight LM cases achieved a high ranking, and only one case (Brazil) obtained a low ranking. By contrast, only one country (Uruguay) with an elitist party system attained a high ranking, while six obtained a low ranking, attesting to the political and organizational fragmentation of union movements where vigorous partisan leadership was lacking. These findings are indicative of more pluralistic civil societies and representational forms in the elitist cases, as opposed to more corporatist patterns in the LM cases with their logic of centralized and monopolistic organization.

In short, labor movements in the LM cases were typically stronger along the two key dimensions that are stressed in the comparative study of labor's political influence: the level of trade union density and the degree of organizational concentration. The first dimension attests to the representativeness of the union movement and its capacity for collective action and organizational encapsulation. The second measures its political cohesion or capacity for unified political action (Golden 1993; Mitchell 1996).

Following the aforementioned party system and union density criteria, Argentina, Bolivia, Brazil, Chile, Mexico, Peru, Venezuela, and Nicaragua (post-1979 revolution) are coded as LM party systems during the ISI era, while Colombia, Costa Rica, the Dominican Republic, Ecuador, Honduras, Panama, Paraguay, and Uruguay are coded as elitist. Challenges to categorization in several cases due to hybrid features, transformation over time, or the distorting effects of authoritarian rule are discussed in the next section. Cuba is excluded from the categorization because its revolution set the country on a very different path of development. Guatemala and El Salvador are also excluded because their conservative reactions to popular mobilization led to prolonged and highly repressive military dictatorships that truncated party system development until the end of their civil wars in the 1990s, after the ISI era had already closed.

Continuity and Change in Elitist Party Systems

Two different subtypes of party system development were found in both the elitist and LM categories. In the elitist category, a basic distinction existed between party systems where 19th-century oligarchic parties remained electorally dominant following the onset of mass politics (Colombia, Uruguay, Honduras, and Paraguay) and those where such parties were displaced by

---

[4] Clearly, shifting from raw scores to a rank order entails some loss of information about union concentration, but the available data are too imprecise to report raw scores with confidence.

newelite, middle-class, or personality-based parties that provided little impetus to labor mobilization (Costa Rica, Ecuador, Panama, and the Dominican Republic). In the first set of cases, party systems during the ISI era continued to be structured around a central intra-oligarchic political cleavage that predated extensive labor mobilization. The parties that organized this divide could be traced back to 19th-century oligarchic disputes between rival leadership factions or liberal and conservative ideological tendencies.

As Coppedge (1998b: 179) argues, periods of partisan-based civil warfare helped to deepen, entrench, and crystallize the organizational cleavages of several oligarchic party systems prior to the onset of mass politics. Colombia, Uruguay, and Honduras all experienced significant civil wars during the formative years of their party systems in the 19th century (as did Costa Rica in 1948). These military conflicts forced elite factions to extend their reach, incorporating individuals into partisan networks that generated new collective identities. Partisan cleavages were then reproduced by the competition for votes and access to state patronage, which formed exclusive and close-knit partisan subcultures (Hartlyn 1988). In the Paraguayan case, an early extension of suffrage rights encouraged elite-based parties to cultivate popular constituencies long before the emergence of a significant labor movement (Abente 1995: 302).

In these cases of oligarchic party system adaptation, elite-based parties had relatively broad bases of support before an extensive process of labor mobilization, allowing them to moderate that mobilization, ward off leftist and populist competitors, and link emerging labor movements to traditional parties. In Colombia and Uruguay, "progressive" factions of traditional oligarchic parties – the Liberals and Colorados, respectively – sponsored the political incorporation of labor without extensively mobilizing workers (Collier and Collier 1991: 272–313). This broadened the electoral base of traditional parties without altering the composition of party systems or their central axis of competition.[5] In Honduras and Paraguay, radical labor unions were repressed, while more compliant unions were created or coopted by dominant parties – the Nationalists in Honduras and the Colorados in Paraguay. Consequently, labor movements in these four countries were relatively weak and subordinate actors, and the onset of mass politics did not reconstitute party systems around a new mass-based LM party. The central cleavage between rival party machines with multi-class support limited party system fragmentation, making the oligarchic cases

---

[5] As discussed in Chapter 7, by the 1960s Uruguay's labor movement had shifted toward an alliance with the partisan left, and a new leftist electoral coalition emerged in 1971 as an alternative to the two traditional oligarchic parties. A military coup in 1973, however, put the development of this left-labor bloc on hold until the critical juncture was underway in the 1980s. As such, the labor component of this left-labor bloc remained too weak, and the partisan component strengthened too late, to place Uruguay in the LM category during the ISI era. Nevertheless, by the 1970s Uruguay possessed certain hybrid features of elitist and LM party systems that marked its critical juncture in distinct ways.

synonymous with bipartyism during the ISI era (though not necessarily beyond it, as we will see).[6]

Political parties in the oligarchic cases were thus vertically organized across class lines, with constituencies that were relatively undifferentiated from each other apart from their partisan identities. Parties were organized by local leadership cadres that were loosely (though often durably) bound to lower-class constituencies by clientelist networks. These networks could be extensive, but they were informally organized, and they did not encapsulate voters in mass, nationally organized party or secondary associations. In Colombia, for example, "the institutionalization of the nation's partisan subcultures was primarily elitist, touching only lightly the lives of the people in the parties' mass bases, especially the rural peasantry" (Archer 1995: 174). Indeed, Archer claims that Colombia's Liberal and Conservative parties decayed organizationally and became "empty shells" when partisan-based civil warfare waned, as "local and departmental directorates ceased to exist, and national directorates became largely ornamental" (1995: 182). Likewise, Gillespie states that Uruguay's two traditional oligarchic parties were "notoriously loosely structured and informally organized," as they lacked "a clearly defined membership or a highly developed party apparatus" (1991: 5).[7]

Parties in oligarchic systems were generally conservative, reflecting their core elite constituencies (Gibson 1996), but they often lacked ideological definition. They tended to be internally heterogeneous, with diverse factions representing a range of ideological positions. As such, they did not rely heavily on programmatic linkages or differentiate themselves sharply from opponents; indeed, they tended to overlap ideologically, given their internal pluralism. Party brands, therefore, were based on the loyalties and subcultural identities generated by exclusive clientelist networks, rather than programmatic or sociological distinctions. Electoral competition was segmented, cutting across class lines to cleave hierarchical and multi-class clientelist machines, while partisan affiliation was individualized, following informal personal or familial networks rather than group membership.

A second type of elitist party system emerged in Ecuador, Panama, and the Dominican Republic, where traditional oligarchic parties declined following the

---

[6] Traditions of bipartyism dating back to the 1840s in Colombia and Uruguay and the 1880s in Paraguay broke down during the neoliberal critical juncture (in Uruguay) or its aftermath period (in Colombia and Paraguay). Only Honduras retained a two-party oligarchic system through the first decade of the 21st century, and its days are likely numbered, as discussed in Chapter 9).

[7] Paraguay may have been a partial exception to this pattern. Although the labor movement in Paraguay was exceptionally weak, the traditional oligarchic parties developed relatively strong grassroots structures around clientelist networks. As stated by Abente (1995: 303), the Liberal and Colorado parties acted "as parties of notables while at the same time developing a mass membership structured along clientelistic lines." Under the authoritarian regime of General Alfredo Stroessner and the Colorado party, the latter developed a disciplined and hierarchical party apparatus with 240 local branches (Abente 1995: 307–308).

onset of mass politics, and new personalistic or patrimonial competitors took their place without sponsoring extensive labor mobilization (see Hartlyn 1998). As Peeler states, these reconstituted party systems contained "popularly supported parties or movements of some durability, but always highly personalistic rather than institutionalized" (1998: 178). Patrimonial party systems shared many of the same features with oligarchic systems: their parties were elite-led, multi-class, and often patronage-based organizations that were ideologically ill-defined. They tended to be organizationally weak, and they attracted support from individual voters through clientelism and candidate appeal rather than the organizational encapsulation of social blocs. Unless a patrimonial system was dominated by rival *caudillos* – as the Dominican Republic was during the 1960s and 1970s by Joaquín Balaguer on the right and Juan Bosch on the left – it was unlikely to have a stable, central divide, and was more prone to multipartyism and electoral volatility than the oligarchic cases.

With the partial exception of the Dominican Republic, patrimonial systems were located on the low end of the spectrum of party system institutionalization – so low, in fact, that some observers questioned whether they even qualified as party systems. Coppedge (1998b: 173), for example, says that such parties may not be "organized well enough to survive the loss of their most important leader," and are not able "to rely on a core of strong party identifiers in the electorate" to ensure that they will not disappear from one election to the next. Nevertheless, patrimonial party systems consistently reproduced personalistic linkages and electoral divides, even when they were organizationally fluid. Although *caudillos* in patrimonial systems often adopted a populist discourse and leadership style – such as Juan Bosch in the Dominican Republic, Arnulfo Arias in Panama, and José María Velasco Ibarra in Ecuador – they did not construct powerful labor movements or labor-based mass parties as in the populist LM cases discussed in the next section. Indeed, military intervention routinely preempted large-scale popular organization in these countries. Patrimonial systems, then, were rife with populist figures, but they did little to empower the lower classes or alter elitist patterns of political domination.

The final elitist case, Costa Rica, developed a hybrid of these oligarchic and patrimonial patterns. Costa Rica's oligarchic party system decomposed during a cycle of labor mobilization and populist reforms in the 1940s. The defeat of populist forces in the 1948 civil war, however, led to the repression of organized labor and a gradual reconstitution of the party system around a central political cleavage between a loose oligarchic coalition and a new multi-class party, the National Liberation Party (PLN). Despite its reputation for social democratic reformism, the PLN was clearly not an LM party; it was formed by the victors in the civil war who had persecuted and demobilized the Communist-led labor movement, and who drew their support predominantly from the middle-class and small-propertied sectors. As Yashar (1995: 85) states, the PLN "lacked a strong working-class constituency and ... failed to cultivate working-class support." Although the party developed some labor ties in the 1960s, it never consolidated a leadership position in Costa Rica's weak and organizationally fragmented labor movement.

Consequently, an aborted process of labor mobilization and the absence of a new LM party placed Costa Rica in the elitist category. But in contrast to Colombia, Uruguay, Paraguay, and Honduras, the critical juncture associated with the onset of mass politics did not lead to the adaptation of an oligarchic party system, but rather to the reconstitution of the party system around new multi-class parties with core oligarchic and middle-class constituencies. A personalistic cleavage between former president Rafael Calderón and PLN leader José Figueres helped to align this new party system, as in the patrimonial cases described previously, but over time this leadership divide congealed into a more institutionalized cleavage between party organizations, much like that between parties in traditional oligarchic party systems.

To summarize, oligarchic and patrimonial party systems in the ISI era were characterized by cadre rather than mass-based organizational forms, weak grassroots participatory structures in parties and civil society, and a heavy reliance on clientelist and personalist linkages. Given the heterogeneous social constituencies of leading parties, electoral competition created segmented political cleavages that cut vertically across class distinctions and limited the politicization of social inequalities. As we will see, however, several of these party systems forged remarkably stable patterns of electoral competition despite their lack of grounding in class distinctions, programmatic differences, and encapsulating organizational forms.

Political Reconstitution in Labor-Mobilizing Party Systems

The durability of elitist modes of political representation in these eight countries differed from the experience elsewhere in Latin America, where the rise of strong labor movements with programmatic linkages to new mass parties produced at least a partial reconstitution of party systems in the ISI era. In these countries, the onset of mass politics politicized social inequalities and transformed political competition. New mass parties polarized the political arena by challenging elite domination, and they created more structurally grounded and stratified cleavage patterns, even where these did not achieve West European levels of class definition.

Under the most common pattern of labor mobilization, populism,[8] the onset of mass politics produced a central cleavage between a mass-based LM party

---

[8] I use the populist concept here in the "classical" sense (de la Torre 2010: 1–27) to refer to political movements, often under charismatic leadership, that mobilize heterogeneous but predominantly lower- and working-class constituencies for social reform and state-led capitalist development (see Conniff 1999). For adaptations of the populist concept to the social and economic landscape of the neoliberal era, see Roberts (1995) and Weyland (1996).

with an ideologically ill-defined reformist agenda and its conservative opponents.[9] Populist LM parties emerged in societies – Argentina, Bolivia, Brazil,
Mexico, Peru, and Venezuela – where a central oligarchic cleavage had not
been institutionalized in the party system prior to the onset of mass politics,
leaving elitist parties with shallow organizational loyalties among popular
sectors. With the expansion of mass political participation, elitist parties in
these countries were quickly eclipsed by new challengers who targeted their
appeals to urban workers, and in some cases to the peasantry and middle-class
sectors as well.

The classic populist parties in Argentina (the Peronist party, officially known as
the *Partido Justicialista* or PJ), Mexico (the *Partido Revolucionario Institucional*
or PRI), Venezuela (*Acción Democrática* or AD), Brazil (the *Partido Trabalhista
Brasileiro* or PTB), Peru (the *Partido Aprista Peruano*, better known as APRA),
and Bolivia (the *Movimiento Nacional Revolucionario* or MNR) made organized
labor a core constituency.[10] They encouraged unionization efforts and articulated
workers' claims for political inclusion and social reform. When these parties
gained access to public office, their corporatist practices awarded organizational
and material benefits to labor unions in exchange for political loyalty. Where
populist parties became politically dominant, as in Mexico and Venezuela (but not
Bolivia), the logic of state corporatist or partisan control tended to supersede that
of grassroots mobilization (Middlebrook 1995; Ellner 1995), creating large but
increasingly docile trade union movements. But even here early spurts of party-
sponsored labor mobilization bequeathed union movements that remained, by
regional standards, organizationally powerful and politically influential, with
centralized national labor confederations operating in close proximity to state
power.

Populist parties' reformist policies and mobilizing strategies elicited hostility
from traditional elites and portions of the middle class, giving their party systems
at least some semblance of a stratified, elite/popular cleavage structure.
Nevertheless, populist parties generally did not construct well-defined class
cleavages like their social democratic counterparts in Western Europe. They
aimed their appeals to a diverse national and "popular" audience that tran-
scended organized labor, attracting elements of the urban and rural poor,
middle-class groups that benefitted from growing public sector employment,
and even industrialists who stood to gain from government protection and
subsidies. And as Gibson (1997) points out, populist parties often relied on

---

[9] Opposition was not exclusively conservative, however, because populist parties also evoked bitter
opposition from the Marxist left, which competed – generally with limited success – to attract
similar working-class constituencies to a more radical project of socialist transformation.

[10] In Bolivia, however, the alliance between the MNR and the more leftist labor movement forged
during the 1952 revolution broke down in the 1960s. In Peru, APRA was a hegemonic force in the
labor movement from the 1930s until the 1960s and 1970s, when it was overtaken by the
Communist Party and a variety of smaller Marxist groups.

conservative, cross-class clientelist networks to mobilize electoral support in rural and peripheral areas, much like elitist parties where segmented cleavage structures prevailed. Likewise, charismatic bonds also served as linkage mechanisms where leaders such as Juan Domingo Perón (Argentina), Victor Raúl Haya de la Torre (Peru), Lázaro Cárdenas (Mexico), and Getúlio Vargas (Brazil) played a central role in populist mobilization.

Given the diversity of their social constituencies and linkage patterns, populist parties eschewed restrictive ideological definitions or class identities. They appealed programmatically to labor and other social groups that stood to benefit from redistributive reforms or state-led development, but they adopted ambiguous or internally pluralistic ideological platforms that emphasized nationalism and social justice rather than socialist transformation. They typically counterposed the interests of *el pueblo* (the people), broadly conceived, against those of the traditional oligarchy, which they portrayed as a narrow elite bound to foreign interests (see Laclau 1977; de la Torre 2010). Consequently, populist cleavages were often highly polarizing politically, but they could be amorphous sociologically and ideologically. Their degree of stratification in electoral behavior ranged from relatively high, as in Argentina (Mora y Araujo and Llorente 1980; Ostiguy 1998), to relatively low, as in Venezuela, where class distinctions were well-defined following the initial rise of AD in the 1940s but gradually diminished as the party moderated in the 1960s and 1970s (Myers 1998). Even where electoral behavior was not strictly differentiated by class, however, the organizational and cultural dimensions of stratified cleavages were present, as populist parties were bound to relatively powerful labor movements and articulated popular identities that sharply contested elite interests (Ostiguy 1998). Furthermore, commitments to land reform allowed populist parties in Mexico, Venezuela, and Bolivia to mobilize substantial peasant support alongside their trade union constituencies.

The organization of mass parties, unions, and peasant associations led to higher levels of voter encapsulation than in the elitist party systems. Voters were bound to populist parties by webs of grassroots representative and participatory structures that fostered collective identities and created more formidable political organizations than the elitist parties they displaced. Although the Argentine PJ had low levels of bureaucratic institutionalization (Levitsky 1998b; McGuire 1997), others like the Venezuelan AD (Coppedge 1994) and the Peruvian APRA boasted centralized, disciplined national organizations that connected the party hierarchy to base-level branches and civic associations. Collier and Collier (1991: 150–151), for example, claim that APRA's "extraordinary organizational capacity" was matched by an "extraordinary capacity to create a sense of community among its members." This sense of community was fostered by extensive grassroots participation in social and political activities, both inside and out of electoral campaigns. Levitsky's (1998a: 458) description of Peronist local branches or *unidades básicas* (UBs) illustrates the range of activities performed by party members:

UBs play a central organizational role during electoral processes, signing up members and providing activists to paint walls, put up posters and mobilize voters for rallies. Between elections, many UBs continue to play an important role in neighborhood life, serving as critical points of access to city and provincial governments. In addition to distributing food, medicines and clothing, providing social services such as legal and medical assistance, school tutoring, and even free haircuts, many UBs administer government social programs and attend to neighborhood infrastructural problems such as sewage, street lights and road surfaces. Many UBs also serve as cultural centers, organizing sports activities for young people, vacation trips for the elderly and parties for neighborhood birthdays.

Although populist forms of labor mobilization were the most common, a more leftist variant developed in Chile and, at the tail end of the ISI era, in Peru, Brazil, and post-revolutionary Nicaragua as well. Under this pattern, labor mobilization was led by socialist parties or revolutionary movements that sharply contested traditional elites and advocated far-reaching social and economic reforms, including basic changes in property relations. These parties prioritized programmatic linkages to the working and lower classes, sometimes creating stratified cleavage structures that aligned social class with ideological distinctions.

In Chile, strong oligarchic Liberal and Conservative parties were formed in the early post-independence period, and were then joined later in the 19th century by the Radical Party, which developed a solid base in middle-class sectors (Remmer 1984; Scully 1992). As industrialization occurred in the 20th century, the industrial and mining proletariat established close ties to newly formed Communist and Socialist parties (Drake 1978; Bergquist 1986: 20–80; Faúndez 1988). Political loyalties under Chile's 1933–1973 democratic regime were more sharply differentiated by class than perhaps anywhere else in Latin America: workers tended to vote Socialist or Communist, middle-class groups were inclined to support centrist parties like the Radicals or Christian Democrats, and elite sectors (and, prior to the 1960s, the rural poor) opted for the Conservative and Liberal parties on the right (Aldunate 1985; Torcal and Mainwaring 2003).

This alignment of class and ideology, while common in Western Europe, was unique to Chile during most of Latin America's ISI era. Elsewhere, leftist parties made limited inroads among workers and did not develop into mass parties, being superseded by populist competitors or weakened by political repression. Nevertheless, leftist variants of labor mobilization did appear toward the end of the ISI era in Peru, Brazil, and Nicaragua as well.[11] In Peru, populist labor mobilization predominated into the 1960s, but thereafter several smaller leftist parties supplanted APRA in the leadership of organized labor. These parties

---

[11] It should be noted that these late-developing patterns of leftist labor mobilization were spawned during the post-Cuban Revolution wave of leftist militancy in the 1960s and 1970s. As such, they were not a product of the labor-incorporating critical junctures that marked the onset of mass politics during the early stages of industrialization.

established ties to labor, peasant, and urban popular movements, and by the mid-1980s their United Left (IU) coalition had become Peru's second largest electoral force (see Huber Stephens 1983; Tuesta Soldevilla 1989; Roberts 1998). In Brazil, the Workers' Party (PT) was founded by militant new industrial unions that challenged the military dictatorship in the late 1970s, which had earlier dismantled the populist PTB. The PT became the dominant party in the labor and peasant movements following the transition to democracy in the mid-1980s (Keck 1992), and it developed into a major electoral force by the end of that decade.

Finally, Nicaragua had long possessed one of Latin America's most narrowly based and authoritarian patrimonial systems, with origins in a Liberal–Conservative divide that became increasingly personalistic under the Somoza family dynasty after the 1930s. The 1979 overthrow of the Somoza dictatorship and the social revolution that followed polarized society between supporters and opponents of the Sandinistas, the socialist-inspired movement that led the insurrection and assumed hegemonic control over the new political order. The Sandinistas sponsored an extensive process of lower-class political mobilization, and they used state power and social reforms, including land redistribution, to establish strong linkages to mass labor and peasant associations. In the process they clashed repeatedly with business sectors and conservative parties. An LM party system thus emerged very late in Nicaragua, but one was clearly in place when the debt crisis erupted in the 1980s.

Leftist parties in these countries developed strong grassroots networks in partisan and civic arenas, and their militants penetrated and mobilized civil society.[12] They forged close ties to class-based secondary associations, and the socialist content of their programmatic appeals accentuated ideological conflicts and class cleavages in Chile, Nicaragua, and (temporarily) Peru. The class cleavage was less well-defined in Brazil, however, even though the PT was founded by union leaders and developed strong ties to other organized popular constituencies. As Mainwaring (1999a: 47) states, "Although the PT espouses class rhetoric, its class base has been highly heterogeneous since at least 1985." This was attributable in part to the PT's ability to draw support from professional, intellectual, and middle-class circles, as well as the tendency of many unorganized poor to vote along clientelist or personalist lines in Brazil.

THE ORIGINS AND IMPLICATIONS OF ELITIST AND LABOR-MOBILIZING PARTY SYSTEMS

This categorization of elitist and LM party systems helps to differentiate national patterns of political representation following the onset of mass politics in the

---

[12] In Brazil, the relationship ran in the other direction, as the PT was clearly a "movement party" (Kitschelt 2006) that was founded by labor and social activists who sought to contest the electoral arena in a context of incipient democratization.

20th century. Although it is beyond the scope of this study to explain why LM party systems developed in some countries but not in others, several observations can be made. First, with respect to structural factors, elitist party systems were more common in the smaller Latin American countries, which lacked the resource base and large domestic markets needed to sustain nationalistic ISI policies. As Alesina and Spolaore argue, small countries benefit from trade openness and international economic integration, which allow them to overcome scale constraints on economic development (2003: 81–94). Consequently, the smaller Latin American countries retained more of an agro-export orientation during the ISI era, and with the exception of Uruguay they lagged behind the regional leaders in the process of industrialization. They thus lacked the dense concentrations of industrial workers that facilitated the rise of powerful labor movements and LM parties.

In contrast, the LM category includes the countries with the largest domestic markets that pursued aggressive ISI policies and acquired dense concentrations of industrial workers (Argentina, Brazil, and Mexico), along with a number of smaller countries that possessed major export-oriented extractive industries (Chile, Bolivia, Venezuela, and to a lesser extent Peru). The mining and petroleum enclaves in these latter countries spawned strong, class-conscious labor movements (Bergquist 1986; Nash 1993), and they generated revenues that could be captured by states and used for statist development policies, even where ISI was slow to develop.[13]

Structural factors alone, however, cannot fully account for these divergent patterns of party system development, as more contingent historical political processes also played a role. As noted above, oligarchic party systems were stronger and more durable where a central organizational cleavage was forged in the midst of armed conflict, encouraging nascent parties of notables to broaden their bases of support prior to the onset of labor mobilization. The development of strong labor movements and LM parties was short-circuited in other countries by periods of civil war or authoritarian rule. By contrast, in the LM camp, periods of revolutionary or leftist government encouraged spurts of labor mobilization that realigned or reconstituted party systems even in the absence of large-scale industrialization, as in Bolivia, Nicaragua, and Peru (under a leftist military regime in the late 1960s). The impact of structural factors on party system development was thus mediated by historical political processes and political agency during labor-incorporating critical junctures or other periods of acute political conflict.

Not surprisingly, then, some party systems manifested hybrid traits, or distinctive subnational variations. In a large, diverse country like Brazil, oligarchic or patrimonial forms of domination prevailed in much of the countryside (Hagopian 1996), while stratified patterns of populist or leftist labor

---

[13] Chile adopted aggressive ISI policies under a center-left governing coalition starting in the late 1930s, but in Bolivia, Peru, and Venezuela ISI did not begin in earnest until the 1950s or 1960s.

TABLE 4.2. *Trade Dependence in Latin America, 1970*

Elitist Party Systems	Imports and Exports (% of GDP)	Labor-Mobilizing Party Systems	Imports and Exports (% of GDP)
Colombia	22	Argentina	11
Costa Rica	56	Bolivia	29
Dominican Republic	37	Brazil	13
Ecuador	28	Chile	26
Honduras	55	Mexico	11
Panama	46	Nicaragua	49
Paraguay	23	Peru	23
Uruguay	22	Venezuela	38
Mean	**36.1**	**Mean**	**25.0**

Source: World Bank, *World Development Indicators* data base (http://data.worldbank.org/data-catalog/world-development-indicators).

mobilization coexisted with patronage machines in urban areas (Keck 1992; Gay 1994). In other cases, the dynamics of political change eventually altered the competitive logic of the party system; as previously mentioned, Peru's populist mode of labor mobilization was transformed into a more class-based, leftist pattern after the 1960s, and Nicaragua's authoritarian-patrimonial system abruptly turned into an LM case after the Sandinista Revolution. Uruguay's longstanding oligarchic party system was eventually modified by the gradual rise of a labor-backed leftist coalition in the 1970s and 1980s, creating hybrid conditions that shaped the national critical juncture, as discussed in Chapter 7.

These caveats and complexities aside, this categorization provides a framework for the comparative analysis of party systems at the dawning of the neoliberal era. It also provides analytical leverage to explore relationships between political institutions and socioeconomic development, as elitist and LM party systems were typically embedded in different political economies. For example, Table 4.2 presents data on trade dependence in 1970, prior to the international shocks that undermined the ISI model. On average, countries with elitist party systems relied more heavily on international markets, with imports and exports accounting for 36.1 percent of gross domestic product (GDP). This compared to 25 percent of GDP in the LM cases, with the three largest countries – Brazil, Mexico, and Argentina – having the lowest levels of trade dependence. These findings conform to the global pattern of economic openness in small countries, and they attest to the inward orientation of ISI models in the larger regional powers.

The two types of party systems are compared along several other dimensions of the state-centric matrix in Table 4.3. The table demonstrates that the LM cases were more highly industrialized, with an average peak score of 24.4 percent of their GDP accounted for by manufacturing activities between 1970

TABLE 4.3. *Party Systems, Industrial Development, and Public Investment in Latin America*

Elitist Party Systems	Manufacturing Share of GDP (Peak Score, 1970–1980)	Public Enterprise Share of Gross Fixed Capital Formation (Peak Score, 1970–1980)	Labor-Mobilizing Party Systems	Manufacturing Share of GDP (Peak Score, 1970–1980)	Public Enterprise Share of Gross Fixed Capital Formation (Peak Score, 1970–1980)
Colombia	19.0	10.3	Argentina	28.0	20.7
Costa Rica	22.2	19.6	Bolivia	15.9	40.9
Dominican Republic	18.5	12.2	Brazil	28.7	22.8
Ecuador	20.2	NA	Chile	25.0	20.0
Honduras	17.0	14.6	Mexico	29.9	29.4
Panama	17.2	27.7	Nicaragua	24.3	NA
Paraguay	17.5	14.5	Peru	25.6	22.1
Uruguay	24.0	18.3	Venezuela	17.7	36.3
Mean	19.5	16.7	Mean	24.4	27.5

Sources: For manufacturing share of GDP, Inter-American Development Bank, *Economic and Social Progress in Latin America: 1980–81 Report*, p. 26. For public enterprise share of gross fixed capital formation, Short (1984: 118–122).

and 1980, the final decade of the ISI era. The only LM cases below 20 percent, Bolivia and Venezuela, had labor movements that were invigorated by mining and petroleum extractive activities, respectively, making them less dependent on the depth of industrialization. The highest scores, once again, belonged to the three LM countries with the largest domestic markets – Mexico, Brazil, and Argentina – which pursued especially vigorous ISI models, trying to "deepen" industrialization by shifting from the production of consumer durables to inter-mediate and capital goods. In contrast, the elitist cases attained an average peak manufacturing score of only 19.5 percent of GDP, indicative of the relatively shallow character of their ISI experiments (with the exception of Uruguay). Table 4.3 also demonstrates that state institutions were more active in using public investment to promote economic development in the LM cases. The peak share of gross fixed capital formation accounted for by public enterprises between 1970 and 1980 averaged 27.5 percent in the LM cases, compared to only 16.7 percent in the elitist cases.[14]

---

[14] This probably understates the difference between the two sets of cases, as the 20 percent figure reported by Short (1984) for Chile – the lowest among the LM cases – appears inaccurate. Given the extensive role of Chile's state development corporation (CORFO) in the industrialization of

TABLE 4.4. *Party Systems and State Interventionism in Latin America*

Elitist Party Systems	Index of State Interventionism (Peak Score, 1975–1995)	Labor-Mobilizing Party Systems	Index of State Interventionism (Peak Score, 1975–1995)
Colombia	6.9	Argentina	7.5
Costa Rica	5.4	Bolivia	6.8
Dominican Republic	6.6	Brazil	8.0
Ecuador	6.0	Chile	7.2
Honduras	4.5	Mexico	6.3
Panama	3.4	Nicaragua	8.8
Paraguay	4.2	Peru	7.0
Uruguay	4.3	Venezuela	6.0
Mean	5.2	Mean	7.2

Source: Derived from Gwartney, Lawson, and Block's (1996) Index of Economic Freedom.

Evidence of broader interventionist tendencies in the LM cases is provided in Table 4.4. The table compares the peak scores of elitist and LM cases on an index of state interventionism derived from Gwartney, Lawson, and Block's 17-indicator "index of economic freedom" (1996).[15] The data demonstrate that the LM cases, on average, had more varied and extensive forms of state intervention during the ISI era, whereas the elitist cases strayed less far from the principles of economic liberalism.

Given higher levels of state interventionism, it is not surprising that partisan competition in the LM systems was more likely to be grounded in programmatic and ideological distinctions. Drawing from Mainwaring and Scully's (1995b: 31) ranking of ideological polarization in Latin American party systems, it can

the country and the widespread nationalization of productive assets in the early 1970s under Allende, it is hard to believe that the 20 percent figure is accurate. Stallings (1978: 47), in fact, reports that "the percentage of gross domestic investment in fixed capital supplied by the state" reached 75 percent even before Allende took office, although this was not necessarily all invested in public enterprises. A more reliable score for Chile would surely accentuate the differences between elitist and LM cases.

[15] The index of state interventionism is calculated by subtracting each country's score on the summary index of economic freedom from 10, so that higher scores reflect greater state intervention in the economy. This 17-indicator index is not ideal, as it includes inflation – a performance variable – with other indicators of policy choice. Nevertheless, it is the most reliable cross-national measure of the generalized patterns of state intervention associated with the ISI model in Latin America. The market reform index developed by Morley, Machado, and Pettinato (1999) does not include all the cases covered here, and although it is very useful for identifying longitudinal patterns of policy change within individual countries, its cross-sectional reliability as a summary measure of state-led development is questionable. Their index, for example, ranks Colombia as considerably more statist than Brazil and Mexico for much of the 1970s, which is at odds with most scholarly assessments of these cases.

TABLE 4.5. *Ideological Polarization in Elitist and Labor-Mobilizing Party Systems*

	Ideological Polarization			
	Low	Moderately Low	Moderately High	High
Elitist Party Systems	Costa Rica Honduras Paraguay	Colombia Panama	Dominican Republic Ecuador Uruguay	
Labor-Mobilizing Party Systems		Argentina	Bolivia Chile Mexico Venezuela	Brazil Nicaragua Peru

Source: Adapted from Mainwaring and Scully (1995b: 31). Since Honduras, Panama, the Dominican Republic, and Nicaragua were not included in the Mainwaring and Scully study, rankings for these cases have been assigned by the author.

be seen that the ideological distance between major parties was generally greater in the LM than the elitist cases (see Table 4.5). Three elitist cases rank in the lowest category for polarization, and none fall in the highest category; among LM cases, three are ranked in the highest category and none in the lowest. The only LM case that Mainwaring and Scully rank moderately low on ideological polarization, Argentina, is difficult to interpret, as the Peronist/anti-Peronist cleavage could be highly polarizing culturally and politically, even if it never fit neatly on a left–right ideological spectrum (Haggard and Kaufman 1995: 167– 168; Coppedge 1997: 8).[16] The particularities of Peronism aside, the differences in ideological polarization across the two sets of cases reflect the historic strength of leftist and populist alternatives in the LM party systems, and the conflicts generated by their challenges to conservative and elite-based parties.

To summarize, although all of Latin America encountered the challenges of economic modernization and labor incorporation in the 20th century, national experiences with ISI and mass politics differed along a number of basic dimensions. These differences created distinct developmental trajectories with interrelated social, economic, and political dimensions. Whereas elitist party systems were associated with shallower industrialization, less extensive state economic intervention, and weak, politically fragmented labor movements, LM party systems were embedded in a developmental matrix that included deeper industrialization, greater state intervention, and more densely organized and politically cohesive labor movements. A principal components factor analysis suggests that these variables were bundled together as elements of an underlying statist development syndrome, with the type of party system and the level of

---

[16] Historically, both Peronism and anti-Peronism spanned the ideological spectrum from left to right. As Ostiguy (1998) argues, this cleavage is better understood in terms of a cultural – political "high" and "low" rather than the more conventional ideological left and right.

TABLE 4.6. *Latin America's State-Centric Matrix (Principal Components Factor Analysis)*

Indicator	Factor Loadings
Labor-Mobilizing Party System	.92374
Labor Union Density	.85435
Ideological Polarization	.75248
Labor Union Concentration	.74875
Trade Dependence	−.73762
State Interventionism	.73411
Manufacturing Share of GDP	.71035
Public Enterprise Share of Gross Fixed Capital Formation	.48483
Eigenvalue	4.53273

TABLE 4.7. *National Rankings on the State-Centric Matrix (Factor Scores) (Principal Components Factor Analysis)*

Labor-Mobilizing Party Systems	Factor Score	Elitist Party Systems	Factor Score
Argentina	1.39	Uruguay	−.05
Mexico	1.16	Ecuador	−.37
Peru	1.01	Dominican Republic	−.57
Brazil	.98	Colombia	−.68
Nicaragua	.97	Costa Rica	−1.14
Chile	.80	Paraguay	−1.25
Bolivia	.36	Panama	−1.29
Venezuela	.27	Honduras	−1.58

trade union density having the strongest correlation with this state-centric matrix (see Table 4.6).[17]

The factor analysis also provides country scores on the principal component that clearly demonstrate the differences between elitist and LM cases: all the LM cases attain a positive factor score, whereas all the elitist cases obtain a negative score (see Table 4.7). Argentina, Mexico, Peru, and Brazil scored highest on the state-centric matrix, while Honduras, Panama, and Paraguay ranked lowest. Uruguay, with its aforementioned hybrid features, was a borderline case that ranked closest to the LM cases among the countries with elitist party systems.

This state-centric matrix began to unravel by the 1960s and 1970s, however, and by the 1980s it confronted a terminal crisis. The collapse of this matrix

---

[17] The factor analysis includes all the variables introduced in this chapter, using interval scales for trade union concentration and ideological polarization, and a dummy variable for the type of party system (LM = 1). The proportion of variance explained by the principal component is .57.

inevitably posed a crisis for the party systems and labor-based forms of political representation that were embedded within it. Given the uneven diffusion of this matrix across the region, the crises that accompanied its demise varied widely in their economic and political severity. This variation was heavily influenced by the differences between elitist and LM cases, transforming these into antecedent conditions for the critical junctures of the neoliberal era.

CONCLUSION

The onset of mass politics in 20th-century Latin America created different patterns of working and lower-class incorporation, distinguishing party systems that were reconfigured by the rise of a mass-based LM party during the ISI era from those that were not. The distinction between elitist and LM party systems is more than a simple descriptive exercise or conceptual mapping; it is a theoretical cornerstone for an explanation of why neoliberal critical junctures were more disruptive in some party systems than others. As intermediaries between states and societies, elitist and LM party systems were elements of broader developmental matrices that indelibly marked national trajectories of political and economic change. These included different associational patterns in civil society, alternative modes of lower-class political incorporation, and distinctive patterns of state economic intervention. As shown in Chapter 5, they also led to different patterns of economic crisis and political disruption during the transition from ISI to market liberalism – patterns that powerfully shaped the dynamics of party system change and continuity.

5

Neoliberal Critical Junctures and Party System Stability

Conventional wisdom suggests that LM party systems entered the 1980s with a series of attributes that should have enhanced their stability. Research on party systems in both the U.S. and Europe has found that aging electoral alignments are less stable than those forged in response to more contemporary issue cleavages (Maguire 1983: 83–85; Carmines, McIver, and Stimson 1987), and the European literature argues that the organization of class cleavages binds voters to parties and limits their mobility (Lipset and Rokkan 1967; Bartolini and Mair 1990). In comparison to their elitist counterparts, LM parties were more densely organized and had more encapsulating linkages to social groups. They encouraged competition that was more likely to be grounded in modern social cleavages and programmatic alternatives rather than disputes from the distant, oligarchic past. Whereas oligarchic party systems seemed anachronistic in the ISI era – the institutional residue of intra-elite conflicts that pre-dated the rise of mass politics – LM party systems were produced by more recent patterns of social mobilization and political competition.

A critical juncture approach suggests, however, that the modern organizational forms of LM party systems were embedded in a state-centric matrix of development that progressively unraveled in the waning decades of the 20th century. The collapse of ISI and the transition to market liberalism eroded the structural foundations of the societal linkage and cleavage patterns that had been spawned by the process of labor mobilization. As such, they exposed LM party systems to more severe exogenous shocks and deeper sociopolitical dislocations than in the elitist cases that experienced more moderate versions of the state-centric matrix.

This chapter provides a brief overview of the economic crisis and the transition to market liberalism, and it explains why this transition exerted differential effects on elitist and LM party systems. It demonstrates that neoliberal critical junctures were especially traumatic and disruptive for countries with LM party systems, and it identifies three basic mechanisms of structurally induced destabilization: the political costs of crisis management, the erosion of party-society linkages, and the weakening of mass-based organizational models in civil and political society. Evidence is presented to show that these destabilizing effects were associated with greater changes in the organizational composition of LM party systems, deeper electoral realignments, and higher levels of electoral volatility. Institutional change during neoliberal critical junctures, therefore, was heavily conditioned by the antecedent properties of party systems during the ISI era.

THE CRISIS OF ISI AND THE TRANSITION TO NEOLIBERALISM

In its heyday, the state-centric matrix incorporated workers in broad multi-class coalitions that supported state efforts to accelerate industrialization by supplying manufactured goods for domestic markets. These coalitions made organized labor an important constituency of governing parties – at least temporarily – in countries like Mexico, Argentina, Bolivia, Brazil, Chile, and Venezuela. By the 1960s, however, both the political and economic foundations of this matrix had begun to crack. Efforts to "deepen" ISI to include capital as well as consumer goods met with limited success, leaving most of the region dependent on imported capital goods and subject to foreign exchange bottlenecks that limited the prospects for growth. Governments overvalued currencies to lower the price of these imports, but overvaluation discouraged agricultural exports that were vital sources of foreign exchange, and it prevented sheltered industries from competing in export markets. Meanwhile, populist spending policies fanned inflationary pressures, while attempts to achieve stabilization by imposing austerity measures exacerbated distributive conflicts between capital and labor (Alesina and Drazen 1991). The tensions between capital accumulation and domestic consumption strained populist coalitions, and states became increasingly dependent on foreign lending to sustain domestic consumption and investment as petrodollars flooded global capital markets in the 1970s (Cardoso and Helwege 1995: 91–99).

Economic growth thus slowed in some of the region's most industrialized countries, and populist coalitions started to unravel at the same time that the Cuban Revolution and the guerrilla movements it inspired intensified ideological conflict. Both the Left and the Right offered proposals to escape the bottlenecks of state-led capitalist development. The Left advocated a deepening of the state-centric model through a transition to socialism, whereby the state would nationalize assets held by domestic elites and foreign investors, redistribute property and income to popular sectors, and stimulate growth through an expansion of the domestic market. Variants of this approach were adopted by the Velasco military regime in Peru (1968–1975), the democratic socialist government of Allende in Chile (1970–1973), and the Sandinista Revolution in Nicaragua (1979–1990), in each case leading to an intensification of popular social and political mobilization.

Alternatives of the Right, on the other hand, sought to reimpose the political exclusion of working- and lower-class groups who had been activated under populism. The first wave of "bureaucratic-authoritarian" military regimes that took power in Brazil (1964) and Argentina (1966) were designed to break with populism – but not the state-centric development model – by repressing LM parties and labor unions. By suppressing popular sector consumption demands, they sought to free up resources for a state-led push toward heavy industrialization (O'Donnell 1973; Skidmore 1977). A second alternative on the Right, however, which began with a new wave of bureaucratic–authoritarian takeovers in Chile (1973), Uruguay (1973), and Argentina (1976), broke with both populism and statism by repressing labor and leftist movements and implementing orthodox structural adjustment programs (Foxley 1983; Schamis 1991). This neoliberal prescription rested on the assumption that economic statism distorted markets and swelled aggregate demand, spawning inflationary pressures, rent-seeking behavior, and economic inefficiency (De Soto 1989; Krueger 1990). As such, neoliberal technocrats sought to stimulate growth by unleashing private entrepreneurship in a competitive marketplace.

The trend toward market liberalization began under the Southern Cone military dictatorships of the mid-1970s, but it took the exogenous shock of the early 1980s debt crisis to seal the fate of the state-centric matrix in Latin America. The ISI model had been shaken by the 1973 oil crisis and the global recession that followed, but it received artificial life support from the flood of cheap petrodollars loaned out by Western banks. The fiscal bases of state-led development were devastated, however, by a confluence of international shocks that followed the second oil crisis in 1979. Interest payments on international loans skyrocketed at the same time that oil import costs soared and a global recession caused export revenues to plunge. These international shocks created severe balance-of-payments deficits, intense inflationary pressures, and extensive private capital flight. When Mexico declared that it could not meet debt service obligations in 1982, the flow of foreign credits to Latin America dried up, state spending plummeted, and the region slid into its most severe depression since the 1930s (Kaufman and Stallings 1989).

The descent into crisis was instrumental in weakening military dictatorships and encouraging regime change (Remmer 1992–1993), but it also saddled new democratic regimes and party systems with the unenviable task of managing stabilization and structural adjustment. Not surprisingly, a number of new democracies responded to the crisis with heterodox adjustment programs, using wage and price controls, fixed exchange rates, and monetary reform to try to contain inflation without the social costs of orthodox austerity measures (Cardoso and Helwege 1992: 188–196). The most prominent of the heterodox programs, however – the Austral Plan in Argentina, the Cruzado Plan in Brazil, and the Inti Plan in Peru – fell victim to hyperinflationary pressures once price controls were lifted, allowing orthodox recipes to sweep across the region by the end of the 1980s (Haggard and Kaufman 1992; Edwards 1995).

The orthodox strategy contained two basic stages, both heavily scripted and closely monitored by the International Monetary Fund (IMF), western governments, and foreign creditors. The first stage prioritized economic stabilization and austerity in an attempt to ease inflationary pressures and balance-of-payments deficits. Stabilization was to be achieved by closing fiscal deficits, slowing the growth of the monetary supply, reducing imports, and expanding exports. Budget deficits were addressed by slashing government spending – including subsidies, social programs, public investment, and public employment – and increasing taxes and fees for public services. Higher interest rates, strict control over monetary emissions, the elimination of wage indexation, and cuts in real wages were also employed to reduce inflation, while currencies were devalued to boost exports and discourage imports. Orthodox stabilization produced savings that could be used to meet debt obligations, but it generally did so by inducing recessions (Cardoso and Helwege 1992: 172), along with a sequel of social costs in the form of underemployment, lower wages, and reduced domestic consumption.

Under the orthodox prescription, stabilization was only the first step toward more far-reaching neoliberal structural adjustment, which aimed to curtail state intervention and reestablish the market as the primary mechanism for allocating goods and services. Tariffs were slashed, price controls were lifted, capital and labor markets were deregulated, public enterprises and services were privatized, and foreign capital was embraced in an ambitious drive to unleash the creative forces of market competition and private entrepreneurship (Williamson 1990; Nelson 1994; Smith, Acuña, and Gamarra 1994; Edwards 1995). Although significant variation existed in the timing, depth, and pace of neoliberal reform, by the early 1990s every country in the region had shifted toward freer markets (see Morley, Machado, and Pettinato 1999; Lora 2001).

Far more than a temporary palliative for the debt crisis, structural adjustment aimed at a complete rupture with the state-centric matrix and a permanent realignment of states and markets in the development process. It also sought to integrate Latin America more thoroughly within global markets at a time when national governments were hard-pressed to maintain sovereign control over fiscal and monetary policies and transnational capital flows (Mahon 1996). In essence, a new mode of capital accumulation had emerged, albeit one with roots in Latin America's 19th-century era of economic liberalism. Rather than domestic consumption and investment serving as the engines of growth under the tutelage of a protective and entrepreneurial state, the region turned anew to commodity-export markets, private capital, and foreign investment to stimulate growth. In the process, states relinquished a broad range of developmental and social welfare responsibilities (Vellinga 1998). States managed the insertion of national economies in global markets and enforced contracts and property rights, but they retreated from responsibilities to develop new productive sectors, control prices, subsidize consumption, redistribute income, and provide an extensive array of social welfare measures.

This crisis-induced realignment of states and markets produced dramatic changes in the organization of societal interests, challenging class-based forms of representation and the programmatic linkages that had been forged between parties and social groups under ISI. It also imposed severe costs of crisis management on many party systems. The political costs of the transition from ISI to neoliberalism were not evenly distributed across party systems, however. As explained below, this critical juncture was more destabilizing for LM than elitist party systems, as the former were prone to more severe and prolonged economic crises, and their organizational and linkage patterns were less compatible with the socioeconomic landscape of the neoliberal era.

PARTY SYSTEMS AND ECONOMIC CRISIS

Economic crises can be highly destabilizing for party systems, as they typically undermine support for parties that are held accountable by voters for economic performance. The more severe an economic crisis, the more likely voters are to punish incumbent officials; the more prolonged a crisis, the more likely it is to erode support system-wide as voters punish successive governing parties. The susceptibility of different types of party systems to economic crises is thus an essential starting point for understanding the divergent outcomes of neoliberal critical junctures.

Several features of LM party systems made them especially vulnerable to severe and prolonged economic crises during the transition to market liberalism. First, as discussed in Chapter 4, LM party systems were typically embedded in more statist political economies; having advanced further with state-led development, they faced a deeper set of adjustment burdens and fell prone to more severe economic disequilibria as ISI entered into crisis. Second, these deeper ISI experiments had generated stronger ISI coalitions, including more densely organized labor movements and LM parties that shared vested interests in the state-centric matrix. These coalitions staunchly opposed adjustment measures that imposed economic hardships on popular sectors.

Consequently, attempts to impose austerity measures generated fierce political resistance and distributive conflicts in the LM cases, often producing political gridlock and policy uncertainties that exacerbated capital flight and deepened economic crises. Structural adjustment was frequently delayed until foreign exchange reserves were nearly depleted and hyperinflation had wreaked havoc on popular living standards (Weyland 2002). Indeed, many of the LM cases tried to avoid orthodox stabilization measures by adopting more politically palatable heterodox reforms that provided short-term relief but ultimately culminated in hyperinflation. In such contexts, LM cases often required more far-reaching structural adjustment packages – the so-called neoliberal "shock" treatments – before they could establish credible commitments to reform and bring their economies into alignment with the market logic of the neoliberal era.

In contrast, most of the elitist cases had not strayed so far from economic liberalism in the middle of the century, and they suffered less severe economic disequilibria during the crisis of ISI and the transition to neoliberalism. Likewise, the political and organizational weakness of labor unions moderated distributive conflicts and the political costs of subjecting labor to the discipline of the marketplace. Simply put, the elitist cases did not have as far to adjust at the onset of the neoliberal era; with shallower versions of the state-centric matrix and relatively mild economic crises, they were able to implement more moderate and gradual adjustment programs.

These disparities between the elitist and LM cases are portrayed in Tables 5.1 and 5.2. Table 5.1 demonstrates that the inflationary crises at the end of the ISI era were far more severe and prolonged in the LM cases, and that the

TABLE 5.1. *Party Systems and Economic Crisis in Latin America*

Type of Party System	Peak Annual Inflation Rate (1970–2000)	Years with Inflation >100 (1970–2000)	Worst Economic Contraction, 1980–2000 (+=multi-year)	1997 Index of Real Minimum Wage (1980 = 100)
Elitist				
Colombia	30.4	0	−4.1	103.8
Costa Rica	90.1	0	−9.6+	135.0
Dominican Republic	59.4	0	−5.7	78.0*
Ecuador	96.1	0	−6.3	50.5
Honduras	34.0	0	−2.2+	78.3
Panama	16.8	0	−15.0+	110.0
Paraguay	38.2	0	−4.0+	107.0
Uruguay	112.5	2	−16.0+	40.8
Mean	**59.7**	**.25**	**−7.9**	**87.9**
Labor-Mobilizing				
Argentina	3079.8	16	−11.2+	78.0
Bolivia	11,748.3	5	−10.9+	32.2
Brazil	2937.8	13	−4.4	73.2
Chile	508	5	−14.7+	102.3
Mexico	131.8	3	−6.2	30.1
Nicaragua	14,295.3	7	−19.8+	NA
Peru	7481.5	7	−23.4+	26.7
Venezuela	99.9	0	−7.8	39.9
Mean	**5035.3**	**7.0**	**−12.3**	**54.6**

* The Dominican Republic's wage index score is for 1996.
Sources: For inflation and economic growth from 1970 to 1997, Inter-American Development Bank, Economic and Social Progress in Latin America, various editions. For 1998–2000, Economic Commission for Latin America and the Caribbean (2001: 68, 95). For minimum wage index, International Labour Organization (1998: 43).

economic recessions and wage cuts associated with stabilization were also much deeper. All six of the countries that experienced annual inflations rates greater than 500 percent in the 1970s and 1980s – Chile, Bolivia, Argentina, Peru, Brazil, and Nicaragua – belonged to the LM camp. The latter five of these cases all experienced hyperinflationary spirals with annual rates that exceeded 2000 percent. Even if Nicaragua's extreme score of 14,295 is excluded, the average peak inflation rate in the other seven LM cases was 3,712 percent, compared to 59 percent in countries with elitist party systems. Among the LM cases, hyperinflation was avoided only in Mexico and Venezuela, where organized labor was allied with – and subordinate to – the governing party for all or most of the period. These two countries used a combination of price controls and wage agreements to contain inflationary pressures, but in the process they pushed much of the burden of economic adjustment onto the backs of workers; as seen in the table, Mexico and Venezuela had the region's second and fourth steepest declines in real minimum wages, respectively, in the 1980s and 1990s.

Even more striking, in the full sample of countries, 56 of the 58 annual inflation rates that exceeded 100 percent were recorded in countries with LM party systems. All of the LM cases experienced at least three years with triple-digit inflation during this time period except for oil-rich Venezuela, which peaked at 99.9 percent. Argentina suffered through no less than 16 years with triple digit rates of inflation, while Brazil followed closely with 13 years. Among the elitist cases, only Uruguay (twice) experienced triple-digit inflation, with a peak rate of 112.5.

Given these dramatic differences in the frequency, duration, and severity of inflationary crises, the costs of economic stabilization – including recessions and wage cuts – were also greater in the LM cases. Table 5.1 lists the deepest single year or consecutive multi-year economic recession experienced by each country between 1980 and 2000; the deepest contraction for elitist systems averaged 7.9 percent, compared to 12.3 percent in the LM cases. Five of the eight LM cases experienced a double-digit contraction, compared to only two elitist countries. The differences between the two sets of countries would be even greater were it not for the anomalous case of Panama, where U.S. sanctions against the Noriega regime caused a severe recession that had little to do with the regional patterns of economic stabilization and adjustment.

Likewise, the decline in the real minimum wage between 1980 and 1997 averaged 45.4 percent in the LM cases, nearly four times the 12.1 percent contraction in countries with elitist party systems. Half of the elitist countries achieved real minimum wage growth between 1980 and 1997, but only Chile – whose economic adjustment occurred before 1980 – had a higher real minimum wage in 1997 than in 1980 among the LM cases.[1] Paradoxically, countries with

---

[1] Economic crisis and reform caused a medium-term decline in real wages in Chile as well. Real wages in 1985 were 17.8 percent below those in 1970, before beginning a gradual recovery that carried into the 1990s (*Economía y Trabajo en Chile: Informe Anual* 1993–1994: 221).

the strongest party-labor blocs suffered the most severe cuts in real wages during this period of economic crisis and adjustment. Among the elitist cases, Uruguay registered the worst score on all of these indicators of economic crisis and adjustment. This reflects the hybrid features of the Uruguayan case and its intermediate ranking on the state-centric matrix, as discussed in Chapter 4.

Altogether, there is persuasive evidence to suggest that more profound statist development experiments culminated in severe economic crises by the 1980s, which in turn led to comprehensive shock treatments to achieve stabilization. Indeed, patterns of stabilization and adjustment were different across elitist and LM cases. Lora and Panizza (2003: 127–128), for example, single out Bolivia, Peru, Brazil, and Argentina – all LM cases – for aggressive privatization reforms, and they identify the elitist cases of Costa Rica, Uruguay, Paraguay, and Ecuador as relative laggards in the reform process. Stallings and Peres (2000: 48) add Chile to the ranks of aggressive reformers and Colombia to the group of "cautious" reformers, while Edwards (1995: 30) adds the Dominican Republic to the laggard category.[2] In general, the elitist cases adjusted in a gradual and moderate fashion, starting from an intermediate level of state intervention and moving progressively in the direction of greater economic orthodoxy. The impact of exogenous shocks on national economies and adjustment patterns was thus mediated by national political institutions and antecedent development experiences.

If countries with LM party systems experienced more severe economic crises and more wrenching adjustment processes, it follows that they would be especially prone to the kinds of destabilizing, performance-based retrospective vote shifts discussed in Chapter 3. Electoral realignments are likely when large numbers of voters opt to punish an incumbent party during periods of recession or hyperinflation, or reward a party that succeeds at stabilization and recovery. It is important to note, however, that the political costs of anti-incumbent vote shifts were not necessarily borne by LM parties, as these often found themselves out of power when crises erupted. More conservative or centrist parties, for example, were saddled with responsibility for crisis management in Peru and Venezuela in the early 1980s, Argentina in the mid-1980s, and Brazil in the late 1980s and early 1990s. These parties were generally pro-market, but they faced well-organized political resistance to the adoption of orthodox stabilization programs, and they often paid a steep price for policy indecisiveness and ineffectiveness. Consequently, there is little reason to expect the political costs of economic crises to be concentrated on any particular type of *party*; they should, instead, be concentrated on LM party *systems*.

---

[2] Mexico was clearly a case of extensive reform as well, but structural adjustment occurred gradually rather than via shock treatment. Venezuela attempted shock treatment between 1989 and 1991, but political resistance blocked the full implementation of neoliberal reforms.

MARKET REFORM AND PARTY–SOCIETY LINKAGES

If party systems were exposed to the destabilizing political costs of economic crises, so also were they threatened by the erosion of their societal linkage, cleavage, and organizational patterns during the transition to market liberalism. Economic crises and market reforms transformed the social landscape and the organization of societal interests in myriad ways, disrupting established patterns of representation. Although market liberalization could undermine the clientelist linkages of elitist party systems, it typically posed more fundamental threats to the programmatic linkages and stratified cleavage structures of LM party systems.

In theory, market reforms combined with the emergence of urban mass societies should erode the clientelist linkages that historically solidified popular bases for elitist party systems. Patron–clientelism has long thrived in rural Latin America, where population density is lower, material scarcities are acute, and political brokerage can be reinforced by patrimonial social relationships. Although patron–clientelism is surely prevalent in urban areas (Gay 1994; Stokes 1995; Auyero 2000), population density can make it more costly and less inclusive. Clientelist exchanges are more difficult to establish and monitor where social relationships are impersonal, and the sheer weight of numbers makes it expensive and inefficient to mobilize support by doling out particularistic rewards. In short, economies of scale may exist in the programmatic provision of public or collective goods (rather than particularistic rewards) in urban mass societies. Likewise, citizens with higher incomes and education levels tend to be less susceptible to clientelist manipulation (see Stokes 2005), as they are more economically independent and have access to political information that reduces their reliance on fixed partisan identities. And by privatizing social programs and cutting public employment, state subsidies, and regulatory intervention, neoliberal reforms should limit the economic resources and policy tools that parties traditionally used to fuel patronage networks. With universal rules for market competition and a level playing field, it should be more difficult for parties to use economic rewards to manipulate political loyalties (De Soto 1989; Geddes 1994).

In practice, however, the effects of market reform on clientelist practices were mixed. According to Valenzuela (1977: 154), clientelism flourishes under conditions of scarcity that undermine universalistic social programs and encourage a resort to particularistic criteria in the allocation of public resources. By slashing broad-ranging forms of social protection, preventing states from responding to collective claims, and disarticulating lower-class collective action, liberalization could encourage the pursuit of particularistic political ties and economic rewards as a shield against market insecurities. As Ames (2001: 36) states, "pork barrel politics does not require that the government supply large quantities of resources ... If resources are plentiful, in fact, brokers lose their monopoly and hence their control, so patronage can thrive in situations of scarcity and uncertainty." Scarcity magnifies the impact of available resources and strengthens the leverage of party brokers who control their allocation (Brusco, Nazareno, and Stokes 2004).

Not surprisingly, then, the targeted poverty-relief programs that accompanied market reforms were often prone to clientelistic political manipulation (Dresser 1991; Roberts 1995; Graham and Kane 1998), and parties that suffered an erosion of corporatist and programmatic linkages to labor unions leaned more heavily on patron–clientelism to secure the loyalty of the unorganized poor (Gibson 1997; Auyero 2000; Levitsky 2003). Neoliberal reforms may have placed boundaries on clientelist practices and eroded the patronage bases of some traditional parties like those in Uruguay (Luna 2006), but they hardy foreclosed clientelistic forms of party–society linkage. Indeed, clientelism provided a mechanism of hierarchical class control that complemented the disorganization of popular subjects from below. From a structural perspective, the vertical linkages of patron–clientelism were a more natural fit in a fragmented social landscape than programmatic linkages based on horizontal, class-based organizations and collective action. Clientelist modes of party–society linkage thus remained prevalent, even if they had a diminishing capacity to reproduce mass partisan loyalties.

Latin America's economic transition, however, posed major threats to party-society linkage and cleavage patterns that were based on ISI-era programmatic ties between parties and organized class constituencies – that is, the social foundations of partisan competition in LM systems. Economic crisis, market liberalization, and state retrenchment (and sometimes repression) altered the organization of interests and the party-mediated mechanisms for transmitting societal claims to state institutions and policymaking arenas – what Collier and Handlin (2009) label the "interest regime." Indeed, the realignment of states and markets led to the political demobilization and disarticulation of mass party and secondary associations that incorporated workers and peasants during the ISI era. In so doing, it undermined all three of the core dimensions of stratified sociopolitical cleavages: their structural basis in class distinctions, the organizational encapsulation of rival social blocs, and the cultural or ideational dimension of collective identities (see Bartolini and Mair 1990).

As Wright (2000: 962) argues, the political leverage of workers has both structural (or market) and associational bases. Structural power is enhanced when workers' skills are in scarce supply or their strategic location allows them to disrupt vital economic activities. Associational power, on the other hand, is a function of workers' capacity for collective action. The disarticulating logic of neoliberal critical junctures was rooted in the joint erosion of these two sources of power. Recessions, trade liberalization, privatizations, and sub-contracting transformed labor markets and class structures, producing job losses in the most heavily unionized, formal sectors of the economy that were conducive to collective action in the workplace. Meanwhile, employment swelled in the informal and temporary contract sectors of the workforce (Portes and Hoffman 2003), where irregular, small-scale, heterogeneous, and unregulated economic activities diffused collective identities and discouraged class-based collective action. By 1998, the International Labour Organization (1998: 1) reported that 59 percent of non-agricultural employment and 85 percent of new job growth in Latin America were in the informal and micro-enterprise sectors, which relied heavily on temporary workers and non-contract forms of employment. Such precarious employment was encouraged in many countries by reforms that deregulated or "flexibilized" labor markets in the name of economic efficiency: restrictions on hiring and firing were relaxed, employee benefits were slashed, collective bargaining was restricted, and union influence over the workplace was curtailed (see Cook 2007; *El Sindicalismo Ante los Proceses de Cambio Económico y Social en América Latina* 1998).

Paradoxically, these structural changes deepened social inequalities in Latin America (see Chapter 6) but diffused the political articulation of class distinctions. Labor movements had little success organizing the informal sectors, and their representational role was increasingly restricted to workers in formal, large-scale enterprises and a shrinking public sector. Trade union membership entered into a steep decline, especially in countries with LM party systems that had attained relatively high rates of unionization in the ISI era. As shown in Table 5.2, every country except Paraguay and Brazil had experienced significant reductions in trade union density by the 1990s,[3] but on average the declines were much steeper in the LM cases. Unionization plunged from an average peak rate of 31.9 percent in the LM cases to a late 1990s average of 16.1 percent; in the elitist cases, the decline was from a peak average of 13.9 percent to a 1990s average of 9.9 percent. Unionization rates declined by nearly 50 percent or more in Argentina, Bolivia, Chile, Nicaragua, Peru, and Venezuela, all LM cases. Among the LM cases, only Brazil avoided a sharp decline in trade union density, as union membership grew rapidly during the democratic transition of the 1980s before leveling off as market reforms were adopted (Sandoval 2001). Most countries with elitist party systems also experienced significant percentage-rate declines in trade union density, but they started from a much lower base level, so absolute declines were far smaller than in the LM cases. Since parties in the elitist systems had never relied heavily on unions to secure lower-class support, de-unionization posed little threat to their organizational and linkage patterns.

Market liberalization also transformed social and productive relationships in Latin America's rural economies (Kurtz 2004b). Agricultural commercialization turned traditional *haciendas* into capitalist enterprises, whose labor needs were met by seasonal and migratory wage laborers rather than resident peasants operating under semi-feudal forms of social control (de Janvry 1981; Gómez

---

[3] In Paraguay the union movement was so emasculated by political repression and cooptation under the Stroessner dictatorship that some sort of strengthening was perhaps inevitable following his ouster in 1989. Paraguay's trade union density thus peaked in the 1990s, although it remained low in comparative terms.

TABLE 5.2. *Changes in Trade Union Density in Elitist and Labor-Mobilizing Party Systems*

Type of Party System	Peak Trade Union Density	1990s Trade Union Density	Net Change in Trade Union Density
Labor-Mobilizing			
Argentina	50.1	22.3	−27.8
Bolivia	24.8	8.7	−16.1
Brazil	24.3	23.8	−.5
Chile	35.0	13.1	−21.9
Mexico	32.1	22.3	−9.8
Nicaragua	37.3	19.4	−17.9
Peru	25.0	5.7	−19.3
Venezuela	26.4	13.5	−12.9
Mean	**31.9**	**16.1**	**−15.8**
Elitist			
Colombia	9.2	5.9	−3.3
Costa Rica	15.4	11.7	−3.7
Dominican Republic	17.0	14.4	−2.6
Ecuador	13.5	9.0	−4.5
Honduras	8.5	5.7	−2.8
Panama	17.0	10.4	−6.6
Paraguay	9.9	9.9	0.0
Uruguay	20.9	12.0	−8.9
Mean	**13.9**	**9.9**	**−4.0**

Source: International Labour Organization (1997b: 235), supplemented by the sources listed in Footnote 3 of Chapter 4.

and Klein 1993; Kay 1999). Likewise, it encouraged the parcelization of communal or cooperative landholdings in countries like Chile, Mexico, and Peru that were often the fruit of historic peasant mobilizations and a structural basis for rural associational life (McClintock 1981; Snyder and Torres 1998). These trends fragmented and diversified the interests of rural producers, discouraging collective action around land conflicts and shifting the focus of agrarian claims to issues of wages, benefits, credits, and support services. Meanwhile, urban migration and economic modernization shrank the relative size of the peasantry, limiting its significance as a political force. Although collective struggles over land continued in countries like Brazil and Ecuador (Wolford 2010), they were far less salient in most of the region than they were during the ISI era, when demands for land reform inspired large-scale peasant mobilizations (Paige 1975; Thiesenhusen 1995; Kurtz 2004b). Once again, the disruptive political effects of these social and economic changes should be more pronounced in LM than elitist party systems, given the historic bonds between peasant associations and populist or leftist parties.

In both urban and rural areas, therefore, lower-class producers became more dispersed and heterogeneous, while their economic roles and collective welfare were increasingly subjected to the individualizing discipline of the marketplace rather than political bargaining or class-based collective action. The demise of mass labor and peasant movements and the emergence of a more fragmented and pluralistic social landscape (Oxhorn 1998) eroded the organizational bases of stratified cleavages where they had existed in the LM cases. Parties were forced to mobilize support across class distinctions in an increasingly atomized electorate that delivered a diminishing number of votes from organized social blocs. Not surprisingly, then, parties distanced themselves from organized labor (Levitsky 1998a) and downplayed class identities and ideology (Torcal and Mainwaring 2003), giving party leaders more autonomy to manage economic reforms and market their appeals to independent and unorganized voters. Neoliberal critical junctures thus accentuated social inequalities but undermined their political organization and articulation.

In much of the region, this disarticulation of class-based political competition was magnified by the partisan dynamics of market reform, as conservative, pro-market parties rarely took the lead in the adoption of structural adjustment policies in countries with LM party systems. In five of the eight LM cases, either the historic LM party (the Peronists in Argentina, the PRI in Mexico, AD in Venezuela, and the MNR in Bolivia) or an independent leader elected by popular sectors (Alberto Fujimori in Peru) eventually assumed political responsibility for structural adjustment, despite their initial opposition to it.[4] Since conservative parties encountered well-organized opposition to neoliberal reforms in these countries, parties with historic ties to organized labor had a comparative advantage in the reform process: they could offer inducements for cooperation, co-opt union leaders, and draw upon reservoirs of political capital and trust to contain popular mobilization (Murillo 2000; Burgess 2004).

Such bait-and-switch reforms, however, entailed a sharp departure from established policy commitments, undercutting the programmatic linkages that bound LM parties to working and lower class constituencies. In countries like Argentina, Mexico, and Peru, the policy about-face made it possible to garner new support (at least temporarily) from middle- and upper-class constituencies that were poised to benefit from economic liberalization (Gibson 1997; Roberts and Arce 1998). As such, the policy shift was not necessarily costly at the ballot box in the short term (Stokes 2001a), especially if it helped stabilize a crisis-ridden economy (Weyland 2002).

---

[4] In the other three LM cases, conservative *actors* led the process of market reforms, but conservative *parties* played a limited role. In Chile, reforms were imposed by the Pinochet military dictatorship. In Brazil, major reforms began under a maverick conservative leader (Fernando Collor) with little partisan base, then continued under a centrist-led partisan coalition formed by Fernando Henrique Cardoso. In Nicaragua, reforms occurred under a loose center-right electoral front formed in opposition to the Sandinista revolutionary government.

Nevertheless, these dramatic policy shifts were programmatically de-aligning, as LM parties historically served as systemic fulcrums – for supporters and opponents alike – which aligned group interests with partisan programs. By shifting to the right and embracing free markets, they could undercut business and middle-class support for conservative parties that were more consistent – but often less politically effective – proponents of market reform (Gibson 1996). At the same time, policy shifts strained political ties to labor and popular constituencies, leaving a political vacuum to the left of center that could be filled by new parties or populist figures. These shifts flagrantly violated candidates' and parties' electoral mandates, reshuffled and loosened partisan loyalties (Lupu 2011), and eroded stratified partisan cleavages. Ultimately, they left party systems vulnerable to protest voting and out-flanking on the left, should extra-systemic actors succeed in channeling societal dissent that had no effective institutional outlets.

As shown in Chapter 7, bait-and-switch reforms occurred in several elitist party systems as well – namely, Costa Rica and Ecuador – subjecting them to similar de-aligning effects. The competitive alignments of most elitist party systems, however, had never been well-defined by ideological or programmatic differences, and the narrowing of policy space under the technocratic consensus for market reform posed fewer challenges to partisan brands that were already predominantly pro-business and pro-market. For LM party systems, however, programmatic distinctions had been a cornerstone of appeals to both labor and capital, and policy convergence inevitably weakened group-based appeals system-wide.[5] Business interests had little incentive for partisanship when their policy preferences were seemingly dictated by global market constraints regardless of the party in office, while popular sectors that bore the material hardships of economic adjustment were often left without partisan vehicles to defend programmatic alternatives.

To summarize, neoliberal critical junctures posed a series of potentially destabilizing challenges to party systems in Latin America. Parties had to contend with the political costs of crisis management, as well as the disarticulation of established linkage, cleavage, and organizational patterns. These challenges were more formidable in LM party systems, whose defining features were deeply embedded in the state-centric matrix and more prone to disruption during the transition to market liberalism. Indeed, LM party systems increasingly converged on the representational patterns that characterized elitist party systems: segmented cleavage structures, professional-electoral party organizations, and linkages based on a mixture of clientelism, personalism, and image marketing. The section that follows explores how these changes affected electoral alignments and the stability of partisan competition.

---

[5] This does not mean that such appeals completely evaporated. As Murillo (2009) shows, labor-backed parties adopted some regulatory reforms that appealed to their union constituencies. They did so, however, within a larger context of macroeconomic policy convergence.

PARTY SYSTEM CONTINUITY AND CHANGE

As explained in Chapter 3, change and continuity in party systems can be tracked along a number of different dimensions. Two of the most basic indicators are the organizational composition of a party system – that is, the political identity of the major party organizations – and the competitive balance (or distribution of vote shares) among these parties. More disruptive critical junctures are likely to produce significant changes in the organizational composition and/or the distribution of vote shares in a party system. A third basic indicator, electoral volatility, provides a short-term measure of stability and change from one election cycle to the next. As shown below, change along all three of these dimensions was more extensive in LM than elitist party systems during the transition from state-led development to market liberalism.

Minor parties rise and fall in many countries without becoming major power contenders or exerting a significant effect on a party system's competitive dynamics. To screen out such "noise," I use a 10 percent threshold of seats in the lower house of congress as the criterion to identify major parties, and measure change in organizational composition and vote shares from the beginning of the "third wave" of democratization in 1978 until 2000. This time span captures the decisive period of economic crisis and market liberalization in every country except Chile, and it makes it possible to establish baseline assessments of partisan strength before the onset of the critical juncture or in its early stages (for countries that returned to democratic rule after the debt crisis began in the early 1980s). It also provides an endpoint that coincides with the region-wide closing of the critical juncture in the late 1990s and the beginning of the post-adjustment or aftermath period. Although national critical junctures in some countries ended earlier in the 1990s (see Part II), the time period analyzed here makes it possible to measure cross-national variation in party system change during a common period when economic crisis and market reforms dominated the agenda of democratic regimes in Latin America.

To smooth out short-term voting fluctuations associated with democratic transitions, the baseline strength of major parties is measured by averaging their legislative seat shares during the first two elections that followed the onset of the "third wave" in 1978; for countries that did not hold two elections before 1985, I used the first available election in the 1980s to measure parties' baseline strength.[6] Parties are coded as major parties if they win at least 10 percent of legislative seats in either the baseline elections or the last election in the time period (i.e., 2000 or before). A change in organizational composition

---

[6] In some countries, such as Mexico, Honduras, Panama, Nicaragua, and Paraguay, these early election cycles did not necessarily occur in contexts where the full panoply of liberal democratic civil and political rights were in force. Nevertheless, the election results presented here provide a reasonable assessment of the relative baseline strength of the major competing party organizations, and are thus useful for measuring change over the course of the critical juncture.

occurs when a major party in the baseline elections disappears before the last election, or when a major new party emerges. Continuity in organizational composition exists when a party (or a re-named successor party) passes the 10 percent threshold in the first and last elections, or when it wins seats in both elections and surpasses the threshold in at least one of them.

As seen in Table 5.3, the differences between elitist and LM party systems during the critical juncture are striking. Continuity in organizational composition existed in six of the eight elitist cases; although significant vote shifts sometimes moved individual parties into or out of major-party status in these countries, only Ecuador had a major party (the populist CFP) disappear during the critical juncture, and only Paraguay had a new one form (with the PEN barely, and briefly, reaching the 10 percent seat threshold). Otherwise, all the major parties in the baseline election cycles remained competitors at the end of the 1990s, and all the major parties at the end of the critical juncture had competed in the baseline election cycles.

By contrast, seven of the eight LM party systems experienced a change in organizational composition due to the collapse of a major party and/or the rise of a new one. The sole outlier, Chile, was an anomalous case – the only country in the region where structural adjustment was completed under military rule, allowing the party system to avoid the political dislocations of crisis management and market liberalization following the country's long-delayed democratic transition in 1989–1990. For the Chilean case, a more accurate measure of the impact of the critical juncture on the party system might be obtained by using the last election before the military coup (1973) as the baseline, rather than the first election following the restoration of democracy (1989). With that adjustment, the Chilean case would include two major parties that were casualties of the critical juncture (the Communist Party and the conservative National Party) and three major new parties that were spawned by it (the center-left PPD and the rightist RN and UDI).[7]

In the other LM cases, changes in organizational composition were more common due to the formation of new parties than the extinction of old ones. Indeed, major new parties emerged in all of these LM cases, whereas major parties only disappeared from congress in Nicaragua (the conservative PCDN) and Peru (the leftist IU). But even if major party extinctions were relatively rare, massive vote losses were common in the LM systems during the critical juncture, and they afflicted parties across the full range of the ideological spectrum – including the right (AP in Peru and COPEI in Venezuela), the center (UCR in Argentina, MNR in Bolivia, PMDB in Brazil, and PRI in Mexico), and a variety of populist and left-leaning alternatives (UDP in Bolivia, FSLN in Nicaragua, APRA in Peru, and AD in Venezuela).

---

[7] The Chilean Communist Party survived the dictatorship and competed in elections through larger coalitions following the return to democracy, but its candidates were not elected to congress until 2009. The RN incorporated leaders from the pre-1973 National Party, but was founded as a new party organization during the democratic transition.

TABLE 5.3. *Major Party Vote Shares and Electoral Realignment, 1978–2000 (percentage of seats in lower house of congress)*

Country/Major Parties	Baseline Elections (average)	Last Election	Change in Seat Shares (%)	Net Change in Seat Shares
Elitist Party Systems				
Colombia	1978/1982	1998		
PL	56.8	51.5	−5.3	14.8
PSC	41.5	17.2	−24.3	
Costa Rica	1978/1982	1998		
PLN	50.9	40.4	−10.5	9.2
PU/PUSC	39.5	47.4	+7.9	
Dominican Republic	1978/1982	1998		
PRD	52.2	55.7	+3.7	33.4
PR/PRSC	44.5	11.4	−33.1	
PLD	2.9	32.9	+30	
Ecuador	1979/1984	1998		
CFP	26.9	–	−26.9	
ID	28.3	12.5	−15.8	48.7
PSC	8.2	21.7	+13.5	
DP-UDC	3.5	26.7	+23.2	
PRE	2.1	20.0	+17.9	
Honduras	1981/1985	1997		
PL	51.9	54.1	+2.2	2.6
PN	44.3	41.4	−2.9	
Panama	1984	1999		
PRD	50.7	47.9	−2.8	
PPA	19.4	25.4	+6.0	8.9
PALA/ MORENA	10.4	1.4	−9.0	
Paraguay	1989	1998		
ANR-PC	66.7	56.3	−10.4	12.5
PLRA	29.2	33.8	+4.6	
PEN	–	10.0	+10.0	
Uruguay	1984	1999		
PC	41.4	33.3	−8.1	20.3
PN	35.4	22.2	−13.2	
FA	21.2	40.4	+19.2	
				Elitist Average = 18.8
Labor-Mobilizing Party Systems				
Argentina	1983/1985	1999		
UCR	51.0	31.9	−19.1	18.4
PJ	41.8	38.5	−3.3	
FREPASO	–	14.4	+14.4	
Bolivia	1979/1980	1997		
MNR	33.6	20.0	−13.6	
ADN	17.4	24.6	+7.2	34.1

TABLE 5.3. (cont.)

Country/Major Parties	Baseline Elections (average)	Last Election	Change in Seat Shares (%)	Net Change in Seat Shares
UDP/MIR	34.3	17.7	−16.6	
CONDEPA	–	14.6	+14.6	
UCS	–	16.2	+16.2	
Brazil	1986	1998		
PMDB	53.4	16.2	−37.2	
PFL	24.2	20.5	−3.7	36.6
PT	3.3	11.3	+8.0	
PDS/PPB	6.8	11.7	+4.9	
PSDB	–	19.3	+19.3	
Chile	1989	1997		
PDC	31.7	31.7	0.0	
PPD-PSCh	13.3	22.5	+9.2	9.6
RN	24.2	19.2	−5.0	
UDI	9.2	14.2	+5.0	
Mexico	1979/1982	2000		
PRI	77.2	44.8	−32.4	
PAN	12.3	30.2	+17.9	34.9
PRD	–	19.4	+19.4	
Nicaragua	1984	1996		
FSLN	63.5	38.7	−24.8	42.3
PCDN	14.6	–	−14.6	
AL	–	45.2	+45.2	
Peru	1980/1985	2000		
APRA	45.8	5.0	−40.8	
AP	30.0	3.3	−26.7	75.6
IU	16.1	–	−16.1	
C90/NM	–	43.3	+43.3	
Perú Posible	–	24.2	+24.2	
Venezuela	1978/1983	2000		
AD	50.4	18.2	−32.2	
COPEI	36.1	4.9	−31.2	59.7
MAS	5.3	12.7	+7.4	
MVR	–	48.5	+48.5	
				LM Average = 38.9

Source: Calculated from electoral data provided in Nohlen (2005).

Major parties suffered large vote losses in a number of elitist party systems as well, with conservative parties, in particular, downsizing in Colombia, the Dominican Republic, Paraguay, and Uruguay. On average, however, realigning vote shifts – whether from one established party to another, or from older parties to new contenders – were much less extensive in the elitist than the LM party systems (see Table 5.3). Adding together major party gains and losses, and dividing by two to establish a 100-point scale, elitist party systems averaged a net shift of 18.8 percent of legislative seats from the baseline elections to the last election in the period under study – less than half the average net shift of 38.9 percent in the LM cases.[8] The only elitist system to surpass the LM average was Ecuador, where the party system was largely reconstituted in the early 1980s as the critical juncture was getting underway. On average, then, LM party systems were more likely to undergo change in their organizational composition during the critical juncture, and more likely to experience major electoral realignments that altered their competitive balance.

Where countries entered the critical juncture with a dominant or hegemonic party – in Mexico, Paraguay, and Nicaragua – electoral realignment entailed a shift toward more competitive and pluralistic partisan politics. Otherwise, electoral realignment did not follow a uniform pattern or direction during the critical juncture in either elitist or LM party systems. Given the historic dominance of relatively conservative parties in most of the elitist cases, vote shifts were more likely to weaken the right and strengthen centrist (Paraguay) or leftist (Uruguay and the Dominican Republic) alternatives. In Costa Rica, however, votes shifted in the opposite direction, while in Ecuador parties from across the ideological spectrum lost ground to new conservative, centrist, and populist contenders. In Colombia, both traditional parties of the right lost seat shares, but no major new party capitalized on their losses – signifying a process of electoral de-alignment more than realignment. In LM party systems, new left-of-center parties gained ground in Argentina, Brazil, Mexico, and Venezuela, but older ones lost ground in Nicaragua, Bolivia, Peru, and Venezuela. Conservative parties strengthened in Chile, Mexico, and Nicaragua, while votes swung toward the centrist PSDB in Brazil and personalistic parties in Peru and Bolivia (prior to the rise of the MAS in the aftermath period).

Consequently, partisan realignments manifested centrifugal tendencies in a number of countries, with left and/or right poles strengthening at the expense of the center, but centripetal patterns were also present. Indeed, the generalized shift of the left toward centrist positions (prior to the rise of Hugo Chávez at the end of the period) and the growing adherence to democratic norms on both the left and the right were indicative of a region-wide process of ideological de-polarization during the latter half of the 1980s and 1990s – the heyday of the Washington Consensus, when programmatic options increasingly narrowed to variants of market liberalism.

Clearly, however, this *programmatic* shift toward the right was not accompanied by a generalized *electoral* realignment toward the right in most of the region. In most countries, conservative parties neither led nor capitalized politically on the process of market liberalization. Indeed, several of the leftist parties and movements that eventually came to power in the post-adjustment period were slowly accumulating forces during the critical juncture, including the FA in

---

[8] If the 1973 election is used as the baseline for Chile, the aggregate national change in vote shares increases from 9.6 to 29.0, and the LM average increases to 41.3.

TABLE 5.4. *Changes in Organizational Composition and Electoral Alignments during Neoliberal Critical Junctures*

Change in Organizational Composition	Party System Adaptation	Minor Electoral Realignment	Major Electoral Realignment	Decomposition and Partial Reconstitution
No	*Colombia Costa Rica Honduras Panama*	*Uruguay*	*Dominican Republic*	
Yes	*Paraguay*	Argentina Chile	*Ecuador* Brazil Bolivia Mexico Nicaragua	Peru Venezuela

Note: *Elitist party systems in italics.*

Uruguay, the PT in Brazil, the Socialist/PPD bloc in Chile, and the varied leftist tendencies that converged under *Chavismo* in Venezuela.

What stands out during the critical juncture, then, is not a common pattern of electoral realignment, but simply the generalized disruption of antecedent competitive alignments and the heightened susceptibility of LM party systems to destabilizing pressures. Changes in organizational composition and electoral alignments are summarized in Table 5.4, drawing from the typology of party system change introduced in Chapter 3. Party systems are coded as experiencing adaptation, minor realignment, major realignment, or decomposition and partial reconstitution based on the data on net changes in legislative seat shares presented in Table 5.3; for the Chilean case, I use the revised measure of net changes in seat shares calculated from the 1973 baseline election, which yields a more accurate score of 29 percent (rather than the score of 9.6 percent calculated from the 1989 election). Five party systems that experienced net shifts in seat shares of less than 15 percent – all from the elitist category – are coded as cases of adaptation. Net shifts of 15 to 30 percent are coded as minor electoral realignments, a category that includes Uruguay, Argentina, and Chile. Net shifts of 30 to 50 percent are coded as major realignments, including two elitist cases (Dominican Republic and Ecuador) and four LM cases (Brazil, Bolivia, Mexico, and Nicaragua). The final category of decomposition and partial reconstitution includes the two remaining LM cases, Peru and Venezuela, which experienced net shifts greater than 50 percent and a generalized breakdown of the party systems that entered the critical juncture.

The disruptive effects of neoliberal critical junctures on LM party systems are readily apparent in Table 5.4. Simply put, LM party systems were more likely to experience changes in their organizational composition, along with major electoral realignments (or breakdowns). The cumulative effects of severe and prolonged economic crises, the management of structural adjustment, and the social and political dislocations of party–society linkage, cleavage, and organizational patterns clearly took their toll on LM party systems.

TABLE 5.5. *Average Electoral Volatility in Elitist and Labor-Mobilizing Party Systems, 1978–2000 (Pedersen index of volatility)*

Type of Party System	Volatility in Presidential Elections	Volatility in Legislative Elections	Combined Average Volatility
Labor-Mobilizing			
Argentina	23.0	14.1	18.6
Bolivia	27.3	27.6	27.5
Brazil	38.4	23.0	30.7
Chile	21.8	10.0	15.9
Mexico	20.0	15.7	17.9
Nicaragua	51.3	47.7	49.5
Peru	39.9	49.6	44.8
Venezuela	37.8	28.9	33.4
Mean	**32.4**	**27.1**	**29.8**
Elitist			
Colombia	13.2	10.8	12.0
Costa Rica	8.7	11.9	10.3
Dominican Republic	18.5	18.1	18.3
Ecuador	37.7	29.2	33.5
Honduras	6.2	7.9	7.1
Panama	26.7	46.6	36.7
Paraguay	24.7	16.1	20.4
Uruguay	11.5	11.2	11.4
Mean	**18.4**	**19.0**	**18.7**

Source: Calculated from electoral data provided in Nohlen (2005).

Not surprisingly, these disruptions were also manifested in short-term patterns of electoral volatility, measured from one election cycle to the next. As seen in Table 5.5, LM party systems on average were far more volatile than their elitist counterparts during neoliberal critical junctures. Volatility scores from 1978 to 2000 averaged 27.1 in congressional elections for the eight LM cases and 32.4 in presidential elections, compared to 19.0 in congressional elections for the elitist cases and 18.4 in presidential elections.[9] The four most stable party systems – Honduras, Costa Rica, Uruguay and Colombia – all belonged to the elitist category, whereas five of the seven most volatile party systems belonged to the LM category. Chile was the most electorally stable of the LM cases, while Costa Rica and the four party systems with 19th-century oligarchic roots – those in Honduras, Uruguay, Colombia, and Paraguay – stood out for their stability among the elitist cases. Oligarchic parties in these four countries not only adapted

[9] Since the first election in each country is a baseline for calculation, actual volatility scores are not recorded until the 1980s.

to the era of mass politics at the beginning of the 20th century, but they remained electorally dominant through neoliberal critical junctures as well.[10] The more recent, patrimonial variants of elitist party systems found in Ecuador and Panama were less stable, however, with Panama experiencing relatively high levels of short-term volatility despite little net change in the party system over time.

In short, despite entering the critical juncture with a series of organizational attributes that should, in theory, have enhanced their electoral stability, LM party systems were more susceptible to the traumatic social and political dislocations of neoliberal critical junctures. The organizational features and societal linkages of LM party systems were precisely those that were most incongruent with the socioeconomic and political landscape of the dawning neoliberal era. Rather than sources of stability, then, these attributes were precursors to political crises and electoral realignment or organizational decomposition. Patterns of party system stability and instability in the recent Latin American experience thus diverge sharply from those found historically in Western Europe, and they defy much of the conventional wisdom on the subject.

CONCLUSION

The transition from ISI to neoliberalism posed challenges to party systems throughout Latin America, but its disruptive effects were heavily conditioned by the antecedent sociological foundations of different types of party systems. LM party systems encountered more severe economic crises than elitist party systems, and they faced greater threats to competitive alignments that were grounded in programmatic and organizational linkages between mass parties and organized class constituencies. As such, they were highly prone to institutional instability during the critical juncture, including changes in their organizational composition, major electoral realignments, and generalized electoral volatility.

Antecedent conditions, however, do not explain the effects of market liberalization on the programmatic alignment of party systems, which was heavily contingent on the partisan configuration of leadership and opposition to the market reform process. As the following chapter shows, reform alignments weighed heavily on competitive dynamics in the aftermath period. These alignments shaped the political expression of societal resistance to market liberalization, largely determining whether it would be channeled into or against the party systems in place at the end of the critical juncture. As such, they conditioned the reactive sequences of the aftermath period, the character of political turns to the left, and the longer-term stability of partisan competition – in short, the institutional legacies of neoliberal critical junctures.

---

[10] As we will see, however, traditional oligarchic parties finally lost their grip on power in Uruguay, Colombia, and (temporarily) Paraguay in the early years of the 21st century, in the aftermath to neoliberal critical junctures.

6

Programmatic (De-)Alignment and Party System Stability in the Aftermath Period

As shown in Chapter 5, antecedent structural and institutional conditions weighed heavily on the political dynamics of neoliberal critical junctures. The transition from ISI to market liberalism was associated with more severe economic crises, greater electoral volatility, and deeper electoral realignments in countries that developed LM party systems during the ISI era. If political outcomes were fully determined by antecedent conditions, however, there would be no reason to characterize the transition to neoliberalism as a critical juncture; political change would merely reflect the unfolding of earlier, path-dependent development trajectories beset by exogenous shocks. For this transition to constitute a critical juncture, political outcomes and their institutional legacies must also be conditioned by the competitive alignments and strategic choices of political actors who ultimately decide on policy and/or institutional change.

During neoliberal critical junctures, the most important strategic choice was the adoption of structural adjustment policies in response to the exhaustion of the ISI model and the exogenous shock of the debt crisis. Although every country in the region adopted market reforms, the political consequences of such reforms varied widely depending on the political orientation and partisan alignment of supporters and opponents of the reform process. These alignments enhanced the programmatic structuring of some party systems – in both elitist and LM cases – contributing to relatively stable forms of post-adjustment partisan competition. In others, however – a majority of cases – they undermined or failed to produce programmatic structuration, destabilizing party systems in the aftermath period. Indeed, reactive sequences in the aftermath period – driven largely by societal resistance to market liberalism – sometimes altered the institutional outcomes of the critical juncture itself; party systems that were relatively stable during the critical juncture encountered new disruptive forces in the aftermath period, while in a few cases inchoate and volatile party systems progressively consolidated.

These divergent institutional legacies were not predetermined by the antecedent properties of elitist and LM party systems. In short, programmatic alignment and de-alignment during the critical juncture were not endogenous to party system types, nor were they strictly determined by historical development trajectories or levels of programmatic structuration during the ISI era (Kitschelt et al. 2009). As noted in Chapter 5, de-aligning or bait-and-switch patterns of reform were especially likely in LM party systems, where the strength of ISI party–labor blocs made it difficult for conservative parties to impose structural adjustment measures. Nevertheless, several elitist party systems also experienced de-aligning critical junctures, while aligning critical junctures occurred in several LM party systems. Patterns of alignment and de-alignment, therefore, were determined by historically contingent political dynamics and partisan configurations during the market liberalization process.

This chapter explains how partisan reform alignments structured or destructured party systems programmatically, and how these alignments shaped the political articulation of societal resistance, the reactive sequences of the aftermath period, and the institutional legacies of stable and unstable partisan competition. These institutional legacies heavily conditioned the character of the political turn to the left in the post-adjustment era, including the propensity of new leftist governments to break with the neoliberal model.

PARTY SYSTEMS AT THE END OF THE CRITICAL JUNCTURE

As explained in Chapter 3, party systems at the end of the critical juncture could be differentiated along two primary dimensions: their level of institutionalization and their degree of programmatic structuration (see Figure 3.1). With the exception of Peru and Venezuela, which experienced party system decomposition and the emergence of populist outsiders during the critical juncture, all the other countries exited the critical juncture by the second half of the 1990s with relatively intact party systems. Although many of these party systems had experienced changes in their organizational composition, major electoral realignments, and/or high levels of electoral volatility (Ecuador in particular), electoral competition continued to be dominated by two or more established parties through the end of the critical juncture (see Table 5.3). For our purposes, these party systems could be considered relatively institutionalized as they moved into the aftermath period, even if they varied considerably in their electoral stability.

Even where neoliberal critical junctures left party systems intact, however, they often de-aligned them programmatically. Programmatic alignment and de-alignment depended on the political orientation of leading market reformers and their opponents. Market reforms aligned party systems programmatically when they were adopted by conservative political actors – whether parties, militaries, or personalist leaders (such as Fernando Collor in Brazil) – and consistently opposed by a major party of the left that was out of office during the decisive period of reform. Bait-and-switch reforms imposed by historic populist or center-left parties, or populist figures who campaigned against structural adjustment policies (such as Alberto Fujimori in Peru), were programmatically de-aligning. Finally, market liberalization was neutral in its effects on programmatic alignments when it was led by conservative actors but no major party of the left existed in opposition. Under these latter two patterns of reform, critical junctures ended with party systems and competitive dynamics that were not programmatically aligned by a central cleavage between supporters and opponents of the liberalization process.

Table 6.1 charts the countries that experienced these different types of critical junctures and the political leaders who adopted the most important reforms, drawing from the reform indices developed by Lora (2001) and Morley, Machado, and Pettinato (1999) to identify the peak periods of market

TABLE 6.1. *Market Reforms, Partisanship, and Types of Critical Junctures (1973–1998)*

Country/Type of Critical Juncture	Leading Reformer(s)	Peak Years of Reform	Party/Political Orientation	Leading Rivals
Aligning				
Brazil (LM)	Sarney	1988–1989	PFL (right)	PT (left)
	Collor	1990–1992	Right/personalist	
	Cardoso	1994–1999	PSDB (centrist)	
Chile (LM)	Pinochet/ Military regime	1974–1979	Right	PDC (centrist) PSCh (left)
Dominican Republic (elitist)	Balaguer	1990–1995	PRSC (right)	PLD (centrist PRD (center-left)
El Salvador	Cristiani	1990–1993	ARENA (right)	FMLN (left)
Mexico (LM)	De la Madrid	1983–1988	PRI (centrist/center-right)	PRD (center-left)
	Salinas de Gortari	1989–1994		
Nicaragua (LM)	Chamorro	1990–1994	Multi-party coalition (center-right)	FSLN (left)
Uruguay (elitist)	Military regime	1973–1981	Right	FA (left)
	Lacalle	1990–1994	PN (right)	
De-aligning				
Argentina (LM)	Menem	1989–1992	PJ (populist)	UCR (centrist)
Bolivia (LM)	Paz Estenssoro	1985–1989	MNR (Populist)	Varied

TABLE 6.1. *(cont.)*

Country/Type of Critical Juncture	Leading Reformer(s)	Peak Years of Reform	Party/Political Orientation	Leading Rivals
Costa Rica (elitist)	Monje	1982–1986	PLN (center-left)	PUSC
	Arias	1986–1990	PLN	(center-right)
Ecuador (elitist)	Borja	1989–1992	ID (center-left)	Varied
	Durán Ballén	1992–1995	PUR (personalist/right)	
	Bucaram	1996–1997	PRE (populist)	
Peru (LM)	Fujimori	1990–1994	Personalist/populist	Varied
Venezuela (LM)	Pérez	1989–1992	AD (center-left)	COPEI (center-right)
Neutral				
Colombia (elitist)	López Michelson	1974–1978	PL (center-right)	PSC (right)
	Gaviria	1992–1993	PL	
Guatemala	Cerezo	1986–1988	PDC (centrist)	Varied
Honduras (elitist)	Callejas	1991–1993	PN (right)	PL (center-right)
Panama (elitist)	Pérez Balladares	1994–1998	PRD (center-right)	Varied
Paraguay (elitist)	Rodríguez	1989–1993	ANR (right)	PLRA (centrist)

Sources: Morley, Machado and Pettinato (1999); Lora (2001).

liberalization. For this analysis, I include El Salvador and Guatemala in the sample of cases; these countries could not be meaningfully categorized in the earlier typology of elitist and LM party systems due to the truncation of party system development in the ISI era by military rule, but both had party system alignments in place during the period of market liberalization that allow them to be placed in the comparative analysis undertaken here.

Bait-and-switch patterns of reform produced de-aligning critical junctures in four LM cases – Argentina, Bolivia, Peru, and Venezuela – as well as two elitist cases – Costa Rica and Ecuador. In these countries, historic populist or center-left parties or, in the Peruvian case, an independent populist figure (Alberto Fujimori) played major roles in the adoption of market reforms.[1] Although

---

[1] The Ecuadorean case is mixed, as conservative, populist, and center-left parties took turns implementing market reforms during the critical juncture and the early aftermath period. As discussed in Chapter 7, the overall dynamic was one of programmatic de-alignment. Stokes (2001a) identifies

market reforms also began in Mexico in a bait-and-switch fashion under a historic LM populist party, the PRI, the hegemonic status and internal hetero-geneity of this party produced a different reform alignment; conflicts surround-ing the policy shift split the PRI relatively early in the critical juncture, producing a major new party of the Left (the PRD), while the PRI moved in a conservative direction to help align partisan competition along programmatic lines (see Bruhn 1997). Mexico's critical juncture, then, approximated those of countries where market reforms were implemented by conservative or centrist leaders and consistently opposed by a major party of the Left: Brazil, Chile, El Salvador, Uruguay, and, more ambiguously, the Dominican Republic (Morgan, Hartlyn, and Espinal 2011) and Nicaragua.[2] In these countries, including both elitist and LM cases, critical junctures aligned party systems along a left–right axis of competition that was grounded in programmatic distinctions.

In the remaining countries – Colombia, Guatemala, Honduras, Panama, and Paraguay – neutral patterns of reform occurred under conservative leadership in the absence of a major leftist competitor. Endogeneity clearly exists in this category, as all the countries had elitist party systems during the ISI era except for Guatemala, where military rule precluded any sort of popular alternative. Consequently, none of these countries had a major populist or leftist party available to lead market reforms, in a bait-and-switch fashion, or oppose them, in an aligning fashion. Like the de-aligning, bait-and-switch cases, critical junctures in these countries ended with forms of partisan competition that were not well structured by pro-grammatic distinctions, as opponents of the neoliberal model were absent or electorally marginal.

Combining the two dimensions of party system institutionalization and pro-grammatic alignment, it is now possible to locate countries in the 2 × 2 table of the institutional outcomes of neoliberal critical junctures presented in Chapter 3 (see Figure 3.1). The upper left cell includes the cases of *contested liberalism*, where party systems were both institutionalized and programmatically aligned

---

other cases of policy switches where conservative leaders adopted orthodox reforms after cam-paigning on platforms that promised economic "security," but in such cases it is deceptive election campaigns – not post-election policy choices – that are out of sync with parties' programmatic orientations. Such electoral opportunism is not uncommon, and it should not have the same systemic de-aligning effects as the dramatic policy reversals adopted by historic statist and LM parties during the critical juncture.

[2] In Nicaragua, painful austerity measures were adopted – under acute, war-time hyperinflationary pressures – by the revolutionary Sandinista government in 1988. More comprehensive structural adjustment policies were adopted by the conservative governments that took office after 1990, with the Sandinistas reverting to an opposition stance on the left. Clearly, civil wars in the 1980s created strong left–right cleavages in Nicaragua and El Salvador prior to the configuration of reform alignments around the process of market liberalization.

Programmatic Structuring of Political Competition	Institutionalized Party System	Non-Institutionalized Party System
High	*Contested Liberalism* Brazil Chile Dominican Republic El Salvador Mexico Nicaragua Uruguay	*Polarized Populism/Political Movements* Venezuela
Low	*Neoliberal Convergence* Argentina Bolivia Colombia Costa Rica Ecuador Guatemala Honduras Panama Paraguay	*Serial Populism* Peru

FIGURE 6.1. National Outcomes of Neoliberal Critical Junctures

between centrist or conservative parties that supported market orthodoxy and leftist parties that challenged it: Brazil, Chile, El Salvador, the Dominican Republic, Mexico, Nicaragua, and Uruguay. The lower left cell of *neoliberal convergence* includes the countries with relatively institutionalized major parties that oversaw the liberalization process, but no major party of the Left in opposition: Argentina, Bolivia, Colombia, Costa Rica, Ecuador, Guatemala, Honduras, Panama, and Paraguay. These were all cases of either neutral or de-aligning patterns of market reform. The lower right cell of *serial populism* is occupied by Peru, where the party system decomposed during the critical juncture and was replaced by a series of populist or personalist electoral vehicles, none offering clear programmatic alternatives to market liberalism. Finally, Venezuela occupies the upper right cell of *polarized populism/political movements*, where party systems decompose and more polarizing populist figures or political movements arise to challenge the neoliberal model. These outcomes – the new institutional baselines for party systems in the aftermath period – are depicted in Figure 6.1.

What, then, were the implications of these different types of critical junctures for party system stability in the aftermath of the reform period? As shown below, party systems characterized by neoliberal convergence, especially those produced by de-aligning, bait-and-switch patterns of reform, were highly susceptible to destabilizing reactive sequences as the Washington Consensus broke down and popular resistance to market liberalism intensified. In short, neoliberal convergence was an unstable equilibrium in the aftermath period: some party systems, such as those in Ecuador and Bolivia, decomposed and moved toward the categories of serial or polarized populism, while others (such as Costa Rica) shifted toward the more programmatic forms of competition associated with contested liberalism. By contrast, the outcome of contested liberalism channeled popular resistance into institutionalized forms of representation with relatively stable patterns of partisan competition. These divergent paths suggest that neoliberal critical junctures produced institutional legacies that varied widely in their ability to withstand the social and political challenges of the post-adjustment era.

THE CHANGING POLITICAL LANDSCAPE
OF THE POST-ADJUSTMENT ERA

Low levels of programmatic alignment were not necessarily destabilizing for party systems during neoliberal critical junctures. Indeed, given the crisis of the state-centric matrix in the 1980s, party systems could avoid some forms of disruption if statist and labor-based alternatives were never very strong to begin with, as in most of the elitist cases. With ISI and socialist models discredited, organized labor in decline, and inflationary crises pushing structural adjustment to the top of the policymaking agenda, popular sectors had little capacity to mobilize on behalf of alternatives. Consequently, party systems that offered no clear channels for dissent from market orthodoxy could sometimes ride out the critical juncture with a minimum of political disruption – as was the case, for example, in Honduras, Costa Rica, Colombia, and Paraguay.

The stability of programmatically non-aligned partisan competition, however, proved to be context dependent, as it was contingent on a particular confluence of socioeconomic and political conditions in the transitional period – namely, the political demobilization and disarticulation of neoliberalism's opponents in a context of structurally constrained programmatic space. These conditions changed along several key dimensions in the post-adjustment period, weakening and eventually fracturing the Washington consensus, while strengthening the social and political expression of resistance to market liberalization.

By the middle of the 1990s, when Brazil became the last country in Latin America to defeat hyperinflation, the primary tasks of economic stabilization had been accomplished and major structural reforms had been adopted throughout the region. The pace, breadth, and depth of the reform process are depicted in Figure 6.2, which tracks change from 1975 to 2000 in the regional average of the general reform index developed by Morley, Machado, and Pettinato (1999), as updated by Escaith and Paunovic (2004). The mean regional trend line moved in the direction of freer markets over the latter half of the 1970s, then declined slightly over the first half of the 1980s, reflecting the prevalence of heterodox

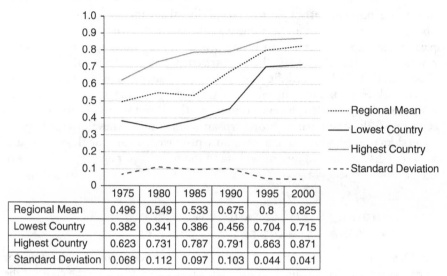

	1975	1980	1985	1990	1995	2000
Regional Mean	0.496	0.549	0.533	0.675	0.8	0.825
Lowest Country	0.382	0.341	0.386	0.456	0.704	0.715
Highest Country	0.623	0.731	0.787	0.791	0.863	0.871
Standard Deviation	0.068	0.112	0.097	0.103	0.044	0.041

FIGURE 6.2. General Index of Market Liberalization in Latin America, 1975–2000 (regional average)
Source: Escaith and Paunovic (2004). Higher scores on the index are associated with greater market liberalization.

adjustment measures during the early stages of the debt crisis. The policy divergence between orthodox and heterodox strategies can be seen in the growing gap in the early 1980s between the most liberalized economy and both the regional average and the least liberalized economy. The divergence is also reflected in the relatively high standard deviation on the market reform index during this period.

A more steeply sloping upward trend line in the mean index score resumes over the second half of the 1980s into the early 1990s – the decisive phase of the critical juncture in most countries – when heterodox experiments collapsed and the Washington Consensus reached its apogee. The consensus is demonstrated by the narrowing gap between the regional mean and the index score of the most liberalized economy, and by the sharp decline in the region-wide standard deviation. The trend line of the regional mean flattens out over the second half of the 1990s, as the deepest reforms had been completed by the middle of the decade.

Although political resistance blocked the full implementation of the neoliberal model in a number of countries, the regional economic landscape was dramatically different at the end of the 1990s than it had been a decade before. Between 1985 and 1990, only four countries in the region – Costa Rica, Honduras, Panama, and Chile – had average annual inflation rates below 20 percent (see Figure 6.3). Eight countries had average inflation rates between 20

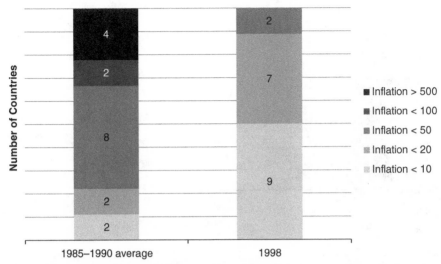

FIGURE 6.3. Average Annual Inflation Rates in Latin America, 1985–1990 and 1998
Source: Economic Commission for Latin America and the Caribbean (2000: 94–95).

and 50 percent, two others averaged between 50 and 100 percent, and four (Argentina, Brazil, Nicaragua and Peru) had average annual inflation rates greater than 500 percent (that is, at hyperinflationary levels). By 1998, only Ecuador and Venezuela had inflation rates greater than 20 percent (40.8 and 35.7, respectively); the other 16 countries were all below 20 percent, nine of them having driven inflation down to single-digit levels.

Stabilization and structural adjustment, however, yielded only modest gains in economic growth. Per-capita GDP in Latin America and the Caribbean grew at an average annual rate of 1.75 percent from 1991 to 2000. This was a marked improvement over the "lost decade" of the 1980s, when per-capita GDP declined at an average annual rate of –0.82 percent. Nevertheless, it still lagged behind the ISI-era average growth rates of 2.63 percent in the 1960s and 3.46 percent in the 1970s (see Figure 6.4), not to mention the 1990s growth rates of 5.53 and 3.34 percent in East and South Asia, respectively. Furthermore, the liberalization of capital markets left the region exposed to domestic and international financial crises, including the Mexican peso crisis of 1994–1995 and the Asian financial crisis of 1997–1998, both of which reverberated across the region. The Asian crisis, in particular, caused growth to stagnate in Latin America at the end of the 1990s, casting doubt on the promise of liberalized economies to generate greater prosperity.

If financial crises and stagnant growth at the end of the 1990s helped erode the Washington Consensus, more fundamental questions were raised by the generalized failure of liberalized economies to make a serious dent in the region's accumulated social deficits of poverty, inequality, and underemployment.

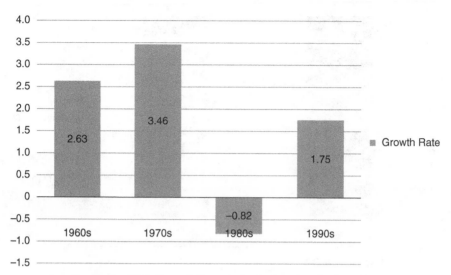

FIGURE 6.4. Per-Capita GDP Growth Rates in Latin America, by Decade
Source: Loayza, Fajnzylber, and Calderón (2004: 67).

During the 1980s the number of people living below the poverty line in Latin America increased by nearly 65 million, while the percentage of the population below the poverty line rose from 35 to 41 percent over the course of the decade before gradually dropping back to 36 percent in 1997 (Echeverría 2000). Likewise, the Gini coefficient of inequality increased from 48.9 in the early 1980s to 52.6 in 2000 (Cornia 2012), the highest average of any region in the world, while the income ratio of the richest to the poorest quintile of the Latin American population increased from less than 16:1 in 1982 to greater than 22:1 in 1995 (Inter-American Development Bank 1997: 41). Income concentration was so powerful in the 1980s that the bottom nine income deciles – that is, the bottom 90 percent of the population – all lost relative income shares, while the top decile increased its share by 10.6 percent (Londoño and Székely 2000: 105–106; see also Altimir 2008).

Despite the relative economic recovery of the 1990s, the average real industrial wage in Latin America in 1996 remained five percent below that of 1980, while the average real minimum wage fell by 30 percent between 1980 and 1997 (International Labour Organization 1998: 43). Many workers in the informal sector, however, did not even make the legal minimum wage; according to the ILO (1997a: 15), over one-third of micro-enterprise workers received less than the legal minimum wage, and over 70 percent lacked pension and health care coverage. Not surprisingly, with income and social benefits so closely tied to precarious employment opportunities, unemployment consistently ranked first on the region-wide list of national concerns from 1995 to 2008 (Latinobarómetro 2010: 7).

These social concerns were often relegated to the margins of democratic competition during the critical juncture, when popular demobilization insulated governments from societal pressures and allowed them to prioritize the urgent tasks of stabilization and structural adjustment. Indeed, given the devastating impact of hyperinflation on wages and consumption, stabilization measures could be beneficial to low-income groups. As such, they often received broad-based societal support (Armijo and Faucher 2002) – or at least tacit consent – whatever their distributive consequences over the longer term. Once inflation had been tamed and the region entered the post-adjustment era, however, democratic competition and new patterns of social mobilization increasingly politicized the social deficits of the neoliberal model. In so doing, they put the Washington Consensus on the defensive and fueled a Polanyian backlash that shaped the reactive sequences of the aftermath period.

This backlash was expressed in a number of different political arenas, and it took a variety of forms. Public opinion surveys, for example, demonstrated broad support for some aspects of market liberalization, but hardly a hegemonic ideological consensus to match its technocratic dominance in policymaking circles. Indeed, public opinion was highly statist in some policy spheres, and it became more so as the region exited the critical juncture and veered toward the left in the aftermath period.

Rather than treating the new economic model as an undifferentiated whole, citizens tended to disaggregate the package of free market reforms, with some measures being more popular than others. Free trade generally received wide-spread support, as it offered consumers access to a broader range of affordable imported goods. Consequently, a region-wide average of over 70 percent expressed support for free trade in the late 1990s (Baker 2003: 425). A majority of survey respondents also expressed general sympathies for market economies and private enterprise, although this support dwindled after the late 1990s (see Figure 6.5 below). Ambiguity toward the market model may have reflected short-term hardships, as satisfaction with the *performance* of the economy fell to a low of 16 percent in 2003 during the final stages of the regional downturn that followed the Asian financial crisis (before tracking upward again as a new commodity boom began in the middle of the decade; see Latinobarómetro 2005: 63).

More specifically, public opinion was unfavorable toward the privatization of basic utilities like water, electricity, and telecommunications. Even when privatizations aimed to broaden access or improve the quality of such utilities, they raised fears of higher prices (Baker 2009). Consequently, the percentage of survey respondents who said privatizations had benefited their country declined after the late 1990s, reaching a low of 21 percent in 2003 before partially recovering as economic conditions improved (see Figure 6.5). Indeed, large and growing majorities expressed support for state control not only over basic

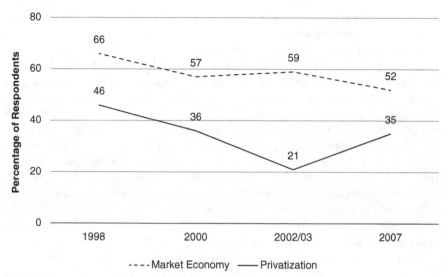

FIGURE 6.5. Support for Privatizations and a Market Economy, 1998–2007 (regional average)

Source: Latinobarómetro (2007: 25–26). The graph shows the region-wide average percentage of survey respondents who either agreed or strongly agreed with the statements "A market economy is best for the country" and "Privatizations of state enterprises have been beneficial for the country."

utilities, but also over oil and gas industries and social programs like pensions, education, and health care systems. As Figure 6.6 shows, support for public ownership averaged over 80 percent of survey respondents in most of these sectors of the economy by 2008. In short, preference ratios for state over private control exceeded 4:1 in major sectors of the economy, especially those concerned with social welfare like primary and university education, health care, and pension systems.

Clearly, many Latin American citizens looked to the state rather than the market to provide basic services and safeguard social welfare. Social inequalities, moreover, were widely seen as unjust, with large majorities – ranging from 75 to 85 percent of survey respondents – consistently saying that the distribution of income in their country was unjust, and half of them saying it was "very unjust" (see Figure 6.7).

These public sentiments demonstrated the underlying social and political fragility of the technocratic consensus that was forged around the neoliberal model in the 1990s. Market liberalization was often imposed by parties and leaders who had campaigned against it, and its limited democratic mandate rested primarily on the dearth of viable alternatives in inflationary contexts and the political disarticulation of opponents, rather than a broad-based ideological consensus. Both of these conditions changed in the aftermath period. Economic stabilization and, after 2003, the onset of a new commodity export

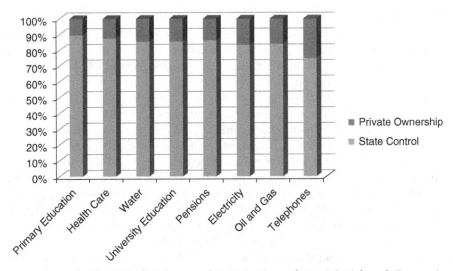

FIGURE 6.6. Preferences for State and Private Control over Social and Economic Activities, 2008 (regional average)
Source: Latinobarómetro (2008: 38).

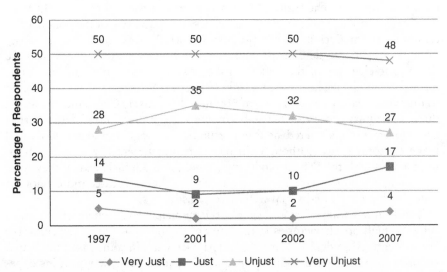

FIGURE 6.7. Public Opinion Toward Income Distribution in Latin America, 1997–2007 (regional average)
Source: Latinobarómetro (2007: 36). The question asked "Do you believe the distribution of income in your country is just?"

boom relaxed market constraints on macroeconomic and social policies. This relaxation gave governments greater latitude to experiment with alternatives to market orthodoxy (Murillo et al. 2011), and it provided incentives for voters to support parties that promised to address social concerns (Remmer 2012). Meanwhile, a revival of popular mobilization in a number of countries reflected a growing politicization of neoliberalism's social deficits, contributing to a re-articulation of partisan and electoral alternatives on the left.

Indeed, the most dramatic expressions of the Polanyian backlash were found not in public opinion surveys, but on the streets and in the ballot box – that is, in forms of social and electoral protest that targeted governments and ruling parties that administered the neoliberal model. As Rice (2012: 7) demonstrates, levels of social protest fell sharply in Latin America during the late 1980s and early 1990s, the peak years of structural adjustment, but protest activities surged again by the late 1990s. Although organized labor remained far weaker than in the past, other popular subjects – especially indigenous groups, but also the urban poor and unemployed workers – were increasingly capable of mobilizing resistance through marches, road blockages, and occupations of public sites (Yashar 2005; Silva 2009). In some cases, they forged political ties between diverse social actors who shared little in common other than their grievances against market liberalization and their contempt for the political establishment.

In this context, leftist political forces progressively strengthened and broadened their support. The regional Left was reeling at the end of the Cold War, deeply uncertain as to the content – much less the viability – of the political and economic alternatives it offered (Roberts 1998). As Castañeda (1993) recognized, however, the demise of Leninist revolutionary models liberated more democratic elements of the Left from the yoke of Soviet communism, not to mention the reflexive hostility of a Cold War-era U.S. hegemon that was poised to intervene against a wide range of popular alternatives. Consequently, as the threat of military coups receded and democratic regimes stabilized, leftist parties and movements discovered new opportunities to politicize social needs and make electoral gains. Although citizens were not necessarily more likely to self-identify with the Left ideologically (Arnold and Samuels 2011), they were increasingly willing to vote for leftist alternatives that advocated more vigorous state developmental and social welfare responsibilities.

This shift in voting behavior began at the municipal level, where leftist parties achieved high profile victories in the late 1980s and 1990s in major cities like Porto Alegre, Montevideo, Caracas, and Mexico City. In some cases, municipal victories gave these parties an opportunity to acquire valuable governing experience (Baiocchi 2003; Chávez and Goldfrank 2004; Goldfrank 2011), setting the stage for unprecedented electoral gains at the national level starting in the late 1990s. By the time Lula was elected to the presidency of Brazil in 2002, for example, his PT had already established a track record of governance in 172 municipalities where it elected a mayor (Baiocchi 2003: 38). Ten other countries in the region elected left-leaning national governments between 1998 and 2011.

Neither social protest nor the "left turn," however, assumed homogeneous political forms. Levels of social protest varied widely across the region, as did the character of the parties and movements that were elected to public office as the region veered leftward in the post-adjustment era. On both fronts, variation was heavily conditioned by the partisan alignments and institutional outcomes of market liberalization during the critical juncture.

REACTIVE SEQUENCES AND INSTITUTIONAL LEGACIES

As explained in Chapter 3, social and political resistance to market orthodoxy played a central role in the reactive sequences of the aftermath period. This resistance found expression in three basic forms: (1) mass social protest; (2) electoral protest, or support for extra-systemic political movements or populist figures; or (3) electoral support for institutionalized parties of the left. Whereas the first two forms of resistance were often complementary, the third followed a very different political logic, reflecting distinct types of critical junctures and institutional legacies.

Although localized or sector-specific protests occurred throughout the region, mass uprisings involving multiple social groups with diverse claims against the neoliberal model were less common. Four cases – Venezuela, Ecuador, Argentina, and Bolivia – stand out for the scale and intensity of mass protests, as each of them experienced a veritable popular rebellion that led, directly or indirectly, to changes in national political leadership. In Venezuela, this rebellion erupted during the critical juncture itself when the mass urban riots known as the *caracazo* greeted the initial adoption of bait-and-switch reforms by Carlos Andrés Pérez of the center-left AD. Pérez never recovered politically from the riots and the state violence that was employed to suppress them, and he was eventually impeached after two military coup attempts – the first led by Hugo Chávez. Venezuela's critical juncture culminated in party system decomposition and the election of Chávez as a populist outsider and trenchant critic of the neoliberal model.

In Ecuador, major social protests also began during the critical juncture with a series of indigenous rebellions after 1990, but they peaked in the early aftermath period when indigenous groups joined with urban popular movements to drive three successive elected presidents from office in 1997, 2000, and 2005. The resulting demise of established parties set the stage for the 2006 election of populist outsider Rafael Correa to the presidency. Argentina's *piquetero* (picketers) movement of largely unemployed workers emerged in the second half of the 1990s and played a leading role in the mass uprising that forced Fernando de la Rua to resign from the presidency during the financial crisis of late 2001. Finally, in Bolivia, indigenous communities, coca growers, workers, and urban popular sectors converged in waves of mass protest known as the "water war" and the "gas war" in 2000 and 2003–2005, respectively (see Silva 2009). These uprisings drove presidents from office in 2003 and 2005, paving the way for the election of Evo Morales and his new movement party, the *Movimiento al Socialismo* (MAS), in 2005.

These four cases were strikingly different along many dimensions, including their levels of economic development, the strength of their democratic regimes and traditional party systems, the severity of their economic crises, and the depth and effectiveness of their market reform programs. All four cases, however, experienced de-aligning bait-and-switch patterns of market reform that left their party systems without an effective institutional outlet for societal resistance. Ambitious structural adjustment policies were adopted by the most important populist or center-left party in each country – the AD in Venezuela, the MNR in Bolivia, the Peronist PJ in Argentina, and the ID in Ecuador. Indeed, secondary populist or center-left parties also adopted or continued neoliberal reforms in subsequent governments that they led (the MIR in Bolivia and the PRE in Ecuador) or participated in (the MAS in Venezuela).

The convergence of established parties around the neoliberal model encouraged dissent to be channeled into extra-systemic forms of social and electoral protest, convulsing national party systems. The leading centrist and conservative parties were eclipsed in all four countries, as were the leading populist or center-left parties in Venezuela, Bolivia, and Ecuador. Only the Argentine Peronist party (PJ) was left standing among the traditional leading parties in these four countries – a singular example of a party that led the process of market reform in the 1990s and then veered back to the left to channel societal resistance in the aftermath period (after the neoliberal model unraveled, under the watch of rival parties, in the financial crisis of 2001–2002).

Decomposition was thus limited to the anti-Peronist side of the party system in Argentina, but it was systemic in the other three countries, where societal resistance found electoral expression in anti-system political movements or populist figures who outflanked traditional parties on the left. In all three countries, reactive sequences that began with mass social protest led to the overthrow or impeachment of elected presidents, the decomposition of established party systems, the election of anti-system populist or leftist alternatives in frontal opposition to the neoliberal model, and institutional ruptures that produced new constituent assemblies and the re-founding of constitutional orders.

The other two countries with de-aligning critical junctures – Peru and Costa Rica – also experienced considerable party system turmoil, albeit with different results. In Peru, the party system decomposed at an earlier stage of the critical juncture, a victim of the hyperinflationary crisis of the late 1980s and the brutal Maoist insurgency of the Shining Path. Structural adjustment policies were thus imposed by a populist outsider, Alberto Fujimori, who had campaigned against neoliberal shock treatment, while traditional parties were displaced by a series of independent personalities – the pattern I call serial populism. In Costa Rica, the adoption of market reforms by the traditional center-left (but not labor-mobilizing) PLN in the mid-1980s was followed by a major electoral realignment and a partial reconstitution of the party system in the aftermath period, but social protest was less explosive than in the aforementioned cases. A new left-populist challenger emerged to outflank the PLN on the left, while the PLN moved rightward and largely displaced the corruption-tainted conservative party.

As shown in Table 6.2, electoral volatility increased in the aftermath period in all six of these cases of programmatic de-alignment. Party systems that were relatively stable during the critical juncture in the 1980s and 1990s – namely, those of Costa Rica and Argentina – became less stable after 2000, whereas those

TABLE 6.2. *Electoral Volatility during Neoliberal Critical Junctures and Their Aftermath Periods (Pedersen index of volatility)*

Country	Net Volatility 1980–2000	Net Volatility 2000–2010	Change in Net Volatility
Dealigning Critical Junctures			
Argentina	18.6	35.0	16.4
Bolivia	27.5	50.7	23.2
Costa Rica	10.3	25.6	15.3
Ecuador	33.5	44.7	11.2
Peru	44.8	48.5	3.7
Venezuela	33.4	41.3	7.9
Average	28.0	41.0	13.0
Neutral Critical Junctures			
Colombia	12.0	37.4	25.4
Guatemala	45.4	49.4	4.0
Honduras	7.1	9.7	2.6
Panama	36.7	23.2	−13.5
Paraguay	20.4	26.9	6.5
Average	24.3	29.3	4.0
Aligning Critical Junctures			
Brazil	30.7	22.0	−8.7
Chile	15.9	19.6	3.7
Dominican Republic	18.3	21.0	2.7
El Salvador	22.2	11.3	−10.9
Mexico	17.9	20.0	2.1
Nicaragua	49.5	21.7	−27.8
Uruguay	11.4	12.6	1.2
Average	23.7	18.3	−5.4

Sources: Calculated from Nohlen (2005) and Georgetown University's *Political Database of the Americas* (http://pdba.georgetown.edu/). Net volatility is the combined average of volatility scores for all presidential and legislative elections in each country.

in the other four countries that were already unstable during the critical juncture became even more volatile in the aftermath period. As measured by the Pedersen index, net electoral volatility (the average aggregate vote shifts in presidential and legislative elections) increased from a six-country average of 28.0 percent from 1980–2000 to 41.0 percent between 2000 and 2010.

In all six countries, bait-and-switch market reforms left party systems without a major challenger to the neoliberal model – in short, with a competitive dynamic of neoliberal convergence or, in the Peruvian case, serial populism. Both proved to be an unstable equilibrium as societal resistance to the neoliberal model strengthened. Venezuela began the reform process as a case of neoliberal convergence – that is, in the lower left cell of Figure 6.1 – but shifted in response to early reactive sequences and ended the critical juncture as a case of polarized populism (i.e., the upper right cell). Bolivia made a similar shift from the lower left to the upper right cell with the rise of a new movement party in the aftermath period. Ecuador, on the other hand, shifted from neoliberal convergence to serial populism as the party system decomposed, then moved to the category of polarized populism with the election of Correa in the aftermath period. Peru has also wavered between polarized and serial populism since Ollanta Humala emerged as a left-leaning populist figure in 2006. Costa Rica, on the other hand, arguably shifted from neoliberal convergence to the upper left cell of contested liberalism with the rise of a new partisan rival to the left of an increasingly conservative PLN. Traditional centrist or conservative parties entered into steep decline in all six countries, while political space that was vacated to the left of center was occupied by new populist or leftist contenders that offered more vigorous opposition to the neoliberal model (except in Argentina, where the PJ tacked sharply to the left to occupy this space). The general trend, therefore, was movement away from neoliberal convergence toward greater programmatic contestation of the neoliberal model in the aftermath period.

Neoliberal convergence was also unstable in the aftermath period, although less dramatically so, in the countries that experienced neutral critical junctures – that is, those where market liberalization was led by conservative parties with no major party of the left in opposition. Net electoral volatility averaged 24.3 for Colombia, Honduras, Panama, Paraguay, and Guatemala from 1980 to 2000, then increased to 29.3 in the aftermath period between 2000 and 2010. Reactive sequences in the aftermath period were more moderate in these countries; none experienced the types of mass protest movements that convulsed the aforementioned bait-and-switch cases, and only Colombia experienced party system decomposition, a fate that was more attributable to the country's distinctive security challenges than to the politics of economic adjustment.

Although traditional conservative parties entered into decline after 2000 in several of these countries – most notably Colombia and, temporarily, Paraguay – this pattern was less consistent than in the bait-and-switch cases. Likewise, outflanking on the Left associated with the rise of new populist or leftist contenders occurred in the aftermath period, especially in Paraguay and eventually in Honduras, but this dynamic was more moderate and fragile in comparison to the explosive growth of radical movements in several of the bait-and-switch cases. In Honduras – until recently home to Latin America's most stable party system in the post-1980 period – a left-populist alternative initially emerged *within* one of the two traditional conservative parties in the form of iconoclastic Liberal President Manuel Zelaya. A military coup against Zelaya in 2009 restored conservative dominance, fractured the Liberal Party, and triggered the rise of a new movement-left party under the leadership of Zelaya and his wife, who finished a close second in 2013 presidential elections – the first serious challenge to the two-party oligarchic system in Honduran political history. By the second decade of the 21st century, therefore, the exceptional stability of Honduras' party system was clearly breaking down, and the regional outlier began to converge on the modal patterns found elsewhere in the region.

Finally, programmatically aligning critical junctures produced a legacy of contested liberalism that was relatively stable, and even stabilizing, in the remaining set of cases (Brazil, Chile, the Dominican Republic, El Salvador, Mexico, Nicaragua, and Uruguay). In these countries, dissent from market orthodoxy in the post-adjustment period could be channeled into the party system by an established party of the left. None of these countries experienced destabilizing mass protests in the early aftermath period,[3] and none saw their party system outflanked by the rise of a major new populist or leftist contender. Instead, institutionalized leftist parties progressively strengthened in most of these countries, altering the competitive balance but avoiding destabilizing patterns of outflanking and party system decomposition. Equally striking, where an institutionalized leftist party was a serious competitor, centrist or conservative parties remained electorally viable in the aftermath period to defend market liberalism and temper the statist inclinations of leftist rivals when they accessed executive office – as they eventually did in every country but Mexico. Consequently, electoral competition reproduced and reinforced contested liberalism in the aftermath period, rather than eroding it.

The stable institutional legacies of aligning critical junctures can be seen in Table 6.2 and Figure 6.8. None of the countries with aligning critical junctures experienced a sharp increase in electoral volatility in the aftermath period, and three of them – Brazil, El Salvador, and Nicaragua – saw volatility decline. In this set of cases, the net average volatility score declined from 23.7 percent in the 1980s and 1990s to 18.3 percent from 2000 to 2010, less than half the level of volatility recorded in countries that experienced de-aligning critical junctures.

These findings suggest that aligning and de-aligning critical junctures had very different legacies for party system stability. Aggregate measures of electoral

---

[3] Chile and Brazil did, however, experience significant new protest cycles in 2011–2012 and 2013, respectively, with popular movements generally demanding deeper social and/or political reforms. The implications of these movements for the institutional legacies of aligning critical junctures are addressed in Chapter 10.

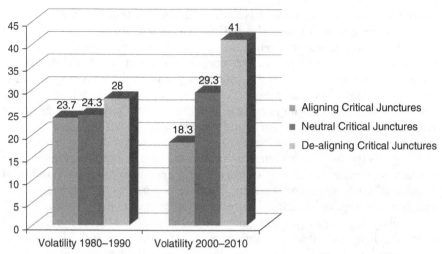

FIGURE 6.8. Net Electoral Volatility and Types of Critical Junctures
Source: See Table 6.2.

volatility, however, only tell us what percentage of votes (or seats) shift in a given election cycle; they don't distinguish between votes that are shifting among established party organizations (i.e., intra-systemic volatility) and those that are going to new parties or "outsider" candidates (i.e., extra-systemic volatility). An alternative approach to assessing volatility, then, is to develop a direct measure of extra-systemic vote shifts. Although this could be done on an election-by-election basis (see, for example, Powell and Tucker 2009), a cumulative measure is more theoretically useful for assessing the legacies of a critical juncture over time. Consequently, I have calculated for each election the aggregate presidential vote and legislative seat shares for all parties or political movements that were formed in 1990 or thereafter – roughly the mid-point of the critical juncture and the onset of the Washington Consensus, when every country in the region had begun to liberalize markets. The indicator thus captures the cumulative development of new parties – whether pro- or anti-market reform – following the initial adoption of liberalization policies by different reform alignments.[4]

As shown in Figure 6.9, this measure of new party votes varies dramatically across countries with different types of critical junctures. Critical junctures that aligned party systems programmatically – that is, those that produced a legacy of contested liberalism – created highly resilient competitive alignments. Indeed, established parties largely "closed off" the electoral marketplace to new

---

[4] Parties were coded as "new" only if they were not organized before 1990. Parties formed after 1990 as a result of name changes or mergers, or coalitions formed among pre-1990 parties, were coded as successors to previous parties rather than new parties.

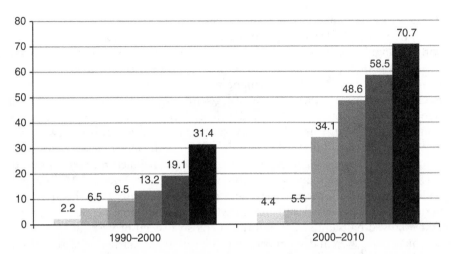

FIGURE 6.9. Aggregate Vote for New Political Parties under Different Types of Critical Junctures, 1990–2010 (presidential and legislative elections)
Note: Percentage includes the vote for all political parties founded in or after 1990.

competitors, which averaged only 6.5 percent of the presidential vote and 2.2 percent of legislative seats in the 1990s. These percentages stayed remarkably flat in the aftermath period, as parties formed after 1990 earned a mere 5.5 percent of presidential votes and 4.4 percent of legislative seats in the first decade of the 21st century. Although leftist forces gradually strengthened over this period in most of these countries, this growth occurred among established leftist parties that were in opposition during the period of market liberalization, rather than new extra-systemic populist or leftist alternatives. Likewise, established conservative parties remained electorally competitive. In short, where conservatives led the process of market reform and a major party of the left remained in opposition, critical junctures bequeathed an institutional legacy of programmatically structured and stable electoral competition.

Competitive dynamics could hardly have been more different where critical junctures produced an institutional outcome of neoliberal convergence. The vulnerability of this legacy to reactive sequences that spawned and empowered new parties is clear in the data. In countries that experienced neutral critical junctures, parties or movements formed after 1990 averaged a relatively modest 13.2 percent of the presidential vote and 9.5 percent of legislative seats in the 1990s. Over the next decade, however – that is, in the aftermath period – average levels of support for new parties surged, even taking into account the notable exception of Honduras (which recorded a score of zero on this indicator for both presidential and legislative elections in both decades, but experienced the rise of a major new leftist rival in 2013). Cumulative support for new parties in this set of cases rose to an average of 48.6 percent of the vote in presidential elections and 34.1 percent of legislative seats between 2000 and 2010. And in countries with de-aligning critical junctures, the vote shift toward new parties in the aftermath period was massive and systematic; between 2000 and 2010, parties formed after 1990 captured a stunning 70.7 percent of the vote in presidential elections, along with 58.5 percent of legislative seats. In short, where market reforms were adopted in a bait-and-switch manner, voters abandoned traditional parties *en masse* and threw their support to a diverse array of new parties and movements, on both the left and right sides of the ideological spectrum.

If the institutional legacies of de-aligning critical junctures were prone to destabilizing reactive sequences, so too were their policy legacies. Aligning and de-aligning critical junctures were both prone to "left turns" in the aftermath period, but these political shifts produced very different policy effects. Left turns that followed bait-and-switch reforms, explosive social protest, and partial or complete party system decomposition produced much sharper departures from neoliberal orthodoxy, as redistributive measures in Venezuela, Argentina, Ecuador, and Bolivia were embedded in more statist macroeconomic policies. Policy reversals in these countries were aided by the demise of centrist and conservative opposition parties that might have placed institutional constraints on leftist rulers in legislative and policymaking arenas. Indeed, the leftist alternatives that arose in Venezuela, Bolivia, and Ecuador were all "new lefts" shaped by the social and political backlash against neoliberalism and the democratic regimes that introduced it; in office, they quickly resorted to plebiscitary measures to convoke constituent assemblies and re-found democratic regimes, thus weakening institutional constraints on executive power and maximizing policy flexibility (Madrid 2009; Levitsky and Roberts 2011a).

By contrast, where institutionalized parties of the Left came into power in the aftermath to aligning critical junctures, redistributive policies were generally adopted in an overarching context of both regime and macroeconomic policy continuity (Weyland, Madrid, and Hunter 2010; Flores-Macías 2012). In countries like Chile, Brazil, and Uruguay, which retained electorally competitive centrist or conservative parties, leftist rulers operated within the confines of established democratic regimes and introduced relatively moderate social reforms that were compatible with the liberalized economies they inherited.

These policy trends are depicted in Table 6.3, which tracks change in the "Index of Economic Freedom" developed by the Heritage Foundation and the *Wall Street Journal*.[5] The region-wide average score on this index – a basic measure of economic liberalism ranging from zero to 100 – declined modestly by 3.9 points after 2000, reflecting the turn away from economic orthodoxy in the aftermath period. Most of this downward trend, however, is accounted for by the four cases that turned sharply in a statist direction following bait-and-switch

---

[5] This index is used in lieu of the structural reform index of Escaith and Paunovic (2004; see Figure 6.2), which is not available past 2000.

TABLE 6.3. *Left Turns and Change in the Index of Economic Freedom, 2000–2012*

Country	2000 Index Score	2012 Index Score	Net Change
Regional Average	64.8	60.9	–3.9
Aligning Critical Junctures			
Brazil	61.1	57.9	–3.2
Chile	74.7	78.3	3.6
Uruguay	69.3	69.9	0.6
De-aligning Critical Junctures			
Argentina	70.0	48.0	–22.0
Bolivia	65.0	50.2	–14.8
Ecuador	59.8	48.3	–11.5
Venezuela	57.4	38.1	–19.3

Source: Heritage Foundation/*Wall Street Journal* "Index of Economic Freedom," (http://www. heritage.org/index/default).

market reforms and mass social protest – Venezuela, Argentina, Bolivia, and Ecuador. The index score declined between 11.5 and 22.0 points in these four cases. Left turns that followed aligning critical junctures in Chile, Brazil, and Uruguay, on the other hand, did not produce dramatic shifts in public policy; Brazil's index score declined by only 3.2 points, while those of Uruguay and Chile actually increased, reflecting the efforts of institutionalized leftist parties to address social concerns within the constraints of relative macroeconomic orthodoxy. More recently elected leftist leaders in El Salvador, Paraguay, and Nicaragua – none of them in countries that experienced bait-and-switch reforms or mass social protest in the aftermath period – also avoided dramatic departures from market orthodoxy during their early years in office. Major policy reversals, therefore, were concentrated in the cases with bait-and-switch reforms, de-aligning critical junctures, explosive social protest, and partial or complete party system break-downs that magnified the policy latitude of new leftist leaders.

As such, neither the institutional nor policy legacies of neoliberal critical junctures were set in stone. Aligning critical junctures produced legacies that moderated reactive sequences and stabilized electoral competition in the aftermath period. Both institutional and policy continuity resulted. De-aligning critical junctures, on the other hand, bequeathed legacies that were predisposed toward disruptive reactive sequences in the post-adjustment era, leaving a sequel of on-going institutional change and dramatic policy reversals. These divergent pathways could not be predicted by antecedent conditions alone; they were the product, instead, of historically contingent (though structurally constrained) policy choices and the political alignments that undergirded them during the turbulent transition from ISI to neoliberalism.

CONCLUSION

Latin America's technocratic consensus for market liberalization may have provided political cover for structural adjustment in contexts of acute financial and inflationary crises in the 1980s and 1990s, when popular movements were in decline and on the defensive. It was not, however, a stable equilibrium in post-adjustment contexts where popular sectors were capable of politicizing social exclusion and inequality. In such contexts, programmatic forms of electoral competition helped to anchor electorates and stabilize party systems. Economic shocks that induce parties to renege on programmatic commitments and converge on policy platforms can erode societal linkages and blur the partisan cleavages that structure electoral competition. By weakening voters' attachments to established parties, they open the door to extra-systemic and non-partisan alternatives that capitalize on societal discontent with the status quo.

These effects are evident in the crisis-induced transition from ISI to neoliberalism. Conservative-led market reforms that were consistently opposed by a major party of the Left aligned party systems programmatically, producing legacies of relatively stable partisan competition. Reforms adopted in a bait-and-switch fashion by populist or center-left parties, however, de-aligned party systems and left them vulnerable to destabilizing reactive sequences as societal opposition to market liberalization intensified in the aftermath period.

Leftist alternatives emerged or strengthened in virtually every country in the region in the post-adjustment period – even where they did not come into power – but different types of critical junctures produced distinct "left turns." Aligning critical junctures allowed societal claims for protection against market insecurities to be institutionally channeled and tempered by established parties. Political shifts to the Left thus occurred by means of an institutionalized alternation in power within relatively intact party systems. Conversely, where critical junctures de-aligned party systems, societal resistance to market liberalism was more likely to be expressed in mass protest movements that challenged the entire political establishment and spawned more radical, extra-systemic populist and leftist alternatives.

Thus far, these divergent patterns of institutional change and continuity have been analyzed in general terms, from a region-wide perspective. Part II of this volume shifts the analytical focus to different national experiences. Chapters 7 and 8 provide comparative analyses of party system adaptation, realignment, and decomposition during the critical juncture in select elitist and LM party systems, respectively. Chapter 9 adopts a comparative perspective on these cases to explore competitive dynamics in the aftermath period. Taken together, the comparative case studies chronicle the divergent fate of Latin American party systems during the transition from ISI to neoliberalism, while tracing the causal pathways that produced different outcomes.

PART II

NATIONAL EXPERIENCES
IN COMPARATIVE PERSPECTIVE

7

Critical Junctures in Elitist Party Systems

To understand variation in the stability of party systems during and after neoliberal critical junctures, it is essential to know how different party systems managed the transition from ISI to neoliberalism, and how they were transformed by that process. As Chapter 5 demonstrated, elitist party systems, on average, faced less-disruptive political and economic challenges during this period of transition and were less electorally volatile than their LM counterparts. As a theoretical first-cut, this generalization suggests that antecedent patterns of political and institutional development during the ISI era accounted for a significant portion of the variation in party system stability during the critical juncture. This generalization, however, masks significant variation in the stability of national party systems *within* each of the two categories, and it glosses over quite distinct patterns of change and continuity. It cannot explain why some parties thrived and others floundered in the same party system, or what adaptive strategies were more or less successful under certain conditions. Neither does it tell us whether electoral volatility reflected vote shifts among established parties or the rise of extra-systemic challengers. Most important, it does not identify the more contingent political processes and alignments within the critical juncture itself that shaped different outcomes.

Elitist party systems amply demonstrate how neoliberal critical junctures produced divergent political outcomes. Although the transition to market liberalism was less economically traumatic and politically destabilizing, on average, in countries with elitist party systems, they nonetheless experienced widely varying patterns of party system change and continuity during the critical juncture. Some party systems adapted to the new policy landscape with no change in their organizational composition and minimal shifts in their electoral balance of power; Honduras and Costa Rica (in the short term) are the obvious examples. Others, like Uruguay, kept the same organizational composition but experienced electoral realignment, with one party (on the left) growing at the expense of conservative rivals. Still other party systems, like that of Ecuador, were both organizationally and electorally fluid. Although no elitist case experienced party system decomposition during the critical juncture, several did in the aftermath period (i.e., Ecuador and Colombia). And while some elitist party systems were programmatically aligned by the process of market liberalization (namely Uruguay's), others were de-aligned (such as those in Ecuador and Costa Rica). Diverse institutional outcomes reflected both distinct antecedent conditions – in particular, party systems that began the critical juncture with widely varying levels of institutionalization – and different political dynamics during the period of economic crisis and reform.

This chapter thus provides a comparative analysis of the critical junctures in four elitist party systems: Costa Rica, Ecuador, Honduras, and Uruguay. The cases are selected to provide maximum variation within the elitist category on the dependent variable of party system stability. They also illustrate a wide range of variation in the patterns of party system change, from adaptation (Costa Rica and Honduras) to electoral realignment (Uruguay) and decomposition (Ecuador in the aftermath period). Likewise, they provide examples of programmatically aligning, de-aligning, and neutral processes of market reform that produced both durable and fragile institutional outcomes. The four cases experienced quite different patterns of popular resistance to market liberalization, spawning reactive sequences during and after the critical juncture that reshaped their competitive alignments and institutional legacies.

Honduras and Costa Rica had the two most stable party systems in all of Latin America during the critical juncture. With low levels of electoral volatility, little cumulative change in the competitive balance of power, and low-to-moderate levels of resistance to market liberalism in both societal and electoral arenas, they are paradigmatic cases of party system adaptation culminating in an institutional outcome of neoliberal convergence. The challenges posed to the reproduction of this outcome in the aftermath period are analyzed in Chapter 9. Uruguay, on the other hand, is a case of relative electoral stability but cumulative or progressive party system realignment. This electoral realignment reflected the gradual decline of the two traditional parties that led the process of market reform and the strengthening of a leftist coalition that effectively channeled resistance to it, producing a highly resilient institutional outcome of contested liberalism. Ecuador, by contrast, had one of the most unstable party systems in the region during the critical juncture, with chronically high levels of electoral volatility. It also experienced multiple periods of bait-and-switch market reform that spawned powerful cycles of mass social protest, as opposition to the neoliberal model was poorly channeled within partisan and electoral arenas. Highly destabilizing reactive sequences in the aftermath period thus culminated in a decomposition of the party system and its displacement by a series of dominant personalities; the initial outcome of neoliberal convergence gave way to a legacy of serial populism, with tendencies toward growing polarization in the aftermath period.

These cases also facilitate comparative analysis because partisan competition during their critical junctures turned heavily on issues related to macro-economic performance and neoliberal reform. In other elitist cases, competitive dynamics were heavily influenced by less systematic sources of variation. In Colombia, for example, the political challenges associated with economic adjustment were almost surely secondary to those rooted in the country's con-vulsive mixture of guerrilla insurgency, paramilitary violence, and drug traffick-ing. Likewise, in Paraguay, Panama, and the Dominican Republic, patterns of party system change were skewed by the rise and fall of authoritarian person-alities through the 1980s and even beyond, meaning that economic issues were often clouded by lingering conflicts over the political regime. In Honduras, Ecuador, and Uruguay, however, not to mention Costa Rica, democratic tran-sitions occurred earlier, and post-transition partisan competition was less tainted by authoritarian legacies. These latter cases, therefore, are more comparable units that provide a measure of control for various types of non-systematic variation. They are thus more amenable to the search for gen-eralizable patterns of party system change in response to the region-wide process of market liberalization.

The comparative analysis starts with an overview of the antecedent party system characteristics in each of the four countries, then proceeds to examine the politics of economic crisis and reform and its impact on partisan competition during national critical junctures. Institutional outcomes reflect the influence of antecedent conditions as well as factors embedded in the critical juncture itself – namely, the allocation of political costs and rewards associated with economic crisis and reform, the programmatic alignment (or de-alignment) of partisan competition resulting from the reform process, and the mobilization and channeling of societal resistance to market liberalization. The resiliency of these institutional outcomes in the face of post-adjustment reactive sequences will be assessed in Chapter 9. The analysis in this chapter demonstrates that elitist party systems were hardly immune from pressures for change during the critical juncture, even if these pressures were less acute than those in the LM cases.

PARTY SYSTEM ADAPTATION AND NEOLIBERAL CONVERGENCE IN HONDURAS AND COSTA RICA

Party systems in Honduras and Costa Rica were the most electorally stable in Latin America during the regional critical juncture, and the two countries illustrate well the dynamic interplay between change and continuity in processes of party system adaptation. Neither country experienced a significant change in the composition of its party system during the critical juncture, as two major parties remained dominant in each country throughout the period of transition (although, as we will see, major changes in organizational composition occurred in both countries in the aftermath period, when new leftist parties emerged). Likewise, neither country experienced a significant realignment in the electoral balance of power among the dominant parties during the critical juncture. Both countries exited the critical juncture with a competitive dynamic of neoliberal convergence, although they arrived at this outcome via different pathways: Honduras by means of a neutral critical juncture, with market reforms led by traditional conservative parties in the absence of a major leftist contender, and Costa Rica by means of a de-aligning "bait-and-switch" process of reform led by the center-left (but not labor-mobilizing) PLN. Since neither party system offered voters a well-defined alternative to the neoliberal model, the reproduction of the institutional outcome was contingent on maintaining low levels of societal resistance in the aftermath period. As this resistance increased at the beginning of the 21st century, both party systems were challenged by destabilizing reactive sequences that spawned major new leftist alternatives.

Antecedent Conditions and Party System Development

Honduras and Costa Rica both entered the critical juncture with elitist party systems and weak, organizationally fragmented labor movements, but in other respects their antecedent conditions were quite different. Honduras made a transition from military to civilian rule in 1981–1982, shortly before the debt crisis erupted, whereas Costa Rica entered the critical juncture with the region's longest-standing democratic regime, dating to the country's political reconstruction following a short-lived civil war in 1948. Honduras retained an oligarchic party system throughout the ISI era, with two major parties – the *Partido Liberal de Honduras* (PLH) and the *Partido Nacional de Honduras* (PNH) – that were both founded around the turn of the century prior to any significant process of labor mobilization in an overwhelmingly agrarian economy. Likewise, Honduras maintained one of the most liberal economies and limited states in the region throughout the ISI era, despite a series of transitions between civilian and military regimes. In contrast, Costa Rica's unstable oligarchic party system was eclipsed during a period of populist mobilization in the 1940s, and the party system was reconstituted following the civil war that aborted the populist experiment. The victors in the civil war founded the *Partido Liberación Nacional* (PLN) in 1951, and despite repressing and demobilizing the Communist Party-led labor movement, they continued some of the populist reforms and expanded the developmental and social welfare roles of the Costa Rican state. The PLN was opposed by a fluid set of conservative parties that ultimately merged into the *Partido Unidad Social Cristiana* (PUSC) in 1983.

The oligarchic party system in Honduras was relatively late to form, as the *caudillos* who waged a series of civil wars and insurrections in the middle of the 19th century were not clearly rooted in a liberal-conservative ideological cleavage, and their conflicts did not generate durable political organizations. Indeed, Honduras' period of liberal reform, which started in the early 1870s and eventually spawned the oligarchic party system, was imposed through military intervention by El Salvador and Guatemala (Mahoney 2001a: 98–99). Liberals committed to the separation of church and state and agricultural commercialization founded the Liberal Party in 1891, but leadership disputes produced a schism at the end of the decade that led to the formation of a conservative splinter in 1902, and eventually to the founding of the National Party (Paz Aguilar 1992: 162; Ajenjo Fresno 2003: 197, 236–237). The PNH was staunchly Catholic and closely tied to the interests of traditional landed elites, whereas the PLH tended to represent the interests of urban commercial and professional sectors. In general, however, Honduran elites were quite weak relative to the foreign banana companies that invested heavily in the country during the period of Liberal hegemony, and the two major parties developed political alliances with rival foreign firms that intervened repeatedly in local political affairs. Indeed, Taylor-Robinson (2006: 110) states that the two parties "were established as tools in the competition between the international banana companies operating in the country."

At first glance, the continuity of Honduras' oligarchic two-party system throughout the ISI era seems surprising, as the country had a very limited democratic experience with relatively few competitive elections in which to institutionalize partisan loyalties. Given numerous authoritarian interludes and restrictions on suffrage and competition even during periods of civilian rule, Smith (2005: 351) categorizes Honduras as "semi-democratic" for only five years (1958–1962) prior to the 1981 transition, and he does not place Honduras fully in the democratic camp until 1998. Both major parties experienced cycles of organizational decay and reconstruction, and prior to the 1980s they only faced off against each other in competitive (though not entirely free) elections in 1923, 1928, 1932, 1954, and 1971. Neither party, however, relied solely on electoral mobilization as a source of political power. Both drew heavily on the economic resources and political leverage of their rival banana companies, and both cultivated societal linkages through clientelist exchanges and episodes of armed insurrection that erupted repeatedly between 1902 and 1932. The PNH, in particular, became an ally of the armed forces and the dominant U.S.-based United Fruit Company, and it collaborated with several military regimes that allowed the party to draw upon the coercive power and resources of the state.

Moreover, Honduras' very slow pace of economic development moderated the pressures placed on the party system by social mobilization from below. The country's foreign-owned banana enclaves provided little stimulus to other sectors of the economy, and the state made no concerted effort to promote industrialization. Labor unrest began to stir on the banana plantations in the 1920s, encouraging the development of a union movement, but political repression in the 1930s curtailed labor mobilization and prevented newly emerging leftist parties from gaining a stronghold among organized labor. Unions and collective bargaining rights were not legally recognized until a second wave of strikes broke out on the banana plantations in 1954. Thereafter national labor and peasant federations were formed, but they remained organizationally fragmented and largely on the margins of the party system. The largest labor and peasant confederation affiliated with the U.S.-based AFL-CIO's anti-communist Inter-American Regional Organization of Workers, but it remained independent of parties inside Honduras. Smaller confederations emerged from Catholic and leftist organizing efforts and aligned, respectively, with the National Party and the electorally marginal Communist Party. Military coups and repression blocked Liberal Party-led governments from implementing land and labor reforms that might have fostered stronger ties to organized popular sectors. Paradoxically, the primary impetus for land reform occurred under a short-lived military regime in the early 1970s that galvanized some labor support and provoked business opposition (see Pearson 1987; Posas 2002, 2004; del Cid 1990).

Consequently, as Honduras returned to civilian rule in the early 1980s, it approached the neoliberal critical juncture with a political economy that had been only lightly touched by the rise of mass politics and the region-wide experiment with ISI. The party system was dominated by two parties with oligarchic roots and little tradition of mass electoral mobilization, much less social mobilization. As stated by Taylor-Robinson, the Liberal Party "has always been conservative," despite its name and the presence of internal factions supporting progressive social reforms; both established parties, therefore, "defend traditional elite interests," and "neither is ideological" (2006: 299 fn 5). Without a major party to champion their interests, labor and popular movements were politically weak and organizationally fragmented, and the economy remained heavily dependent on agricultural exports. Not surprisingly, then, Honduras had the lowest score on the state-centric index of any country included in this study (see Table 4.7).

Costa Rica, on the other hand, was more heavily marked by the rise of mass politics and the regional shift toward expanded state economic and social welfare activities in the middle of the 20th century. As in Honduras, an oligarchic party system was slow to develop in the 19th century, as repeated military coups and *caudillo* rivalries failed to establish a well-defined political cleavage or durable organizational forms. Rival members of the coffee elite dominated the political arena, forming several new parties in the late 19th and early 20th centuries that were, as Vega Carballo (1992: 204) states, "appendages of the modernizing agro-exporting oligarchy." These parties remained vehicles of dominant personalities, however, and electoral fraud and military insurrections were pervasive. Suffrage was restricted until a series of electoral reforms in the early decades of the 20th century, which facilitated the rise of new parties advocating social reform and, finally, the founding of a Communist Party in 1931 with a growing base of support among artisans and banana plantation workers (Yashar 1995: 73–74).

The turning point in Costa Rica's party system development came in the 1940s, and it was intimately tied to the rise of mass politics and the divisions this provoked within the political elite. Rafael Angel Calderón, a scion of the coffee oligarchy from the dominant *Partido Republicano Nacional* (PRN), was elected to the presidency in 1940, but he turned the tables by unleashing a process of populist mobilization that thoroughly altered the national political landscape. In a most unusual populist coalition, Calderón allied with reformist sectors of the Catholic Church, the Communist Party, and Communist-led labor unions to launch a series of ambitious social reforms, including social security legislation, the country's first labor code, and taxes on income and property (Yashar 1997: 72–86). As the pace of unionization accelerated, these reforms precipitated a backlash among elite and middle-class groups, with the latter founding the *Partido Social Demócrata* (PSD) out of university networks that supported more vigorous state developmental and social roles but bitterly opposed Calderón's collaboration with the Communist Party. The PSD allied with Calderón's oligarchic opponents in national elections in 1948, and following charges of electoral fraud it launched a short-lived civil war that culminated in the defeat of the Calderón–Communist populist bloc.

PSD leader José Figueres Ferrer presided over a newly formed revolutionary junta, but his alliance with conservative forces quickly unraveled as the institutional foundations for a new political order were established. Figueres maintained many of the social welfare provisions adopted during the 1940s, and he antagonized elite sectors by nationalizing the banking system, imposing new taxes, and disbanding the army. The party system was largely reconstituted, with Figueres and the PSD founding the PLN in 1951, and conservative forces regrouping in shifting multi-party coalitions – ironically, with Calderón and his PRN playing a prominent role. The PLN of Figueres emerged as the country's dominant electoral force, claiming the presidency and a majority of legislative assembly seats for all but eight years between 1953 and 1978 (Alfaro Salas 2003: 46, 48). During this time the PLN expanded the state's economic and social responsibilities in multiple arenas. ISI policies began in earnest in the late 1950s, with increased tariffs to protect local producers, multiple exchange rates to facilitate the importation of capital goods, and credits and subsidies to nurture favored industries. The state heavily regulated prices in the domestic economy, and it assumed a more direct entrepreneurial role by establishing a public development corporation in 1972 and over one hundred autonomous institutions to manage public utilities and services. Meanwhile, access to higher education was gradually expanded, and a social safety net was created with pension and national health care systems that were among the most generous and extensive in Latin America (Mesa-Lago et al. 2000: 412–434; Sandbrook et al. 2007: 101–105).

These social policies secured the PLN's reputation as one of Latin America's most successful center-left or social democratic parties, and the party was a prominent regional member of the Socialist International. As Bowman (2002) demonstrates, PLN reforms were deeply polarizing in the 1950s, sparking such intense opposition from elite groups that the democratic regime was nearly toppled on several occasions. It is thus misleading to characterize Costa Rica's post-1948 democratic regime as the product of an elite political consensus. Nevertheless, political conflict was tempered by the relatively low level of popular mobilization, a reflection of the fact that the PLN – despite its social democratic reputation – was most definitely *not* an LM party. Indeed, following their victory in the 1948 civil war, Figueres and the PSD took concerted measures to repress and demobilize the labor movement and its Communist Party sponsors, going so far as to dismiss all public sector employees and authorize private firms to fire workers who were politically suspect. While tolerating church-based union organizing, they dissolved communist-led unions, forced labor activists into exile or jail, and banned both the Communist Party and its affiliated labor confederation, the country's largest (see Booth 1987; Yashar 1997: 185–187). As Yashar (1997: 187) states, by 1953 "the number of unions registered with the Ministry of Labor declined from 204 to 74," and new labor laws restricted the collective rights of workers, including the rights to organize unions and engage in strikes or political activities.

Neither the labor movement nor the Marxist left ever fully recovered from this aggressive demobilization, as labor remained organizationally weak and highly fragmented in the absence of cohesive partisan leadership. By the 1950s, a Catholic-inspired labor confederation founded as an alternative to Communist unions had established ties to the PLN, but the largely middle-class party showed little interest in labor mobilization. The confederation dwindled in size and ended the 1950s with a minuscule membership of some 4,000 workers (Booth 1987: 222). Other unions retained residual loyalties to Calderón despite his return to conservative politics, while some new unions grew out of leftist organizing attempts in the 1950s and 1960s. Four national confederations competed for worker loyalties by the 1970s, but the largest – affiliated with the newly re-legalized but electorally marginal Communist Party – had a membership of only 20,000, and more than half of all unionized workers belonged to unions that were independent of the national confederations (Booth 1987: 223, 233). Indeed, the government made it easier for workers to gain legal recognition for private "solidarity" associations than labor unions, thus steering workers into business-sponsored organizations that emphasized class harmony and provided workers with credit unions and other services if they relinquished their right to strike. Over 1,200 solidarity associations were legally recognized in the late 1980s, compared to only 436 labor unions (Upham 1996: 101–102).

Consequently, in comparison to most other countries with elitist party systems, Costa Rica entered the neoliberal critical juncture with a more advanced developmentalist state, more extensive social welfare provisions, and greater programmatic structuring of partisan competition. It did not, however, possess the type of strong labor movement that was typically associated with these developmental traits, given the reconfiguration of its party system around an anti-populist and anti-Communist process of labor repression in the late 1940s.

Neoliberal Critical Junctures and Party System Adaptation

With small economies that depended heavily on agricultural exports, Costa Rica and Honduras were vulnerable to the series of shocks that struck the international economy in the late 1970s and early 1980s. The second oil shock in 1979 increased the cost of imports, while the global recession that followed in its wake led to steep cuts in commodity export revenues. The 1982 debt crisis caused private capital flows to dry up, at the same time that interest rates on international loans rose sharply. Although these exogenous shocks plunged both countries into economic crises that eventually led to the adoption of neoliberal reforms, by regional standards their crises were relatively mild and short-lived, allowing party systems to contain their political costs. Aggregate vote shifts were thus small and entirely intra-systemic (i.e., among established parties) during the critical juncture. The major parties in both countries adapted programmatically to the neoliberal model and shared in its implementation. Since neither party system was anchored in extensive labor mobilization, the social dislocations that accompanied economic adjustment were less severe than in many other countries, and popular mobilization against market reforms was modest in scope. Indeed, levels of social protest were among the lowest in the region. Although neoliberal convergence left both party systems vulnerable to destabilizing reactive sequences, these would not emerge until the aftermath period, as established party systems seemingly passed through the critical juncture unscathed.

In the Honduran case, the transition to civilian rule in 1981–1982 following seventeen years of nearly uninterrupted military dictatorship occurred shortly before the debt crisis exploded in the region, saddling the newly elected Liberal government of Roberto Suazo Córdova with the burdens of crisis management. The economic crisis was comparatively mild, however, as would be expected in the country with the region's lowest score on the state-centric index. Honduras' peak inflation rate of 29.5 percent was the third lowest in the region, following only Panama and Colombia. Similarly, Honduras' worst economic recession, –2.2 percent in 1982–1983, was the smallest of any country in the region during the 1980s and 1990s (see Table 5.1). Suazo Córdova thus played for time and put off the adoption of structural adjustment policies, while the economy rebounded to grow at a modest 4.0 percent annual rate for the rest of the decade, moderating the political costs of the economic crisis. Unlike ruling parties in most of the region during this period of crisis, the PLH was able to avoid large anti-incumbent vote swings and retain both the presidency and its legislative majority in 1985 elections (see Appendix, Tables 11 and 12).

A gradual process of market reform began under Suazo Córdova's Liberal successor, José Azcona del Hoyo, who took initial steps to liberalize trade and exchange markets and privatize public enterprises (Pino and Hernández 1990: 56–64). Although the economy grew in the late 1980s, inflationary pressures started to build, and the growth that occurred was not sufficient to reverse a decade-long slide in real wages and per-capita GDP. Not surprisingly, then, after two Liberal administrations and nearly a decade of economic austerity, the PLH lost votes (a relatively modest 6.7 percent of the aggregate presidential vote) to the more conservative opposition party, the PNH, in the 1989 national election. This election produced the first alternation in executive office in

Honduras' new democratic era, with Rafael Callejas of the PNH winning the presidency.

Callejas took office as inflation was rising into the double digits – a high rate for Honduras, though it paled in comparison to the hyperinflationary levels found in other parts of the region at the time. In response, Callejas adopted the country's most ambitious package of structural adjustment measures in the early 1990s. Under IMF supervision, the new president slashed public spending and employment, devalued the currency, lowered business taxes, liberalized trade and financial markets, strengthened agrarian property rights, and encouraged the development of a free-trade zone for foreign investors in export manufacturing activities. Given the shallowness of antecedent statist and ISI development strategies in Honduras, however, the orthodox policy shift of the late 1980s and early 1990s was clearly less dramatic than that in most of the region. On the structural reform index, Honduras ranked as the least statist economy in the region during the ISI era, and the decisive period of orthodox reform under Callejas increased the country's score on the index by a relatively modest .127 points, from .620 in 1990 to .747 in 1993 (Escaith and Paunovic 2004, appendix). Although the early stages of economic adjustment triggered a wave of public-and private-sector strikes, with the number of labor disputes rising from only fourteen in 1985 to ninety-three in 1990 (Wilkie et al. 2002: 429), political divisions within organized labor and government concessions on wage demands led to a decline in strikes thereafter. The strike wave did not trigger widespread social protest, much less pose a threat to the political establishment or the party system.

Indeed, Honduras' party system adapted to this policy shift with remarkably high levels of continuity in its organizational composition and competitive alignment, at least through the end of the critical juncture and the immediate aftermath period. Although Callejas' National Party was defeated in the presidential elections of 1993 and 1997, it remained highly competitive (and would, in fact, return to the presidency on several occasions after 2000). Short-term vote shifts away from the PNH returned to the PLH, producing electoral outcomes in 1993 and 1997 that were virtually identical to those of 1981 and 1985 at the beginning of the critical juncture (see Appendix Tables 11 and 12). Electoral support for the traditional party of the Left, PINU-SD (*Partido de Innovación y Unidad-Social Demócrata*), remained flat and insignificant with less than three percent of the presidential vote and legislative seats, while new contenders – including a reconfigured leftist coalition PUD (*Partido Unificación Democrática*) in the 1990s – made little headway. Both the PLH and the PNH relied heavily on clientelist linkages to reproduce popular support, a tendency that was magnified by their internal factionalism and an electoral system that made legislators highly dependent on party leaders by prohibiting split-ticket voting until 1993 (see Taylor 1996). In comparison to programmatic linkages with their redistributive implications and mobilizing potential, the PNH and PLH found the delivery of clientelist payoffs to be an effective way to secure the loyalties of low-income voters without challenging the interests of traditional elites (Taylor-Robinson 2006: 123).

The Liberal successors to Callejas thus maintained and deepened the process of market reform, ratifying the policy shift in the arena of partisan and electoral competition; the major parties alternated in office, but electoral competition did not lead to a rejection of the neoliberal model. As such, Honduras' critical juncture effectively ended with the 1993 electoral ratification of a market-reform process that involved both major parties and left their clientelist control of the electorate intact. In comparative perspective, this adaptation of a two-party oligarchic system to the neoliberal era was remarkably free of political turbulence; the two major parties shared governing responsibilities, converged programmatically on market liberalization policies, and avoided major electoral realignments and outsider challenges. The institutional outcome of neoliberal convergence was produced by means of a neutral critical juncture, with market reforms led by a traditional conservative party and supported by its center-right rival, with no major party of the left in opposition. The reform process, therefore, did not de-align the party system programmatically, but neither did it align it for the aftermath period around an axis of support and opposition to the neoliberal model. As shown in Chapter 9, the durability of this competitive equilibrium would hinge on the containment of popular mobilization and intra-elite factionalism in the aftermath period, when challenges to neoliberal orthodoxy began to emerge.

In short, Honduras entered – and exited – the critical juncture with a two-party oligarchic system that institutionalized the dominance of traditional political and economic elites, along with the sociopolitical disorganization of working and lower classes. Given the high degree of political continuity, a case could easily be made that in strictly national terms, the transition to neoliberalism did not constitute a critical juncture for Honduras – a bump in the road, perhaps, but not a decisive turning point in party system development. No significant change occurred in the composition or competitive alignment of the party system, and since traditional parties had never developed strong programmatic linkages or mass-based organizational forms in civil or political society, changes in clientelistic linkage patterns were limited as well. It is only in the larger regional context of political transformation that Honduras can be seen as anchoring a pole of adaptation and continuity in the neoliberal critical juncture; Honduras' elitist, two-party system rode out the critical juncture and its immediate aftermath with fewer disruptions than any other in Latin America.

Costa Rica's party system was also highly stable during the critical juncture. Like Honduras, Costa Rica ended the critical juncture with a form of neoliberal convergence, although this outcome was produced by a de-aligning process of market reform that required more significant adaptive measures by established parties, and it proved to be more vulnerable to reactive sequences in the aftermath period that altered the established two-party system. Indeed, by the early 2000s the party system was undergoing a significant electoral and programmatic realignment, with the decline of the established conservative party (PUSC), a shift toward the right of the traditional center-left party (PLN) that led the process of market reform, and the emergence of a major new center-left alternative that mobilized opposition to basic elements of the neoliberal model. As such, Costa Rica's party system weathered the critical juncture intact, but its mode of adaptation created institutional legacies that were susceptible to erosion and the political mobilization of new contenders.

Having adopted extensive forms of state economic intervention and ambitious social welfare programs during the ISI era, Costa Rica confronted more significant adjustment burdens during the critical juncture than Honduras. Indeed, PLN governments in the 1970s expanded the state's developmental responsibilities, relying heavily on foreign lending to finance new public investments in a broad range of agricultural and industrial activities (Mesa-Lago 2000: 423–427; Sandbrook et al. 2007: 104–105). Starting in the late 1970s, however, the economy was buffeted by falling export prices, rising international interest rates on the public debt, higher prices for imported oil, and a sharp decline in external private capital flows. These changes in global markets created a deficit in the balance of payments that compounded Costa Rica's chronic fiscal deficit. The conservative coalition government of Rodrigo Carazo (1978–1982) was determined to uphold the value of the national currency and maintain a fixed exchange rate, leading to widespread capital flight and an ominous four-fold increase in the external debt between 1976 and 1982 (Mesa-Lago 2000: 520). The economy slid into recession in 1981 and then bottomed out in 1982 as the debt crisis spread across the region, leading Costa Rica to default on its national debt. The economy contracted by –2.3 percent in 1981 and –7.3 percent in 1982, while inflation peaked the same year at over 90 percent. The crisis weakened political support for the governing conservative coalition – soon to reorganize as the PUSC (*Partido Unidad Social Cristiano*) – and helped produce a temporary 15-point vote swing that brought the PLN a landslide victory in the 1982 national elections (see Appendix Tables 7 and 8).

Under the presidency of Luís Alberto Monge, the PLN launched a series of austerity and liberalization measures to address the economic crisis. As Seligson and Martínez Franzoni (2010: 312–323) argue, the reform process begun by Monge and extended by his PLN successor, Oscar Arias, did not constitute radical neoliberal "shock therapy," despite being implemented under terms of IMF conditionality. Instead, PLN reformers selectively borrowed from the neoliberal "package" of adjustment measures, adopting reforms in a gradual and piecemeal fashion that progressively whittled away at the statist development policies that their party had played such a prominent role in crafting since the early 1950s. Monge took steps to stabilize the economy and cut the fiscal deficit by reining in government spending, expanding the tax base, unifying exchange rates, devaluing the currency, and renegotiating debt service payments. Partial structural reforms followed over the second half of Monje's term, including tariff reductions, cuts in state subsidies, and price liberalization (see Wilson 1994).

Taken together, these reforms began a general shift from ISI to export-promotion development policies, a reorientation that was formalized through a series of agreements with the IMF and the World Bank. Market reforms were also heavily subsidized by U.S. assistance, reflecting Costa Rica's strategic location during the 1980s Central American conflicts (Carranza and Chinchilla 1994: 40–41). Indeed, U.S. aid between 1983 and 1985 was equivalent to more than one-third of the government's budget and roughly 10 percent of GDP (Edelman 1999: 76–78). This financial assistance helped the economy rebound quickly; by 1984 inflation had fallen to 12 percent and a decade-long expansion with nearly 5 percent average annual growth rates had begun. By regional standards, then, Costa Rica's economic crisis was painful but short-lived, and neoliberal reforms began relatively early – especially for a democratic government – and met with above-average macroeconomic success.

Economic stabilization and recovery helped the PLN achieve re-election in 1986, albeit with a diminished majority of the vote. Although the immediate crisis had passed, the new government of Oscar Arias consolidated and deepened the orthodox turn in the PLN's development strategy. Under Arias the PLN slashed tariffs, eliminated non-tariff barriers to trade, dismantled public monopolies in the import sector, promoted non-traditional exports, expanded private sector banking activities, and developed a plan to privatize firms in the main state holding company. These orthodox measures increased Costa Rica's score on the structural reform index from .474 in 1984 to .769 in 1990 (Escaith and Paunovic 2004, appendix), a net change of .295 that was substantially greater than that of Honduras.

The new policy orientation was controversial inside the PLN, and it met with a fair measure of societal resistance. The urban poor protested against electricity rate hikes, public sector employees opposed privatization policies, and farmers periodically protested cuts in price supports and credit programs (Edelman 1999; Sandbrook et al. 2007: 108). Nevertheless, popular mobilization was neither widespread nor sustained. A short-lived spike in labor disputes occurred in 1990, but overall strike levels dropped sharply over the course of the 1980s as the economy was liberalized and worker militancy declined (Wilkie et al. 2002: 429). The organizational fragmentation and political weakness of organized labor undoubtedly helped alleviate societal pressures on the PLN as it progressively turned in a more orthodox direction.

Although the PUSC defeated the PLN in 1990 general elections, this was not part of a reactive sequence against the neoliberal model, as the conservative party had provided ideological and legislative support for the market-reform process. Despite populist campaign promises, the PUSC continued neoliberal policies after taking office, supporting reforms of the public pension system and efforts to increase private sector participation in the provision of education and health care services. As Seligson and Martínez Franzoni state, "Each subsequent administration made a steady but selective turn towards a neoliberal developmental style" (2010: 316). The neoliberal model, therefore, was reproduced without a major political backlash in successive rounds of electoral competition, and Costa Rica's critical juncture effectively ended with this 1990 electoral ratification of the policy shift that occurred in the 1980s.

As in Honduras, then, Costa Rica's critical juncture produced an institutional outcome of neoliberal convergence, with two established parties alternating in office and maintaining thorough command of the electoral arena, at least through the early stages of the aftermath period. No significant changes in the organizational composition or competitive balance of the party system occurred during the critical juncture, other than the unification of an existing conservative coalition under a single party, the PUSC, in the early 1980s. As such, the party system became *more*, not less, institutionalized during the critical juncture. The conservative bloc bore the brunt of the political costs of crisis management in the early stages of the critical juncture, but the PUSC recovered to capture the presidency and the largest block of legislative seats in 1990 and 1998. The two major parties won between 87.8 and 94.8 percent of the legislative seats and between 91.6 and 98.7 percent of the presidential vote in every election from 1982 to 1998. Although a number of minor parties competed in national elections, none experienced significant electoral growth during the critical juncture or its immediate aftermath, and no major new parties or populist rivals emerged to challenge the electoral dominance of the PLN and the PUSC until the aftermath period.

But in contrast to Honduras, where parties had never embraced ambitious state-led development models or social welfare programs, party system adaptation during Costa Rica's critical juncture entailed a relatively high degree of programmatic change on the part of the PLN. Neoliberal convergence, therefore, was a product of programmatic de-alignment that left the party system without a well-defined institutional outlet for opposition to the neoliberal model. The major policy shift overseen by the PLN in the mid-1980s may have allowed the party to avoid the political costs of a deepening crisis and reap the rewards of stabilization and recovery, but it strained the party's societal linkages and eroded partisan and political cleavages grounded in ISI-era programmatic distinctions. Although it was never an LM party, the PLN had long cultivated programmatic linkages to multi-class constituencies that stood to gain from vigorous state developmental and social welfare activities, and these linkages were difficult to sustain once the party had adopted market reforms and consolidated a more technocratic leadership team.

Consequently, in keeping with its social democratic traditions, the PLN was loath to make an explicit ideological commitment to neoliberalism. The party leadership maintained its distance from elected officials who were responsible for implementing the policy shift, and PLN candidates for public office continued "to campaign on the party's traditional social democratic platform, regardless of the policies pursued by their own party in government" (Wilson 1999: 764). Those policies, moreover, were crafted so as to minimize the risks of an electoral or social backlash; indeed, the orthodox turn was much more pronounced in macroeconomic than social policy spheres. With reforms adopted in a gradual and piecemeal fashion, rather than by comprehensive shock therapy, political opposition could be fragmented and final intentions were obfuscated. Foreign pressure was invoked as justification for unpopular measures, and targeted social benefits helped to cushion the impact of broader spending cuts on the most vulnerable sectors of the population (see Wilson 1999; Carranza and Chinchilla 1994). Indeed, neither the state's developmental roles nor its social welfare responsibilities were slashed as deeply as in some other countries in the region, and both PLN and PUSC governments consulted with interest groups and made policy concessions in response to societal pressure.

Market reforms, therefore, streamlined public administration and expanded private sector participation in a broad range of productive and social-service sectors, but they did not culminate in widespread cuts in public employment or government spending on health care and education. Little was done to deregulate labor markets, and political opposition limited government efforts to privatize the pension system and major public utilities like electricity. Consequently, as Sandbrook et al. (2007: 115) state, economic liberalization in Costa Rica did not lead to "a substitution of the state by the market," but rather to "a complicated and evolving interrelationship" between them.

This policy moderation, gradualism, and pragmatism undoubtedly helped contain, or at least delay, the political mobilization of programmatic opposition to market reforms. They also limited the social costs of structural adjustment, especially in a context of relatively robust economic growth after 1983. During the economic crisis of the early 1980s, unemployment and poverty rates increased, while real wages fell by nearly 30 percent and the percentage of the population covered by public health care and pension programs declined (see Mesa-Lago 2000: 522–532). By the mid-1990s, however, the country had returned to or surpassed pre-crisis levels on most of these social indicators. Indeed, Costa Rica was one of only three countries in the region to have higher real wages and real minimum wages in 1990 than in 1980 (International Labour Organization 1997a: 50).

In comparative perspective, therefore, Costa Rica's moderate course of market liberalization was relatively successful in producing economic growth with stability, and it strained but did not rupture the country's vaunted social safety net. This performance record helped the dominant parties ride out a programmatically de-aligning critical juncture without electoral upheavals or a major social backlash. Although the outcome of neoliberal convergence was destined to encounter disruptive reactive sequences after 2000, it was, as in Honduras, a stable equilibrium during the period of economic adjustment and its immediate aftermath.

The short-term stability of neoliberal convergence in Costa Rica and Honduras, however, was not replicated in other countries that experienced neutral or de-aligning critical junctures. As the following section shows, neoliberal convergence in Ecuador – the product of a tumultuous, de-aligning critical juncture – was a highly unstable competitive alignment, and it was prone to immediate and convulsive reactive sequences in the context of an under-institutionalized party system and mobilized societal resistance to the neoliberal model.

NEOLIBERAL CONVERGENCE AND PARTY SYSTEM CHANGE IN ECUADOR

Among countries with elitist party systems during the ISI era, Ecuador stands out for its chronic electoral volatility and for the recent formation – and eventual decomposition – of the party system that managed the transition from ISI to neoliberalism. Ecuador also stands out among the elitist cases for the scope, intensity, and duration of social mobilization against market reforms outside formal electoral arenas. Societal resistance left Ecuador's neoliberal model incomplete, politically unconsolidated, and highly vulnerable to policy reversal, and it posed formidable challenges to a party system that could neither channel nor contain it. These outcomes were shaped by the interplay between antecedent conditions in Ecuador's party system and the distinctive political dynamics of the critical juncture itself.

In contrast to Honduras and Costa Rica, Ecuador entered the critical juncture with an inchoate and fragmented party system. These antecedent conditions made the country vulnerable to electoral volatility and political deinstitutional-ization, especially in a critical juncture that encouraged programmatic de-alignment, imposed political costs across a wide range of governing parties, and failed to generate a stable neoliberal growth model to help secure partisan loyalties. Furthermore, in contrast to these other countries, Ecuador's critical juncture spawned a powerful new indigenous social movement which served as a focal point for popular resistance, thus compensating for the traditional weakness of organized labor. The capacity for social mobilization set the stage for powerful reactive sequences in the aftermath period that produced a decomposition of the party system and a pattern of serial populism that eventually turned in a more polarizing direction.

The distinctive features of the Ecuadorean case can be traced back to the onset of mass politics in the 1930s and 1940s, when a unique and highly personalistic brand of populism eclipsed the traditional oligarchic parties but failed to recon-figure the party system around a new labor-mobilizing alternative. The patri-monial party system that emerged at the middle of the century was very weakly institutionalized, and following a long series of populist cycles, military inter-ventions, and regime breakdowns, a new and largely reconstituted party system struggled to consolidate after Ecuador made a transition to democracy in the late 1970s. The management of economic crisis and market reform in the years that followed compounded the pressures on this fledgling party system, but it hardly created them; the critical juncture did not dislodge an established party system so much as it impeded the consolidation of one.

Antecedent Conditions: Populism and Ecuador's Patrimonial Party System

Like many other countries in Latin America, Ecuador had developed both Conservative and Liberal oligarchic parties by the late 19th century. The conservatives defended the Catholic Church and the economic interests of highland agrarian elites, who dominated the political arena until the 1895 "Liberal Revolution." The Liberals held sway thereafter, advocating a more secular state while defending commercial and agro-export interests on the coast, where production of the leading export commodity – cocoa – was concentrated. These oligarchic parties thus gave institutional form to a regionally based, coastal – highlands political cleavage that would outlive the parties themselves.

In a familiar pattern, oligarchic rule was undermined in the 1920s and 1930s by changes in the export-led growth model and the early stages of political mobilization by urban popular sectors. Plant disease in the 1920s damaged cocoa production and weakened the financial and political dominance of the Liberal agro-export elite. By the time the Great Depression arrived, further damaging the export economy, Ecuador's oligarchic order was in retreat, and mass politics lay just around the corner.

What set Ecuador apart, however, was the distinctive character and political impact of the populist experience that followed this onset of mass politics. This populist experience lasted from the 1930s to the 1970s in its original form, and continued thereafter under a plethora of different leaders. As such, it was far more extensive than anything experienced in Honduras and Costa Rica, yet it failed to reconfigure Ecuador's party system around a new mass-based alternative as in the LM cases. The leading populist figure – five-time president José María Velasco Ibarra – was a charismatic but highly contradictory leader who appealed to the masses but made little effort to organize them in a political party or labor unions. A fiery orator, Velasco Ibarra employed anti-oligarchic rhetoric to gain his first election to the presidency in 1933. But in contrast to other mid-century populist figures like Perón, Cárdenas, Vargas, and Haya de la Torre, who created mass-based party and/or labor organizations, Velasco Ibarra was not an institution builder. Indeed, he was contemptuous of political institutions that restricted his autonomy or mediated his relationship to mass constituencies. As stated by Sosa-Buchholz (1999: 147), Velasco Ibarra's "disdain for party organization" was revealed by his signature statement to "give me a balcony and I will make myself President." Likewise, Velasco Ibarra courted workers' votes, but he remained aloof from the union movement and at times actively repressed organized labor and its political allies (Martz 1980: 298). Consequently, a military regime – not a populist figure – passed the first labor code that gave legal recognition to unions in Ecuador (Conaghan and Malloy 1994: 33).

Like other populists, Velasco Ibarra appealed to multi-class and politically eclectic constituencies, unifying them around his personal leadership by attacking the political establishment and cultivating an image as an independent outsider. Despite his anti-oligarchic rhetoric, however, he drew surprising support from traditional landed elites. As Conaghan and Malloy (1994: 33) state, Velasco Ibarra was a "fundamentally conservative and virulently anticommunist" leader who paved the way for a "dominant class co-optation of populism" from the 1930s through the 1960s. Elite groups had little to fear from his mobilizing strategies or economic programs, as Velasco Ibarra did not adopt significant redistributive measures, nor did he pursue aggressive ISI policies to industrialize Ecuador's agro-export economy. Instead, he exploited divisions within the Liberal and Conservative parties, at times winning over these parties or their dissident factions; indeed, his opportunism exacerbated their factionalism. He also wooed a fluid and heterogenous mix of Socialists, rightists, regional bosses, and students (see, for example, de la Torre 2000: 37). Velasco Ibarra's poorly organized electoral coalitions quickly dissolved after he took office, however, making his governments both autocratic and highly unstable; elected five times to the presidency between 1934 and 1968, he was deposed four times before the end of his term.

In short, populism in Ecuador was far less embedded in the larger ISI/state-centric matrix than it was in most other Latin American countries. It introduced mass politics, but not mass parties or labor organizations, and it did not create a state committed to industrialization, redistribution, or corporatist control of labor and popular mobilization. Ecuador departed from economic liberalism during the Great Depression, but it did not launch significant ISI policies, and a boom in banana exports after World War II helped to restore the traditional agro-export development model. Indeed, the manufacturing share of GDP actually declined between 1940 and 1960, making Ecuador a notable outlier to the regional post-war industrialization trend (see Thorp 1998: 162). State industrial promotion policies began under a civilian government in the late 1950s, but the major push toward ISI occurred belatedly, under nationalistic military regimes in the 1960s and 1970s (see Fitch 1977). Likewise, military regimes initiated land reform and the corporatist organization of the peasantry (Zamosc 1994: 45–47; Yashar 2005: 91), and they supported wage increases and other pro-labor policies in the 1970s.

These statist and nationalist policies incurred the wrath of business groups, which became increasingly vocal proponents of democratization and market liberalization (Conaghan and Malloy 1994: 77–98).[1] Even with military support, however, Ecuador's labor movement could not overcome the constraints of the country's shallow industrial base, its lack of a significant mining sector, and the absence of a labor-mobilizing populist party. Trade union density lagged

---

[1] Clearly, the experience with military rule in Ecuador in the 1970s (and in the neighboring Andean countries of Peru and Bolivia) contrasted with that in Brazil and the Southern Cone countries of Chile, Uruguay, and Argentina. In the Andes, nationalistic, left-leaning military regimes were associated with statism and redistributive social reforms, and business groups often believed democracy would better protect their interests and provide institutionalized channels for policy influence. In the Southern Cone, on the other hand, business groups often turned to the military for protection from the radical forms of social mobilization that occurred under democracy.

well behind that in the LM cases, reaching only 15 percent of the labor force at its peak (see Table 4.5). Similarly, the union movement remained politically fragmented for most of the ISI era between rival Christian Democratic, leftist, and U.S.-affiliated confederations.

Ecuador's populist experience, then, did not reconfigure the party system around a mass-based, labor-mobilizing alternative. Instead, it alternated with military rule in a pattern that weakened, fractured, and gradually displaced traditional oligarchic parties, while limiting their control over the state resources needed to cultivate durable clientelist linkages to popular sectors. This limitation was compounded by literacy restrictions that disenfranchised much of Ecuador's rural indigenous population, depriving the Liberals and Conservatives of the broad peasant bases that helped oligarchic parties weather the rise of urban mass constituencies in other Latin American countries. Consequently, after the arrival of Velasco Ibarra on the political scene, only once did a traditional oligarchic party capture the presidency (the Liberals in 1940). Populism injected a large dose of personalism and fluidity into the party system, given Velasco Ibarra's aversion to organization and his constantly shifting tactical alliances. The party system remained elitist, though highly fragmented and patrimonial in character, with fluid and de-institutionalized patterns of political representation.

Therefore, in contrast to Costa Rica and Honduras, Ecuador did not enter the critical juncture with an institutionalized two-party system – an antecedent condition that weighed heavily on political dynamics during the transition to neoliberalism. Instead, as Ecuador began a democratic transition in 1978 after six years of reformist, post-Velasco military rule – under a new constitution that dramatically expanded the electorate by enfranchising illiterates – the secular decomposition of the oligarchic party system continued, and a partial reconstitution occurred around a fluid set of alternatives with strong patrimonial characteristics. The Liberal (PLRE) and Conservative (PCE) parties progressively moved to the political margins; these parties had captured nearly 60 percent of the congressional vote in 1947, but this figure shrank to 38 percent in 1954, 15.8 percent in 1979, and a paltry 8.1 percent in 1984 (Nohlen 2005: 387–389, vol. 2). Taking their place was a strikingly diverse set of new parties and splinter groups, several of which had emerged from splits in the Liberal or Conservative parties themselves. The most important of these were the *Partido Social Cristiano* (PSC), which split from the Conservative Party in 1951, captured the presidency with its support in 1956, and then displaced it as the leading party of the right in the late 1970s; the *Izquierda Democrática* (ID), which was formed by Liberal Party dissidents in 1970 and became the leading party of the center-left during the regime transition; the *Concentración de Fuerzas Populares* (CFP), a populist party devoted to regional strongmen in Guayaquil and the coastal region; the *Partido Roldosista Ecuatoriano* (PRE), which emerged from a split within the CFP in the early 1980s and largely displaced it; and *Democracia Popular-Unión Demócrata Cristiana* (DP-UDC), a centrist party with Christian Democratic leanings and political roots in both the Conservative Party and the

PSC (Conaghan 1995: 439–444; Freidenberg 2003). These parties bore primary responsibility for managing economic crisis and market reform during Ecuador's neoliberal critical juncture.

The Critical Juncture and Programmatic De-alignment in Ecuador

Ecuador's economy plunged into crisis in 1982 with the rest of the region, but the crisis had been brewing since the beginning of the decade, when prices for the country's petroleum exports began to fall and interest rates on its skyrocketing foreign debt sharply increased. Ecuador had become an oil exporter in 1972, just in time to reap the windfalls from the dramatic rise in international oil prices in the mid-1970s. The nationalist military regime led by General Guillermo Rodríguez Lara responded to the oil bonanza by embarking on a spending spree that subsidized both investment and consumption in the domestic economy. The regime invested heavily in new public enterprises and infrastructure development, expanded the public payroll, provided subsidies and tax credits for private businesses, and subsidized consumption of food, gasoline, and electricity. Despite higher oil revenues, fiscal and balance-of-payments deficits worsened as government spending increased and the demand for imports swelled. The government resorted to massive international borrowing to cover these deficits; as Conaghan and Malloy (1994: 111) state, "From 1975 to 1980 Ecuador's foreign debt increased sevenfold, and its debt service ratio climbed from 4 to 19 percent."

Consequently, the new democratic regime that took office in 1979 encountered a rapidly deteriorating international economic environment. The first civilian president, Jaime Roldós of the populist CFP, initiated austerity measures as early as 1981 when oil prices began to fall and global interest rates spiked. The situation worsened in 1982 when the regional debt crisis caused a sharp decline in the flow of private bank credits. Roldós' successor, Osvaldo Hurtado of the centrist DP,[2] responded to the crisis with a stabilization package that included devaluing the currency, raising taxes and interest rates, cutting state subsidies, and increasing the price of gasoline and electricity. He also negotiated a standby agreement with the IMF, paving the way for a rescheduling of Ecuador's debt with private creditors (see Schuldt 1994:122; Conaghan and Malloy 1994: 112–113). When these austerity measures provoked street protests and a series of national strikes by organized labor, Hurtado responded by declaring a state of emergency.

By regional standards, the crisis of the early 1980s in Ecuador was relatively mild. The economy sank into recession in 1983, with a –2.8 percent growth rate, while the rate of inflation tripled that same year to 48.4 percent. By 1984, however, inflation was moderating and a recovery was under way, with the

---

[2] Hurtado had been vice president under Roldós, the fruit of an electoral pact between their two parties. He assumed the presidency when Roldós was killed in a plane crash in 1981.

economy growing by more than 4 percent. Recovery aside, the crisis and unpopular austerity measures took their toll on the incumbent parties. Riven by factionalism, the CFP lost three-quarters of its congressional seats and half its presidential vote in the 1984 national elections, the beginning of a downhill slide that would thoroughly marginalize the party by the early 1990s (see Appendix Tables 9 and 10). Hurtado's DP remained electorally marginal, leaving the conservative PSC to face off against the center-left ID in the 1984 presidential race. The contest was won by León Febres Cordero of the PSC, a former president of Guayaquil's Chamber of Industry and a prominent critic of state intervention in the economy.

Although Hurtado had recognized the need for fiscal belt-tightening after the spending binge of the 1970s, he was hardly committed to a neoliberal restructuring of state–market relations. By contrast, Febres Cordero was a staunch supporter of structural adjustment policies, albeit one who masked his policy preferences behind populist promises on the campaign trail. Operating largely through executive decrees, Febres Cordero eliminated exchange rate controls, liberalized financial markets, deregulated foreign investment, and reduced price controls, subsidies, and state spending. These reforms were implemented gradually rather than through shock treatment, as the economic recovery of the mid-1980s and the absence of hyperinflation alleviated the sense of urgency. The package of reforms did not include major privatization initiatives, and given Febres Cordero's close ties to industrialists, he moved slowly to reduce trade protectionism. Shaken by a new downturn in oil prices and rampant currency speculation, Febres Cordero reversed course on exchange rate liberalization near the end of his term, thus abandoning a centerpiece of his structural adjustment program (Conaghan and Malloy 1994: 179).

Ecuador's first major attempt at neoliberal reform thus ended in a partial retreat, and Febres Cordero left office with a structural reform index (.539) that was virtually identical to that when he entered (.537) (see Escaith and Paunovic 2004). Economic performance also deteriorated over the latter part of his term, as a serious recession in 1987 produced an economic contraction of 6 percent. Mounting inflationary pressures compounded the crisis, reaching 75.6 percent in 1989, ensuring that economic adjustment would remain a salient issue on the political agenda of Febres Cordero's successor.

With the PSC vote cut nearly in half following Febres Cordero's rocky tenure, the center-left ID defeated the new populist party PRE in the 1988 election behind presidential candidate Rodrigo Borja. Although Borja was a long-time critic of the neoliberal model, he did not attempt to reverse the reforms of Febres Cordero. Instead, he proved to be a pragmatic market reformer in office, liberalizing foreign trade, exchange rates, and labor markets, and increasing Ecuador's score on the structural reform index from .539 in 1988 to .754 in 1992 (Escaith and Paunovic 2004, appendix). As these reforms were adopted by the country's leading left-of-center party, they were clearly programmatically de-aligning for Ecuador's fragile party system, and the ID paid a steep price at the ballot box for abandoning its traditional platform. The party's share of the first-round presidential vote fell from 24.5 percent in 1988 to 8.5 percent in 1992, while its share of legislative seats steadily declined, from 43.7 percent in 1988 to 18.3 percent in 1990 and a meager 9.1 percent in 1992.

By 1992, then – a mere decade after the start of the debt crisis – Ecuador's most important right, center, populist, and leftist parties had all taken a hand at managing economic stabilization and reform. All the incumbent parties (with the exception of Hurtado's very small DP) had suffered major vote losses, and votes were beginning to shift to new and sometimes ephemeral parties or independent figures. Meanwhile, the economy remained mired in a type of low-growth, partial-reform equilibrium (Hellman 1998) that was vulnerable to financial instability, especially given the dependence of the Ecuadorean economy on volatile international commodity prices.

A third major push for neoliberal reform thus occurred under Borja's conservative successor, Sixto Durán Ballén. Durán Ballén broke with the PSC to launch an independent electoral vehicle, the *Partido Unión Republicana* (PUR), in the 1992 campaign. Strongly committed to scaling back the public sector, the new president proposed a series of privatizations along with cuts in public spending and employment. With World Bank assistance, he passed laws to open the petroleum sector to foreign investment, and he proposed an agricultural modernization plan that would have ended land redistribution, weakened communal land rights, and promoted private property rights to land and water resources. Some of Durán Ballén's ambitious restructuring plans were watered down by congressional opposition or popular resistance, however, as a strengthening indigenous movement protested against the government's oil policies and forced it to renegotiate agricultural reforms (Sawyer 2004: 109–110; Yashar 2005: 147–148).

Although orthodox policies under Durán Ballén cut the inflation rate from 54.3 percent in 1992 to 24.4 percent in 1996, Ecuador was not able to reach the single-digit inflationary levels of many other countries in the region by the mid-1990s. Economic growth remained anemic, while declining oil prices contributed to larger financial difficulties and a looming bank crisis that would afflict the economy over the latter half of the 1990s. At the end of Durán Ballén's term in office, the PUR largely disappeared from the political arena, and more established parties returned to the forefront in the 1996 election campaign. Campaigning as a fiery, anti-establishment defender of the poor, the eccentric populist leader Abdalá Bucaram of the PRE mobilized a "multiclass alliance of the marginalized" (de la Torre 2010: 108) to defeat the conservative candidate of the PSC and the business establishment, Jaime Nebot, along with independent television personality Freddy Ehlers, who was backed by the newly formed indigenous party *Pachakutik*.

Like most populist figures, Bucaram's mass appeal was not grounded in well-defined programmatic positions. Although he vaguely promised to support the economic interests of the poor, oppose monopolies, and defend labor unions against liberalization policies, he was not explicitly anti-neoliberal; instead, he pledged to "popularize" capitalism by helping small businesses and the poor to reap the benefits of market reforms that had previously been captured by privileged elites (de la Torre 2010: 98–99). This ambiguity aside, however, Bucaram clearly emerged as the popular alternative to the establishment's orthodox neoliberal project, making his subsequent embrace of structural adjustment policies at least a partial case of de-aligning, "bait-and-switch" liberalization. To alleviate the fiscal burdens of falling oil prices and crushing debt repayments, Bucaram immediately adopted a package of austerity and liberalization measures, including privatizations, a major devaluation, cuts in job security, and huge price hikes for subsidized public services like gas, electricity, transportation, and telephones. The political backlash developed quickly, and it was strikingly diverse in its social composition. Within six months, Bucaram was embroiled in corruption scandals, and business leaders had joined organized labor and the indigenous movement in a civic strike and mass protests that paralyzed the national economy. Congress responded, on dubious constitutional grounds, by removing Bucaram from the presidency for reasons of "mental incapacity" in February 1997.

Ecuador's critical juncture had a less precise end-point than the others analyzed here, as the cycle of economic crisis, partial market reform, and political reaction played out over successive administrations and continued into the aftermath period. The popular uprising that triggered the downfall of Bucaram, however, arguably brought the critical juncture to an end, as the prospects for comprehensive market liberalization had been closed by the rapid development of popular movements in opposition – a "social veto," so to speak, that drove the reactive sequences of the aftermath period. From then on, market reformers were put on the political defensive, as Bucaram became the first of three consecutive elected presidents to attempt market reforms and be driven from office in contexts of mass social protest. The exercise of this social veto, and the resounding rejection of the political establishment that it embodied, set the stage for the arrival of a more leftist and staunchly anti-neoliberal populist leader, Rafael Correa, in 2006.

Ecuador's powerful reactive sequences were conditioned by three primary characteristics of the country's critical juncture: the failure to institutionalize and programmatically align the party system that emerged during the early stages of the democratic transition, a pattern of intermittent market reform that failed to produce stable growth and left the economy susceptible to repeated financial crises, and the gradual development of a powerful, indigenous-led protest movement that frontally challenged both the neoliberal model and the nascent party system. A series of new and established parties alternated in the presidency and seemingly offered voters a range of ideological and programmatic choices. In office, however, there was little to differentiate their policy orientations. Although conservative leaders like Febres Cordero and Durán Ballén were more ideologically committed to neoliberal reform, centrist, populist, and leftist leaders were also pressured to adopt austerity and liberalization measures. Indeed, the adoption of market reforms by the country's leading leftist (ID) and populist (PRE) parties during the critical juncture created an overarching dynamic of programmatic de-alignment. Neoliberal convergence undermined parties' programmatic linkages to voters, and even clientelist linkages were shallow in a context of repeated fiscal adjustment and rapid alternation in office. By default, then, parties relied heavily on personalistic linkages. Levels of party discipline and identification were so low that widespread party-switching was commonplace in the congress (see Conaghan 1995).

Neither was partisan competition durably aligned by the allocation of costs and benefits associated with crisis management. The major parties absorbed the costs of economic crisis and reform, as seen in a consistent pattern of anti-incumbent vote swings, but none reaped any rewards for effective performance. The PSC, ID, and PUR all suffered steep electoral declines after governing the country and administering market reforms. These anti-incumbent vote shifts accounted for much of Ecuador's notorious electoral volatility, which averaged 37.7 percent in presidential campaigns and 29.2 percent in congressional races during the 1980s and 1990s. During the critical juncture itself, this volatility was largely intra-systemic; that is, it reflected vote shifts from one established party to others. Rather than decomposing, therefore, the party system experienced a serial pattern of short-term electoral realignments. By the 1990s, however, large blocs of voters had begun to support independent figures (such as Durán Ballén in 1992 and Ehlers in 1996) or new political parties (such as *Pachakutik*), foreshadowing the process of party system decomposition that would occur in the aftermath period.

Given its debt service burden, Ecuador remained in a state of nearly perpetual fiscal crisis and economic stagnation, producing chronic pressures for unpopular adjustment measures to streamline spending and eliminate market distortions. Recessions occurred in 1983 and 1987, and adjustment measures did not yield a stabilizing growth pattern. Growth rates averaged only 2.3 percent in the 1980s and 1.9 percent in the 1990s, lagging behind the rate of population growth, leading to a 5.2 percent decline in per-capita GDP from 1980 to 2000 (World Bank 2008). The costs of prolonged economic stagnation, moreover, were heavily concentrated on low income groups. The real minimum wage, for example, lost two-thirds of its value in the 1980s and remained at less than half its 1980 value through the end of the 1990s (International Labour Organization 1998: 43, 2005: 102). In contrast to Costa Rica, then, Ecuador did not experience a stabilizing growth pattern – or possess an effective social safety net – to cushion the impact of market liberalization on popular living standards and moderate the reactive sequences that followed in the wake of bait-and-switch reforms.

Likewise, Ecuador's economy remained subject to inflationary pressures throughout the 1990s, well after stabilization had been achieved in most other countries of the region. Ecuador did not, however, suffer the ravages of a hyperinflationary spiral that might have weakened social resistance to structural adjustment policies or produced political dividends for parties that achieved stabilization. Inflation reached 75.6 percent in 1989 and 96.1 percent in 2000, but generally remained between 20 and 50 percent – high enough to generate discontent, but a far cry from the hyperinflationary rates that provided political cover for neoliberal shock treatment in neighboring countries. In general, then, stagflation combined with persistent cuts in state subsidies and social programs to impose the political costs of crisis management on successive governing parties, rather than realigning the party system around the political gains of parties that achieved stabilization and growth.

With all the major parties converging on variants of the neoliberal model, at least when saddled with governing responsibilities, resistance to market liberalization was channeled into forms of social protest that targeted the political establishment. Initially, organized labor tried to spearhead popular resistance, with the largest labor confederation declaring a series of general strikes to protest the austerity and liberalization measures adopted by Hurtado and Febres Cordero (Conaghan and Malloy 1994: 149). The number of strikes swelled in the late 1980s, from 72 strikes involving 9,248 workers in 1985 to 169 strikes involving 51,175 workers in 1989. Labor mobilization declined precipitously, however, as market liberalization deepened in the early 1990s; by 1994, a mere 14 strikes occurred, involving 1,888 workers (Wilkie, Aleman and Ortega 2001: 429).

By the 1990s, however, the locus of resistance had shifted to the agrarian sector, and from class-based demands to a combination of class and ethnic claims, as Ecuador developed the region's strongest and most sustained pattern of indigenous political mobilization during the critical juncture. For several decades, churches, small leftist parties, and unions had worked at the grassroots level to organize indigenous communities around claims for land and local autonomy. By 1980, indigenous federations had emerged in both the highlands and the Amazon to articulate claims for cultural rights as well, creating new popular subjects that were not present in Honduras and Costa Rica with their far smaller indigenous populations. In 1986 these federations merged to form the *Confederación de Nacionalidades Indígenas del Ecuador* (the Confederation of Indigenous Nationalities of Ecuador, or CONAIE), a national organization based on a "fusion of material and cultural demands" (Yashar 2005: 133) that was without precedent in the region.

As Yashar (2005) convincingly demonstrates, neoliberal reforms created a series of economic and political grievances that became inextricably linked to claims for cultural rights and community autonomy for indigenous peoples in Ecuador. In the Andean highlands, market reforms threatened the communal land rights, corporatist recognition, and state resources that had been extended as part of the land reform policies of the 1970s military regime. In the Amazon lowlands, the desire to attract foreign investment in oil production encroached on traditional land-use practices and communal autonomy (Sawyer 2004).

Demands for ethnic cultural recognition thus became inseparable from those related to the control of land and natural resources. At the same time, indigenous organizations spoke out against neoliberal policies that exposed them to the vagaries of the marketplace, including low prices for agricultural products, high prices for inputs, and reduced government credits, subsidies, and social programs. These diverse grievances were largely articulated outside the party system, as established parties made little effort to represent indigenous peoples or give them political voice. Openly disdainful of a party system that excluded them and a democratic regime that had reversed some of the social gains made under military reformers, indigenous organizations became advocates of electoral abstention by the mid-1980s – just a few short years after constitutional reforms had extended suffrage rights to most of the indigenous population (Yashar 2005: 142–143).

Indigenous resistance to the neoliberal model was thus channeled outside and against the party system, with a "National Indigenous Uprising" orchestrated by CONAIE in May of 1990 inaugurating the first in a long series of massive social protests. For 10 days, protesters cut off roads, withheld farm produce from markets, marched on provincial capitals, and occupied local government agencies and churches. This uprising, which Zamosc (1994: 37) characterized as a "general civic strike," forced both provincial authorities and the Borja administration to negotiate with indigenous representatives over economic grievances and land conflicts.

In the years that followed, the indigenous movement reached out to other popular organizations that had their own grievances against the neoliberal model. Indigenous groups joined labor confederations in a 1993 general strike, and they worked with environmental organizations to protest new oil concessions. In 1994 indigenous activists briefly occupied oil wells and the Ministry of Energy and Mines, then joined labor, peasant, and student organizations in mass demonstrations against an austerity-induced hike in domestic oil prices. These demonstrations, which included road blockages, school closures, and the shutdown of public transport, occurred across much of the country, and turned violent in some localities (Sawyer 2004: 112–114). CONAIE also led protests in 1994 against the agricultural modernization plan of Durán Ballén, and in 1995 against his proposal to privatize social security. In both cases the protests forced the government to water down or abandon its liberalization plans. Two years later, CONAIE made an important strategic shift: after boycotting parties and elections for 10 years, the national confederation decided to create its own party organization, *Pachakutik* (officially, the *Movimiento de Unidad Plurinacional Pachakutik-Nuevo País* [MUPP-NP]), and to contest political power in the electoral arena (Van Cott 2005: 112–123).

The rise of this indigenous protest movement, combined with its ability to forge alliances with labor unions, environmental organizations, and other groups that shared grievances against the neoliberal model, provided graphic evidence of the crisis in Ecuador's party system and representative institutions. Mobilization from below would subsequently drive the reactive sequences of the aftermath period, but it would not, however, resolve the crisis of partisan representation, even with the formation of *Pachakutik*. As shown in Chapter 9, Ecuador's inchoate party system largely decomposed in the post-adjustment era, but it was not reconstituted by new party organizations with stable mass constituencies. Instead, the unstable equilibrium of neoliberal convergence gave way to a dynamic of serial populism and, eventually, a more polarizing variant of populism under leftist leader Rafael Correa. In the process, Ecuador's contentious process of market liberalization would be reversed by one of Latin America's most vigorous advocates of state-led development.

PROGRAMMATIC ALIGNMENT AND CONTESTED LIBERALISM IN URUGUAY

Neoliberal critical junctures in Honduras, Costa, Rica, and Ecuador were all neutral or de-aligning in their programmatic effects, producing institutional outcomes of neoliberal convergence that varied widely in their relative stability. Not all elitist party systems, however, experienced neutral or de-aligning critical junctures; consequently, not all entered the post-adjustment era with a competitive alignment of neoliberal convergence. The Uruguayan case, in particular, experienced a conservative-led process of market reform that aligned its party system programmatically, producing an outcome of contested liberalism that was a relatively stable competitive equilibrium – both during the critical juncture, when Uruguay's party system was nearly as stable as those of Honduras and Costa Rica, and during the aftermath period, when it proved to be more resilient in the face of potentially destabilizing reactive sequences. Uruguay also provides an unusually clear-cut example of cumulative or progressive electoral realignment over the course of multiple election cycles, without triggering high levels of electoral volatility within any particular cycle. In short, Uruguay shows how the competitive balance of a party system can change over time within an overarching framework of institutional continuity.

In Uruguay, as in Costa Rica, the two leading traditional parties supported the adoption of market reforms, and a new leftist competitor arose in part by defending a relatively strong (by regional standards) welfare state. But whereas Costa Rica's new leftist alternative only emerged in the post-adjustment era, Uruguay's was spawned by the social ferment of the 1960s and early 1970s, and it progressively strengthened (and moderated) during the critical juncture that followed. Uruguay's historic two-party system thus realigned electorally during the critical juncture, and the new balance of forces tilted even further in the aftermath period when the leftist *Frente Amplio* (Broad Front, or FA) won national elections for the first time in 2004. Like Ecuador, then, Uruguay veered to the left in the post-adjustment era, but it did so under the auspices of an institutionalized leftist party rather than a populist outsider, reflecting the very different institutional legacies of programmatically aligning and de-aligning critical junctures.

Antecedent Conditions: Uruguay's Oligarchic Party System in Transition

Prior to the rise of the *Frente Amplio*, Uruguay boasted one of the world's oldest and most durable two-party systems. Indeed, González (1995: 140) states that the two dominant parties, the Colorados and Blancos (officially known as the National Party), "preceded the truly unified nation-state." These parties first emerged in the late 1830s as *caudillo*-led political–military organizations – in short, the partisan armies of military strongmen – during the 1839–1851 civil war that followed the formation of the Uruguayan state. During the war the Colorados held power in Montevideo, while the Blancos laid siege from the countryside – the genesis of the party system's eventual urban–rural cleavage. Although the parties grew out of oligarchic factionalism, military mobilization allowed them to penetrate society and acquire popular followings long before suffrage reform brought about mass electoral participation in the second decade of the 20th century. Partisan sub-cultural identities were reproduced through patron–client linkages; although the Colorados dominated the national government and its clientele system for over a century, they entered into a series of power-sharing arrangements to end repeated Blanco insurrections, leaving the latter in charge of a number of provincial governments and their patronage networks.

Like conservative parties elsewhere in Latin America, the Blancos were closer to rural landed interests and the Catholic Church, whereas the Colorados reflected the more urban, commercial, and anticlerical positions of Latin American liberalism. These distinctions were far from iron-clad, however. As González (1995: 141) argues, "both parties represented cross sections of Uruguayan society," drawing support across religious, ideological, and class lines, and thus leaving the urban–rural divide as "the only significant social cleavage" to align electoral competition. The heterogeneous, catch-all character of the parties' social composition was reinforced by their factionalism, which allowed competing ideological tendencies to exist within each party as well. Uruguay's "double simultaneous vote" electoral system fostered this factionalism, as it allowed voters to select the party of their choice as well as an intra-party factional list preference. This system, adopted in 1910, promoted electoral stability and discouraged fragmentation, as it gave voice to dissidents and provided "incentives for the smaller groups to remain within the larger umbrella" (Morgenstern 2004: 44). Factions had little reason to split from established parties, since their prospects at the presidential level were enhanced if they remained within their party's "pooled" vote.

Uruguay's two-party system was, in fact, exceptionally stable, one of only a handful in the region to manage the rise of mass politics in the early 20th century with minimal disruptions. Indeed, the Colorado Party, which controlled the presidency until 1958, sponsored the process of labor incorporation during the two presidential terms of José Batlle y Ordóñez early in the century. Batlle was a social reformer who sought to mobilize support among workers – a largely untapped political resource – by creating free public education, promoting industrialization, and giving workers an eight-hour work day, social security, and new rights to vote, unionize, and strike (see Collier and Collier 1991: 275). Batlle's reforms promoted unionization and garnered support among urban workers and the middle class, but they largely failed to bind unions to his party. Instead, his reforms alienated conservatives in the Colorado party and exacerbated its factionalism, without securing the loyalty of a nascent labor movement that was predominantly anarchist and socialist in inspiration. Consequently, as suffrage reforms expanded the electorate, conservatives in both major parties relied heavily on clientelist linkages to mobilize working- and lower-class support.

The combination of social reforms and patronage politics thus enabled the traditional parties to broaden their electoral base at a relatively early stage in the country's socioeconomic development. Since these reforms were adopted prior to widespread industrialization and unionization, they had a preemptive effect that dampened subsequent labor mobilization in both partisan and union spheres. Indeed, they largely separated these spheres, creating a type of "political dualism" whereby workers joined unions led by small leftist parties but continued to vote for the traditional Colorado or Blanco parties (Lanzaro 2004a: 30; Drake 1996: 91–92). Reformist factions in the Colorado Party appealed to workers programmatically, but they did little to organize workers on the ground, and the party remained too internally divided over labor issues to provide cohesive political leadership of the union movement. Anarchists, Socialists, and eventually Communists, on the other hand, organized unions and supported workers' more militant demands, but they were unable to translate their organization in the workplace into mass appeal in the electoral arena. Consequently, although Uruguay adopted relatively ambitious ISI policies after the 1930s and developed the most industrialized economy and the strongest labor movement of any Latin American country with an elitist party system, it did not possess a mass-based labor-mobilizing party, and it fell short of the levels of trade union density attained in countries with LM party systems (see Table 4.1).

The cycle of reform was repeated in the 1940s, when Colorado governments adopted new measures to strengthen job security, increase wages and social benefits, and establish corporatist tripartite wage councils that gave workers a voice in the formulation of public policies (Collier and Collier 1991: 641–642). Although linkages to organized labor remained weak, the Blancos and Colorados maintained their electoral dominance, jointly averaging 88.9 percent of the vote for the lower house of congress and 86.7 percent of the presidential vote between 1934 and 1966. Meanwhile, the Socialist and Communist parties together averaged a mere 5.1 percent of the vote during this period (Nohlen 2005: 502–527, vol. 2). Clearly, then, industrialization and mass politics did little to alter the two-party system that was a primary legacy of the oligarchic order.

This alignment of sociopolitical forces began to change along several key dimensions by the late 1960s and early 1970s, in the process eroding the political dualism of workers and moving Uruguay closer to the representational patterns of the LM cases. First, the labor movement became more organizationally cohesive, eventually forming a centralized national confederation (the *Convención Nacional de Trabajadores*, or CNT) in 1966 that incorporated virtually all unionized workers under leftist (primarily Communist) political leadership. Second, the partisan left also unified and strengthened under the banner of the FA in 1971, which brought together the historic Socialist and Communist parties along with Christian Democrats and leftist splinters from the Blancos and Colorados. Electoral support for the left increased sharply that year, when the fledgling FA won 18.3 percent of the vote nationwide, nearly double the best previous combined electoral showing of diverse leftist groups. During this period the Uruguayan political system was also shaken by the development of an urban guerrilla movement known as the *Tupamaros*, who conducted a series of armed robberies, kidnappings, and prison breaks in the name of social revolution.

By the early 1970s, therefore, the traditional political order in Uruguay was being challenged on several different fronts. The spreading sense of political crisis was compounded by chronic economic stagnation and growing inflationary and balance-of-payments pressures. Although industrialization began relatively early in Uruguay and ISI policies met with initial success, the small size of the domestic market placed severe constraints on an inward model of industrialization. These constraints tightened as early as the mid-1950s, when prices for agricultural exports began to fall and trade deficits mounted. As growth slowed and inflation increased, the tenuous social pacts of the ISI era began to unravel; rural producers mobilized opposition to the urban-industrial bias in macroeconomic policies, and workers resorted to increasingly militant strike tactics to counteract falling real wages and rising unemployment. With conservative factions on the ascendance in the Colorado party, a succession of Blanco and Colorado governments tried, with limited success, to stabilize the economy through austerity measures and stimulate growth with orthodox liberalization policies. They also resorted to increasingly harsh emergency powers to crack down on strike activity and, eventually, the *Tupamaro* insurgency.

Therefore, as in its Southern Cone neighbors Chile and Argentina, the ISI model began early in Uruguay but ran out of steam in the 1950s, producing a series of economic bottlenecks that hindered growth and exacerbated distributive conflicts. As Ramos (1986: 25) states, between 1945 and 1973 "per capita income in Uruguay grew by a mere 0.7 percent per year, the slowest growth rate in Latin America except for Haiti." The early exhaustion of ISI created a political gridlock and ideological polarization, with Uruguay's growing Left advocating socialist reforms and redistributive policies, and its traditional right supporting a shift toward economic orthodoxy and market liberalization. Following a declaration of internal war in 1972 and a militarization of counterinsurgency tactics against the *Tupamaros*, the stage was set for a military takeover in 1973 that was brokered by the Colorado government of Juan Bordaberry and supported by sectors of both traditional parties (González 1995: 153–154).

This military takeover inaugurated over a decade of highly repressive authoritarian rule that froze the party system in place until Uruguay returned to democratic rule in the mid-1980s. Arguably, the party system was in transition from an elitist to an LM system at the time of the 1973 democratic breakdown. This transition, however, was short-circuited by military intervention. The military took power shortly after the founding of the FA, when it had only competed in one election cycle and still presented a relatively weak third-party alternative to the two traditional parties. Certainly, the FA had yet to establish itself as a durable power contender. Given the unchallenged electoral hegemony of two 19th-century parties throughout the ISI era – and well into the critical juncture of the 1980s – Uruguay clearly belonged to the category of elitist party systems, even if the country had developed certain hybrid features by the 1970s. By the time the FA was able to seriously contest state power – in the elections of 1994 – market restructuring had been underway for two decades, the ISI era was a distant memory, and the labor movement was in decline. Indeed, the FA steadily gained strength during the latter stages of the critical juncture and the aftermath period not by riding the crest of an expanding ISI model, but by defending its last bastions – the Uruguayan welfare state and public sector – against market pressures to downsize and privatize.

These market pressures had progressively strengthened since the orthodox policy shift that began under the military regime. As in Chile and Argentina, military repression provided political cover for neoliberal technocrats to launch structural adjustment programs in the mid-1970s, prior to the onset of the region-wide debt crisis. The impetus for early reform came from short-term inflationary and balance-of-payments crises, as well as prolonged economic stagnation and chronic disequilibria. Consequently, the military and its civilian technocrats tried to stimulate export-led growth by liberalizing an economy characterized by high levels of trade protectionism, widespread wage and price controls, and an extensive system of pensions and social services. The military devalued and unified the exchange rate to promote exports, lifted some price controls and import quotas, cut wages and pension benefits, and liberalized financial markets. Despite the regime's pro-market discourse, however, essential features of neoliberal orthodoxy were left aside; tariff reductions were announced but largely unimplemented, and the regime did little to liberalize labor markets, privatize public enterprises and services, or reduce the number of public sector workers (Ramos 1986: 29–32; de Sierra 1994: 197–198).

In the short term, this partial model of neoliberal reform produced mixed economic results. Economic growth accelerated to a 4 percent annual rate between 1974 and 1980, but unemployment reached over 12 percent of the workforce, real wages fell by over 20 percent, and inflation remained stubbornly high, averaging over 60 percent annually (Ramos 1986: 26). The growth that did occur, moreover, came at the cost of sharply increased external debt at the end of the 1970s. This left the Uruguayan economy in a highly vulnerable position when the regional debt crisis caused a steep decline in international capital flows after 1982. The debt crisis erupted at a time when the government had increased interest rates to fight inflation and allowed the currency to appreciate, thus hampering export growth. The net result was a severe recession, with the economy contracting by more than 17 percent between 1982 and 1984. The economic crisis inflamed civilian opposition to the military regime, provoking a wave of strikes and mass protests in 1984. Having already lost a 1980 referendum on a proposed set of constitutional reforms to institutionalize military tutelage of the political process, the military had little choice other than to negotiate its return to the barracks.

In contrast to Chile, then (see Chapter 8), market liberalization under Uruguay's military rulers was incomplete and unsuccessful, and the military regime was not able to withstand the economic downturn of the early 1980s. Economic adjustment, therefore, remained front and center on the political agenda of the new democratic regime. Whereas the politically decisive period of market reform in Chile's critical juncture occurred under military rule, that of Uruguay would follow the democratic transition, when the party system assumed responsibility for crisis management. Uruguay's authoritarian decade was thus more of an interlude or a holding pattern than a critical juncture in party system development; the latter occurred when established parties returned to office and aligned themselves in support or opposition to deeper structural adjustment.

Programmatic Alignment and Contested Liberalism in Uruguay's Critical Juncture

If leftist social and political mobilization in the 1960s and early 1970s was nipped in the bud before it could establish an LM party system, it nevertheless launched a long-term process of party system realignment – both electoral and programmatic – that was eventually consolidated during the neoliberal critical juncture. This realignment had two central elements. First, it entailed a basic shift in the party system's organizational composition and in the electoral balance of power between the two dominant traditional parties and their emerging competitor on the left; in essence, a historic two-party system evolved into a two-and-a-half-party system (González 1995: 152), and eventually into a three-party system (with other minor competitors on the margins of the party system). Second, realignment consolidated an axis of programmatic competition between the traditional parties, which supported the general thrust of market liberalization, and the FA, which staunchly criticized the neoliberal model and defended state developmental and welfare roles. This programmatic structuring of partisan competition was in sharp contrast to historic patterns; prior to the rise of the FA, programmatic differences shaped internal factions within the major parties, but they cut across partisan lines rather than sharply differentiating Blancos from Colorados. The new alignment thus strengthened programmatic party-society linkages, at the same time that state retrenchment jeopardized the reproduction of clientelist linkages (Luna 2006).

A decade of military rule put this process of realignment on hold, but it failed to reverse it. Indeed, authoritarianism had remarkably little effect on the competitive balance of the party system. Despite severe repression against the partisan and social left, both the labor movement and the FA were revived during Uruguay's 1984–1985 democratic transition, and partisan vote shares in 1984 were strikingly similar to those in the last pre-coup election in 1971. The Colorado presidential vote share held steady at around 41 percent of the electorate, while the Blanco vote fell from 40 to 35 percent and the FA vote rose slightly from 18.3 to 21.3 percent (see Appendix Tables 13 and 14).

Crucially, the political dynamics of market reform following the democratic transition helped to consolidate the electoral and programmatic realignments that had begun in the 1960s and early 1970s. The Colorados and Blancos alternated in power for the first 20 years of the new democratic regime, with the Colorados capturing the presidency in 1984, 1994, and 1999, and the Blancos triumphing in 1989. As such, the traditional conservative parties bore political responsibility for managing the economic crisis they inherited and deepening the process of structural adjustment that had begun under authoritarian rule. Although the leaders of both traditional parties generally supported a deepening of market reforms – in particular, privatizations and social security reform – they faced significant opposition from dissident factions inside their parties, as well as from the FA and various social actors. Consequently, crisis management and market liberalization proved to be politically costly; the electoral dominance of the two traditional parties gradually eroded, while the FA attracted new constituencies and grew toward the political center. The FA moderated its initial socialist tendencies, but still channeled societal opposition to neoliberal orthodoxy.

The first new civilian president, Julio María Sanguinetti of the Colorados, cautiously introduced deregulatory policies and a modest program of privatizations, but political opposition limited the scope of his liberalization measures. The economy rebounded strongly from the debt crisis during the early years of the democratic transition – GDP growth averaged 8.5 percent in 1986 and 1987 – but it deteriorated once again during Sanguinetti's final two years in office. Economic growth ground to a halt in 1988, and a gaping fiscal deficit sent inflation soaring past the 80 percent mark in 1989 and over 100 percent in 1990 and 1991, making Uruguay the only country with an elitist party system to reach triple-digit rates of inflation during the critical juncture.

Electoral support for the Colorados declined in 1989, but voters sent a mixed message to the political establishment. At the municipal level, the FA began a string of electoral victories in the capital city of Montevideo, demonstrating the growing strength of the Left's urban base. Municipal administration allowed the FA to demonstrate its capacity for effective governance by promoting decentralization, improving service delivery, and opening channels for popular participation in budgeting and program implementation (Winn and Ferro-Clérico 1997; Schelotto 2004). It also propelled the FA's first mayor of Montevideo, Tabaré Vászquez, to national prominence as a serious presidential contender.

At the national level, however, votes shifted from the Colorados to the Blancos in 1989, giving the presidency to Blanco leader Luis Alberto Lacalle. Lacalle quickly embarked on the most ambitious attempt to deepen neoliberal reforms that Uruguay's democratic regime would see. Lacalle helped found the MERCOSUR regional trade pact, and he cut the fiscal deficit to reduce inflationary pressures. His attempts to privatize the social security system and major public enterprises encountered greater societal resistance, however, including two general strikes. Pension reforms were blocked in congress, and a major piece of legislation to privatize state-owned enterprises was overturned in a popular referendum by 70 percent of the voters. An earlier referendum, passed by 82 percent of voters, increased social security benefits by indexing payments to salaries. As such, Uruguayan citizens employed a constitutionally sanctioned mechanism of direct democracy to defend the welfare state and exercise veto power over new market reforms – a type of policy leverage that was largely denied citizens in other Latin American countries (de Sierra 1994: 199; Filgueira and Papadópulos 1997).

Market restructuring thus remained incomplete as Uruguay's critical juncture drew to a close with the 1994 national elections, when voters cast judgment on the most important democratic attempt to impose comprehensive neoliberal reforms. The Colorados captured the presidency in a very narrow three-way race with 32.3 percent of the vote, allowing former president Sanguinetti to return to executive office. This election marked the definitive rise of the FA to the status of a major power contender, with Vászquez at the head of the front's ticket. The growth of the FA from 21.2 percent of the vote in 1989 to 30.6 percent in 1994 occurred primarily at the expense of the incumbent Blancos, producing a gradual realignment in the electoral balance of power that would continue – and deepen – in the aftermath period. It also deprived Sanguinetti's Colorado party of a congressional majority, inducing the Colorados and Blancos to forge a conservative legislative coalition in support of the market model.

Indeed, Uruguay's three-party system was increasingly transformed into a two-block alignment that was structured by a programmatic cleavage between the two traditional conservative parties and their rising leftist rival. Uruguay's aligning critical juncture, with market reforms adopted by conservative parties and consistently opposed by an institutionalized party of the left, thus produced an outcome of contested liberalism as the institutional baseline for the aftermath period. Vote shifts during the critical juncture (and its aftermath) occurred between the Blancos and Colorados and, in a cumulative fashion, from these parties to the strengthening FA. Aggregate volatility remained quite low by regional standards, however, averaging slightly over 11 percent on the index of volatility for both presidential and legislative elections in the 1980s and 1990s.

The key contrast to Honduras, Costa Rica, and Ecuador – which experienced neutral or programmatically de-aligning critical junctures – was the presence of an institutionalized party of the Left in consistent opposition to market reforms that were led by conservative actors. Societal resistance to market liberalization in Uruguay thus had an institutionalized outlet of expression that was lacking in the other three cases, and the impressive growth of the FA during the latter stages of the critical juncture clearly reflected its effectiveness at channeling this societal resistance. Labor unions, pensioners, and other social groups – often with political ties to the FA – organized campaigns to gather petitions and vote in the referendums against privatization, providing ample opportunities for the FA to appeal to new constituencies. At the same time, the partial state retrenchment that occurred under Uruguay's neoliberal model eroded the clientelist linkages that had traditionally bound the urban and rural poor to the Blancos and Colorados, making it possible for the FA to penetrate social sectors where it was previously weak (Lanzaro 2004a: 57–65; Luna 2006). Consequently, the FA expanded its vote in rural areas and low-income sectors in the 1990s, complementing its traditional multi-class but predominantly urban strongholds among organized labor, younger voters, and the better-educated middle class. In so doing, the FA (which included elements of the old *Tupamaros* revolutionary movement) moderated its discourse and occupied the center-left programmatic space, targeting a broad range of interests with diverse claims related to employment, wages, and social benefits.

Ultimately, then, Uruguay's party system, like those of Honduras and Costa Rica, was highly stable electorally during the critical juncture. Unlike those others, however, it was programmatically aligned by the process of market reform, and it entered the aftermath period with a competitive dynamic of contested liberalism that reproduced itself over time. Reactive sequences in the aftermath period did not alter the institutional baseline of contested liberalism, as they did with neoliberal convergence; instead, they reinforced it, as the FA continued to strengthen in the aftermath period, and Uruguay turned to the Left by means of a highly institutionalized alternation in power. The divergent fate of these party systems in the post-adjustment era is explained in Chapter 9; a summary of their respective critical junctures is provided in Table 7.1.

TABLE 7.1. *Overview of Critical Junctures in Countries with Elitist Party Systems*

	Onset of Crisis	Initial Policy Response	Decisive Stage of Market Reform	Political Response and Effects	End of the Critical Juncture
Honduras	1982	Policy continuity 1982–1985; moderate reforms 1985–1990	1991–1993: reforms of public sector, taxation, trade, finance, agriculture, foreign exchange and investment	Moderate strike wave; alternation in office of two leading parties, but ratify policy shift in electoral competition; party system adaptation	1993 election; outcome of neoliberal convergence by means of a neutral critical juncture
Costa Rica	1981–1982	Austerity and moderate reforms 1982–1984	1984–1990: major reforms in fiscal policy, foreign trade, taxation, finance, price deregulation	Moderate level of social protest; alternation in office of two leading parties, but ratify policy shift in electoral competition; party system adaptation	1990 election; outcome of neoliberal convergence by means of a de-aligning critical juncture
Ecuador	1982	Austerity 1982–1984; erratic market reforms 1984–1988	1988–1995: major reforms to liberalize financial markets, foreign trade and investment, foreign exchange, deregulate prices and labor markets, privatizations	Moderate strike wave, then intensifying indigenous-led social protest after 1990; widespread anti-incumbent voting, high levels of electoral volatility; social resistance blocks some reform measures	1997 popular uprising vs. Bucaram establishes social veto against deeper reform; outcome of neoliberal convergence by means of a de-aligning critical juncture
Uruguay	1982	Continue incomplete neoliberal model of military regime 1982–1985; moderate market reforms under new democratic regime 1985–1989	1990–1994: major reforms of foreign trade, fiscal policy, attempts at privatizations and social security reform	Social resistance channeled into popular referendum campaigns; alternation in office of two traditional conservative parties, but electoral realignment due to strengthening of leftist opposition	1994 election; outcome of contested liberalism by means of an aligning critical juncture

CONCLUSION

Although elitist party systems were, on average, more stable during the transition from ISI to neoliberalism than LM party systems, this chapter has demonstrated the range of variation that existed within the elitist category. Whereas party systems in Honduras, Costa Rica, and Uruguay were electorally stable during the critical juncture, that of Ecuador was extremely volatile. This variation was undoubtedly related to the degree of institutionalization of antecedent, ISI-era party systems, and it was not strictly determined by the *type* of critical juncture each country experienced. Indeed, countries with programmatically neutral (Honduras), aligning (Uruguay), and de-aligning (Costa Rica) critical junctures remained electorally stable throughout the 1980s and 1990s. Elitist party systems that were reasonably well-established before the critical juncture, therefore, were generally able to weather the storm with minimal disruptions in the short term, no matter what political alignments undergirded their process of market reform.

These alignments, however, varied widely in their capacity to articulate and channel societal resistance to the neoliberal model – and, consequently, to weather the reactive sequences of the aftermath period. As Chapter 9 shows, different institutional outcomes generated distinct types of reactive sequences, some of which reinforced and reproduced existing competitive alignments, and others which undermined or transformed them, producing longer-term institutional legacies that diverged sharply from the outcomes of the critical juncture itself.

Before analyzing these reactive sequences in the aftermath period, however, it is necessary to explore neoliberal critical junctures in countries with LM party systems. In these countries, the transition from ISI to neoliberalism was typically marked by much deeper economic crises and higher levels of political disruption, including electoral volatility and major realignments or systemic decomposition. In contrast to the elitist cases analyzed above – where relative stability during the critical juncture was at least partially endogenous to antecedent levels of party system institutionalization during the ISI era – the fate of LM party systems during the critical juncture was more independent of antecedent institutional development, and thus more contingent on the political dynamics of crisis management and reform during the critical juncture itself.

8

Critical Junctures in Labor-Mobilizing Party Systems

In contrast to elitist party systems, LM systems were partially or wholly reconfigured by labor mobilization and the rise of mass politics in the middle of the 20th century. Deeply embedded in the state-centric logic of ISI, these party systems encountered fierce distributive conflicts and highly disruptive political upheavals as the ISI model entered into demise in the 1970s and 1980s. At a minimum, all of the LM party systems experienced major electoral realignments during the transition to neoliberalism; none, in other words, rode out the critical juncture with the type of party system continuity and adaptation seen in the Honduran and Costa Rican cases in Chapter 7. Most LM party systems, in fact, witnessed the rise of major new partisan contenders, while two of them – Peru and Venezuela – experienced party system decomposition.

Nevertheless, some LM party systems were realigned or reconfigured during the critical juncture in ways that were conducive to institutional stability in the aftermath period, whereas others were prone to destabilizing reactive sequences and ongoing institutional change. This chapter attempts to explain such variation through a comparative analysis of four LM cases: Argentina, Brazil, Chile, and Venezuela. The cases were selected to offer a wide range of variation on the key outcomes of interest – namely, the stability of party systems and their patterns of change over time, both during the critical juncture and in the aftermath period. The set of cases thus includes the most electorally stable LM party system (Chile), as well as a case where the party system decomposed by the end of the critical juncture (Venezuela). These cases also vary on a number of potential explanatory variables of interest, including the level of institutionalization of antecedent party systems, the gravity of economic crises during the critical juncture (in particular, the existence of hyperinflationary crises), and the political identity of leading market reformers and their opponents.

These cases demonstrate that the relative stability of party systems in recent decades is not simply an endogenous, path-dependent legacy of historical patterns of institutional development. Party systems that appeared institution-alized during the ISI era sometimes destabilized (Argentina) or decomposed (Venezuela) during the critical juncture or its aftermath. The obverse can also be found, where a traditionally inchoate party system progressively institution-alized during the same period (i.e., Brazil). Likewise, the cases demonstrate that electoral stability and volatility are not simple functions of economic performance or crises, nor of systemic properties such as the fragmentation and ideological polarization of party systems. Although these factors may play a role in particular cases, they do not clearly differentiate stable from unstable party systems in contemporary Latin America. Instead, they cut across the level of stability, with both stable and unstable party systems located at widely varying levels of these other indicators.

What does clearly differentiate stable from unstable party systems is the programmatic alignment or de-alignment of political actors during the process of market liberalization. Although the impact of programmatic alignments was not always apparent during the critical juncture itself, when the organized popular constituencies of LM party systems were disarticulated and demobi-lized, such alignments weighed heavily on competitive dynamics in the aftermath period as societal resistance politicized the neoliberal model. The reactive sequences of the aftermath period are analyzed in Chapter 9; this chapter compares and contrasts the critical junctures that spawned and conditioned them. It starts with a short overview of historical patterns of party system development in the four cases, explaining how oligarchic party systems gave way to LM party systems following the rise of mass politics, and how LM systems were embedded in the state-centric logic of ISI. It then examines how LM party systems managed the politics of crisis and reform during the transition from ISI to market liberalism. It concludes by explaining how the political dynamics of support and opposition to market reform either aligned or de-aligned party systems programmatically, producing institutional outcomes with greater or lesser vulnerability to destabilizing reactive sequences in the aftermath period.

FROM OLIGARCHIC RULE TO MASS POLITICS

Although Argentina, Brazil, Chile, and Venezuela all developed LM party systems in the 20th century, they arrived there along very different routes, and the oligarchic party systems that they displaced varied dramatically. Of the four cases, Chile possessed by far the strongest and most competitive oligarchic party system. Although suffrage rights were highly restricted – slightly over one percent of the population voted in elections in the early 1870s (Scully 1995: 104) – partisan competition had become institutionalized in Chile by the late 1850s, with a competitive axis grounded in a clerical-anticlerical cleavage between Conservatives and Liberals. An even more anticlerical Radical Party split off from the Liberals in 1861 (Remmer 1984; Scully 1992). In a pattern that was common in Europe but unusual in the Latin American experience, Chile's oligarchic party system gradually added new party organizations with distinctive social and ideological appeals as economic modernization and suffrage reforms transformed the political landscape. The Radical Party developed into the primary representative of emerging middle sectors, while the growth of a mining and industrial proletariat helped spawn labor-mobilizing Communist and Socialist parties in 1922 and 1933, respectively.[1] Chile's LM party system was in place, therefore, by the 1930s, with the Liberals and Conservatives on the right, the Radical Party in the center, and the Socialists and Communists on the left – Chile's famous "three-thirds" alignment.

Venezuela stood at the opposite end of the spectrum of party system development. The wars of independence in Venezuela bequeathed a legacy of civil strife, authoritarianism, and political fragmentation, weakening the oligarchy and blocking the establishment of central state authority. Nineteenth-century "parties" were thus regionally based political–military factions dominated by local *caudillos*. As Kornblith and Levine state, these parties were "little more than armed bands" that "left no trace at all" in the development of Venezuela's modern party system (1995: 39, 40). Indeed, these proto-parties were swept away in the early 20th century by the military dictatorship of Juan Vicente Gómez, who seized power in 1908 and repressed all forms of social and political mobilization. A national party system only began to form following the death of Gómez in 1935, which led to a groundswell of labor, student, and political mobilization that culminated in the founding of *Acción Democrática* (AD) in 1941. In effect, Venezuela's modern party system was born labor-mobilizing, in contrast to that of Chile, which evolved from oligarchic to labor-mobilizing through a gradual process of accretion.

Party systems during the oligarchic era in Argentina and Brazil lay between these polar extremes. In contrast to Venezuela, the powerful agrarian oligarchy in Argentina overcame its early post-independence period of regional fragmentation and *cuadillismo* to create a hegemonic party, the *Partido Autonomista Nacional* (PAN), in the latter half of the 19th century (Gibson 1996: 46–47). The PAN relied on coercion, fraud, and suffrage restrictions on immigrant workers to dominate the electoral arena from 1880 to 1909, but it did not institutionalize partisan competition during the oligarchic era as did the traditional parties in Chile. Moreover, the PAN did not survive the transition to mass politics, as did its oligarchic counterparts in Chile. A regional cleavage between provincial and coastal elites prevented oligarchic interests from organizing effectively at the national level, and the PAN splintered "into a multitude of conservative provincial parties beholden to local landowners and allied professional and commercial groups" (McGuire 1995: 204). The electoral dominance of oligarchic parties was eroded by suffrage reforms in 1912 that reduced electoral fraud,

---

[1] The Workers' Socialist Party was founded by a small group of miners and shoemakers in 1912, then changed its name to the Chilean Communist Party in 1922.

along with the absence of a large "sedentary" peasantry to support conservative parties out of deference to landlord patrons (McGuire 1995: 203–206; Gibson 1996). With the rise of mass politics, then, oligarchic parties were eclipsed first by the middle-class-dominated *Unión Cívica Radical* (UCR) from 1916 to 1930, and then by the labor-mobilizing populism of Juan Perón after the mid-1940s.

Finally, in Brazil, oligarchic interests were politically dominant but very poorly organized in the partisan sphere prior to the onset of mass politics. Liberal and Conservative parties were active in parliament under the post-independence monarchy, but they were highly dependent on local bosses with fluid partisan loyalties (Graham 1990). With the end of the monarchy, Brazil's "Old Republic" (1889–1930) "became the quientessence of oligarchical politics" with "untethered rule by local political bosses" (Mainwaring 1999a: 69), but partisan organization was radically decentralized and underdeveloped. A dominant oligarchic machine existed in each of the major states, linking governors to local notables while competing to forge alliances and control the national government. An alliance between the coffee oligarchy of São Paulo and the cattle barons of Minas Gerais effectively dominated the politics of the republic. As Mainwaring (1999a: 67, 69) states, "there was nothing resembling free and fair political competition until the 1930's," contributing to "a complete absence of national parties."

Of the four countries, then, only Chile possessed a nationally organized oligarchic party (or, in the Chilean case, parties) to defend elite interests in the electoral arena as economic modernization transformed the social landscape and suffrage reforms enfranchised the working and middle classes. Economic and political changes by the early decades of the 20th century made it impossible to reproduce exclusive oligarchic regimes by electoral means: either exclusion had to be enforced through political coercion and authoritarianism – the "conservative reactions" analyzed by Collier and Collier (1991) – or popular sectors had to be incorporated into the political process. In none of these LM cases, however, were new popular subjects incorporated by traditional oligarchic parties, as they were in several of their elitist counterparts like Uruguay and Colombia. Instead, party systems were at least partially reconstituted by the rise of new LM parties with strong ties to organized labor and core electoral constituencies in urban working, middle-class, and popular sectors. Likewise, in none of these countries did labor incorporation occur without a breakdown in democratic rule and some type of authoritarian interlude; oligarchic political orders were not able to make a smooth transition to competitive mass politics in contexts of significant lower-class political mobilization.

LABOR-MOBILIZING PARTY SYSTEMS AND STATE-CENTRIC DEVELOPMENT

Although the four countries varied in their pace of industrialization, all developed vibrant labor movements by the early decades of the 20th century, along

with a variety of populist and leftist parties or movements that promoted unionization and competed for influence in the working class. Likewise, all eventually
embraced vigorous state-led development models, combining ISI policies with a
variety of social welfare and redistributive measures.

In three of the four countries, populist leaders and parties were dominant
actors in the process of labor mobilization and political incorporation. Only in
Chile did the Marxist left consistently take the lead, although it might have
elsewhere (Brazil in particular) in the absence of political repression. Chile's
northern nitrate and copper mining camps were breeding grounds of a militant
labor subculture in the early 20th century, with anarcho-syndicalist and Marxist
currents that diffused to urban-industrial centers and nurtured the rise of the
Workers' Socialist Party (POS), renamed the Chilean Communist Party (PCCh)
in 1922 (DeShazo 1983; Bergquist 1986). By 1920 the POS was the dominant
force in Chile's first national labor federation, and an estimated 10–15 percent of
the workforce was unionized, an unusually high percentage for this period in
Latin America (Faúndez 1988: 22). The POS/PCCh entered the electoral arena in
the early 1920s, but the rise of mass politics proved destabilizing for Chile's
oligarchic form of democracy; five military coups occurred between 1924 and
1932, and the PCCh and labor unions were repressed under authoritarian rule
from 1927 to 1931.

Democracy was restored in 1932, however, and Chile's left-labor bloc
resumed its political development. The PCCh acquired a stronger working-
class base than any other Communist Party in the Americas, despite having to
compete with a Socialist Party (PSCh) that also mobilized substantial labor
support. The PSCh was founded in 1933, blending Marxist and populist
influences in a nationalist alternative of the Left (Drake 1978), and it joined
with PCCh and Radical Party (PR) activists to found a new national labor
confederation in 1936. These three parties also formed a "Popular Front"
coalition that elected three consecutive PR presidents in 1938, 1942, and
1946. The Popular Front governments initiated an aggressive program of
state-led industrialization, while union membership increased more than
five-fold between 1932 and 1952 (Roberts 1998: 90). By 1941 the PCCh and
PSCh combined for a third of the vote in congressional elections, creating a
Marxist electoral bloc without parallel in the Americas.

Although the Popular Front dissolved and the PCCh was banned and
repressed for a decade in response to Cold War pressures after World War II,
the basic configuration of Chile's ISI-era party system remained intact. Unique in
Latin America, the "three thirds" alignment was structured by the competition
between three distinct ideological tendencies, each represented by two major
party organizations that jointly mobilized around a third of the electorate. In
addition to the PCCh and PSCh on the left, the right continued to be represented
by the historic Liberal and Conservative parties, while the center was occupied
by the PR and, after the late 1950s, the Christian Democratic Party (PDC).
Centrist parties could build a political majority by forging alliances with the

either the left or the right, or they could run their own ticket in highly competitive and unpredictable three-way races. The party system managed a developmentalist state that was among the most active and interventionist in Latin America (Stallings 1978), with industrial promotion policies that included trade protectionism and public investments through the State Development Corporation (CORFO), which provided loans to private businesses and founded numerous industries through joint public–private ventures.

In the other LM cases, the Marxist left was eclipsed by populist rivals in the mobilization and political incorporation of the working class. Labor shortages and a relatively early process of industrialization gave Argentina the strongest union movement in Latin America in the early 20th century, but linkages to parties were fragile, in part because large numbers of immigrant workers lacked voting rights. Anarchists and syndicalists wielded significant influence in the labor movement but did little to build party organizations. The UCR, meanwhile, made overtures to labor after capturing the presidency in 1916, but the centrist party ultimately failed to consolidate an alliance when a 1919 strike wave provoked a violent conservative backlash (Bergquist 1986: 101–138; Godio, Palomino, and Wachendorfer 1988). Union membership thus declined in the early 1920s even before the Great Depression undercut Argentina's export-based economy and its long tradition of civilian government. A 1930 military coup against the UCR ushered in 13 years of conservative military-oligarchic rule, which imposed new repressive measures against a labor movement that was fractured between competing syndicalist, socialist, and communist tendencies.

The post-1930 oligarchic restoration deepened the accumulation of pent-up demands that exploded after Perón and other dissident army officers led a new military coup in 1943. Influenced by the corporatist principles of European fascism, Perón used his post as the minister of labor to mobilize a personal base of support by encouraging union organizing, establishing a minimum wage, expanding social security, and backing labor in collective bargaining disputes. He also used the power of state recognition to marginalize autonomous and leftist-led unions and create "parallel" unions that owed him allegiance. Socialist and communist currents in the labor movement were thus overwhelmed by the rise of Peronism, which captured control of the central labor confederation (the *Confederación General del Trabajo*, or CGT) and increased union membership nearly five-fold between 1941 and 1954 (Collier and Collier 1991: 337–341).

This popular mobilization proved threatening to other members of the military regime, who had Perón arrested in 1945, until mass protests organized by the CGT secured his release. Perón and loyal union leaders then created the Labor Party in October 1945, which marked the effective beginning of Argentina's LM party system. The Labor Party (PL) and allied groups elected Perón to the presidency in 1946, and although Perón subsequently dissolved the PL, some type of labor-mobilizing Peronist party became a permanent fixture in

Argentine politics (McGuire 1997). Indeed, Peronism was electorally dominant; in the absence of a nationally organized conservative party (Gibson 1996), the UCR became the de facto defender of elite interests and the multi-class meeting ground for all anti-Peronist groups, but the factionalized UCR could not match the Peronists' mobilizational capacity from below. Consequently, elite opposition to Perón turned repeatedly to military intervention to negate Peronism's electoral hegemony, with the military coup that sent Perón into exile in 1955 merely the first of many efforts to use authoritarian measures to exclude the populist movement from power (see O'Donnell 1973: 167–201). Even during Perón's 18-year exile, however, his legacy endured in Latin America's most powerful labor movement and a highly statist economic model. Perón had greatly accelerated the ISI policies that began tentatively during the Great Depression, with the state subsidizing and protecting domestic industries by hiking tariffs, establishing public enterprises in a broad range of utilities and basic industries, awarding lucrative state contracts, and providing industrialists with subsidized foreign exchange for imported capital goods. State spending increased 87 percent between 1944 and 1950, while public sector employment expanded 144 percent between 1943 and 1952 (Teichman 2001: 33).

In Venezuela as well, the onset of mass politics spawned competition between a Communist Party and a more center-left, national populist alternative. Although authoritarianism and delayed industrialization slowed the development of the labor movement, labor mobilization began in earnest when oil displaced coffee as the primary export commodity in the 1920s, attracting workers from all over Venezuela to the oil camps in the Maracaibo Basin (Bergquist 1986: 217–226). Although the repressive tactics of the Gómez dictatorship kept a lid on popular mobilization, the dictator's death in 1935 unleashed a torrent of popular protest and a wave of strike activities in the oil sector. As Communist (PCV) and social democratic activists competed for influence in the nascent labor movement – the latter would found the AD in 1941 – Gómez's military successors responded with an erratic sequence of reformist and repressive measures. The AD capitalized on selective repression of PCV organizations to consolidate its leadership of labor and peasant unions in the early 1940s, permanently marginalizing the PCV from popular constituencies (Bergquist 1986: 251; Collier and Collier 1991: 253). Shortly thereafter, the AD joined a military conspiracy that gave the party a leading role in a governing *junta* for a three-year period (1945–1948) known as the *trienio*.

The *trienio* marked "the definitive introduction of mass politics into national life" (Kornblith and Levine 1995: 42), and it established the basic contours of Venezuela's LM party system. In 1946 alone, over 500 new unions were recognized by the AD government, more than triple the number that had existed previously (Collier and Collier 1991: 265). The AD founded a new petroleum workers' union and a national labor confederation, the Confederation of Venezuelan Workers (CTV), which incorporated virtually all of Venezuela's organized workers and peasants. The government supported workers' wage and benefits demands in collective bargaining and promised land reform for its peasant supporters, overseeing a nine-fold increase in the number of peasant unions (Powell 1971: 79). AD's social reforms and popular mobilization, however, triggered a backlash from conservative sectors of the military, the Catholic Church, and the business community. A new party of Christina Democratic inspiration known as COPEI was formed in 1946, giving conservative elites a serious partisan vehicle to represent their interests for the first time in Venezuelan history.

More ominously, the conservative backlash triggered a new military coup in 1948 that unleashed a wave of repression, rolled back social reforms, and drove AD underground for ten years. Nevertheless, the partisan alignment forged in the 1940s proved to be highly durable, as AD and COPEI set aside their differences to join other opposition forces in overthrowing the Pérez Jiménez dictatorship in 1958. A negotiated pact between the two parties and other actors laid the foundations for a new democratic regime (Karl 1987), which AD and COPEI would dominate for the next forty years. Following the intense ideological polarization of the *trienio*, the two parties moved toward the center and forged a broad consensus for a state-led model of development that used ample oil revenues to moderate distributive conflicts.

Although the ISI model had been slower to consolidate political support in Venezuela than in Chile and Argentina (Echeverría 1995), the AD government in the 1940s used a new oil tax to provide fiscal revenues for industrial promotion policies. The AD founded the Venezuelan Development Corporation (CPV) and formed a national petroleum company and other state enterprises (Karl 1997: 84–96). Following the democratic transition in 1958, ISI "became the axis of the model of growth" (Bitar and Meíias 1995: 106), one which created "a permanent predominance of the public sector matched in Latin America only by socialist Cuba" (Karl 1997: 90). Both AD and COPEI subscribed to this development model as they alternated in office, shared the spoils of state patronage, and made massive investments in steel, aluminum, hydroelectric, and petrochemical industries to diversify the economy. By the early 1980s public enterprises accounted for 29.4 percent of GDP, and the state employed 22.5 percent of the workforce (Crisp 2000: 122). Meanwhile, the private sector benefitted from low taxes, subsidized credits, and a system of import licensing that offered protection as high as 940 percent despite the maintenance of low tariff levels (Naím 1993: 41). Some 362 bureaucratic agencies and 303 consultative commissions helped govern the economy (Crisp 2000: 97–98, 123), facilitating semi-corporatist participation by business and labor in the policymaking process.

Finally, in Brazil, the establishment of an LM party was more heavily dependent on state initiative than oppositional mobilization. In line with regional patterns, worker militancy intensified in major urban centers in the early 20th century, and a strike wave rocked the oligarchic establishment after

World War I. After the foundation of the Brazilian Communist Party (PCB) in 1922, anarchist influence among unions gave way to communist leadership, making the PCB "the dominant force in the labor movement" by 1930 (Collier and Collier 1991: 71). Repeated cycles of proscription and repression, however, combined with state-led efforts to incorporate labor from above, prevented the PCB from consolidating its leadership and developing a stable mass base of electoral support like the Communist Party in Chile.

Indeed, organized labor was brought under state control following the arrival to power of Getulio Vargas in 1930. Vargas put an end to the decentralized oligarchic rule of Brazil's First Republic; he centralized state power, adopted social welfare measures, and passed a labor law that granted legal recognition to unions within an elaborate set of state corporatist institutions (Schmitter 1971). Vargas' corporatist model gave the state control over union finances, leadership selection, and social and economic activities, while curtailing collective bargaining, strikes, and political activities. Unions were purged of Communist leaders or denied legal recognition, and the labor confederation founded by the PCB was outlawed. The PCB responded by leading an armed revolt in 1935, but this only provided a pretext for harsher authoritarian measures. With military support, Vargas closed congress in a 1937 coup and created a fascist-inspired *Estado Novo* ("New State") that included "the most full-blown system of corporatism" in Latin America (Collier and Collier 1991: 186; see also Weinstein 1996: 58–62).

Vargas changed course once again in 1943, however, when the impending Allied victory in World War II encouraged him to start a process of democratization and turn in a populist direction to build mass support. Corporatist controls over labor unions were relaxed, the PCB was re-legalized, and Vargas bestowed new benefits on workers in an effort to build a state–labor alliance. Shortly before being overthrown in a 1945 military coup, Vargas also founded two political parties that would be major players in Brazil's first period of mass democratic politics from 1945 to 1964. The Social Democratic Party (PSD) was formed by state governors appointed by Vargas, who built a strong base of rural support around local party machines with centrist or conservative political orientations. Vargas also used his Ministry of Labor to build a new working-class party, the Brazilian Labor Party (PTB), which became the most important partisan expression of the labor movement and the political left following yet another proscription of the PCB as the Cold War got underway in 1947. Anti-Vargas conservatives also founded a new party of the Right in 1945, the National Democratic Union (UDN), giving the country three major party organizations that covered a broad range of the ideological spectrum during this initial period of experimentation with mass democratic competition (Mainwaring 1999a: 70–71).

If Vargas laid the foundations for Brazil's ISI-era party system, he also gave a jump-start to state-led industrialization. Vargas intervened aggressively during the Great Depression: the state purchased coffee to support prices when export markets collapsed, created marketing boards for agricultural exports, provided debt relief to local producers, and prohibited textile and machinery imports in order to save foreign exchange and stimulate domestic industry (Baer 1989: 36–37; Weinstein 1996: 59). With staunch support from the military and many industrialists, Vargas proceeded to stimulate private industry by providing tax credits, subsidized loans, import quotas, and exchange controls, and the state invested heavily in infrastructure projects and new public or mixed public–private enterprises in steel, automobile, railroad, mining, and oil industries (Skidmore 1967: 41–47). State-led development continued in the 1950s with the creation of a national development bank to channel investments toward infrastructure projects and favored industries, along with a multiple exchange-rate system to prioritize imports of raw materials and equipment that were essential for industrialization. The government of Juscelino Kubitscheck (1956–1961) made a major push to deepen ISI to the capital goods sector, promising "fifty years of progress in five" (Skidmore 1967: 164). The state raised tariffs and encouraged foreign investment in manufacturing activities behind tariff walls, adopted ambitious targets for infrastructure and industrial development, and built a new capital city in Brasilia to promote development in the country's vast interior. Economic growth averaged 7 percent a year, while industrial production increased by 80 percent between 1955 and 1961.

To summarize, the transition from oligarchic to mass politics led to polarization and upheaval in all four countries, including democratic breakdowns and military repression of popular movements. Given the strength of mobilization from below, however, conservative forces were unable to exclude labor and popular sectors from the political arena through long-term authoritarian solutions (as in countries like El Salvador and Guatemala), and neither were they able to incorporate them politically through traditional oligarchic parties (as in Colombia and Uruguay). In all four countries, then, party systems were reconfigured in the mid-20th century by the rise of a new, mass-based, labor-mobilizing populist or leftist party (or parties, in the Chilean case). In each case, the cleavage between the LM party and its centrist or conservative rivals became a central fault line in the political order. In Venezuela and Argentina, this cleavage congealed into party systems with two major power contenders; in Brazil and Chile, major centrist parties occupied the space between the left and right partisan poles. Only in Chile did traditional oligarchic parties remain dominant on the right, and only in Chile and Argentina did middle-class parties that predated the onset of mass politics remain significant players. In Brazil and Venezuela, party systems were thoroughly reconstituted following the onset of mass politics.

These LM party systems were embedded in statist development models that – in the short-run, at least – generated rapid growth and industrialization after the crisis of the 1930s. The state-centric matrix, however, was riven by internal political and economic contradictions that eventually undermined economic performance and frayed the tenuous multi-class coalitions undergirding ISI policies. In most cases (excepting Venezuela), these contradictions destabilized democratic regimes and produced military interventions in the 1960s and 1970s that helped set the stage for neoliberal critical junctures. These military interventions, and the political crises that spawned them, shaped the character of the political actors and the balance of power among them during the process of market liberalization. As such, they weighed heavily on the reform alignments that differentiated national experiences during the critical juncture.

PRELUDE TO CRITICAL JUNCTURES: POPULAR MOBILIZATION, DEMOBILIZATION, AND MILITARY RULE

In all four LM cases analyzed here, critical junctures were preceded by experiments with leftist or populist governments in the 1960s or 1970s. These experiments deepened state interventionism and, with the partial exception of Venezuela, mobilized popular sectors behind redistributive platforms that challenged elite interests. Neoliberal critical junctures, therefore, entailed much more than a shift toward economic orthodoxy; they had a political correlate as well, involving the subordination, if not outright exclusion and repression, of labor and popular sectors who were wedded to ISI. This subordination helped to shield technocratic reformers from societal pressures, whether the regime was authoritarian or democratic. It also moderated demands for higher wages and consumption, thus alleviating inflationary pressures. The conservative reactions that demobilized popular alternatives, however, varied in their timing relative to the adoption of neoliberal reforms (Schamis 1991); dismantling the state-centric matrix had both political and economic dimensions, but they did not always temporally coincide.

Brazil, Argentina, and Chile were – along with Uruguay – the classic cases of "bureaucratic-authoritarianism" (BA) in the 1960s and 1970s, whereby professionalized militaries came into power with long-term projects to modernize economies and politically deactivate the party–labor blocs of the ISI era (Stepan 1971; O'Donnell 1973). Despite their similarities, BA regimes varied in their approaches to market liberalization and, therefore, in their relationships to neoliberal critical junctures. Brazil's military regime put an end to populist redistributive policies but continued the country's statist development model, leaving market liberalization on the agenda of its civilian successors in the aftermath to the early 1980s debt crisis. Argentina's first BA regime in the 1960s also continued along a statist trajectory, while its second – like Uruguay in the 1970s – imposed partial neoliberal reforms but failed to achieve economic stabilization. As in Brazil, it left the burdens of structural adjustment to fall on civilian successors. In both countries, therefore, party systems had to manage the politics of economic crisis – including hyperinflation – and market reform. As such, their critical junctures effectively began with their respective democratic transitions in 1983 (Argentina) and 1985 (Brazil), after the debt crisis had weakened incumbent military rulers (Remmer 1992–1993).

In Chile, on the other hand, the military regime imposed and consolidated comprehensive market reforms, while absorbing the political costs of the early 1980s financial crisis. Alone in the region, Chile's party system was insulated from the direct political costs of both crisis management and structural adjustment in the 1980s. Since the decisive period of market liberalization occurred under military rule, the onset of Chile's critical juncture must be dated earlier, to the 1973 military coup that ended Allende's socialist experiment and ushered Pinochet into power.

In these three countries, the party systems that managed – or, in the Chilean case, inherited – market liberalization had all been subjected to extended periods of military repression, political exclusion, and social demobilization. As party systems reemerged from military rule during the democratic transitions of the 1980s, however, they varied dramatically in their levels of continuity with the pre-authoritarian, LM party systems of the ISI era. Military rule essentially froze Argentina's party system in place, while it largely reconstituted Brazil's party system and partially reconstituted and electorally realigned that of Chile. Most important for our purposes, the political dynamics of market liberalization in the three countries created different types of critical junctures: bait-and-switch reforms were programmatically de-aligning in Argentina (as well as Venezuela), whereas conservative-led reforms opposed by major leftist parties were programmatically aligning in Brazil and Chile. Chile's party system, therefore, was relatively stable throughout the new democratic period, while those in Argentina and Brazil evolved in opposite directions: Argentina's established party system was relatively stable during the critical juncture but prone to disruptive reactive sequences in the aftermath period, whereas Brazil's reconstituted party system was volatile during the critical juncture but increasingly stable and institutionalized in the aftermath period. Venezuela's highly institutionalized party system progressively decomposed over the latter part of the critical juncture.

These different types of critical junctures depended on the programmatic alignment of actors who made strategic choices to adopt (or oppose) structural adjustment policies, but such alignments were conditioned by military regimes (except in Venezuela) and their political legacies – in particular, the balance of power they left behind between elite and popular sociopolitical blocs. That is self-evident in the Chilean case, where the military regime itself was strong enough to impose and consolidate Latin America's most far-reaching market revolution over the bitter opposition of the region's most powerful partisan Left. The Brazilian case was less obvious, but perhaps more instructive; the military did not carry out a market revolution, but it left behind a conservative-dominated political order (Power 2000) that would eventually liberalize the economy as the partisan left was re-building. Both of these military regimes were, in their own terms, relatively "successful"; although they failed to consolidate permanent forms of authoritarian rule, they modernized economies, strengthened business elites and their conservative political allies, controlled the terms and pace of regime transitions, imposed institutional rules to safeguard conservative influence, and reversed (at least temporarily) the political ascendance of popular and leftist movements. If Chile's military regime imposed a conservative, programmatically aligning critical juncture, Brazil's laid the foundations for one.

The Argentine case was strikingly different, as the authoritarian regime crumbled in response to military defeat in the Malvinas War and the economic debacle of the early 1980s. Authoritarian rule did not leave behind a major conservative party to advance the military's aborted neoliberal project (Gibson 1996), and for all its brutal repression, the military failed to suppress the mobilizational capacity of a Peronist labor movement that wielded an effective social veto against any process of structural adjustment attempted by non-Peronist parties. Given this configuration of organizational power and political resources in Argentina's new democratic order, conservative, anti-Peronist forces were not well-positioned to lead a process of market liberalization; indeed, Peronism had a comparative advantage in dismantling the state-centric matrix it had earlier built (Murillo 2000), enhancing the probability of a programmatically de-aligning process of market reform.

Brazil

The rise of BA regimes was a conservative reaction to the strengthening of LM parties and their affiliated popular movements in the ideologically polarized context of post-Cuban Revolution Latin America. The first BA regime put an end to Brazil's post-war democratic experiment in 1964, shortly after conservatives lost control of governing institutions to ascendant populist and leftist forces arrayed behind President João Goulart of the PTB, a former Minister of Labor who had been a protégé of Vargas. For most of the 1946–1964 democratic period, the more conservative of Vargas' two parties, the PSD, was Brazil's largest party, followed by the conservative and anti-Vargas UDN. The two parties controlled nearly 80 percent of the seats in the lower house of congress at the beginning of the democratic period, while the PSD elected presidents in 1945 and 1955 and a UDN-led coalition won in 1960 (Vargas himself captured the presidency on a PTB-led ticket in 1950, only to commit suicide before the end of his term). Both conservative parties lost vote shares over the course of the democratic period, however, while the left-leaning PTB progressively strengthened. By 1962 the PTB had overtaken the UDN in both houses of congress, and by the following year defections from other parties left the PTB with the largest bloc of seats in the lower house (Power 2000: 54). The shifting balance of power was accentuated by the ascendance of then-Vice President Goulart to the presidency in 1961 after the abrupt resignation of the isolated incumbent Jânio Quadros. Initially stripped of full presidential powers by means of a constitutional amendment that was passed by congress to assuage conservative and military fears, Goulart won a 1963 plebiscite to restore executive authority, and proceeded to align himself with the more leftist, pro-labor wing of the PTB (Mainwaring 1999a: 82).

Indeed, by the early 1960s organized labor, while politically divided, had become increasingly independent of state corporatist controls. Labor activists affiliated with the Communist Party and the left wing of the PTB took the lead in the formation of a new national labor confederation, which generally supported Goulart but pushed his administration even further to the left (Collier and Collier 1991: 546–555). A sharp increase in strike activity ensued, at the same time that Brazil experienced an unprecedented wave of political mobilization by rural workers and peasants. Long excluded from corporatist institutions for labor representation, the rural poor had begun to organize in peasant leagues and unions by the latter half of the 1950s, especially in the northeastern sugar cane region. With support from Communist and Catholic activists, rural unions organized strikes in support of wage claims and labor rights, while peasant leagues occupied large estates and demanded their expropriation (Pereira 1997: 23–35).

This groundswell of labor and peasant mobilization was one of the first victims of the military coup that deposed Goulart in April of 1964. Peasant leagues were banned, and the military intervened in some 500 labor unions and federations to purge leftist leaders and reassert strict corporatist controls. Strike activity and collective bargaining all but vanished, and real wages fell sharply. As Drake (1996: 82) states, "The number of strikes fell from 192 in 1963–64 to 25 in 1965 and 0 in 1971." This demobilization of popular sectors was reinforced by their political exclusion. Although congress continued to function for most of the authoritarian period, it was purged of its leftist opposition, and the pre-1964 parties were all dissolved in October 1965. In their place, the military created an official two-party system, composed of a pro-regime conservative party, ARENA (National Renovating Alliance), and an officially sanctioned "opposition" party, the MDB (Brazilian Democratic Movement). ARENA absorbed much of the political elite from the old UDN, PSD, and other conservative parties that largely supported the coup, while the MDB provided an outlet for tightly constrained dissent (see Power 2000: 54–60).

These two parties would provide the initial building blocks for the reconstituted party system that emerged during Brazil's democratic transition – a party system that would, eventually, assume responsibility for market reform. Following the populist cycle of the early 1960s, the military regime had adopted some orthodox measures to reduce the fiscal deficit and tame inflationary pressures, including wage cuts, credit tightening, and increased taxes and utility rates. This belt-tightening, however, occurred within an overarching commitment to state-led industrialization in alliance with private capital (Evans 1979). Massive investments in heavy industry and infrastructure projects produced explosive growth between 1968 and 1974 – the "miracle years," when the economy expanded at an annual rate of 11.3 percent. The state played a prominent role as both entrepreneur and financier, as public enterprises accounted for an estimated 74 percent of the combined asset value of the country's 100 largest firms, and state banks provided much of the funding for industrial expansion (Baer 1989: 80, 86).

When the 1973 international oil shock caused a surge in the price of oil imports and a growing trade deficit, the military regime resisted the adoption of austerity measures. Instead, it relied on foreign lending to maintain its investment programs and stimulate growth. The economy continued to grow at a 7 percent annual rate through the end of the decade, albeit at the cost of a four-fold increase in the foreign debt – from $12.5 billion in 1973 to $53.8 billion in 1980. The growing debt burden left the country vulnerable to a series of new international shocks, including the second oil shock in 1979, the surge in international interest rates caused by rising global inflation, and the regional debt crisis triggered by Mexico's 1982 default, which caused a steep drop in private international capital flows. With interest payments on the national debt rising nearly 15-fold between 1973 and 1982 (calculated from Baer 1989: 106), the Brazilian economy fell into recession in both 1981 and 1983, contracting by more than seven percent – the first time since the 1930s that the country had experienced a recession. To compound the crisis, the rate of inflation reached triple digits for the first time, averaging 142 percent a year from 1980 to 1985. No longer able to stake its claims for political legitimacy on superior economic performance, the military regime had little choice but to follow through on a decade-long process of political liberalization that ultimately led to a highly restrictive democratic transition in 1985 – one that ensured the country's new and inchoate party system would be saddled with the burdens of crisis management and structural adjustment.

Argentina

The prelude to Argentina's critical juncture differed from that of Brazil's in three fundamental ways. First, it allowed Argentina to enter the critical juncture with a far more institutionalized party system. In contrast to Brazil – where the military regime dismantled the LM party system and founded a new one – military rulers in Argentina left the Peronist (PJ) and Radical (UCR) parties intact as the dominant actors in the party system. Second, elements of the neoliberal model were adopted in Argentina by the military regime in the late 1970s, although reforms ultimately failed to achieve stabilization. Third, Argentina's military regime did not empower conservative forces to dominate a new democratic order.

The relatively early adoption of neoliberal reforms reflected the fact that the ISI model ran out of steam in Argentina long before it did in Brazil. Annual GDP growth in Argentina averaged a modest 3.8 percent from 1945 to 1972, below the regional average of 5.0 percent, and well below Brazil's region-leading 6.9 percent. Only Uruguay, Bolivia, and Paraguay recorded lower average growth rates than Argentina during this peak phase of ISI. Argentina's slow rate of growth was attributable in part to chronic inflationary and balance-of-payments problems that forced governments to adopt periodic austerity measures. Indeed, Argentina recorded the highest average annual inflation rates in the region from the 1940s to the 1960s (calculated from Thorp 1998: 318, 322), leading to repeated stabilization measures that made the country notorious for its boom-and-bust economic cycles. As early as 1949, Perón had been forced to tighten credit, rein in government spending, and cut real wages in response to imbalances generated by his initial expansionary policies (Skidmore 1977: 158–164). The UCR administrations of Arturo Frondizi (1958–1962) and Arturo Illia (1963–1966) that governed while Perón was in exile tried to promote industrial development and woo labor support, but Frondizi ended up implementing an IMF stabilization plan, and Illia was paralyzed by a wave of strikes and factory takeovers launched by Peronist unions (Smith 1989: 39–40). Both Radical presidents were overthrown in military coups that sought to block the reincorporation of Peronism into the democratic arena.

With a Peronist electoral victory looming on the horizon, the military coup that toppled Illia in 1966 created the first of two BA regimes in Argentina. As in Brazil, the first BA regime combined orthodox and statist economic measures, seeking to control inflation at the same time that it deepened ISI (Smith 1989: 74–100). Cuts in wages and workers' benefits, however, helped trigger a 1969 uprising in the industrial city of Córdoba that severely weakened the military regime. Labor and student unrest spread, while inflation mounted, business support faltered, and the military regime was challenged by both leftist and Peronist guerrilla movements. After eighteen years of alternating military and UCR rule that demonstrated the impossibility of governing Argentina in opposition to Peronism (O'Donnell 1973: 167–201), the military stepped down in 1973 and acceded to Perón's triumphant return from exile, hoping that the aging populist leader could discipline his increasingly fractious movement.

Following a landslide presidential victory in 1973, Perón negotiated a social pact with business and labor confederations that called for a price freeze and wage restraint. This social pact quickly unraveled, however, and Perón's failing health and untimely death in 1974 created a leadership vacuum that unleashed violent conflict between the Peronist left and right. The weak successor government led by Perón's widow, Isabel, acceded to the wage and price demands of both business and labor, while continuing "to print money at full speed to finance massive deficit spending" (Smith 1989: 229). The government tried to implement orthodox stabilization measures in June 1975 but quickly capitulated as labor strikes and popular protests spread. By the first quarter of 1976 inflation had surged to a 3,000 percent annual rate and foreign exchange reserves were virtually depleted. The military intervened once again in March 1976, putting a bitter end to the Peronist restoration and installing the country's second BA regime.

In contrast to previous military regimes, however, the *junta* that took power in 1976 sought to break with state-led development by imposing an ambitious program of market reform. A technocratic team led by Economy Minister José Martínez de Hoz devalued the currency, tightened the money supply, cut wages and the fiscal deficit, eliminated price controls and subsidies, liberalized credit markets, slashed tariffs, and lifted nontariff restrictions on trade (Foxley 1983: 117; Ramos 1986: 39). Although little effort was made to privatize state-owned enterprises – in part due to their pivotal role in the country's military-industrial complex – market liberalization was sufficiently deep to move Argentina from .405 on the structural reform index in 1976 (the second lowest in the region) to .691 in 1980 (the third highest in the region following Chile and Uruguay, which also had BA military regimes; see Escaith and Paunovic 2004). On the political front, Argentina's military regime violently repressed Peronist and leftist guerrilla movements and their suspected sympathizers, decimating their ranks and producing thousands of "disappearances." Partisan political activity was suspended, but in contrast to Brazil, the military did not create a pro-regime party or reconstitute the party system. The national labor confederation was placed under government trusteeship, strikes were banned, and hundreds of union and party activists were imprisoned (McGuire 1997: 170–171).

The military's attempt to stabilize the economy achieved modest short-term success, but it quickly faltered under the weight of a growing external debt, a still-overvalued currency, and high interest rates that stifled domestic investment. The inflation rate averaged over 150 percent annually between 1977 and 1980, and with the onset of the global financial shocks of the early 1980s, the economy fell into a steep recession. With the economy contracting by 6.6 percent in 1981 and 4.9 percent in 1982, the military retreated from orthodox measures and the rate of inflation rose above 300 percent in 1983. The foreign debt, which stood at less than $10 billion in 1976, ballooned to more than $46 billion by 1983 (Smith 1989: 261). As labor unrest and popular protests spread, the military made a desperate gambit to shore up national unity by invading the Malvinas Islands in 1982, culminating in a disastrous military defeat at the hands of Great Britain. Thoroughly discredited, the military was forced to accept a democratic transition in 1983 and the subsequent trial and conviction of *junta* members for human rights violations (Brysk 1994; Munck 1998). Argentina's new democratic rulers thus inherited a partially liberalized economy suffering from severe recession and acute inflationary pressures. The UCR and Peronists returned to the forefront of democratic competition, but spent the rest of the decade grappling with the burdens of economic stabilization and structural adjustment.

Chile

In contrast to Argentina and Brazil, Chile pushed beyond ISI policies to adopt major socialist and redistributive reforms in the period preceding the critical juncture. Since Chile's socialist experiment unfolded under a democratic regime and entailed exceptionally high levels of lower-class social mobilization

(Winn 1986), the military coup that brought it to a violent end was designed to deactivate and repress popular sectors, much like the coups that installed BA regimes in Brazil and Argentina. In contrast to those countries, however, Chile's military regime withstood the economic debacle of the early 1980s and remained in power through the end of that decade. It also imposed the region's most thorough process of market liberalization, largely insulating the party system from the political costs of crisis management and structural adjustment in the 1980s. Alone in the region, Chile's party system inherited, rather than implemented, structural adjustment policies, and it governed the country following the 1990 democratic transition during a period of unprecedented economic expansion. As such, the onset of Chile's critical juncture predated both the democratic transition and the 1980s debt crisis; it began with the overthrow of Allende in 1973 and the reversal of his socialist development model by military successors. Chile's critical juncture, therefore, was conditioned more heavily by the endogenous political crisis of state-led development than by the exogenous international shocks of the early 1980s.

In Chile as in Argentina, ISI policies were adopted early but lost much of their dynamism by the 1950s. The economy was plagued by chronic inflation, and per-capita GDP growth from 1950 to the mid-1970s was less than half the Latin American average outside the Southern Cone (Ramos 1986: 46). An orthodox attempt to stimulate the economy received a brief trial from 1958–1964 under conservative president Jorge Alessandri, who had narrowly defeated Allende – the candidate of a newly formed leftist alliance – in a close three-way race. Alessandri sought to cut state spending, lower taxes and tariffs, and relax state controls on prices, wages, and foreign exchange (Stallings 1978: 80–81). Orthodox measures sparked labor unrest, however, and the partisan Right opted to support Christian Democratic (PDC) leader Eduardo Frei in the 1964 presidential campaign, rather than risk a leftist victory in a three-way race.

Under Frei the state returned to an active developmentalist role and promoted social reform, including land redistribution. Land reform came on the heels of suffrage reforms in 1958 that reduced vote buying in the countryside and gave the rural poor a secret ballot for the first time. Together, these reforms undermined landed elites' political control of the countryside, the historic bastion of Chile's Liberal and Conservative parties. In so doing, they unleashed a wave of rural political mobilization in the 1960s, with the PDC competing with the Socialists and Communists to organize peasant unions and capture the votes of the rural poor (Scully 1992: 106–170). Frei's reforms triggered virulent opposition from the political right, which broke with the PDC to run Alessandri for the presidency once again in 1970. In a tight three-way race, Allende's leftist coalition won a narrow plurality to claim executive authority for the first time in Chilean history. Thus began Chile's "peaceful road to socialism," arguably the most radical experiment in democratic social and economic reform ever seen.

Allende's Popular Unity coalition attempted to shift from state-led capitalist development to a socialist model in which the state assumed control over the commanding heights of the economy. In three short years, the Allende regime completed the nationalization of the copper industry, took over fourteen of the seventeen commercial banks, transferred hundreds of industries into the hands of the state, and expropriated 60 percent of agricultural land. By 1973 the state owned nearly 600 industries, and its expenditures accounted for 45 percent of GDP (Stallings 1978: 131–132; Teichman 2001: 25). Real wages rose sharply and price controls were established on basic consumer goods; when supply bottlenecks emerged the state intervened to establish grassroots distribution networks.

Initially, Allende's reforms placed the conservative opposition on the defensive, while robust economic growth in 1971 helped to broaden his coalition's base of support in municipal elections. By 1972, however, socialist reforms had triggered a furious backlash from the private sector, which responded by hoarding goods, engaging in economic sabotage, and unleashing a wave of capital strikes. Negotiations between the government and Christian Democratic leaders failed to produce an accord on the scope of nationalizations, and the militant wing of Allende's coalition pledged to "advance without compromise." Meanwhile, social mobilization from below escaped the government's control and increasingly forced its hand on nationalization policies (Winn 1986). Peasants seized land-holdings and workers occupied over 350 industries, linking factories together in *cordones industriales* to defend the Allende government. Street protests and counter-protests occurred almost daily as class conflict intensified in 1973.

As political mobilization – both pro- and anti-government – exceeded the institutional confines of Chile's democratic regime (Valenzuela 1978), the combination of economic disruption and a U.S.-orchestrated international financial blockade created a severe economic crisis. Lacking a congressional majority, Allende was unable to finance ambitious social programs through tax increases, creating a gaping fiscal deficit. The inflation rate reached triple digits in 1972 and surged past 500 percent in 1973, while the economy contracted by more than 10 percent during Allende's final two years in power. Shortages of basic consumer goods exacerbated economic hardships and encouraged black market activity. The military intervened on September 11, 1973, attacking the presidential palace to depose Allende in one of the most violent coups in Latin American history. The coup ended forty years of uninterrupted democratic rule and ushered in nearly seventeen years of harsh military dictatorship under General Augusto Pinochet. Although it took a year and a half for the Pinochet regime to define a new economic model, Chile's critical juncture – and Latin America's neoliberal era – had begun.

MARKET REFORM AND ALIGNING CRITICAL JUNCTURES: CHILE AND BRAZIL

As described above, orthodox stabilization measures were hardly unknown to Latin America when the neoliberal era began. They had been standard fare for conservative rulers, both civilian and military, in response to fiscal and balance-of-payments imbalances throughout the ISI era. These conventional measures, however, paled in comparison to the structural adjustment programs adopted during neoliberal critical junctures. The latter reform packages were far deeper, more comprehensive, and more ideologically grounded, initially in the Chicago School monetarism of Chilean technocrats, and by the 1980s in the authoritative conditionality of international financial institutions like the IMF and the World Bank.

Structural adjustment was especially deep in the LM cases because they had pushed further along the path of state-led development. Indeed, market liberalization was integral to a larger conservative project of weakening the partisan and labor blocs that were embedded in the state-centric matrix. The party systems that emerged from neoliberal critical junctures had largely ceased to be labor-mobilizing; even where populist or leftist parties retained organizational linkages to unions, labor movements were smaller and weaker than they were before the critical juncture in all the LM cases with the exception of Brazil, and they were less central to the political identities and mobilizational strategies of their partisan allies. Nevertheless, neoliberal critical junctures had varied effects on the stability and programmatic alignment of LM party systems. As shown below, military regimes in Chile and Brazil created forms of conservative political dominance that encouraged programmatically aligning critical junctures, with stabilizing effects on party competition in the post-adjustment era.

Chile: Military Repression, Market Reform, and Programmatic Alignment

Although Chile had strong parties with deep social roots before the 1973 coup, the ability of the party system to withstand the military dictatorship – and the critical juncture it wrought – was far from assured. As the Venezuelan case demonstrates (see next section), even the most institutionalized party systems could break down during the transition to neoliberalism, and Venezuela's parties were hardly subjected to the violent repression and authoritarian political engineering that Chile's parties were forced to endure. Chile's military regime aimed, in the short term, to extirpate Marxism from the body politic and dismantle the democratic institutions that allowed it to flourish. Over the longer term, it sought to create permanent institutions of authoritarian governance and reconfigure social and economic relationships around a logic of market individualism that would preclude a revival of leftist mobilization. As stated by Valenzuela and Valenzuela (1986: 191), the "cardinal objective" of this "regenerative project" was "to do away with the traditional party system."

In short, the military dictatorship sought to re-found the social, economic, and institutional bases of political order in Chile. It immediately declared a state of emergency and claimed executive, legislative, and constitutive powers, while subordinating the judiciary to its authority. Military forces occupied factories, universities, and shantytowns, arresting and torturing tens of thousands of persons and dismissing 160,000 from their jobs (Remmer 1980: 282). The military proceeded to close congress and local governments, burn the electoral registry, dissolve labor and peasant confederations, and prohibit elections in social organizations. Following the democratic transition in 1990, an official investigative commission documented 2,279 cases of political killings or disappearances, along with nearly 1,600 additional unconfirmed cases (Chilean National Commission for Truth and Reconciliation 1991: 1122).

From the outset the discourse of the military regime vilified parties and their leaders for political extremism and irresponsibility, depicting parties as "the principal source of Chile's social and economic ills" (Scully 1995: 122). Marxist parties were immediately banned, while their assets were confiscated and their leaders hunted down by Pinochet's ruthless intelligence agency. The PSCh and PCCh both had their internal directorates decapitated multiple times during the first three years of the dictatorship, forcing remaining party leaders to operate from East Berlin and Moscow, respectively (Roberts 1998: 95–98). Both parties had their ranks decimated by repression, political withdrawal, and exile, as some 200,000 Chileans fled the country. Non-Marxist parties, meanwhile, were decreed to be in indefinite recess. The Christian Democratic Party (PDC) was subsequently outlawed in 1977, and the National Party (formed through the 1966 merger of the traditional Conservative and Liberal parties) voluntarily disbanded, in gratitude to the military and in anticipation of a long-term authoritarian project. A new constitution imposed in 1980 created a framework for permanent military tutelage of the political process, while banning parties that advocated class struggle and prohibiting civic and labor leaders from belonging to political parties (see Barros 2002; Ensalaco 2000: 133–135).

Having inherited a severe inflationary and balance-of-payments crisis, the military regime immediately adopted orthodox stabilization measures. The exchange rate was devalued, public spending and wages were slashed, and strict monetary policies were adopted (Foxley 1983: 49–52). Liberalization measures were also adopted, as price controls were lifted, tariffs were cut, restrictions on foreign investment were relaxed, factories nationalized by Allende were returned to their previous owners, and agricultural cooperatives were privatized (Ramos 1986: 16–20). This initial adjustment produced a severe recession in 1975, when GDP plummeted by 12.9 percent and unemployment jumped from 9.2 to 16.3 percent (Foxley 1983: 50).

Nevertheless, the military regime persevered with market reforms, launching a more ambitious program of neoliberal restructuring in mid-1975. This new program, which was unprecedented in its scope, reflected the ascendance of University of Chicago-trained technocrats within Pinochet's management team and the growing predominance of internationally oriented financial and export conglomerates within the Chilean economy. Government spending slashed another 27 percent, tariff reductions and privatizations were accelerated, and interest rates and capital markets were liberalized (Silva 1996: 110–111). By

1980 tariffs had been fixed at 10 percent, a new labor code had been passed to liberalize labor markets and sharply restrict union and collective bargaining rights, and reforms leading to the privatization of social security had been initiated. Of the nearly 600 enterprises in the public sector at the time of the coup, only fifteen remained in 1980, while public sector employment had been cut by 21 percent and nearly 65 percent of land-reform properties had been parceled out to private owners (Foxley 1983: 61–67). The rate of unionization, which surpassed 30 percent under Allende – even among rural workers – plunged below 10 percent by the mid-1980s, and a mere 6.5 percent in the agricultural sector. Labor militancy all but evaporated; Chile averaged almost 3,000 strikes per year involving 350,000 workers in 1971 and 1972, but a mere thirty-seven strikes per year involving 3,583 workers in 1983 and 1984, a nearly one-hundred-fold decline (Roberts 1998: 152, 158; Kurtz 2004b: 120). By 1981, Chile's score on the structural reform index had jumped from .352 in 1973 to .769, giving it the most liberalized economy in the region (Escaith and Paunovic 2004).

Chile's market revolution thoroughly transformed the social landscape, but it left the political alignments that undergirded the party system largely intact. Although parties were forced to withdraw from active political life for most of the first decade of military rule, they returned to the forefront in 1983, when a financial crisis and severe recession spawned a three-year cycle of mass protests against the dictatorship. Following a spurt of economic growth between 1976 and 1981, when GDP expanded at an annual rate of 7.2 percent, Chile's fixed exchange rate produced a sharp appreciation of the currency and mounting trade and current accounts deficits. Foreign exchange reserves were depleted, while capital inflows slowed and interest rates soared (Foxley 1983: 60). With borrowers unable to repay loans, the financial system teetered on the brink of collapse, and the government was forced into a series of bank interventions and a massive currency devaluation (Ramos 1986: 22–23). An unprecedented recession ensued, with GDP declining nearly 15 percent in 1982–1983, making Chile's open economy the most severely affected in the Latin American region by the global debt crisis.

The onset of mass protests in early 1983 brought partisan activities back into the open and forced parties to define their strategic stance toward regime change. The traditional three-thirds alignment of Right, Center, and Left quickly reemerged, albeit with significant modifications from the pre-coup party system. Indeed, the party system was partially reconstituted in the 1980s, and major coalitional realignments occurred, effectively translating the traditional "three-thirds" into two blocs: a rightist bloc that defended the military regime and staunchly supported its neoliberal project, and a center-left bloc that vigorously opposed the dictatorship along with major elements of its economic model. From the outset, then, the reemerging party system was programmatically aligned around a regime cleavage, as well as support and opposition to the neoliberal model.

The partisan Right, which had voluntarily dissolved after the coup, confident that its interests were secure under Pinochet, was largely reconstituted in the 1980s in anticipation of a potential regime transition. Pinochet's closest civilian advisors and neoliberal technocrats, led by his political architect, Jaime Guzman, formed the *Unión Demócrata Independiente* (UDI) in 1983, while remnants of the old National Party formed a new partisan vehicle, *Renovación Nacional* (RN), in 1987. Although the UDI more forcefully defended the dictatorship and its plans for a tightly controlled regime transition – in reality, a constitutionally prescribed effort to institutionalize authoritarian rule – both parties supported the regime's economic model, which had begun a new and more sustainable growth phase in the mid-1980s. Likewise, both parties had strong ties to business interests that overwhelmingly supported the economic model and feared a return to unrestricted democratic competition (Silva 1996: 217–227; Garretón 2000).

Greater organizational continuity existed on the partisan Center and Left – ironically, where military repression had been most fierce. The PDC remained the dominant party of the Center and the country's single largest party. In contrast to the 1960s, however, when its *camino propio* (independent path) strategy led it to eschew alliances and create centrifugal competitive dynamics (Valenzuela 1978), the party entered into a strategic alliance with smaller centrist and leftist parties to contest the dictatorship after 1983. This alliance was facilitated by changes within both the PDC and the highly fragmented partisan Left. Not only did the PDC become more amenable to alliance building (Huneeus 2003: 142), but it also adopted a more resolute opposition stance against the dictatorship after the late 1970s. Much of the party leadership had supported the coup in 1973 in order to avoid social revolution, expecting a short-lived military intervention, but the party gradually moved into opposition because of the dictatorship's human rights violations and Pinochet's increasingly transparent designs to institutionalize authoritarian rule for the long term (Garretón 1989a: 406–407).

As the PDC shifted toward the opposition camp, it began a strategic convergence with part of the Socialist Party (PSCh). Under Allende, the PSCh anchored the more militant wing of the Popular Unity coalition, as the party had been heavily influenced by revolutionary currents in the 1960s. After the coup, however, exiled Socialist leaders began a critique of their party's role under Allende, arguing that its radicalism had prevented the Popular Unity from building a multi-class democratic majority for reform. This self-criticism reflected the influence of Gramscian intellectual currents on Socialist and Christian Left leaders exiled in Europe, and it became the starting point for a broader process of ideological renewal. The "Socialist Renovation" broke with revolutionary Leninism and reconceptualized the Socialist project as an open-ended process of deepening democracy – one that required broad popular majorities and flexible political alliances (see Garretón 1987; Walker 1990; Roberts 1998).

Leaders of the Socialist renovation believed that Pinochet could only be defeated through an alliance with the centrist PDC and its middle-class constituencies. The traditional Socialist–Communist alliance, they thought, was a recipe for political isolation and exclusion, especially in a context where the PCCh was becoming increasingly radicalized. Although the PCCh had been an architect of Allende's *vía pacífica* (peaceful road) and a moderate voice in his governing coalition, the party decided in the early 1980s that Pinochet would never relinquish power peacefully, and could only be driven from office by force – that is, through an insurrectionary "popular rebellion" backed by the force of arms. The party thus created an armed insurgent force, and its youthful cadres in urban shantytowns played a major role in the explosion of social protests between 1983 and 1986 (Roberts 1998).

This insurrectionary strategy was tentatively backed by the orthodox branch of the now-splintered Socialist Party, but it was opposed by the Socialists' more "renovated" factions as well as the Christian Democrats. These latter parties supported mass protests but not armed insurrection, which they considered futile and counter-productive against a ruthless and professionalized military apparatus. Indeed, they supported protests primarily to create fissures in the military regime and provide political leverage for a negotiated transition to democracy, as they did not believe Pinochet could be forced from office by societal pressure alone. Consequently, the PDC, renovated Socialists, and other small parties formed the first in a series of center-left coalitions in 1983, privileging elite negotiations for a "pacted" transition, while the PCCh and orthodox Socialists created a rival front to pressure the regime from below. The democratic opposition was thus split during the peak phase of the protest cycle. The level of social protest declined by the second half of 1986, however, as the economy began to rebound and the fear of spiraling violence made the Christian Democrats and Socialists back away from militant tactics. Middle-class and organized-labor participation in the protests diminished, leaving the most radicalized youth in poor *barrios* as the central protagonists (Garretón 1989b: 267–270; Oxhorn 1995).

Indeed, by 1987 the locus of regime contention had begun to shift from the streets to the electoral arena. Having survived the financial crisis, the protest cycle, and an armed attack on his presidential motorcade, Pinochet began to implement his plan for a controlled transition, starting with a 1988 plebiscite to extend his presidential term for eight more years. Meanwhile, the opposition – having failed to drive Pinochet from power or negotiate a return to unfettered democracy – set out to defeat Pinochet where he was weakest: at the ballot box. A new law allowed parties to gain legal recognition and engage in a voter registration drive; to circumvent a continued ban on Marxist parties, the renovated Socialist branch created a new "instrumental" party, the *Partido por la Democracia* (PPD). The PPD coalesced with the PDC to anchor a seventeen-party opposition bloc known as the *Concertación* (Concertation), while the Communist Party – left outside the *Concertación* and increasingly isolated in its commitment to mass insurrection – reluctantly called for its members to vote against Pinochet as well.

The opposition defeated Pinochet by a vote of 54.7 to 43 percent, forcing the dictatorship to negotiate a package of constitutional reforms and schedule competitive national elections for December 1989. The *Concertación* elected PDC leader Patricio Aylwin to the presidency with 55.2 percent of the vote, defeating a rightist candidate who had been Pinochet's economy minister during the recovery of the late 1980s. Aylwin's triumph was the first of four consecutive presidential victories by the center-left coalition, which also captured a majority of seats in the lower house of congress (see Appendix Tables 5 and 6).

Upon the return to democracy, the party system quickly congealed, with the three ideological tendencies crystallizing into two primary political blocs. On the Right, the RN and UDI formed a new opposition coalition, albeit one that was stronger than the pre-coup Right. Whereas the National Party had averaged 20.7 percent of the congressional vote in 1969 and 1973, combined rightist forces obtained 34.2 and 36.7 percent of the vote in 1989 and 1993, respectively, while obtaining over 40 percent of the seats in the lower house thanks to a binomial electoral law that over-represented the second-largest bloc. The center-left *Concertación* was led by the PDC, the newly re-legalized and reunified PSCh – which absorbed a number of smaller Christian Left parties – and the PPD, which acquired an independent identity and formally separated from the PSCh, while retaining a sub-pact with the latter inside the governing coalition.[2] The PDC vote was virtually unchanged from the pre-coup period; the party averaged 29.5 percent of the congressional vote in 1969 and 1973, and 26.6 percent in 1989 and 1993. Although the PSCh vote declined – from 18.7 percent in 1969 to 11.9 percent in 1993, when it was first allowed to compete again on its own label – it was reinforced by the PPD, which averaged 11.7 percent in 1989 and 1993. The Communist Party was the primary vote loser during the critical juncture; the PCCh averaged 16.1 percent of the congressional vote in 1969 and 1993, but the coalitions it led after the transition averaged only 5.9 percent of the vote in 1989 and 1993, preventing the party from obtaining seats in congress under the highly disproportional electoral system.

Chile's critical juncture, then, produced a complex mixture of change and continuity within the party system. The organizational composition of the party system changed with the displacement of the National Party on the right by RN and UDI and the formation of a new secular center-left party, the PPD, which essentially occupied and expanded the political space of the historic Radical Party, now much diminished in importance. Organizational continuity existed

---

[2] Initially some activists were members of both the PSCh and the PPD, but they were required to choose sides when the parties separated in 1992. Ricardo Lagos – the Socialist leader who played a central role in the founding of the PPD – remained the de facto head of both parties, however, helping to secure their close alliance within the larger *Concertación*.

through the PDC, the PSCh, and the PCCh, but electoral and coalitional realignments had altered competitive dynamics; the radical left around the PCCh emerged much weakened from the dictatorship, whereas the center-left PSCh-PPD bloc strengthened, broke with the radical left, and forged a new majoritarian alliance with the centrist PDC.

This new competitive alignment was forged by two basic, mutually reinforcing sociopolitical cleavages that divided the Right from the center-left *Concertación*. One cleavage was structured by support and opposition to the military dictatorship and its institutional legacies; the conservative parties had not only supported the dictatorship, but also defended the restrictions it imposed on democracy afterwards, including the disproportional binomial electoral system, senators designated by the military regime that gave the right an unelected majority in the upper house, military tutelage of the political process, and legal immunity for human rights violations that occurred under military rule (Siavelis 2000). The *Concertación* chafed at these restrictions and progressively whittled them down, but contestation over basic democratic rules created a durable political cleavage over the nature and extent of popular sovereignty in Chile.

Superimposed on this political divide was a programmatic cleavage structured by support and opposition to the dictatorship's neoliberal model – albeit a cleavage that softened over time. Whereas the business community and the partisan right staunchly supported market liberalization, from the outset organized labor, the partisan Left, and much of the PDC had opposed it. This opposition was tempered after the mid-1980s, when a more pragmatic team of neoliberal technocrats took the helm after the financial crisis and the economy began an unprecedented period of expansion, driven largely by new agricultural and natural resource exports (Silva 1996). Consequently, as the democratic transition drew near, the PDC and PSCh promised to address the "social deficits" of the neoliberal model while reassuring the business community that they would not attempt a sharp break with the status quo, much less roll the clock back to the statism of the past.

Once in office the *Concertación* moved cautiously to increase the minimum wage, strengthen the public sectors of largely privatized health care and pension systems, and negotiate a modest tax increase that allowed for greater spending on poverty-relief programs. Bolstered by its unelected Senate majority, the conservative opposition blocked deeper reforms, especially to the liberalized labor code. The popular bases of the left often chafed at the relative continuity with the neoliberal model under the *Concertación*, but the commitment of the center-left coalition – especially the PSCh within it – to modify social policies and promote "growth with equity" (Weyland 1997) clearly differentiated its programmatic positions from the rigid orthodoxy of a partisan Right that was steeped in the market fundamentalism of Pinochet's Chicago School technocrats. The Aylwin government did, in fact, sustain rapid economic growth – averaging 7 percent a year between 1990 and 1993 – while reducing unemployment, raising the minimum wage by one-third, and cutting the rate of poverty from 44 percent of the population to 28.5 percent in 1994 (see Roberts 1998: 149).

Chile's critical juncture effectively ended with the 1993 electoral ratification of the partisan and programmatic alignments that congealed during the democratic transition. The *Concertación* elected the PDC's Eduardo Frei – a son of the former president – to the presidency with 58.0 percent of the vote, a slight increase over 1989, while the composition of the legislature was virtually unchanged. This electoral continuity clearly reflected the stabilizing effects of Chile's stellar economic performance; at a time when neighboring countries were still grappling with hyperinflation and structural adjustment, Chile was basking in a period of rapid growth, low inflation, and improving social indicators. Having demonstrated that it could manage a contentious regime transition while sustaining pro-growth policies that addressed the needs of the poor, the *Concertación* successfully reproduced its electoral support.

Electoral stability, however, was also buttressed by the competitive alignment of the party system around a basic cleavage between conservative and center-left blocs – a cleavage that was grounded in both regime preferences and programmatic distinctions. This cleavage had obvious roots in the pre-1973 ideological structuring of the Chilean party system, but it was reinforced and reconfigured by political alignments during the process of market liberalization under military rule – that is, during a critical juncture that bequeathed an institutional legacy of contested liberalism. Market reforms that were imposed by a military dictatorship and opposed by a thoroughly excluded left helped to align the party system programmatically as Chile returned to democratic rule. As shown in Chapter 9, this basic alignment of programmatic and partisan competition would endure well into Chile's aftermath period, making its party system the most stable of the LM cases in the neoliberal era. It also contained social protest for the better part of two decades, at a time when many neighboring countries were roiled by mass movements that challenged both the party system and the neoliberal model.

Brazil: Democratization, Market Reform, and Party System Alignment

In many respects the Brazilian case might appear to be the opposite of Chile – and a "least likely" case for party system stabilization during the neoliberal era. Brazil's military regime (1964–1985), while conservative and exclusionary, was nevertheless notable for its economic statism; in contrast to Chile, it did not oversee structural adjustment or insulate the party system from its costs. The Brazilian party system, moreover, did not have deep historical and social roots in earlier democratic periods like that of Chile. The parties that dominated the Second Republic from 1945 to 1964 were dissolved by the dictatorship, and the party system was thoroughly reconstituted during military rule and the democratic transition of the 1980s. Brazil's fledgling and inchoate post-transition party system thus resembled that of Ecuador (see Chapter 7) more than those in Argentina or Chile with their strong traditional parties.

Brazil's new parties were notoriously weak, in a country with a long tradition of party system underdevelopment. In an influential study, Mainwaring (1999a: 5) called Brazil "an exceptional case of party weakness," noting that the country has had "seven distinct party systems" since the first parties of notables emerged in the 1830s. Contemporary parties, he argues, "have weak roots in society and limited legitimacy, and exercise little influence over congressional representatives." Not surprisingly, then, Brazil manifested the standard traits of under-institutionalization following its democratic transition: electoral volatility, susceptibility to populist and "outsider" challenges, widespread party switching among elected representatives, and a reliance on patronage to leverage political support. Party weakness was reinforced by electoral institutions, such as open-list proportional representation, that encouraged personalized voting and undermined organizational discipline (Mainwaring 1999a: 243–262).

Nevertheless, the Brazilian party system began to show signs of progressive institutionalization by the latter half of the 1990s, when the critical juncture drew to a close and the aftermath period began. This institutionalization undoubtedly benefited from the stabilization of the economy in 1994–1995, when Brazil finally defeated hyperinflation and eliminated a major source of performance-based electoral volatility. The comparative record in Latin America demonstrates, however, that economic stabilization alone did not suffice to institutionalize electoral competition; it mattered greatly whether structural adjustment aligned or de-aligned party systems programmatically. In Brazil, structural adjustment was unusually transparent in its aligning effects, as market reforms were adopted by a series of conservative and center-right coalition governments starting in the late 1980s, and they were consistently opposed by a new party of the left that progressively strengthened over the course of the critical juncture. The consolidation of this basic cleavage helped the major parties build stronger organizations, construct name-brand loyalties, and channel societal dissent into the party system. In so doing, it transformed a notoriously inchoate party system into one that was well above the Latin American average for electoral stability in the post-adjustment era.

As in Chile, this central political cleavage was initially shaped by the alignment of forces in support and opposition to military dictatorship. In contrast to Pinochet, however, Brazil's military rulers began the reconstitution of the party system by forming a pro-government party of the right, ARENA, and an official opposition party, the MDB, which lacked a well-defined ideological stance but was clearly located near the political center. As stated by Power (2000: 55), the October 1965 decree that established these two parties and abolished their predecessors "marked the beginning of a political cleavage that would characterize Brazilian politics for a generation or more: authoritarians versus democrats." Upon its formation, ARENA incorporated all the sitting governors into its ranks, giving it effective political control over the vast interior of Brazil through clientelist networks in small towns and rural areas. The MDB, on the other hand, obtained significant support in legislative elections in more urban and industrial areas, especially in the south and southeast of the country. The MDB strengthened and elections became more competitive after 1974, when the regime relaxed repressive measures and began a gradual process of political liberalization (Mainwaring 1999a: 85–86; Power 2000: 57–60).

This post-1974 political opening also provided an impetus to labor mobilization, which played a major role in the reconstitution of the partisan left as Brazil entered its democratic transition. Although the military had purged unions of leftist leaders following the coup, it left the basic structure of trade unionization intact, while reasserting the state corporatist controls that had progressively unraveled in the 1950s and early 1960s. Indeed, the dramatic expansion of heavy industry caused the number of workers in manufacturing and construction to increase nearly four-fold between 1960 and 1980, while trade union membership actually quintupled between 1964 and 1980 to reach 22.5 percent of the wage labor force (Drake 1996: 80, 82). Over the second half of the 1970s, a new breed of Catholic and leftist union activists formed factory commissions and independent, grassroots unions that operated outside the state corporatist system of constraints. Centered in the metallurgical unions in the automobile industry around São Paulo, this militant "new unionism" sparked a massive wave of strikes in the late 1970s and launched the political career of its charismatic young leader, Luis Inácio "Lula" da Silva. In 1980, Lula joined other union leaders, intellectuals, and grassroots Catholic activists to found the Workers' Party (PT) – in essence, a new partisan vehicle for a plethora of social movements that flourished in the 1970s (see Keck 1992).

Although social mobilization and deteriorating economic conditions in the early 1980s put the military regime on the defensive, it held fast to its plan for a gradual, controlled democratic transition. Fearing that the MDB would serve as a broad opposition front to contest national elections, the regime adopted a new political parties law in 1979 that was designed to fragment opposition forces (Mainwaring 1999a: 89–91). The law dissolved the two established parties and encouraged new parties to form. ARENA was re-baptized the Democrátic Social Party (PDS), anchoring the Right, while the MDB was renamed the Party of the Brazilian Democratic Movement (PMDB), a centrist party with both conservative and social democratic flanks. On the Left, the PT emerged to compete with the Democratic Labor Party (PDT) of Leonel Brizola, a former PTB leader with family ties to Goulart.

The regime held legislative elections in 1982, with the PDS and PMDB capturing over 90 percent of the seats in the lower house, demonstrating the weakness of the partisan Left in the latter stages of the military regime (see Appendix, Table 4). The military proceeded with plans for an indirect presidential election in 1985, with a president to be chosen by an electoral college composed of the national congress and representatives from the ruling party in each state (a majority held by the rightist PDS). With the economy rapidly deteriorating, a massive protest movement erupted in 1983–1984 calling for a constitutional amendment to allow for direct presidential elections. The protest movement provided a shot in the arm to the PT and other opposition forces, while creating new fissures in the conservative bloc, some of whose leaders supported the call for direct elections. The protest movement narrowly failed to induce congress to pass the constitutional amendment, but the conservative PDS split when forced to choose a presidential candidate; defectors led by former party president José Sarney formed the Liberal Front Party (PFL), which negotiated an alliance with the PMDB and supported its presidential candidate, Tancredo Neves. Neves won the vote in the electoral college but died before he could assume office, allowing Sarney – a long-time leader of ARENA and supporter of the military regime – to become an unlikely first civilian president after twenty-one years of military rule (Power 2000: 66–68).

The party system was thus in a state of flux as Brazil returned to civilian rule in 1985 and entered its critical juncture. The PMDB won a majority of seats in both houses of congress in 1986, along with 22 of 23 gubernatorial races, while the PFL displaced the PDS as the leading party on the right. Many PDS legislators switched over to the PMDB or PFL to exploit patronage opportunities (Mainwaring 1999a: 102); others joined several newly founded conservative parties, further fragmenting the partisan Right. Despite its growing strength in civil society, the PT (as well as the PDT on the Left) remained a minor electoral force at this stage of the democratic transition.

Clearly, the influx of ex-ARENA/PDS leaders into the PMDB, combined with the latter's governing alliance with the conservative PFL, blurred the political cleavage between authoritarians and democrats that had structured the party system for the better part of two decades. The PMDB became increasingly conservative and clientelistic in its mode of governance, creating disillusionment within the party's more social democratic tendencies. Dissenters broke with the party in 1988 to form the Brazilian Social Democratic Party (PSDB), which became a major force in the broad Center and center-left space in the party system.

Discontent was compounded by the economic travails of the Sarney administration. Heavily dependent on debt-fueled growth in the 1970s, Brazil had been hit hard by the global economic crisis of the early 1980s. The economy experienced recessions in 1981 and 1983, while inflation surged to 142 percent in 1983 – the first of twelve consecutive years of triple- or quadruple-digit inflation rates. When Sarney took office, the new civilian government adopted a heterodox stabilization program in early 1986 known as the Cruzado Plan, which froze wages and prices, eliminated indexing, and introduced a new currency, bringing temporary relief. The respite was fleeting, however, as Sarney's failure to achieve a fiscal adjustment prevented him from breaking inflation's inertial logic. Instead, the economy experienced "an explosion of suppressed inflation" that exacerbated distributive conflicts and encouraged business and labor groups to defect from the Cruzado Plan (Kingstone 1999: 41). Inflation rose to over 200 percent in 1987 and 682 percent in 1988 as the economy sank into yet another recession. Sarney finally began a tentative shift toward orthodox measures late in his term, in particular by initiating trade liberalization (Weyland 2002: 81–89).

This belated turn to orthodoxy by a conservative government did not contain Brazil's hyperinflationary spiral. Indeed, inflation surged to 1,287 percent in 1989 and a staggering 2,938 percent in 1990. The orthodox turn did, however, contribute to an emerging alignment of the party system along a programmatic axis of competition, at a time when the authoritarian-democratic cleavage had weakened. By the late 1980s, business interests in Brazil – long dependent on varied forms of state protection and subsidization – became increasingly critical of state intervention and the distortions it created in the economy (Kingstone 1999: 51–52). At the same time, both centrist and conservative parties were gravitating toward support of structural adjustment policies to contain hyper-inflationary pressures. In the 1989 presidential election – the first in the new democratic era – the candidates of the PDS and PSDB "played to business community audiences with mildly liberalizing and antistate appeals" (Kingstone 1999: 150). Similar appeals were made by the maverick conservative figure Fernando Collor de Mello, who combined support for market reforms with populist, anti-corruption critiques of established parties and business elites. Although Collor had begun his political career in the rightist PDS, he formed a new personalist party vehicle, the National Reconstruction Party (PRN), to support his independent presidential campaign.

Meanwhile, on the left the PT clearly differentiated itself programmatically from these centrist and conservative alternatives. The PT defined itself as socialist, proposed a nationalization of the financial sector, supported labor rights, and assumed "a leading role in opposing trade liberalization, privatization, labor 'flexibilization,' and measures to institute greater fiscal efficiency in the social sectors" (Hunter 2010: 26). The party's distinctive programmatic stance was buttressed by its growing track record of municipal governance; after electing only two mayors in 1982 and one in 1985, the PT captured thirty-six mayorships in 1988, including three state capitals. These elections placed 10 percent of the Brazilian population under a municipal government of the PT (Hunter 2010: 81). Many of these municipal administrations made notable innovations in the style and substance of local governance by introducing participatory budgeting procedures, stipends for schoolchildren, and new programs for public education, health care, and housing (Baiocchi 2003; Goldfrank 2011).

The growth of the PT, especially in the more industrialized south and southeast of the country, allowed Lula to finish second in the first round of the 1989 presidential election and pass into the second-round run-off against Collor. Brizola of the leftist PDT finished a close third and proceeded to support Lula in the runoff. Nevertheless, Collor narrowly won the run-off election by a vote of 53 to 47 percent (see Appendix, Table 3), combining support from the business community with effective populist appeals to the unorganized poor who were outside the PT's movement networks (see Kingstone 1999: 152). The

1989 election provided graphic evidence of the extraordinary volatility of the party system at this stage of the critical juncture. The party of Collor, the PRN, had only recently been formed and had a minimal presence in congress. The parties of the second- and third-place contenders, the PT and PDT, had combined for barely 8 percent of the lower house seats in the 1986 elections. Wracked by hyperinflation, the two governing parties, the PMDB and the PFL of Sarney, were decimated at the ballot box in 1989, their candidates winning only 4.7 and 0.9 percent of the presidential vote, respectively. Anti-incumbent voting was virtually universal, as voters supported candidates who were largely outside the party system (Collor) or in opposition to the status quo (Lula).

Following the tepid orthodox measures adopted by Sarney, Collor embarked on a far more ambitious program of stabilization and structural adjustment. Indeed, he "chose the most radical measures that his aides were considering" (Weyland 2002: 115), issuing decrees from his second day in office to cut tariffs and government spending, close government agencies, increase taxes, privatize major state-owned industries, and deregulate the economy. Most controversially (and contrary to orthodox economic principles), he also froze financial assets, including bank savings, for an eighteen-month period. Although Collor initially tried to govern in an autocratic and independent fashion "above" established parties, by late 1990 he made a concerted effort to build a coalition in congress among conservative parties, especially the PFL and PDS, bringing several of their leaders into his cabinet (Power 2000: 191–195). In the process, Brazil's partisan Right aligned itself behind Collor's market reforms, along with much of the business community (Kingstone 1999: 164–168). The new model was vehemently opposed by the PT and the country's largest labor confederation, the PT-affiliated Unified Workers Central (CUT).

Despite this opposition, Collor's audacious shock treatment initially received a favorable response in public opinion surveys (Weyland 2002: 127–128). Public approval was fleeting, however, as shock treatment produced a major recession in 1990, with the economy contracting by 4.4 percent and remaining stagnant for the next two years. Moreover, structural adjustment achieved only partial and temporary success in reining in inflation, in part due to Collor's failure to complete the process of fiscal adjustment. Inflation dropped from 2,938 percent in 1990 to 441 percent in 1991, but by 1992 it was back over 1,000 percent, and in 1993 it surpassed 2,000 percent again. By then Collor was gone; buffeted by corruption scandals, including incendiary charges of influence peddling made by his own brother, Collor became a target of popular protests, and his conservative support base crumbled. The anti-corruption crusader resigned from office in December 1992 in the midst of an impeachment trial for corruption.

Collor was replaced in office by his vice president, Itamar Franco, formerly of the PMDB. An early critic of Collor's shock treatment, Franco slowed down the process of market liberalization but did not make a serious attempt to reverse it. With hyperinflation raging, he went through several finance ministers before finally settling on PSDB leader and Senator Fernando Henrique Cardoso, formerly a prominent leftist intellectual who had become a leader of the democratic opposition against the dictatorship. Despite his social democratic leanings and his firm opposition to Collor, Cardoso believed it was necessary to deepen the process of market liberalization and achieve stabilization once and for all. Cardoso convinced centrist and conservative forces in congress to accept a fiscal adjustment that would limit federal transfers to states and municipalities, then implemented a multi-stage process of currency reform that was designed to break the inertial inflationary effects of indexation (Weyland 2002: 222–225). This reform culminated in the adoption of a new currency pegged to the dollar through the Real Plan in July 1994, which finally brought hyperinflation under control (Kingstone 1999: 195). The inflation rate fell from 2,076 percent in 1994 to 66 percent in 1995 and a mere 15.8 percent in 1996. This stabilization, moreover, was achieved without plunging the economy into recession; indeed, GDP grew by 5.3 percent in 1994 and 4.4 percent in 1995.

The political effects of stabilization were immediate and dramatic. In June 1994, just prior to the adoption of the Real Plan, Lula was heavily favored in public opinion surveys of voter preferences for the October 1994 presidential elections. By August, he had been overtaken in the polls by Cardoso (Weyland 2002: 225), who formed an electoral alliance with his former adversaries on the right, in particular the PFL, in order to block Lula from the presidency and forge a governing coalition in support of market reforms. Cardoso proceeded to win the election in the first round by a vote of 54.3 to 27.0 percent for Lula. Upon taking office, Cardoso solidified his center-right governing coalition, bringing the PMDB and several smaller conservative parties into the fold. This alliance-building strategy gave the president a legislative majority, albeit one that was neither disciplined nor cohesive. Cardoso made a major push to privatize state-owned firms, deregulate the economy, liberalize foreign investment laws, and limit federal spending, but he also sought to balance orthodox reforms with social policy initiatives to provide poverty relief and improve public health care and education.

Arguing that more time was needed to complete economic and institutional reforms, Cardoso won a constitutional amendment that allowed him to run for re-election in 1998. He defeated Lula and the PT by a vote of 53.1 to 31.7 percent, virtually replicating the partisan alignment and competitive balance of the 1994 election. This re-election drew Brazil's critical juncture to a close, as the main tasks of stabilization and structural adjustment had been completed and ratified at the ballot box. The net change in the economy over the course of the critical juncture was dramatic; as late as 1987, Brazil had recorded a score of .465 on the structural reform index, but this score rose to .663 in Sarney's last year in office, .707 in Collor's final year, and .770 when Cardoso was re-elected (Escaith and Paunovic 2004).

Likewise, after years of tumult, the party system had also begun to show signs of consolidation. The dominant parties at the beginning of the democratic transition, the PMDB and the PFL, had ceased to be contenders in the presidential arena, although the latter recovered some ground through alliance strategies and both parties retained significant blocs of legislative seats. The PSDB and the PT, on the other hand, became the major contenders in presidential elections in the 1990s and steadily increased their presence in congress. These four major parties controlled two-thirds of the seats in the lower house of congress by 1998, and electoral volatility sharply declined. In presidential elections, volatility fell from 60.0 in 1994 to 16.8 in 1998, while in legislative elections it declined from 39.4 in 1990 to 16 in 1994 and 13.6 in 1998.

Clearly, economic stabilization after 1994 contributed to this declining electoral volatility, as it eliminated the inflationary spirals that encouraged anti-incumbent voting during the earlier stages of the critical juncture. Electoral stability, however, was also enhanced by the programmatic alignment of partisan competition that occurred during Brazil's market-liberalization process, which produced an institutional legacy of contested liberalism. Structural adjustment policies were begun by the conservative leaders Sarney and Collor, and continued under the center-right coalition governments headed by Cardoso. Opposition to these reforms was consistently championed by the PT and its affiliated labor and popular constituencies, and the leftist party strengthened electorally as the critical juncture unfolded. As shown in Chapter 9, this basic alignment would remain intact in the aftermath period, even as the competitive balance shifted in favor of the PT and the party moderated its opposition to market liberalism.

MARKET REFORM AND DE-ALIGNING CRITICAL JUNCTURES: ARGENTINA AND VENEZUELA

In contrast to Chile and Brazil, market reforms in Argentina and Venezuela were neither led by conservative political actors nor consistently opposed by a major party of the Left. Both countries experienced de-aligning critical junctures, with bait-and-switch patterns of market reform led by historic LM parties. Although Argentina's party system weathered the critical juncture largely intact, it suffered highly destabilizing reactive sequences in the aftermath period. In Venezuela, on the other hand, the party system decomposed toward the end of the critical juncture and was displaced by the polarizing populism of Hugo Chávez. This section analyzes party system dynamics in these two countries during their respective critical junctures; Chapter 9 explores the legacies of those critical junctures in the aftermath period.

Argentina: Bait-and-Switch Reform and Party System De-alignment

In contrast to Brazil, Argentina entered its democratic transition – and its neoliberal critical juncture – in 1983 with two major parties that long pre-dated its BA military regime, along with a myriad of smaller, often provincially based alternatives. Between them, the UCR or Peronists had won every competitive presidential election since 1916. The partisan Right, however, was notoriously weak (Gibson 1996), and the military regime did not bequeath a conservative-dominated political order to lead the process of market liberalization, as did the military regime in Brazil. In the first election cycle after the military regime in 1983, the Peronist PJ was defeated in a presidential election for the first time in the party's history, and UCR leader Raúl Alfonsín – a staunch critic of the dictatorship and its human rights violations – became the first new civilian president. Argentina thus began the new democratic era with no major conservative party, a traditional centrist party in power, and a Peronist opposition that remained highly statist in its programmatic orientation.

The PJ was thoroughly dominated by its labor wing and partially discredited by its role in the economic mismanagement and political violence of the 1970s (Munck 1998; McGuire 1997). Although the party and its union base had been weakened by repression and partial economic restructuring under the dictatorship, it retained substantial influence over labor and social mobilization. Indeed, Peronism wielded an effective social veto against democratic attempts to impose new structural adjustment policies by political actors from outside its ranks.

Alfonsín assumed the presidency with a strong democratic mandate, having defeated the PJ candidate by a vote of 48.8 to 39.1 percent, while helping the UCR capture a narrow majority of seats in the lower house of congress (see Appendix, Tables 1 and 2). Nevertheless, he inherited an economy in shambles. In contrast to Chile, the military regime's neoliberal reforms had failed to produce a viable growth model, tame inflation, or capture the political allegiance of the business community. Furthermore, the military abandoned power in the midst of the global debt crisis in the early 1980s. Consequently, Alfonsín had to contend with a gaping fiscal deficit, a slow recovery from the 1981–1982 recession, massive capital flight, and an inflation rate that would top 600 percent in each of his first two years in office (see Smith 1989: 271). The president initially took a firm stand in opposition to IMF prescriptions for orthodox stabilization policies, only to accept an IMF plan that he could not fulfill in September 1984. Early efforts to negotiate a social pact between capital and labor failed, and the economy sank into a new recession in 1985, contracting by 6.6 percent.

In June 1985 a new economic team adopted a heterodox stabilization program known as the Austral Plan that included a wage and price freeze, the creation of a new, devalued currency, price hikes for public services, and restrictions on monetary emissions. Inflation declined and the economy experienced a new spurt of growth, but distributive conflicts between business and labor led to a loosening of controls by the middle of 1986 and a resurgence of inflationary pressures. Unions mobilized to recoup wage losses, which combined with business price hikes, capital flight, and opposition to tax increases to torpedo government efforts to lower the fiscal deficit and control wages and prices. By early 1987 the government had negotiated a more orthodox stabilization plan with the IMF, but it failed to prevent a return to triple-digit inflation, leading to series of ill-fated adjustment packages (Acuña 1994: 32–37; Smith 1989: 269–285).

In this context of deepening economic crisis, the UCR lost its majority in the lower house of congress in 1987 mid-term elections. The PJ and a new conservative party, the Union of the Democratic Center (UceDé), picked up a number of new seats, while Peronism trounced the UCR in the provinces, winning seventeen of the twenty-two governorships. Following its first-ever electoral defeat in 1983, the PJ had undergone a process of organizational "renovation," with a new set of leaders who sought to diminish trade-union control of the party, broaden its appeal to non-working-class constituencies, and democratize and institutionalize its notoriously informal organizational structure (Levitsky 2003: 109–118).

Renovation aside, the PJ retained political control over the national labor confederation, the CGT, and it used its influence over social mobilization to pressure Alfonsín as the economy deteriorated. The Peronist labor movement declared thirteen general strikes during the Alfonsín years, while the total number of strikes jumped from 321 in 1983 to 1,050 in 1985, 699 in 1986, and 638 in 1987 (*La Economía Argentina*, various issues). Conflict over the distribution of the social costs of stabilization repeatedly blocked efforts to reach a truce, as the PJ and the CGT declined to negotiate a "pact of governability" to prevent the economy's descent into chaos (Smith 1989: 293). A series of military rebellions against Alfonsín over human rights trials and pay cuts contributed to the impression of a government under siege.

New elections were held in the midst of yet another severe recession and a hyperinflationary surge that would reach over 3,000 percent in 1989. The PJ selected as its 1989 presidential candidate the colorful governor Carlos Menem, who had been associated with the renovation current but was backed by more traditional trade-union sectors in internal party primaries. Menem won a decisive 49.3 to 32.5 percent victory over UCR candidate Eduardo Angeloz, and assumed office five months early when Alfonsín stepped down so that a new government could tackle the financial crisis. The PJ also captured an absolute majority of seats in the Senate and a near-majority in the lower house. The gravity of the economic crisis clearly weakened the UCR and contributed to anti-incumbent vote shifts; the party's legislative vote share dropped 20 percentage points between 1983 and 1989, and only 58 percent of those who voted for Alfonsín supported the UCR candidate in 1989, with 27 percent shifting to the Peronist column (Catterberg 1991: 97).

Menem had run for office on a traditional populist platform, alluding to the need for a moratorium on debt payments and a major wage hike to keep up with inflation. With inflation running at nearly 200 percent a month, however, Menem's election was followed by one of Latin America's most dramatic bait-and-switch packages of reform. Before taking office, Menem turned over the ministry of economy to executives from one of Argentina's leading agro-export firms, a traditional adversary of Peronism. Other cabinet positions were given to representatives of business associations and the conservative UceDé, a pro-market conservative party that threw its support to Menem. Upon taking office, Menem immediately imposed neoliberal shock treatment. Public spending and tariffs were cut, utility prices were raised, the exchange rate was unified, prices were deregulated, and state-owned enterprises were sold to private investors.

Although inflation sharply declined in response to these measures, the initial stabilization did not hold. The rate of inflation rose above 2,000 percent in 1990, prompting Menem to deepen structural adjustment. Stabilization was finally achieved when Menem and his fourth economy minister, Domingo Cavallo, implemented a "convertibility plan" in April 1991, fixing the peso at one to the dollar and requiring that any monetary emissions be backed by gold or foreign currency. The new economic team took additional measures to liberalize labor markets, reduce union control over social welfare funds, and privatize the pension system. The reforms amounted to "a veritable neoliberal revolution in the model of accumulation and the structure of social relations in Argentina" (Acuña 1994: 47), while Cavallo claimed the administration was "changing everything that Perón did" (*La Nación*, February 11, 1992, p. 13).

Indeed, Latin America's most famous populist party, long synonymous with state-led development, had overseen one of the region's deepest and most comprehensive processes of market reform. Argentina's score on the index of structural reform rose from .642 in 1988 to .856 in 1992, the highest in Latin America at the time (Escaith and Paunovic 1994). By the end of 1991 inflation was under 1 percent a month, dropping to annual rates of 24.9 percent in 1992, 10.6 percent in 1993, and 3.9 percent in 1994. Pro-market policies and the end of hyperinflation helped restore business confidence, and the economy took off on a four-year spurt of rapid growth, expanding by nearly 8 percent a year between 1991 and 1994.

Not surprisingly, Menem and the PJ reaped political rewards from this stabilization and growth. Menem basked in public approval ratings over 50 percent and consolidated his personal control over the party, which began to push for a constitutional reform to allow presidential re-election. Recognizing its dim electoral prospects, the UCR bowed to political realities and negotiated a pact with the PJ to elect a constituent assembly and allow the president to stand for re-election. Menem achieved a resounding victory in 1995 presidential elections, earning 49.9 percent of the vote to only 17 percent for the UCR candidate and 29.3 percent for José Octavio Bordón of the new FREPASO (Front for a Country in Solidarity) alliance. The PJ won a majority in both houses of congress, while the UCR's bloc of seats in the lower house was cut nearly in half between 1985 and 1995. Electoral realignment had thus produced a new Peronist majority and a split opposition comprised of a declining UCR and an emerging coalition of center-left and ex-Peronist forces grouped together in FREPASO.

Menem's re-election demonstrated that he had successfully navigated the political and economic landmines of structural adjustment, transforming a historic populist party into an architect of free-market reforms. This transformation was wrenching within the PJ, however, as opposition to the new economic model was widespread within the traditional labor wing of the party as well as center-left elements within the renovated current (Palermo and Novaro 1996; Corrales 2002). Indeed, a survey of Peronist activists demonstrated that a sizable majority disapproved of all or major parts of Menem's reforms (Levitsky 2003: 191–194). Nevertheless, Menem moved so quickly and decisively that internal opponents had little capacity to resist. As stated by PJ congressional leader Humberto Roggero,

The PJ is a party of leaders, and when Menem acted, the party followed ... Our party's ideology is flexible, and it is part of our culture to recognize when reality changes... We try to understand the historical stage and adapt to it. If you can't change history, you must accompany it. We might fall 20 times, but we'll get up 21 times, because of our vocation for power. (Author's interview, Buenos Aires, May 27, 1999)

Ultimately, defections from the ranks of the PJ were kept to a minimum. At the elite level, the main defection occurred in late 1990 when Carlos "Chacho" Álvarez led a group of eight center-left congressional deputies out of the PJ, and eventually helped to found FREPASO. In response to early dissent, however, Menem gave party leaders a greater role in his cabinet, coordinated policies with the PJ congressional bloc, and invoked Peronist symbols and principles to justify his reforms (Palermo and Novaro 1996; Corrales 2002: 169–185). He also allowed significant autonomy for provincial Peronist governments and funneled resources to them. The PJ's decentralized organization allowed local Peronist leaders to keep the party's patronage machine operating even within the fiscal constraints of an austere neoliberal state, thus securing the PJ's grassroots territorial bases (Gibson and Calvo 2000; Levitsky 2003: 195–209). At the sub-national level, then, traditional Peronist practices and clientelist linkages continued.

The success of Menem's project also required that he win over – or at least neutralize – the other critical bastion of traditional Peronism, the labor movement. This was no easy task, as workers bore much of the brunt of structural adjustment's social costs. Real wages, for example, shrank by more than 25 percent between 1990 and 1993, while the rate of unemployment jumped from 5.8 in 1991 to 18.8 in 1995 despite rapid economic growth (International Labour Organization 1998: 37). Market reforms struck directly at the interests of labor, including layoffs in privatized firms, restrictions on public sector strikes and collective bargaining, the privatization of union-controlled health and pension programs, and the flexibilization of labor markets, which eased restrictions on firing workers and hiring temporary employees. The percentage of the workforce organized in trade unions declined from 36.1 in 1986 to 22.3 in 1995 (International Labour Organization 1997a: 235; McGuire 1997: 268), continuing a steady slide that began in the mid-1970s. Many of Argentina's most prominent unions were decimated by economic restructuring; according to

Levitsky (2003: 146), membership in the metalworkers union "fell from nearly 300,000 to 170,000, railway workers union membership fell from 67,000 to 14,000, oil workers union membership fell from 35,000 to 2,000, and textile workers union membership fell from 74,000 to 44,000." This organizational decline was accompanied by labor's loss of political influence within the PJ, a deliberate component of the renovationists' strategy to enhance the autonomy of the party apparatus.

Organized labor, however – like the PJ itself – was prone to internal hetero-geneity, allowing Menem to play different factions against each other. Ranis (1995), for example, discovered that many workers were open to the potential efficiency gains of economic liberalization, despite their statist traditions. The CGT thus split into pro- and anti-reform tendencies in 1989 before reuniting three years later, while a more critical group of unions led by school teachers and public employees broke with the CGT to form an opposition confederation. The government used traditional party–union linkages to offer inducements for collaboration in the reform process, such as generous retirement packages, control over employee-owned stock programs, and private pension and life insurance plans (Murillo 2001: 142–144).

Consequently, after declaring thirteen general strikes in response to Alfonsín's tepid orthodox reforms, the CGT declared only one general strike against Menem's shock treatment during his first term in office. This acquies-cence was rewarded with modest concessions on labor relations that posed little threat to the core of the neoliberal model. Menem took advantage of the PJ's historic corporatist linkages to neutralize labor resistance and co-opt support. At the same time, however, party reforms and the new economic model eroded the organizational foundations for these corporatist relationships, in the process transforming the PJ from a labor-based mass party to a more territorial and patronage-based machine party that was heavily dependent on local and provincial power brokers (see Auyero 2000; Levitsky 2003: 107–143).

As the PJ de-unionized, the Menem government made a conscious effort to dilute class cleavages by appealing to middle- and upper-class voters who were traditionally averse to Peronism. Menem named business executives and pro-market technocrats to key cabinet positions (Teichman 2001: 123), and forged an alliance with the conservative UCeDé to support market reforms. This alliance allowed the UCeDé to advance its programmatic objectives, albeit at the cost of its own development as a partisan representative of Argentine business interests; the UCeDé suffered an electoral decline and was relegated to the political margins by the late 1990s. As stated by Borón (2000: 160), "the price the UceDé had to pay for this Pyrrhic ideological victory was none other than its political emasculation as a party."

Consequently, Argentina's bait-and-switch process of market reform repro-duced the organizational vacuum on the political right that had existed at the national level since the onset of mass politics in the early 20th century (see Gibson 1996; Borón 2000). A survey conducted shortly before the 1995 election found that 74.7 percent of the upper-middle class and 69 percent of the upper class declared no affiliation or sympathy for any established party, compared to 43.1 percent of the lower class, where Peronist identities were still anchored (*Estudio Mora y Araujo y Asociados*, February 1995). This same survey, however, found that roughly 80 percent of the middle- and upper-class respondents were positive or neutral toward the Menem government and its economic model, while approximately one-third expressed support for Menem's' re-election. Menem thus exploited the organizational vacuum on the Right to attract new support among middle- and upper-class independents while retaining Peronism's core lower- and working-class constituencies (see Gervasoni 1995; Gibson 1997: 364–366). In the process, he softened – at least temporarily – Argentina's ISI-era class cleavage and produced a multi-class electoral coalition comparable to those of patronage-based machine parties elsewhere in Latin America.

Argentina's critical juncture effectively ended when Menem's 1995 re-election ratified the basic policy shift in the electoral arena. The political dynamics of economic crisis and market reform during the critical juncture had realigned the party system electorally, while de-aligning it programmatically. Little change occurred in the organizational composition of the party system during the critical juncture, as the PJ and UCR remained the two leading parties; although new parties emerged on the Right (UceDé) and the Center-Left (FREPASO), neither would consolidate a position as a major power contender in the aftermath period. The electoral balance of power between the UCR and the PJ was altered, as the UCR bore the brunt of the political costs of economic crisis, while the PJ reaped the political rewards of stabilization. Vote shifts from one established party to the other, however – a form of intra-systemic volatility – were relatively modest in comparative perspective. Argentina's combined presidential and legislative electoral volatility in the 1980s and 1990s was 18.6, below the regional mean and much lower than the average score of 29.8 in the LM cases.

As Argentina exited the critical juncture in the mid-1990s, therefore, its party system appeared to be relatively intact, albeit with some fluidity on the anti-Peronist side of the political cleavage. The bait-and-switch process of reform, however, had left the party system without a major conservative party to defend the neoliberal model, or a major party of the Left to contest it. Although the newly formed FREPASO sought to fill the latter political void, it proved incapable of doing so effectively. As shown in Chapter 9, FREPASO would be decimated, along with the UCR, when the two parties formed a governing alliance in the aftermath period and retained Menem's neoliberal model in a context of acute financial crisis and explosive social protest. Argentina's programmatically de-aligning critical juncture, therefore, produced an institutional outcome of neoliberal convergence that was highly susceptible to destabilizing reactive sequences in the aftermath period – very much in contrast to the programmatically aligned party systems of Chile and Brazil, with their legacies of contested liberalism.

Venezuela: Bait-and-Switch Reform, Programmatic De-alignment, and Party System Decomposition

Like Argentina, Venezuela was a classic case of bait-and-switch market reform led by a historic LM party. Unlike Argentina, however, Venezuela's party system decomposed toward the end of the critical juncture, facilitating the rise of an anti-neoliberal populist outsider who would dominate national politics in the aftermath period. In Venezuela, therefore, neoliberal convergence culminated in a process of party system decomposition and an institutional legacy of polarized populism.

Although neoliberal critical junctures produced a number of unexpected political outcomes in Latin America, perhaps none was more shocking than that of Venezuela. The collapse of the Venezuelan party system in the 1990s and the rise of a stridently anti-neoliberal populist figure in Hugo Chávez pose a double paradox that challenges much of the conventional scholarly wisdom. First, decomposition occurred in one of the most highly institutionalized party systems in Latin America. The party system was dominated by the conservative COPEI and the center-left, labor-mobilizing AD – both moderate, nationally organized parties with multi-class bases of support. The two parties were renowned for their discipline, electoral stability, and penetration of civil society (Coppedge 1994; Kornblith and Levine 1995). Between them, the two parties had won every presidential election since Venezuela's return to democracy in 1958, and in the 1970s – when neighboring countries were struggling to dismantle military rule – AD and COPEI jointly captured over 85 percent of the presidential vote and 80 percent of the legislative seats in national elections. Although ample oil revenues led the Venezuelan state and both parties to become riddled by administrative inefficiency and rent-seeking behavior, especially after the mid-1970s oil bonanza, AD and COPEI remained formidable political institutions, and their collapse would have been considered unimaginable prior to the 1990s.

Second, although Venezuela's democratic regime and party system boasted many of the attributes that have been identified by scholars as contributing to the successful adoption of structural adjustment policies, market reform in Venezuela was a more abject political failure than in perhaps any other country in Latin America. Indeed, political resistance limited the scope and depth of market liberalization even before the rise of Chávez, despite seemingly favorable institutional conditions. Venezuela had an institutionalized democratic regime, which should, in theory, lengthen the time horizons of social and political actors and allow them to accept short-term sacrifices in exchange for long-term gains. It also had only two major parties, limiting the number of "veto players" who could block reform, facilitating the construction of legislative majorities, and reducing coordination problems in the policymaking process (Haggard and Kaufman 1995: 166–174; Tseblis 2002). As Geddes states (1994: 187), cooperation for reform "emerges more easily when it involves fewer, relatively stable, disciplined parties" – precisely the attributes of the Venezuelan party system in the 1980s.

These parties, moreover, were not ideologically polarized. The policy distance between them by the 1970s was quite moderate, and they had a history of forging political and economic pacts dating to the 1958 democratic transition (Karl 1987). They also penetrated civil society in ways that gave them a significant measure of control over the articulation of societal demands, especially those of organized labor (Ellner 1995; Burgess 1999; Murillo 2001). Indeed, they had institutionalized political bargaining by giving labor, business, and other social actors representation on hundreds of consultative commissions and public agencies (Crisp 2000). European scholarship has long argued that such participatory, neo-corporatist forms of interest representation can moderate sectoral demands, institutionalize class compromise, and elicit cooperation during periods of economic restructuring (Garrett 1998).

Despite these seemingly favorable institutional conditions, the Venezuelan party system failed to manage the transition from ISI to neoliberalism, and the electorate resisted market reforms more consistently than any other in Latin America. In all four presidential campaigns during Venezuela's critical juncture, voters chose the candidate who appeared to be the most electorally viable opponent of orthodox adjustment. Initially, these opponents were drawn from within the party system – specifically, from AD – but as the two major parties converged on orthodox positions, they were rejected by the electorate and displaced by independent personalities or populist figures who promised to buck the trend. In contrast to Argentina, where bait-and-switch reforms in a context of acute hyperinflation allowed the PJ to reap electoral rewards from stabilization, similar reforms adopted by the AD in Venezuela – in the absence of hyperinflation (see Weyland 2002) – provoked an immediate and powerful political backlash that ultimately contributed to voter detachment from traditional parties system-wide.

Ironically, the economic crisis that triggered Venezuela's critical juncture in the early 1980s followed closely on the heels of the oil export windfalls of the 1970s. Although Venezuela started ISI policies relatively late, oil revenues fueled steady economic growth through the mid-1970s, with growth rates averaging over 5 percent a year in the post-1958 period (Echevarría 1995: 4, 28, 49). Despite the oil boom of the 1970s, however, Venezuela borrowed heavily from international lenders, using its oil reserves as collateral to finance an explosion of state spending on subsidies, social programs, and industrial development. Central government expenditures increased more than six-fold between 1970 and 1981, while the external debt ballooned from less than one billion dollars in 1970 to over 27 billion in 1984 (Karl 1997: 165, 258). Rather than enabling Venezuela to escape the financial and foreign exchange bottlenecks that plagued other Latin American countries, the oil bonanza encouraged state profligacy and inefficiency, leaving the country vulnerable to the global shocks that loomed on the horizon.

The COPEI government of Luís Herrera Campíns was elected in 1978 on a fiscally conservative platform that promised to halt the rampant overspending, corruption, and foreign borrowing that characterized the populist administration of the AD's Carlos Andrés Pérez during the first oil bonanza of the mid-1970s. The second oil boom at the end of the decade, however, encouraged Herrera to forego austerity; instead, he increased public spending and took on new debt, hoping to stimulate an economy that had ceased to grow. Economic conditions deteriorated in 1982, however, when the global recession, falling oil prices, and higher interest rates on the debt plunged Venezuela into crisis. The decline in export revenues caused the fiscal deficit to swell, while an overvalued exchange rate led to widespread capital flight. Herrera abruptly devalued the currency in February 1983, causing purchasing power to plummet, and he established a multi-tiered system of exchange controls that became rife with corruption and rent-seeking (Karl 1997: 175–76). Desperate for revenues, the COPEI government declared a unilateral moratorium on debt repayments and raided the reserve funds of the state oil company. The government hoped to reschedule foreign debt and obtain new loans from the IMF, but it was wary of harsh conditionality terms, and ultimately postponed politically sensitive negotiations until after the December 1983 elections (Echevarría 1995; Karl 1997: 174–177).

During Herrera's five-year term, Venezuela's GDP shrank by 5.1 percent, producing a 16.5 percent reduction in per-capita GDP (Echevarría 1995: 75). Not surprisingly, national elections in 1983 produced a vote shift from COPEI to AD, with the latter electing Jaime Lusinchi to the presidency and capturing a congressional majority (see Appendix, Tables 15 and 16). Despite a grant of special decree powers from congress to tackle economic problems (Crisp 2000: 33–34), Lusinchi postponed serious reform while overseeing a modest – and ultimately deceptive – economic expansion. His government negotiated an accord with foreign banks in 1986 to reschedule Venezuela's foreign debt, without formally adopting IMF conditionality. Nevertheless, Lusinchi failed to implement the orthodox reforms mandated by this accord, and he increased government spending, especially during the election year of 1988 (Karl 1997: 178–179). The economy grew at an average rate of 5.7 percent during Lusinchi's final three years, while price controls kept inflation below 30 percent – a far cry from the hyperinflationary rates in neighboring countries with LM party systems.

This relatively favorable economic performance came at a steep price, however, as severe bottlenecks were developing below the surface. Oil prices fell by more than 60 percent between 1982 and 1986, and Venezuela's external debt ballooned to over $30 billion. By the end of Lusinchi's term both the current account and fiscal deficits were more than 9 percent of GDP, and foreign exchange reserves were virtually depleted. Inflationary pressures were artificially contained by price controls, which spawned hoarding, black market activities, and consumer shortages in the months before the 1988 presidential election (Naím 1993: 35–37).

During the 1988 campaign, neither of the major presidential candidates – Eduardo Fernández of COPEI and former president Carlos Andrés Pérez of the AD – prepared the electorate for the economic shock treatment that lay just around the corner. Fernández advocated market reforms, but denied that an IMF accord would be necessary to secure them. Meanwhile, Pérez fostered expectations that his election would allow a return to the generalized affluence of his first presidential term in the 1970s. Pérez spoke vaguely about the need for economic reforms, but his vocal criticism of the neoliberal model masked the content of the policies he would adopt (Corrales 2002: 92). Later, he would acknowledge that he cloaked his intentions to keep from scaring the populace (interview with the author, Caracas, June 9, 1998).

Indeed, with the economy growing and inflation artificially contained, there was hardly a political consensus on the need for austerity and structural adjustment, despite the evidence of underlying disequilibria. Likewise, economic hardships had not yet driven voters to reject the dominant parties; to the contrary, AD and COPEI jointly captured 81.6 percent of congressional seats and a record 93.3 percent of the presidential vote in 1988. AD retained the presidency behind Pérez with 52.9 percent of the vote, although it lost its congressional majority. Little suggested that an unprecedented period of political turbulence was about to begin.

Following the elections, however, the economic crisis that Lusinchi had kept under wraps was ready to explode. The shortage of foreign exchange hampered imports and exacerbated consumer shortages, leading to rationing and a growing black market fed by suppressed inflation. According to one of the technocratic architects of Pérez' adjustment strategy, former Planning Minister Miguel Rodríguez, operational foreign exchange reserves "were negative by more than $6 billion" when Pérez took office, with liquid reserves more than offset by short-term debts due within the first four months of the administration (Rodríguez 1994: 378). Given this straightjacket, Pérez defied his populist track record and immediately negotiated an orthodox package of reforms with the IMF, turning to technocratic advisors from outside the ranks of AD to implement them. This reform package, known as the *gran viaje* ("great turnaround"), was implemented with "dizzying speed." The government "eliminated exchange controls and established the free convertibility of the bolívar, freed interest rates, liberalized virtually all prices, and increased rates for electricity, water, telephone, gasoline, public transportation, and most other public services" (Naím 1993: 50). Tariff and nontariff barriers to trade were slashed or eliminated, as were restrictions on foreign investment, and a plan was launched to privatize state-owned enterprises and financial institutions. Although congressional opposition blocked the full implementation of privatization and tax reforms, the process of structural adjustment under Pérez was still profound, driving up Venezuela's score on the structural reform index from .465 in 1988 to .609 in 1992 (Escaith and Paunovic 2004).

Indeed, Pérez's shock treatment was more severe than even the IMF required, leading some members of his economic team to question the harshness and speed of the adjustment (Weyland 2002: 110–112). In contrast to Menem in Argentina, Pérez could not use hyperinflation to provide political cover for his policy switch, and many citizens undoubtedly hoped that a new rise in oil prices would make austerity and adjustment unnecessary. In the aftermath to the oil boom, it was easy to blame economic problems on the mismanagement and corruption of political leaders who had squandered their country's wealth (Carrasquero and Welch 2000: 176). As reported by Romero (1997: 21), surveys found that even after a decade of lower oil prices, 91 percent of Venezuelan citizens believed their country was rich, and 94 percent believed "there would be enough money for all and more" if the country "were honestly administered and corruption eliminated." Not surprisingly, then, quarterly surveys conducted in 1989 found that on average only 30 percent of Venezuelans approved of Pérez' reforms, whereas 53 percent preferred a return to the previous economic model (Consultores 21 S.A. 1996: 154).

In this context, societal resistance to structural adjustment did not take long to emerge. On February 27, 1989, within weeks of Pérez' inauguration and eleven days after announcing structural adjustment measures, a 100-percent increase in bus fares triggered a spontaneous five-day rebellion known as the *caracazo* in Caracas and other cities. Rioters took over the streets and looted shops, destroying several thousand stores and business establishments. The government responded by declaring a state of emergency, suspending civil liberties, and sending military troops to suppress the rioters (López Maya 2005: 61–84). Between 246 and 1,500 people were killed in the riots and repression (Silva 2009: 204), and thousands were arrested in military sweeps of lower-class neighborhoods. The *caracazo* was the most widespread and violent of all the popular uprisings – sometimes dubbed "IMF riots" – that greeted initial structural adjustment measures in Latin America.

Smaller-scale social protests continued thereafter, with over 3,000 separate protest events recorded between 1989 and 1993 (López Maya 2005: 90, 94). Protest activities, however, were not well organized by a cohesive central actor; Venezuela did not have a mass-based indigenous movement like those that arose later in Ecuador and Bolivia, and the national labor confederation, the *Confederación de Trabajadores de Venezuela* (CTV), was too closely tied to AD to channel societal resistance. Pérez' about-face was highly controversial within the CTV, as the AD's labor bureau had played a critical role in securing his presidential nomination by the party. Although the CTV leadership expressed grudging approval of the reforms when they were first adopted, after the *caracazo* the labor central temporarily broke ranks and joined independent unions in convoking a general strike – the first in Venezuela since the 1958 democratic transition. As stated by Burgess (1999: 114), the May 1989 strike "was an unprecedented act of norm-breaking voice that brought the economy to a halt and severely damaged the government's credibility." Following the general strike, however, the CTV backed away from social mobilization, and worked with AD dissidents in congress to water down some

TABLE 8.1. *Social Class and Support for Neoliberal Reforms in Venezuela, 1989–1991 (Average Percentage of Respondents)*

	Lower Class	Lower-Middle Class	Middle Class	Upper Class
Support neoliberal reforms	23.8	30.1	40.7	51.5
Return to previous economic model	55.1	54.0	43.3	30.7

Source: Calculated from Consultores 21, "Estudio de Opinión Pública Sobre Temas Económicos," 11 surveys between April 1989 and December 1991. Data from the September 1990 survey were not available.

of Pérez' proposed reforms on labor market flexibilization, wage policies, and social benefits (Burgess 2004: 135–138).

The short-term economic costs of the shock program compounded its political credibility problems and fueled dissent within AD, especially after the party made a poor showing in state and local elections in December 1989. GDP contracted by 7.8 percent in 1989, while inflation rose to a record level of 84.5 percent once price controls were lifted. Although inflation dropped in the remaining years of Pérez' term, it remained above pre-adjustment levels. The economy rebounded strongly after 1989, as a new increase in oil prices helped stimulate an average growth rate of 7.6 percent between 1990 and 1992. Nevertheless, a solid plurality continued to oppose the new economic model in public opinion polls, and by 1992 – when the Pérez government was rocked by two failed coup attempts – opponents outnumbered supporters by 56 to 28 percent (Consultores 21 S.A. 1996: 154). As shown in Table 8.1, opinions toward the neoliberal model were sharply differentiated by social class; lower-income Venezuelans consistently opposed the new model, while the middle class was split and a majority of upper-income citizens offered support. Following several decades of centripetal competition between two moderate parties with multi-class constituencies, this divergence provided early signs of a renewed politicization of class cleavages in Venezuelan society.

This lower-class opposition clearly reflected the social costs of economic adjustment. Continuing a decade-long slide, real wages plunged more than 30 percent between 1989 and 1991, while prices for consumer staples rose as subsidies and price controls were eliminated. Government spending cuts exacerbated the wage contraction and price increases; by 1993 per-capita social spending had fallen by 40 percent below the level of 1980, including real cuts of greater than 40 percent in education programs, 70 percent in housing and urban development, and 37 percent in health care (República de Venezuela 1995: 40). Social spending accounted for 8 percent of GDP in 1987, but only 4.3 percent by 1994 (Evans 1998: 12). The percentage of the population living below the poverty line increased from 36 percent in 1984 to 66 percent in 1995, with the most severe deterioration coinciding with the process of economic adjustment; in 1989 alone the poverty rate increased from 46 to 62 percent of the population, while those living in extreme poverty more than doubled, from 14 to 30 percent (República de Venezuela 1995: 23). The Pérez government targeted new nutritional and medical programs on the poor (Naím 1993: 53–54), but they hardly compensated for these broader economic hardships.

These hardships strengthened the position of Pérez' critics inside AD, who feared the potential electoral costs of unpopular reforms. The national director-ate of AD initially endorsed the new economic model, as did the leadership of COPEI, while the AD's congressional bloc largely adhered to party discipline in passing most of Pérez' reforms. Even pro-reform sectors of AD chafed at the president's technocratic mode of governance, however, as Pérez imposed reforms with little dialogue and – in contrast to Menem in Argentina – never developed a sound strategy to win over his party (Corrales 2000). Pérez paid a steep political price for this relative neglect of AD; by October 1991 his oppo-nents had taken control of the party leadership, and the momentum for reform ground to a halt. The CTV paralyzed Caracas with a general strike in November, and AD congressional deputies joined opposition parties to block further privatizations and pass a labor law that clashed with the general thrust of the market model. Despite the economic revival of the early 1990s, Pérez was increasingly isolated politically and vulnerable to the popular backlash that was brewing in Venezuelan society.

The backlash exploded in February 1992 when Lt. Col. Hugo Chávez led a military rebellion that broke with a generation-long norm of military subordi-nation to civilian authority (Trinkunas 2005). Although the coup attempt was suppressed by loyal military forces, landing Chávez in prison, it stunned Venezuela's political establishment by garnering a significant measure of popu-lar sympathy. In response, Pérez abandoned new economic reforms and brokered a pact of co-governance between AD and COPEI. This accord broke down in June of 1992, however, when COPEI ministers abandoned the cabinet. Although Pérez weathered another coup attempt in November, his administra-tion was paralyzed. Bereft of popular and partisan support, Pérez was suspended from the presidency on May 19, 1993, one day before the Supreme Court ruled that there were sufficient grounds to try him for corruption (Corrales 2002: 64–65).

Following a short-lived interim government, AD selected another market reformer, Claudio Fermín, as its candidate in the 1993 presidential campaign. The party paid a severe price at the ballot box for the national crisis, receiving its lowest vote total in history: 23.6 percent of the presidential vote, and only fifty-five of the 203 seats in the chamber of deputies. The vote shift away from AD, however, did not revert to the COPEI column; the conservative party joined the AD in electoral decline, receiving only 22.7 percent of the presidential vote and 54 seats in the chamber of deputies. Systemic decomposition rather than electoral realignment had become the dominant trend.

Several factors prevented COPEI from capitalizing on AD's decline. As the party in power when the economic crisis erupted in the early 1980s, COPEI had already borne political costs for its mishandling of the economy and never fully recovered. It was also an increasingly fractious party, with internal schisms related to leadership disputes and policy discord. Although COPEI evolved toward support of market reform, a faction led by party founder and former president Rafael Caldera stridently opposed the neoliberal model. Caldera, in fact, had rationalized the first 1992 coup attempt as an expression of outrage at Pérez' reforms, and he broke with COPEI when he failed to win the party's presidential nomination in 1993. COPEI thus failed to project an image of coherent leadership, and it was hard pressed to differentiate its neoliberal program and establishment profile from those of AD, given the parties' longstanding collaboration. The two parties were the architects and pillars of an economic and political order that was rapidly decomposing, and their demise proved to be as mutual as their historic structuring of the post-1958 regime. While 82 percent of Venezuelans blamed AD for the crisis, 65 percent attributed responsibility to COPEI as well (Romero 1997: 16).

Furthermore, Venezuela's bait-and-switch pattern of market reform made it difficult for COPEI to experience an electoral revival in the 1990s. The conservative party was pro-business and increasingly pro-market, but it had relinquished political leadership of the reform process to AD, and the relatively narrow portion of the electorate that supported the new economic model divided its political loyalties between the two parties. Meanwhile, opponents of reform – by all indications a majority of citizens – had no reason to support COPEI as an alternative to AD. Instead, social discontent was channeled toward explicitly anti-neoliberal electoral alternatives outside the traditional two-party system. In a close four-way race, a narrow plurality of 30.5 percent gave the presidency to Caldera in 1993, who ran an anti-neoliberal campaign at the head of a makeshift coalition known as *Convergencia Nacional* (National Convergence, or CN), which included the small leftist party *Movimiento al Socialismo* (Movement to Socialism, or MAS). The demise of the old order was accentuated by the strong showing of Andrés Velásquez of the leftist *La Causa R* party (Radical Cause), which captured 21.9 percent of the presidential vote and an unprecedented forty seats in the chamber of deputies. With roots in a 1970 split of the Venezuelan Communist Party and a strong base among non-AD labor unions, *La Causa R* had won the governorship of the industrial state of Bolívar in 1989 and 1992, along with the mayorship of Caracas in 1992 (see López-Maya 1997). Never before, however, had it received more than 0.3 percent of the presidential vote.

The independent vote for Caldera and the protest vote for *La Causa R* demonstrated that many citizens were detaching from the dominant parties (Alvarez 1996). This detachment was also evidenced by rising levels of electoral abstention, which reached 39.8 percent in 1993, more than double the 18.1 percent recorded in 1988 (Hellinger 2003: 45). Similarly, the percentage of

Venezuelans who claimed to be members or supporters of a party fell to 22.8 percent in 1994, down from 48.7 percent in 1973 and 32.4 percent in 1990 (Molina Vega and Pérez Baralt 1996: 224). Nevertheless, voter detachment during this early stage in the process of party system decomposition was cautious and partial. AD and COPEI jointly retained a majority of seats in congress, and while the electorate chose a president from outside the ranks of the dominant parties, Caldera was hardly an outsider to the political establishment that he now so roundly criticized.

Caldera's new presidential term, however, only accelerated the demise of the old order. The president took office in the midst of a recession and a severe crisis in the newly deregulated banking system. As Weyland (2002: 214) states, "imprudent, speculative and even fraudulent lending practices" had led to a series of bankruptcies and a collapse of trust in financial institutions, ultimately forcing the closure of "seventeen banks that controlled two-thirds of all financial assets." In response to the crisis, Caldera initially remained true to his heterodox platform; he imposed price and exchange controls, took over eight major banks, and bailed out others at enormous cost to the national treasury. He also suspended constitutional guarantees of economic liberties and stimulated growth through lax monetary policies.

After two years of recession, the economy resumed slow growth in 1995, but fiscal and balance-of-payments deficits led to capital flight and acute inflationary pressures. With inflation rising to an unprecedented 99.9 percent rate in 1996, Caldera reversed course and turned toward economic orthodoxy – in essence, the second de-aligning process of structural adjustment in Venezuela's critical juncture. The government negotiated an accord with the IMF and reached an agreement with AD to provide legislative support for an adjustment package devised by new Planning Minister Teodoro Petkoff – ironically, the historic leader of the leftist MAS. Petkoff's "Agenda Venezuela" called for deep budget cuts, the lifting of exchange controls, currency devaluation, increased public-sector prices, and layoffs of government employees (Weyland 2002: 225–226). Although this policy switch did not elicit the types of violent social protest that greeted Pérez' reforms in 1989, neither did it win much support among Venezuelans. By 1997, the administration of the aging Caldera was evaluated negatively by 74 percent of survey respondents (Consultores 21 S.A. 1997; question 22).

With the economy mired in new recessions in 1996 and 1998, Venezuelans approached the 1998 elections having lived through twenty years of recurring economic hardship. Per-capita GDP had declined by 20 percent over this period, returning to levels last seen in the 1960s (Crisp 2000: 175). Wages fell even more sharply than national income; indeed, a 60-percent plunge in real industrial wages from 1980 to 1996 was the steepest in Latin America (International Labour Organization 1998: 43). Economic hardships, therefore, were disproportionately borne by the lower and working classes, exacerbating inequalities. The income share of the poorest 40 percent of the population fell from 19.1 to

14.7 percent between 1981 and 1997, while that of the wealthiest decile increased from 21.8 to 32.8 percent (Economic Commission for Latin America and the Caribbean 1999: 63).

The political costs of this dismal long-term record were profound. Surveys demonstrated that only 6 percent of Venezuelans had confidence in political parties, while 91 percent expressed a lack of confidence (Luengo and Ponce 1996: 70). Not only had a succession of parties failed to reverse the economic slide, but they had proved incapable of offering meaningful programmatic alternatives. Two bait-and-switch processes of market reform had produced an overarching pattern of neoliberal convergence, one that encompassed Caldera and MAS as well as AD and COPEI – thus demonstrating the failure of partisan and electoral competition to generate policy alternatives that accurately mapped onto the programmatic divide in Venezuelan society. Increasingly, then, this programmatic divide became superimposed on an establishment/anti-establishment political cleavage, allowing outsiders to politicize inequalities and mobilize the popular constituencies that consistently opposed the neoliberal model.

The 1998 elections thus deepened the process of party system decomposition, especially in the presidential race, as voters abandoned established parties *en masse* for a diverse array of independent candidates. Initially, surveys indicated that the presidential frontrunner was a former Miss Universe, Irene Sáez, a popular independent mayor from a wealthy district of Caracas. Sáez was endorsed by COPEI, but experienced a steady erosion of support in the months preceding the December election. The decline of Sáez opened space on the Right for Henrique Salas Römer, a proponent of market reform and former COPEI governor who had broken with the party to launch an independent electoral vehicle known as *Proyecto Venezuela* (PV). Unlike COPEI, the AD hierarchy initially imposed party stalwart Luís Alfaro Ucero as a candidate from within its ranks, but the party's regional bases rebelled as Alfaro languished in the polls. Meanwhile, having failed to establish a partisan identity separate from that of the aging President Caldera, *Convergencia Nacional* sank into political oblivion.

All of these candidates had connections to the political establishment and supported the general course of market liberalization. In the end, all were eclipsed by the candidate with the most impeccable outsider credentials and the most strident critique of the neoliberal model – former coup leader Hugo Chávez. After receiving a pardon from President Caldera in March 1994, Chávez left prison and traveled across the country, recruiting supporters for a nationalistic "Bolivarian" political movement that would be built around the clandestine military networks he had been organizing since 1983 (Trinkunas 2005: 180–183). Chávez condemned the traditional parties for their corruption and railed against "savage neoliberalism" and the oligarchic and imperialist interests it served. The centerpiece of his populist campaign was a pledge to convoke a constituent assembly and re-found the republic, promising an institutional rupture with the post-1958 political order that AD and COPEI had so thoroughly dominated.

A year-and-a-half before the election, Chávez's support hovered in the single digits in opinion surveys. His campaign surged, however, as he consolidated a position as the most formidable left-of-center, anti-establishment candidate, allowing him to overtake Sáez in the polls by the summer of 1998. In the process, *Chavismo* captured the political space that might have been occupied by either or both of the small, more established leftist parties that briefly emerged as significant actors in the 1990s – the MAS and *La Causa R*. Neither of these parties, however, was able to do what the PT did in Brazil – that is, progressively strengthen as an opposition force by channeling resistance to the neoliberal model and building a reputation for innovative and effective governance at the local level. The participation of MAS leaders in Caldera's bait-and-switch reforms weakened the party as an outlet for social discontent, while *La Causa R* was politically tainted by an ineffectual term in the mayorship of Caracas in the mid-1990s (Goldfrank 2011: 84–120). The latter party served as a vehicle for electoral protest in 1993, but it never consolidated a mass base of support; with the rise of Chávez, *La Causa R* split, and the majority faction threw its support to the populist leader. MAS, as well, backed Chávez in the 1998 elections, provoking an exodus from the party of Petkoff and other historic leaders.

In a desperate attempt to contain Chávez, the political establishment moved up congressional elections, hoping to take advantage of the organizational weakness of Chávez' *Movimiento Quinta República* (MVR, or Fifth Republic Movement). The MVR, however, finished a strong second to AD in the congressional elections, and with Chávez ahead in the opinion polls for the presidential race, COPEI and AD abandoned the candidacies of Sáez and Alfaro Ucero in order to support the most viable anti-Chávez independent, Salas Römer. This last-ditch opportunism, however, tainted Salas Römer as the candidate of the establishment and crystallized the outsider/establishment cleavage that separated Chávez from the field. Chávez won in a landslide, earning 56.2 percent of the vote compared to 40 percent for Salas Römer.

Chávez' victory left little doubt that a new political era had dawned, and that Venezuela's critical juncture had ended with an electoral rebuke of the neoliberal model and a decomposition of the party system that imposed it. Chávez moved quickly to uphold his campaign pledge to re-found Venezuela's democratic regime, relying heavily on plebiscitarian appeals to circumvent institutional checks and balances. The outsider president purged the judiciary, convoked a popular referendum on the election of a constituent assembly to write a new constitution, and adopted a plurality electoral formula that allowed his coalition to capture 121 of the 131 assembly seats. The assembly quickly asserted "supra-constitutional powers" and dissolved congress and state legislatures, thereby eliminating other elected bodies as institutional checks on Chávez's authority, and effectively excluding traditional parties from governing institutions.

The aftermath to Venezuela's critical juncture would be dominated by Chávez's attempts to consolidate his political authority within this new set of regime institutions. This authority was intensely polarizing, given the erosion of institutional checks and balances, the resort to plebiscitarian appeals to circumvent or rewrite the rules, the political marginalization and discursive demonization of the political establishment, and the ideological offensive against a neoliberal model that reigned supreme elsewhere in the region. Venezuela's critical juncture, then, unfolded through a dynamic of neoliberal convergence that programmatically de-aligned and ultimately decomposed the party system, but it ended with an outcome of polarized populism that structured electoral competition in the post-adjustment era. As explained in Chapter 9, this outcome was poorly institutionalized on both the populist and anti-populist sides of the political divide, impeding a rapid reconstitution of the party system. The cleavage itself, however, was highly durable as a central axis of sociopolitical competition.

CONCLUSION

Countries with LM party systems during the ISI era encountered especially formidable political and economic challenges during the transition to neoliberalism. All experienced acute economic crises, including severe recessions and, in most cases, hyperinflation. The combination of economic crisis and structural adjustment weakened organized labor as a political actor and forced LM parties to develop linkages to new and often unorganized social constituencies if they hoped to remain electorally competitive. Although LM parties in Argentina, Brazil, and Chile adapted in varying ways to these challenges, the AD in Venezuela did not, and the larger party systems in all the LM cases were heavily transformed by neoliberal critical junctures. All experienced changes in their organizational composition and electoral alignments, and that in Venezuela eventually decomposed under the pressures of crisis management and market reform.

Despite similar projects of market liberalization, the political dynamics of economic reform created very different institutional legacies in the four cases analyzed here. Market reforms led by conservative actors and opposed by a major party of the Left were programmatically aligning in Chile and Brazil, creating institutional legacies of contested liberalism that structured electoral competition in the aftermath period. Programmatically de-aligning bait-and-switch reforms imposed by historic LM parties (Argentina and Venezuela), on the other hand, left party systems vulnerable to destabilizing reactive sequences. The pattern of neoliberal convergence bequeathed a legacy of polarized populism where the party system decomposed during the critical juncture

TABLE 8.2. *Overview of Critical Junctures in Countries with LM Party Systems*

	Onset of Crisis	Initial Policy Response	Decisive Stages of Market Reform	Political Response and Effects	End of the Critical Juncture
Chile	1973 Military Coup	Orthodox stabilization 1973–1975	1975–1981 under Pinochet military dictatorship: neoliberal reforms to liberalize foreign trade, privatize industries, deregulate prices, labor, and capital markets, privatize social security	Political repression under Pinochet; mass protests 1983–1986 following financial crisis; democratic transition 1988–1990 under leadership of center-left coalition; reconstitution of partisan right to defend neoliberal model	1993 election returns center-left coalition to power; outcome of contested liberalism by means of a programmatically aligning critical juncture
Brazil	1982 economic crisis; critical juncture begins with 1985 democratic transition	Mix of austerity and heterodox measures 1985–1987	1988–1992 under conservatives Sarney and Collor, 1994–1996 under centrist Cardoso; liberalize foreign trade, privatize industries, deregulate prices and capital markets	Initial electoral volatility and anti-incumbent voting; electoral gains for Cardoso and PSDB following stabilization; societal resistance channeled by strengthening PT	1998 re-election of Cardoso; outcome of contested liberalism by means of a programmatically aligning critical juncture
Argentina	1982 economic crisis; critical juncture begins with 1983 democratic transition	Initial heterodox stabilization plan under Alfonsín 1984–1986; orthodox reforms	1989–1991 bait-and-switch shock treatment under Menem; liberalize foreign trade,	General strikes against Alfonsín; electoral realignment favoring Peronism in 1989	1995 re-election of Menem; outcome of neoliberal convergence by means of a programmatically

		blocked by labor and political resistance 1987–1988	privatize industries, deregulate prices, labor, and capital markets, convertability plan to fix peso to dollar		de-aligning critical juncture
Venezuela	1982 debt crisis	Major devaluation 1983, but postpone structural adjustment under COPEI and AD	1989–1992 under Pérez, 1996–1998 under Caldera, both bait-and-switch; liberalize foreign trade, privatize industries, deregulate prices and capital markets	Massive urban riots follow initial shock treatment; anti-incumbent voting and gradual party system decomposition in 1993 and 1998 elections	1998 election of Chávez; outcome of polarized populism by means of a programmatically de-aligning critical juncture

(Venezuela), and unstable forms of electoral competition where traditional parties survived but encountered new forms of societal resistance in the aftermath period (Argentina). As shown in Chapter 9, all four of these countries would turn to the Left politically in the aftermath period, but their institutional legacies heavily conditioned the type of leftist alternative that emerged, and the ways in which they channeled societal resistance to market liberalism.

9

Aftermath: Reactive Sequences and Institutional Legacies

Critical junctures have lasting effects, but their institutional outcomes vary in their resiliency. That is especially true of critical junctures in party system development, where any given set of parties, or any competitive equilibrium among them, is at least potentially susceptible to the disruptive effects of elite and mass political behavior. Whether motivated by policy or office-seeking goals, the strategic behavior of political elites can destabilize a party system by altering its "supply side" through decisions to split, merge, or form new parties. Likewise, voters are free to alter their partisan preferences in response to changing conditions, preferences, issue saliencies, or performance records. A disillusioned electorate can always "throw the bums out" if it so chooses. To reproduce a competitive equilibrium thus requires that political entrepreneurs have incentives to join and remain in established party organizations, and that citizens be motivated to vote for them in relatively stable proportions.

Why, then, are the institutional outcomes and competitive equilibriums produced by some critical junctures more stable and resilient than others? Stability is not simply a function of institutional strength, as the divergent trajectories of party systems in Brazil and Venezuela amply demonstrate; it also matters how a critical juncture aligns competing political actors and positions them to respond to evolving societal pressures. Such alignments may even condition – in a path-dependent manner – the types and intensities of societal pressures that emerge, as well as their mode of political expression within or against established institutions. Reactive sequences in the aftermath period are thus likely to vary in their capacity to disrupt, transform, or reproduce the institutional outcomes of critical junctures themselves. Some outcomes may be reinforced or "locked in" by reactive sequences that they effectively channel, producing path-dependent institutional legacies; others may be transformed by reactive sequences that disrupt initial outcomes and produce longer-term institutional legacies that diverge sharply from them.

Latin America's post-adjustment era strongly suggests that reactive sequences are shaped by different types of critical junctures and their institutional outcomes. Reactive sequences following economic adjustment had two basic inter-related components: (1) the repoliticization of development policies and social citizenship claims as the technocratic consensus for market orthodoxy broke down in the late 1990s; and (2) the growth of populist and leftist political alternatives, demonstrating a renewed mobilizational capacity on the part of neoliberalism's opponents in both social and electoral arenas. These dual processes unfolded quite differently across cases, however, and they produced divergent institutional effects, depending on the type of critical juncture and the alignment of party systems around the process of market reform.

More concretely, programmatically aligning critical junctures – where conservative actors led the process of market reform and a major party of the Left provided consistent opposition – produced institutional outcomes of contested liberalism that channeled discontent and social citizenship claims into established party systems, thus moderating reactive sequences. Indeed, reactive sequences reinforced contested liberalism as an institutional legacy and produced relatively stable patterns of electoral competition in the aftermath period. The cases of contested liberalism analyzed here – Uruguay from the category of elitist party systems, and Brazil and Chile from the LM category – all turned to the Left after 2000, but they did so by means of an alternation in power between established party organizations, without mass protests or the rise of populist outsider candidates. Ruling leftist parties, moreover, did not break sharply with the neoliberal models they had once bitterly opposed, much less the democratic regimes that nurtured their rise. They experimented with social policy reforms and moderate redistributive measures, but they maintained relatively orthodox macroeconomic policies and they operated within the rules of the game of the established constitutional order (Levitsky and Roberts 2011a: 20–24; Flores-Macías 2012).

By contrast, reactive sequences were much more destabilizing in countries that experienced programmatically neutral or de-aligning critical junctures. Where market reforms were adopted by conservative parties in the absence of a major leftist rival (the neutral pattern), or imposed in a bait-and-switch manner by leftist and labor-based parties or populist figures, a reform dynamic of neo-liberal convergence left party systems without an institutionalized channel for dissent from market orthodoxy and the articulation of claims for social citizenship. In such contexts, reactive sequences took a variety of forms, including mass social protests, the rise of new movement parties or anti-establishment populist figures, and the breakdown or re-founding of democratic regimes. These reactive sequences undermined neoliberal convergence and generated major changes in regime institutions and/or party systems, including major electoral realignments and partial or complete processes of party system decomposition.

In the cases analyzed here – Costa Rica, Ecuador, and Honduras from the category of elitist party systems, and Argentina and Venezuela from the LM category – neoliberal convergence was an unstable competitive equilibrium, if not during the critical juncture then at least in the early aftermath period. Longer-term institutional legacies, therefore, tended to diverge from the initial outcomes of critical junctures themselves. Where mass protests severely disrupted party systems, those legacies included political shifts to the left – as in Venezuela, Argentina, and Ecuador – that broke more decisively with the neoliberal model than the left turns in Brazil, Chile, and Uruguay, where contested liberalism had institutionalized political constraints on new leftist governments.

As such, the antecedent conditions associated with elitist and LM party systems that shaped national crises during the critical juncture were far less important determinants of institutional stability in the aftermath period. Elitist and LM party systems exited the critical juncture with both stable and unstable competitive equilibriums, depending on the alignment of political forces during the period of economic adjustment. Neoliberal critical junctures, then, reshuffled the deck; they largely eroded the antecedent properties that differentiated party systems during the ISI era, and they created new institutional baselines for partisan competition in the post-adjustment era that varied dramatically in their resiliency. It was that capacity to break down and reconfigure partisan competition that made these junctures truly critical.

REACTIVE SEQUENCES AND THE REPRODUCTION OF CONTESTED LIBERALISM: BRAZIL, CHILE, AND URUGUAY

As previous chapters have shown, party systems in Chile, Brazil, and Uruguay entered neoliberal critical junctures with very different antecedent properties. Whereas Uruguay had an elitist party system during the era of state-led development, Brazil and Chile had LM systems. Party systems in Uruguay and Chile were highly institutionalized, whereas Brazil's was historically weak and largely reconstituted as the country exited military rule in the 1980s. Nevertheless, important similarities existed in the critical junctures of these three countries, as market reforms were adopted by conservative rulers or coalitions and consistently opposed by a major party of the left. Market liberalization, therefore, aligned party systems programmatically, producing institutional outcomes of contested liberalism that served as the baseline for partisan competition in the aftermath period.

Aftermath periods in these three countries were also strikingly similar, as established parties of the Left progressively strengthened, moderated their programmatic stands, and came into power after 2000. The strengthening of the Left produced at least moderate forms of electoral realignment, but aggregate electoral volatility in all three countries was relatively low in the post-adjustment period. Centrist and conservative parties remained major power contenders, placing important institutional and policy constraints on leftist parties in public office. Left turns, therefore, occurred by means of highly institutionalized alternation in office, and governments of the Left sought to address social needs within the overarching constraints of inherited market economies. Although Chile and Brazil experienced major cycles of social protest after 2010, with the former developing a powerful student protest movement that challenged the inequities of a highly privatized educational system (Donoso 2013), levels of social mobilization were relatively moderate for most of the aftermath period, and societal resistance to market orthodoxy found channels of expression in partisan and electoral competition.

The origins of programmatically aligning critical junctures in these three countries can be traced to their bureaucratic-authoritarian military regimes in the 1970s, which either fully implemented structural adjustment policies (Chile) or oversaw regime transitions that empowered conservative civilian successors during the crucial phase of market reform in the late 1980s and 1990s (Uruguay and Brazil). Major parties of the left with strong labor ties – the PT in Brazil, the *Frente Amplio* (FA) in Uruguay, and the Socialists and Communists in Chile – staunchly opposed conservative rulers during the decisive periods of market reform. Reactive sequences in the aftermath period weakened conservative or centrist incumbents while strengthening these established parties of the Left.

In Uruguay, this electoral realignment involved a cumulative process of vote shifts from the traditional Blanco and Colorado parties to the leftist FA over the course of three successive election cycles – 1994, 1999, and 2004. Since the founding of the FA as a loose coalition of small leftist parties in 1971, its electoral support had been highly stable; the front obtained 18.3 percent of the presidential vote in 1971, 21.3 percent in 1984, and 21.2 percent in 1989. The FA's vote began a steady rise in 1994, however, following a relatively successful municipal administration in Montevideo under Socialist mayor Tabaré Vázquez and the major push to deepen market reforms by the Blanco administration of Luís Alberto Lacalle in the early 1990s. With Vázquez standing as its presidential candidate, the FA was the primary beneficiary of the vote shift away from the incumbent Blancos in 1994; the leftist coalition's vote increased by nearly 10 percentage points, and it narrowly missed capturing the presidency in a tight three-way race with 30.6 percent of the vote (see Appendix Tables 13 and 14).

As market reforms weakened the clientelist linkages that bound low-income voters to the Blancos and Colorados, the FA mobilized newfound support through its programmatic defense of Uruguay's welfare state (Lanzaro 2004a: 53–59; Luna 2006). Fearful of an FA electoral plurality, the traditional parties worked together to change the rules of the game, passing a constitutional reform in 1997 that called for a second-round run-off when no presidential candidate earned a majority of the vote in the first round. This electoral engineering worked as designed in 1999; although the FA did, in fact, win a first-round plurality with 40.1 percent of the vote, the Blancos and Colorados joined forces to defeat their rival in the second round by a vote of 54.1 to 45.9 percent. Increasingly, the three-party system was shifting toward a two-bloc alignment, with the two historic conservative parties allied against a leftist challenger who they could no longer defeat in a three-way race.

Victory was fleeting, however, as Colorado leader Jorge Batlle took office in 2000 in the midst of a deepening regional economic slump that was exacerbated by financial crises in Asia and Russia. After growing at a 4.8 percent annual rate from 1991 to 1998, the Uruguayan economy entered into a prolonged recession from 1999 to 2002, culminating in contractions of 3.8 and 7.7 percent in 2001 and 2002, respectively. This dismal performance undermined confidence in the ability of Uruguay's liberalized economy to sustain growth, and it further eroded support for Latin America's longest-standing oligarchic party duopoly. Having dominated Uruguayan politics for over 160 years, the two traditional parties were defeated in national elections for the first time in 2004, when Vázquez was elected president on the FA ticket with 51.7 percent of the vote. The FA was re-elected five years later, with former Tupumaros guerrilla leader José Mujica winning a 52.4 percent majority in the second round. The FA also captured a majority of seats in the lower house of congress in both 2004 and 2009.

The vote shifts that produced this secular electoral realignment were substantial, as the FA increased its vote share by over thirty points between 1989 and 2004, while the Colorado party – the primary loser among the traditional parties – lost nearly 20 percent of its vote share. These cumulative vote shifts, however, were relatively modest within individual electoral cycles; indeed, net election-cycle volatility in presidential and legislative elections in Uruguay averaged only 10.6 percent in the 1990s and 12.6 percent in the first decade of the 21st century, the second lowest average in the region after Honduras. Likewise, the composition of the party system was highly stable, as new parties formed after 1990 averaged a mere 2.8 percent of the presidential vote and 2.0 percent of legislative seats in the 2004 and 2009 elections. Consequently, the growth of the FA realigned the party system electorally and altered the competitive balance between the conservative bloc and the Left, but it did not destabilize the party system. To the contrary, it reinforced and reproduced the basic competitive dynamic of contested liberalism, with a central cleavage between a conservative bloc that supported market orthodoxy and an institutionalized partisan Left that advocated redistributive policies and expanded social citizenship rights. Not surprisingly, in their exhaustive empirical analysis of legislative surveys and party ideology in Latin America, Kitschelt et al. (2009: 171) found that Uruguay ranked alongside Chile for the highest level of programmatic structuring of partisan competition in Latin America.

In Brazil as well, the aftermath period was marked by a major electoral realignment, with votes shifting from the center-right bloc that implemented market reforms to the major party of the Left that led the opposition to them. Although the PT's vote share climbed steadily throughout Brazil's democratic period, the decisive realignment occurred more abruptly than in Uruguay, with a major vote shift between 1998 and 2002. Brazil's critical juncture had ended with the 1998 re-election of PSDB leader Fernando Henrique Cardoso, the architect of the stabilization plan that finally put an end to hyperinflation in the mid-1990s. Cardoso's re-election occurred, however, as Asia's financial crisis was spreading to Latin America. Although Brazil, unlike Uruguay, avoided a new recession, Cardoso was forced to devalue the real, and GDP growth slowed to an annual average of only 1.7 percent between 1998 and 2002.

After finishing second in three consecutive presidential elections, Lula and the PT were primed to capitalize on this economic slowdown and pent-up demands to address Brazil's gaping social inequalities. Lula's presidential vote jumped from 31.7 percent in 1998 to 46.4 percent in the first round of the 2002 election, while that of the PSDB plummeted from 53.1 to 23.2 percent for Cardoso's successor as party leader, José Serra. The second-round run-off produced a landslide victory for Lula with 61.3 percent of the vote. The PT victory in the presidential campaign clearly capitalized on Lula's personalistic appeal, which far surpassed the party's own pull; although the PT's legislative representation continued its steady growth, allowing it to capture the largest bloc of deputies in the highly fragmented lower house of congress, it still only captured 17.7 percent of the seats (see Appendix Tables 3 and 4). As such, the PT – in contrast to the FA in Uruguay – would have to govern at the head of a large multi-party coalition that included centrist and conservative parties, placing significant constraints on Lula's ability to shift public policies in a leftward direction.

Despite grumbling from the PT's social bases about the slow pace of social and economic reform, and a major corruption scandal that tainted the PT's hard-earned reputation for clean government, Lula rallied to achieve re-election in 2006 with virtually an identical percentage of the vote. With support from several smaller parties, Lula took 46.6 percent of the first round vote against 41.6 for the PSDB candidate, who ran in alliance with the conservative PFL. The second round produced a comfortable victory for Lula with 60.8 percent of the vote. The same two parties faced off again in 2010, with Lula's hand-picked successor, Dilma Rousseff, taking 46.9 percent of the vote in the first round and 56.0 percent in the second round – the third consecutive national election victory of the PT.

These results demonstrated that Brazil's electoral realignment toward the Left, like that of Uruguay, had not been destabilizing for the party system. To the contrary, electoral volatility diminished sharply once the economy had been stabilized and partisan competition became structured programmatically by the central cleavage between supporters and critics of the market liberalization process. Volatility in Brazilian legislative elections averaged 16.5 on the Pedersen index for the five election cycles between 1994 and 2010, and it averaged 23.9 in the four presidential elections from 1998 to 2010, both well below the regional averages – a striking turnaround for a party system that was long synonymous with under-institutionalization (Mainwaring 1999a). Likewise, although the party system remained highly fragmented, its composition was remarkably stable in the aftermath period, as reactive sequences produced an electoral realignment among established parties rather than their displacement by new contenders. Parties formed after 1990 averaged a mere 2.2 percent of the presidential vote and 1.4 percent of legislative seats in the four national elections between 1998 and 2010. Consequently, a critical juncture that began with a highly volatile and inchoate party system produced a programmatic alignment around center-right and leftist blocs that institutionalized contested liberalism as a durable legacy in the aftermath period.

Finally, in Chile, a partial electoral realignment toward the left also occurred in the aftermath period, but its political dynamics differed from those in Uruguay and Brazil due to the coalitional alignment of the Chilean party system following the country's democratic transition. The center-left *Concertación* alliance placed Christian Democratic leaders in the presidency during the first two elections of the democratic period in 1989 and 1993, but by the late 1990s the balance of power within the alliance had shifted toward the Socialist-PPD bloc, which generally received support as well from the smaller Radical Social Democratic Party (PRSD). The leader of this bloc, Ricardo Lagos, won the *Concertación*'s internal primary for the 1999 presidential campaign with over 70 percent of the vote, then captured the presidency in a tight race against the conservative alliance candidate, Joaquín Lavín of the UDI. Lagos narrowly surpassed Lavín in the first round of the election with 48.0 to 47.5 percent of the vote, and prevailed in the run-off by a 51.3 to 48.7 percent margin (see Appendix Table 5). Six years later, Socialist Michelle Bachelet succeeded Lagos in the presidency, defeating a divided conservative bloc with 46 percent of the first-round vote and 53.5 percent in the second round.

At the legislative level, the Christian Democrats (PDC) also lost ground during this period to the left bloc within the *Concertación*. The PDC's share of seats in the lower house of congress declined from 31.7 percent in 1997 to 16.7 percent in 2005, while that of the PSCh/PPD/PRSC increased from 25.8 to 35.8 percent in the same period (see Appendix Table 6). The gradual decline of Chile's leading centrist party, however, was not solely attributable to vote shifts toward the Left, as the conservative bloc also strengthened at the expense of the center during this period. The conservative alliance increased its share of lower house seats from 39.2 percent in 1997 to 45 percent in 2005, while the internal balance of power within this alliance shifted in favor of the more hard-line UDI, the direct partisan descendant of *Pinochetismo*. Indeed, the UDI established itself as the single largest party in congress starting in 2001, when it captured over a quarter of the lower-house seats.

Rather than a simple electoral re-alignment toward the Left, then, Chile experienced a moderate centrifugal realignment, with votes shifting from the center toward both the left and right sides of the spectrum. These vote shifts, however, did not alter the basic two-bloc alignment of the party system, nor did they produce high levels of electoral volatility by regional standards. Legislative volatility scores on the Pedersen index were 9.2 in 1997, 21.0 in 2001, and 8.8 in 2005; volatility in presidential elections was moderately higher, registering 23.1 in 1999 and 24.6 in 2005, largely because the conservative bloc could not always settle on a single presidential candidate. The organizational composition of the party system was highly stable, with vote shifts occurring almost entirely among established parties. New parties formed after 1990 obtained only 1.3 and zero percent of the presidential vote in 1999 and 2005, respectively, and an average of 7 percent of legislative seats in 1997, 2001, and 2005.

Consequently, in Chile, Uruguay, and Brazil, contested liberalism proved to be a stable institutional outcome of neoliberal critical junctures. In all three countries, conservative-led market reforms that were challenged by established parties of the Left structured electoral competition along programmatic lines – in each case, with reinforcement from a regime cleavage with roots in the struggles against military rule. The central left–right cleavage reproduced itself in aftermath periods as leftist parties strengthened and captured national executive office. Societal dissent from market orthodoxy was largely channeled by these leftist parties, contributing to electoral realignments, but avoiding destabilizing reactive sequences. None of these countries experienced major outbreaks of social protest in the early aftermath period, and none witnessed the rise of major new parties or populist outsider movements.

"Left turns" in these countries, moreover, were not accompanied by an electoral collapse of established centrist and conservative parties. In Uruguay, the Colorado Party lost roughly half its vote share over the course of the aftermath period, but support for the Blancos was relatively stable, and the two-party conservative bloc remained a viable rival to the FA with close to half of the vote. In Brazil, the centrist PSDB remained the PT's major rival, generally in alliance with a weakening but still significant PFL on the right (renamed the Democrats, or DEM, in 2007). The PMDB and several smaller parties continued to be important electoral and legislative coalition partners as well. In Chile, the partisan right – especially the UDI – actually strengthened in the aftermath period, eventually taking the presidency away from the *Concertación* in 2009/10 (see below). In short, centrist and conservative parties that had championed market reforms against serious leftist rivals may have lost elections in the aftermath period, but they remained electorally competitive – something their counterparts in the bait-and-switch cases typically failed to do, as we will see.

Furthermore, the competitiveness of centrist and conservative parties undoubtedly contributed to the progressive moderation of the leftist parties that came to power in all three countries. The Chilean PSCh, the FA in Uruguay, and the PT in Brazil were heterogeneous parties, both socially and ideologically, and all (or their immediate predecessors) were influenced by the revolutionary currents that swept across the regional Left in the 1960s and 1970s. All had significant socialist and Marxist tendencies well into the 1980s and even the 1990s, and all started the critical juncture as virulent critics of the neoliberal model. All three parties, however, underwent significant changes along the path to presidential power. Having lived through the military repression of bureaucratic authoritarianism, all became staunch proponents of democracy and human rights. They worked – often at great risk – to bring about democratic transitions, and they agreed to pursue their socialist and participatory objectives within the institutional rules of new democratic regimes, even when those rules were biased against them and overrepresented the Right. Although they maintained ties to organized labor and other popular constituencies – more so in Brazil and Uruguay than Chile – all three parties became increasingly professionalized and electoralist over time, reaching out to centrist and middle-class voters to broaden their electoral appeal (Roberts 1998; Lanzaro 2004a; Hunter 2010).

These Left parties, moreover, also lived through the debt crisis, inflationary traumas, and the collapse of bureaucratic socialism in the Soviet bloc. Once stabilization had been achieved and market reforms consolidated, they knew that a return to the statist models of the past was neither politically nor economically feasible, and they moderated their programmatic stands while maintaining a critical perspective toward the neoliberal model (Samuels 2004; Hunter 2010). This moderation was reinforced by the electoral strength of centrist and conservative rivals, the ever-present risks of capital flight, and the structural dependence of the state on private capital in highly liberalized economies. The mere expectation of Lula's election victory in 2002 was enough to make Brazil's stock, bond, and currency markets swoon, revealing the formidable structural constraints on the policy latitude of new leftist governments, and forcing Lula to issue public assurances of general macroeconomic policy continuity (Hunter 2010: 137; Campello, forthcoming). Likewise, moderation was buttressed by the institutional checks and balances of increasingly consolidated democratic regimes with strong centrist- and conservative-party representation. Indeed, the PT and the Chilean Socialists had nowhere near legislative majorities from their own ranks (in contrast to the FA in Uruguay), making it essential to negotiate and compromise on policy reforms with more centrist allies as well as conservative rivals.

In office, then, these new leftist presidents continued relatively orthodox macroeconomic policies. They maintained fiscal and monetary discipline as well as open trade regimes, and they did not attempt to reverse the widespread privatization policies of their predecessors (Weyland, Madrid, and Hunter 2010; Flores-Macías 2012). This relative orthodoxy was clearly a significant departure from the policy stands that these parties had taken as opposition forces when market reforms were initially adopted, and it generated considerable discontent among many of their followers who anticipated a sharper break with the neoliberal model.

These parties did not, however, fully abandon the policy commitments that differentiated them from their more conservative rivals and aligned partisan competition along programmatic lines. Indeed, all of them were active on the social policy front to redistribute income and strengthen the social safety net around their market economies. Minimum wages were sharply increased, while tax reforms enhanced progressivity and generated new revenues from income and corporate taxes to be used for social programs (Cornia 2012). In Brazil, Lula oversaw a dramatic expansion of the conditional cash transfer program known as *Bolsa Família* that had begun under Cardoso; by the end of Lula's first term, over 11 million households with roughly a quarter of the Brazilian population received monthly stipends from the program (Lindert et al. 2007: 17). This program was instrumental in allowing the PT to broaden its electoral appeal in underdeveloped northeastern regions of Brazil that were traditional bastions of conservative parties with extensive clientelist networks (Hunter and Power 2007). In Uruguay, Vázquez re-introduced tripartite salary councils, extended collective bargaining to rural and public sector workers, expanded public health and pension systems, and launched new targeted poverty-relief programs focused on family allowances, housing assistance, and nutrition (Lanzaro 2011; Pribble and Huber 2011). In Chile, Lagos launched a cash-transfer program targeted at the poorest sectors of the population, along with jobs training and unemployment insurance programs. More ambitiously, he also implemented a national health plan that provided universal basic coverage for a broad range of medical conditions. Bachelet expanded this health care program along with pre-school, day care, and kindergarten programs in low-income communities. Her signature reform, however, was the adoption of a basic universal pension system that provided coverage for many women and informal sector workers who were effectively excluded from the privatized pension system (Pribble and Huber 2011: 120–121).

Particularly in Chile and Uruguay, then, leftist governments moved beyond targeted poverty relief measures to introduce universal forms of social citizenship that clearly broke with neoliberal conceptions of market-based provisioning for social needs and minimal (or "residual") welfare states. In all three countries, social indicators showed marked improvements, with rising wages, declining poverty levels, and reduced income inequality (see Cornia 2012). These gains were clearly facilitated by improved economic performance, as leftist governments in all three countries were given additional maneuvering space by the region-wide trends toward rising commodity export prices and rapid GDP growth after 2003. The new economic boom reduced debt levels and relaxed fiscal and foreign exchange constraints on national governments, making it possible to address social needs without resorting to more radical and destabilizing redistributive measures. The combination of macroeconomic stability, steady growth, and moderate redistribution undoubtedly contributed to electoral stability as well, as leftist governments were re-elected twice in Brazil and Uruguay (through 2013) and once in Chile (before returning again after one term of conservative government).

As of 2013, the only electoral defeat suffered by these leftist governments came in Chile in 2009–2010, when Bachelet – despite record 80-percent approval ratings in public opinion surveys – was not able to stand for re-election under Chilean electoral laws. When PSCh leaders deferred to their Christian Democratic allies in the selection of the presidential candidate of the *Concertación*, a young Socialist deputy, Marco Enríquez-Ominami, split the coalition by launching an independent bid for the presidency with the backing of several small leftist parties. Enríquez-Ominami obtained 20.1 percent of the first-round presidential vote, and a weakened *Concertación* candidate, former president Eduardo Frei of the PDC, lost in the second round to the candidate of the conservative alliance, Sebastian Piñera, by a vote of 51.6 to 48.4 percent (see Morales Quiroga 2012).

Although the *Concertación* retained half of the seats in the senate and fifty-seven out of 120 lower house seats, this first-ever defeat after twenty years in power raised basic questions about the ongoing resilience of the competitive alignment that had structured Chilean politics since the democratic transition. Volatility remained low in legislative elections, scoring 8.8 on the Pedersen index in 2009, but the defection of Enríquez-Ominami produced a volatility score of 28 percent in the presidential election, a new high for Chile. More ominously, perhaps, other indicators suggested an erosion of the party system's roots in Chilean society. An AmericasBarometer survey in 2010 found that only 11.6 percent of Chilean respondents identified with a political party – shockingly, the lowest score recorded in Latin America. Uruguay, by contrast, recorded the highest level of party identification in the region at 66.2 percent, while Brazil registered 30.2 percent, slightly below the regional average (see Table 2.1). The low level of identification with parties in Chile found parallels in very low levels of participation in party activities; in 2005 only 2 percent of Chilean survey respondents said they had worked for a political party, ranking Chile alongside Guatemala for the lowest score in the region, with less than one-third the regional average (Latinobarómetro 2005: 35). Similarly, voter registration and electoral turnout as a percentage of the voting age population steadily declined during the democratic period; by 2009, only 58 percent of the voting age population cast a ballot, down from 82 percent in 1989 (Morales Quiroga 2012: 84). Many young people, in particular, declined to register to vote, and expressed generalized disillusionment with the political establishment.

Indeed, a major outbreak of student protests had erupted in 2006, combining with other forms of unrest among sub-contracted workers, indigenous and environmental activists, and public transport users to signal the growing ineffectiveness of the *Concertación*'s channeling of societal demands (Donoso 2013; Ruiz 2012). Dissent spread after Piñera took office and his administration was rocked by a massive new outbreak of student protests against educational inequalities, tuition debts, and the widespread privatization of the Chilean educational system. The protests mobilized both secondary and university students around demands for free public education, and led to the occupation of the *Universidad de Chile* and other educational institutions. Labor unions expressed solidarity with the student protesters, as did up to 79 percent of respondents in public opinion surveys (Adimark GfK 2011: 62–65).

Chile's student protests were a frontal assault on a social pillar of the neoliberal model that Lagos and Bachelet had left largely intact. This mobilization clearly outflanked the *Concertación* and the PSCh on the left, suggesting that a new and deeper level of societal contestation had emerged – one that challenged the competitive equilibrium and policy compromises that were major legacies of

Chile's critical juncture. In response, leftists in the *Concertación* induced the coalition – despite Christian Democratic misgivings – to form a new, broader political alliance that incorporated the Communist Party (PCCh), supported Communist and student leaders in congressional races, and sponsored Bachelet's candidacy for a new term in office. Running on a platform that called for tax increases to finance a push toward universal free public education, Bachelet was returned to office with over 62 percent of the second-round vote and a solid majority in both houses of congress (including Communist student leader Camilla Vallejo and five other deputies from the PCCh).

As such, social protests challenged the Chilean party system, but they did not displace it. Instead, student mobilization reinforced the basic alignment of contested liberalism, as it re-politicized social inequalities, pulled the Socialists and the *Concertación* back to a more critical stance toward neoliberal orthodoxy, and encouraged a full reincorporation of the Communist Party into the democratic order. Social pressure from below reactivated Chile's central political cleavage and strengthened programmatic linkages on the left side of the party system where they had progressively weakened after two decades of democratic pragmatism and compromise. The Chilean case suggests that social mobilization and protest can be a reproductive mechanism or positive feedback effect for the institutional legacies of contested liberalism; the cases that follow demonstrate that it can have more disruptive or transformative effects where critical junctures ended with neoliberal convergence.

NEUTRAL CRITICAL JUNCTURES AND REACTIVE SEQUENCES: HONDURAS' OLIGARCHIC SYSTEM IN TRANSITION

In contrast to Brazil, Chile, and Uruguay, the other countries in this study experienced neutral or programmatically de-aligning critical junctures that produced variants of neoliberal convergence – ultimately, a less stable institutional outcome than contested liberalism. The one case analyzed here with a neutral critical juncture, Honduras, appeared until recently to be an outlier to the general patterns, as it boasted the most electorally stable party system in Latin America during the first three decades of the third wave. Outliers, however, can be highly instructive empirical and theoretical reference points. They anchor the end points on continuous measures of many variables, define the boundaries and scope conditions of theoretical generalizations, and aide in the identification of missing variables and conditional or threshold effects. Identifying such effects can be especially revealing when an erstwhile outlier converges on more general patterns, as Honduras eventually did in the second decade of the aftermath period.

In short, Honduras' exceptional electoral stability during the critical juncture and the early aftermath period sheds light on the reasons why most other countries in Latin America were so volatile. Simply put, Honduras was located at the far lower end of the continuum for state-led development and labor and popular mobilization, the antecedent conditions that were associated with deeper economic crises and greater political disruption during the transition to neoliberalism. This transition was less disruptive for Honduras and other countries that retained oligarchic party systems during the ISI era. These party systems, however, did not fare as well in the aftermath period. Uruguay's party system realigned to the Left, as discussed above, while Colombia's decomposed after 2000, with new rightist and leftist alternatives emerging in the void. Paraguay's oligarchic system was outflanked, at least temporarily, by an independent leftist, Fernando Lugo, although the impeachment – in effect, a congressional coup – that removed Lugo from the presidency in 2012 aimed to restore the traditional order.

Although Honduras' two-party oligarchic system held on a bit longer, it also became an increasingly unstable equilibrium in the post-adjustment era. Indeed, the exception eventually proved the rule: that neoliberal convergence was not a durable institutional legacy of neoliberal critical junctures. That legacy temporarily veered off course when maverick president Manuel Zelaya of the traditional Liberal Party turned in a populist direction following his election in 2005. A military coup backed by the conservative Supreme Court and the traditional parties in congress sought to nip this populist experiment in the bud in 2009, but four years later a new leftist movement organized by Zelaya and his wife, Xiomara Castro, mounted the first serious electoral challenge to the National and Liberal parties in Honduran history. Castro ultimately finished a close second to the National Party candidate in a presidential campaign that was marred by violence and allegations of electoral fraud. The Honduran case suggests that the competitive equilibrium of neoliberal convergence is not only contingent on containing popular mobilization from below, but also on maintaining elite political cohesion; indeed, elite "defectors" may try to harness the untapped potential of popular mobilization by sponsoring it "from above" in order to tip the balance in intra-elite conflicts or otherwise challenge the traditional order.

Until 2013, the Honduran party system remained, on the surface at least, highly stable electorally. Since the end of the critical juncture in 1993, the Liberals (PLH) have won the presidency in 1993, 1997, and 2005, while the National Party (PNH) won in 2001 and 2009. Vote shifts between the two dominant parties were very moderate, producing the lowest Pedersen index volatility scores in the region: an average of 8.4 in five presidential elections between 1993 and 2009 and 9.5 in national legislative elections. The two parties jointly garnered over 95 percent of the presidential vote and over 90 percent of the congressional seats in all of these elections (see Appendix Tables 11 and 12). None of the minor parties made significant vote gains, and the vote for new parties formed after 1990 was nonexistent prior to 2013. This electoral stability was reflected as well in voter identification with the two dominant parties; public opinion surveys in 2010 found that 43.7 percent of Hondurans identified with a political party, the fourth highest percentage in Latin America following Uruguay, the Dominican Republic, and Costa Rica (see Table 2.1).

Through 2005, at least, reactive sequences in the aftermath to the critical juncture were extremely mild. They had little or no impact on the party system, and they did not challenge the political reproduction of Honduras' neoliberal model. Populist promises filled election campaigns, with candidates from both parties pledging to create jobs and increase social spending, but both parties supported the basic premises of the development model – namely, free markets and economic integration with the U.S. through the Central American Free Trade Agreement. Although the Liberal Party typically devoted more attention to social welfare concerns, surveys of legislators indicated that both parties located themselves to the right of center (Zoco 2006: 265), minimizing programmatic competition on economic issues. Public opinion also leaned to the Right; indeed, average ideological self-placements in Honduras were the furthest to the Right in the entire region in 1996 and third behind the Dominican Republic and Costa Rica in 2006 (Latinobarómetro 2006: 83–85).

The relative lack of differentiation on economic fundamentals had important implications for electoral competition and popular participation in the democratic process. First, in the country with world's highest murder rate, valence issues related to crime, gangs, and personal security became highly salient during election campaigns and policy debates. Candidates competed to demonstrate their toughness and effectiveness in combating crime, while the death penalty emerged as an issue of programmatic debate. Indeed, Honduran citizens ranked crime as the most important problem facing the country, ahead of unemployment and poverty (Latinobarómetro 2006: 39–40). Second, levels of popular mobilization and political participation remained quite low. In public opinion surveys, Hondurans reported levels of participation that ranked below the regional mean in voting, working for parties, signing petitions, discussing politics, and attending protests (Latinobarómetro 2006: 20–28). Levels of social protest lagged well behind those found in many South American countries. Third, both traditional parties appealed to popular constituencies through clientelist linkages; in comparison to programmatic linkages with their redistributive implications, the PNH and PLH found clientelist payoffs to be a "cheap way" to secure voter loyalties without "threatening traditional elite interests" (Taylor-Robinson 2006: 123).

But if patron–clientelism produced electoral stability, other indicators suggested that it created relatively weak forms of party–society linkage. Indeed, evidence accumulated over the course of the aftermath period that many Honduran citizens were detached from or poorly represented by formal political institutions. Electoral participation, for example, suffered a steep decline during the critical juncture and its aftermath, with the turnout rate declining from 84 percent in 1985 to only 49.9 percent in 2009 (see Appendix Table 11). The stability of partisan vote shares thus found its counterpart in rising voter apathy or even alienation; traditional parties retained roughly equal shares of a dwindling electorate that was increasingly impervious to their mobilizational appeals. Furthermore, surveys of civil society organizations found that they were disproportionately likely to be aligned with small opposition parties rather than the two dominant parties (Dewachter and Molenaers 2011: 127). Public opinion surveys conducted in 2004 ranked Honduras the lowest among nine countries in and around Central America on an index of political legitimacy based on levels of support for democracy, national institutions, and government economic performance (Seligson and Booth 2009: 3). Finally, despite the strong conservative tilt in ideological identities, 23 percent of Hondurans self-located to the Left of Center (Latinobarómetro 2006: 84) – that is, in programmatic space that was organizationally vacant, as it had never been occupied by a partisan contender with significant electoral appeal. There were, then, blocs of potential voters for a new electoral alternative that mobilized support along a programmatic – rather than a clientelistic – axis of competition.

It was in this context that the Liberal Party elected Manuel Zelaya president in 2005. Zelaya, a former leader of Honduras' principal business association who had run for office on a law-and-order platform, unexpectedly veered in a populist direction after his election – a rare case of bait-and-switch toward the Left in the recent Latin American experience. Zelaya launched major new poverty assistance programs, provided loans and subsidies to small businesses and farmers, expanded social security and free public education, and opened new channels for popular consultation on major issues. Most controversially, he decreed a 60 percent increase in the minimum wage in 2009 (Pastor Fasquelle 2011: 17), while steering Honduras into membership in several Venezuela-led economic integration initiatives, including the trade pact known as the Bolivarian Alliance for the Americas (ALBA) and a regional accord that made Venezuelan oil available on favorable terms. Zelaya's populist tilt provoked intense opposition from the business community and the mass media, as well as the PNH and conservative sectors of his own Liberal Party. When Zelaya tried to schedule a non-binding poll on a referendum to convene a constituent assembly, he was detained by military forces on June 28, 2009, removed from office by a vote of congress (controlled by his party), and ushered into exile in Costa Rica.

Not surprisingly, the fractured Liberal Party suffered a significant vote loss in the subsequent 2009 elections, but the vast majority of this vote shift was intra-systemic – that is, toward the National Party, which captured the presidency by a 57 to 38 percent margin over its historic rival. Nevertheless, political developments after the coup increasingly pushed in an extra-systemic direction – namely, toward an outflanking of the traditional parties on the Left. Zelaya's supporters regrouped after the coup, forming an umbrella civic organization known as the *Frente Nacional de Resistencia Popular* (FNRP) which incorporated labor unions, peasant associations, and other community organizations. FNRP-affiliated groups launched a series of land occupations and labor strikes, especially among public sector teachers who opposed a government plan to partially privatize the education system. In the northern part of the country, conflicts between large landowners and peasant organizations involved in land occupations led to rising levels of political violence, with dozens of peasants and security guards killed between late 2009 and the end of 2011 (*LatinNews Daily Report*, July 12, 2012). In May of 2011, Zelaya was allowed to re-enter the country and form a new leftist party, *Libertad y Refundación* (LIBRE), which supported these peasant groups in conflicts with landowners. Behind Xiomara Castro, LIBRE finished second in the 2013 national elections with 28.8 percent of the presidential vote, behind the PNH with 36.9 percent, but ahead of the PLH and another new party founded by a television personality who ran on an anti-corruption platform (the *Partido Anticorrupción*, or PAC). Together, LIBRE and PAC won over 40 percent of the presidential vote and legislative seats, an unprecedented level of support for new, extra-systemic parties in Honduras.

This social and political mobilization outside the two traditional parties clearly challenged the reproduction of neoliberal convergence as a long-term institutional legacy of Honduras' neutral critical juncture. Indeed, the reactive sequences triggered by Zelaya's populist tilt and his post-coup return have undermined the basic precondition for a stable competitive equilibrium of neoliberal convergence: the sociopolitical disorganization of working and lower classes outside the clientelist networks of the traditional parties. The Honduran "exception," then, may have been slower to develop these disruptive reactive sequences than the other countries that experienced neoliberal convergence, but its political trendlines appear to be moving in the same direction. The demise of neoliberal convergence in these other cases is examined below.

PROGRAMMATIC DE-ALIGNMENT AND REACTIVE SEQUENCES: THE LEGACIES OF BAIT-AND-SWITCH REFORM

Chapters 7 and 8 analyzed critical junctures in four countries that experienced bait-and-switch patterns of market reform: Costa Rica and Ecuador from the category of elitist party systems, and Argentina and Venezuela from the LM cases. All of these countries experienced forms of neoliberal convergence during the critical juncture, although party system decomposition in Venezuela led to an outcome of polarized populism. In none of these countries did neoliberal convergence prove to be a stable competitive equilibrium in the aftermath period.

In these four cases, reactive sequences during the critical juncture and/or the aftermath period were dominated by three principal tendencies: (1) rising levels of social protest against market liberalism; (2) the demise of established conservative and/or centrist parties in every case, and the decomposition of entire party systems in Venezuela and Ecuador; and (3) the outflanking to the left of established party systems, with the rise of new leftist parties, movements, and populist figures or, in the Argentine case, a turn toward the left within Peronism. In Venezuela, Ecuador, and Argentina, these left turns followed in the wake of mass protest movements and partial or complete processes of party system decomposition, and they produced new governments that broke more sharply with the neoliberal model than the leftist governments analyzed above in Chile,

Brazil, and Uruguay. Although the PLN provided a measure of continuity in the Costa Rican party system, a new Leftist party eventually captured the presidency in 2014. It is to this case that I first turn.

Costa Rica: From Neoliberal Convergence to Contested Liberalism

Of these four de-aligning cases, Costa Rica had the most stable party system during the critical juncture and the least disruptive aftermath period. Even in Costa Rica, however, the vaunted stability of partisan competition was shaken in the aftermath period: the conservative PUSC entered into decline, the center-left PLN – which had taken the lead in the adoption of market reforms – moved rightward to occupy the space left vacant by the PUSC, and a new leftist party emerged to outflank the establishment and fill the void on the Left. The party system, in short, experienced a partial decomposition (on the Right) and recomposition (on the Left), as well as major electoral and programmatic realignments.

As explained in Chapter 7, Costa Rica's market reforms began relatively early, especially in comparison to other countries under democratic rule, and its critical juncture ended early as well – with the 1990 election victory by the conservative PUSC, which ratified the neoliberal reforms begun by its center-left rival. The PLN and PUSC alternated in power and remained electorally dominant for the first decade of the aftermath period (see Appendix Tables 7 and 8), with very low levels of electoral volatility. The average volatility score on the Pedersen index was only 4.8 percent in the 1990, 1994, and 1998 presidential elections, and 8.8 percent in the three legislative election cycles. As in Honduras, however, growing signs of disenchantment with the political establishment were evident even during this period of electoral stability. As early as the mid-1980s, public opinion surveys began to detect a decline in the legitimacy of the political system, as measured by indicators of trust and support for basic political institutions (Seligson 2002). By the late 1990s, moreover, this declining legitimacy was beginning to influence electoral behavior; voter turnout dipped in the 1998 elections, while support for minor opposition parties and new parties formed after 1990 experienced a modest increase.

According to Seligson (2002: 180–181), much of this decline in systemic legitimacy reflected public opposition to government attempts to open the economy and privatize state-owned utility companies, which were relatively efficient in Costa Rica. Indeed, in Latinobarómetro (1999–2000: 26) surveys conducted in the late 1990s, on average only 38 percent of Costa Ricans said that privatizations had benefited their country – the second-lowest average in the region after Venezuela. With both major parties supporting privatizations and other orthodox reforms, however, societal opposition had no effective partisan outlet, and programmatic distinctions between the two major parties progressively faded. In a 1998 survey, for example, legislators from both the PLN and the PUSC located their party to the right of center, and programmatic differences on economic issues cut "across partisan lines" rather than creating a "significant political divide between them" (Zoco 2006: 265, 270). Consequently, "By the early 1990s, the complaint that the PLN and PUSC were mirroring each other had become a common refrain. Many citizens felt unrepresented by either" (Lehoucq 2005: 147).

As policy convergence eroded programmatic linkages, the two major parties became more dependent on clientelist bonds to secure support. The parties had never relied exclusively on programmatic linkages; as Carey (1996: 103–135) demonstrates, they had long used constituency services and local pork-barrel spending to cultivate particularistic loyalties and patron–client linkages as well. According to Lehoucq (2005: 148), however, "As differences between the PLN and the PUSC eroded, they began to collude at the task of colonizing" once-autonomous public agencies, placing their respective loyalists throughout public administration. Such clientelist practices are vulnerable to political backlash when they become patently corrupt, exclusive, and detached from larger programmatic objectives.

Although the political backlash in Costa Rica was less explosive than that in several of the other countries that experienced bait-and-switch reforms, it nonetheless produced major changes in the party system. Reactive sequences began with a surge in popular mobilization against the neoliberal model. Unprecedented mass protests erupted in the spring of 2000 against a proposed law to open the state electricity and telecommunications monopolies to private competition. Whereas protests in the past "were almost always limited to a specific sector, such as university students or small farmers," the protest cycle in 2000 "spread to all sectors of the population for two weeks and displayed a ferocity uncharacteristic of Costa Rican demonstrations" (Seligson 2002: 181). These protests were a prelude to widespread demonstrations against CAFTA, the regional free trade agreement that was negotiated in 2003–2004. The accord required Costa Rica to further reduce tariff protections and expose state monopolies to foreign competition, raising concerns about its potential effects on farmers, small producers, and subsidized public services.

This social mobilization clearly outflanked the party system to the Left, articulating programmatic preferences that were odds with the policy stands of the two major parties. It also exacerbated dissent within the PLN, energizing factions opposed to the technocratic leadership group that had steered the party line since the 1980s. In late 2000, a dissident group led by former Economics Minister Ottón Solís broke away from the PLN to found the *Partido Acción Ciudadana* (Citizen Action Party, PAC), which quickly occupied vacant political space to the left of center. The PAC opposed privatizations and defended traditional state developmental and social welfare activities. The new party capitalized on public discontent to capture 26.9 percent of the presidential vote for Solís in 2002 and nearly a quarter of the seats in the national assembly – the first clear sign that reactive sequences in the aftermath period were undermining the two-party system and producing a major electoral realignment.

Indeed, not only did a new party of the Center-Left erupt onto the political scene in the 2002 elections, but a strong showing was also made by a relatively new party of the right, the *Partido Movimiento Libertario* (Libertarian Movement Party, or PML). A staunch advocate of free market reforms, the PML was founded in 1994 but remained a minor force until the 2002 elections, when it captured 10.5 percent of the legislative seats. Shortly thereafter, the PML established itself as a leader of the partisan Right when the traditional conservative party, the PUSC, became embroiled in a series of corruption scandals after defeating the PLN in the second round of the presidential elections in 2002. These scandals eventually led to the trial and conviction of two former presidents from the PUSC – Rafael Calderón Fournier (1990–1994) and Miguel Rodríguez (1998–2002) – for receiving kickbacks from foreign companies seeking contracts in Costa Rica's social security and telecommunications systems. The PUSC paid a steep price at the ballot box for these scandals; the party obtained less than 4 percent of the vote in the 2006 and 2010 presidential elections, and its congressional representation dropped to 8.8 percent of the seats in 2006 and 10.5 percent in 2010.

With the PUSC in crisis and the PAC playing a lead role in civic and political mobilization against Costa Rica's ratification of the CAFTA treaty, the PLN became the primary defender of the market-liberalization process it had launched in the 1980s. Behind the candidacy of former president Oscar Arias, the PLN narrowly defeated PAC leader Ottón Solís by a vote 40.9 to 39.8 percent in the 2006 presidential race. During Arias' second term, a contentious debate over CAFTA blocked legislative ratification of Costa Rica's entry into the trade pact, forcing the government to submit the treaty to a popular referendum – the first in Costa Rica's history. In the October 2007 referendum, the government narrowly prevailed by a vote of 51.4 to 48.6 percent, making Costa Rica the last country to ratify its membership in CAFTA.

The vote on CAFTA demonstrated that Costa Ricans remained split down the middle over the basic course of market liberalization. What changed during the first decade of the 21st century, however – the second decade of Costa Rica's aftermath period – was that partisan competition was restructured along this programmatic axis. The neoliberal convergence of the PLN-PUSC duopoly that emerged during the critical juncture broke down after 2000; as the party system was partially reconstituted, it became more programmatically aligned, with relatively well-defined parties on both sides of the central programmatic divide. Arguably, then, in the aftermath period Costa Rica moved from the lower left cell in Figure 6.1 – the domain of neoliberal convergence – to the upper left cell of contested liberalism. New parties on the right (PML) and left (PAC) lent support and opposition, respectively, to the neoliberal model, while the PLN anchored a broad centrist or center-right spectrum that promoted market reforms, but also defended the core universalist features of Costa Rica's traditional welfare state. This new programmatic alignment was reinforced in the 2010 national elections, with the PLN retaining the presidency for its candidate, Laura Chinchilla, who obtained 46.9 percent of the vote against 25.1 percent for Solís of the PAC and 20.9 percent for Oscar Guevara of the PML.

In Costa Rica, then, neoliberal convergence was relatively stable during the critical juncture and the early aftermath period, but in a context of significant societal resistance to market liberalization, it was not a durable competitive equilibrium for the long term. The institutional legacies of the critical juncture diverged sharply from its initial outcome by the second decade of the aftermath period, as reactive sequences exerted their transformative effects. Although the party system did not fully decompose or get displaced by anti-establishment outsiders, it was partially reconstituted by new parties on the Right and Left that realigned the party system both electorally and programmatically. Costa Rica experienced significant social protest, especially after 2000, but market reforms did not produce the kinds of explosive protest movements that toppled governments in several of the other bait-and-switch cases analyzed in the next section. Neither did reactive sequences reverse the process of market liberalization. They did, however, limit market reforms in the social policy sphere, and they generated a new partisan Left that eventually captured the presidency in 2014 for Luís Guillermo Solis of the PAC. Solis won a narrow plurality of the first-round vote and a resounding 77.8 percent of the second-round vote when the PLN candidate read the writing on the wall and attempted to withdraw from the race. Although Solis did not promise a radical break with the neoliberal model, he pledged to reduce social economic inequalities, defend workers' rights in the free trade agreements, and strengthen public health and social security systems.

In short, Costa Rica's programmatically de-aligning, bait-and-switch process of market reform produced an initial outcome of neoliberal convergence that was vulnerable to destabilizing reactive sequences, even if these sequences were more moderate than those experienced in the other bait-and-switch cases. Undoubtedly, Costa Rica's relatively strong economic performance exerted a moderating effect on these reactive sequences; the country avoided a recession during the regional downturn at the end of the 1990s, and per-capita GDP growth during the lean years from 1990 to 2003 averaged 2.6 percent, the fourth-highest rate in Latin America (Rodríguez 2010: 94). Steady growth helped to cushion living standards from the social costs of structural adjustment; although real minimum wages were relatively stagnant and income inequality worsened in the aftermath period, with Costa Rica's score on the Gini index rising from 44.0 in 1990 (one of the lowest in the region) to 50.2 in 2009 (near the regional mean; see Cornia 2012), the percentage of the population living below the poverty line gradually dropped from 23.7 percent in the 1980s to 21 percent in the 1990s and 18.5 percent by 2010 (Huber and Stephens 2010: 158; Economic Commission for Latin America and the Caribbean 2011: 65).

Furthermore, structural adjustment did not lead to a dismantling of Costa Rica's welfare state, as both PLN and PUSC governments resisted World Bank pressures to radically privatize health care and pension systems. Instead, they adopted a limited private pension program to supplement the public system, maintaining the latter's broad coverage (Madrid 2003: 188–189), and they introduced market incentives to enhance the efficiency of the public health care system while keeping the private sector "narrowly confined" (Weyland 2006: 151). A comparative perspective thus suggests that although Costa Rica's social democratic traditions did not block the process of market liberalization, they nonetheless limited its scope by shielding the social safety net from the pressures for market orthodoxy. In so doing, they moderated the political backlash against market reforms in the aftermath period – and, arguably, made the neoliberal model more politically sustainable than in the other bait-and-switch cases analyzed in the following section.

Argentina: Economic Crisis, Social Protest, and the Peronist Left Turn

Like Costa Rica, Argentina ended the critical juncture with two major parties that generally supported the market reforms adopted by Peronist President Carlos Menem – in short, with neoliberal convergence. Also like in Costa Rica, reactive sequences in Argentina's aftermath period decimated the major party that had *not* led the reform process (the Radical Party, or UCR), while leaving the reform leader (the Peronist PJ) as the dominant actor in the party system. In contrast to Costa Rica, however, reactive sequences in Argentina were conditioned by a severe financial crisis and a deep recession in the late 1990s and early 2000s. This new cycle of economic crisis triggered an explosion of social protest that forced the resignation of the UCR-FREPASO government and produced a thorough decomposition of the non-Peronist side of the party system. The Peronists survived this upheaval – indeed, they capitalized on it – but, in contrast to the PLN in Costa Rica, they veered back in a more statist and heterodox direction after returning to power, ultimately abandoning the neoliberal course the party had adopted under Menem after 1989. Alone in the region, the PJ led the process of structural adjustment during the critical juncture and then channeled much of the social backlash against it in the aftermath period, emerging politically hegemonic as the unlikely beneficiary of Argentina's "left turn" after 2003.

Argentina's critical juncture ended with Menem's convincing re-election in 1995, which ratified the process of market liberalization at the ballot box following the defeat of hyperinflation. During Menem's second term, however, new strains developed within the economic model, and the PJ's political leadership began to falter. The Mexican peso crisis contributed to a recession in Argentina in 1995, demonstrating the country's continued vulnerability to international financial shocks. Although growth resumed at a healthy rate in 1996 and 1997, it stalled again in 1998, and by 1999 the economy had slipped into a recession that would last for four years and drive unemployment and poverty rates to unprecedented levels. The convertibility plan that fixed the Argentine peso to the dollar kept the inflation rate in the low single digits, but it caused the peso to be overvalued, leading to a growing trade deficit and high interest rates that discouraged investment. The key economic measure that allowed Menem to defeat hyperinflation during the critical juncture thus limited the government's policy flexibility in the aftermath period, setting the stage for a new and politically devastating economic crisis at the end of the decade. These problems were compounded by the financial crisis in Asia and Brazil, which led to a devaluation of the Brazilian currency in January 1999 and a slump in Argentina's exports to its primary MERCOSUR trading partner.

Although currency overvaluation was clearly creating economic imbalances, the fear of a revival of inflationary pressures and the loss of international confidence led the government to stick to its course and reject calls for the lifting of convertibility. Menem's thinly veiled intention to run for a third consecutive term in office generated internal schisms within Peronism, given the emergence of rival leaders in the PJ. The most prominent of these, Eduardo Duhalde – Menem's first vice-president and the governor of Buenos Aires province – stood at the apex of the PJ's formidable patronage machine in the densely populated province.

With the PJ mired in internal conflict over presidential succession, a process of realignment and alliance building occurred within the anti-Peronist bloc. The UCR had emerged from the 1995 election in a weakened state, having finished third in the presidential race with a mere 17.0 percent of the vote and capturing only 26.5 percent of the seats in the lower house of congress, barely half of the PJ's 51 percent (see Appendix Tables 1 and 2). The UCR's prospects, however, were buttressed by the possibility of an electoral alliance with FREPASO to contest Peronism. FREPASO first emerged as a significant force when its predecessor alliance, the *Frente Grande* (Big Front), won 13.6 percent of the vote in the 1994 constituent assembly elections. It followed this up with a second-place finish in the 1995 presidential campaign and the election of twenty-two deputies to the lower house of congress. FREPASO was an internally heterogeneous front that brought together several small leftist parties, moderate independents, and left-leaning Peronist splinters under the leadership of former Peronist deputy Carlos "Chacho" Alvarez. FREPASO had ties to public sector labor unions that rejected the neoliberal model, as well as middle-class and professional circles that were critical of the corruption of the Menem government, the patronage politics of lower-class Peronism, and the social costs of neoliberal orthodoxy. As such, FREPASO positioned itself to fill the political void left by the decline of the UCR in the Center and the PJ's programmatic shift toward the neoliberal Right (Novaro and Palermo 1998). FREPASO made effective use of the mass media to appeal to voters on valence issues related to the rule of law and clean government, but it invested little in the development of grassroots party organs, especially outside the capital.

Although FREPASO adopted a cautious critical stance toward Menem's neoliberal model, it accepted the general thrust of market reforms, making it ideologically compatible with the pro-market UCR. Since the two parties shared a common interest in contesting Peronist dominance of Argentine politics, they forged an alliance in anticipation of the 1997 mid-term congressional elections (Novaro and Palermo 1998). Although the PJ retained its majority in the senate, it lost its majority in the lower house, claiming 46.3 percent of the seats as compared to 40.5 percent for the UCR-FREPASO alliance. The alliance with FREPASO and the 1997 elections breathed new life into the UCR, as they demonstrated that Argentine politics continued to be cleaved along a Peronist/ anti-Peronist axis, and that the anti-Peronist bloc – now represented by two major parties – could still compete at the national level.

The UCR-FREPASO alliance was clearly encouraged by the apparent vulnerability of Menem and the PJ. Menem's public-approval ratings plummeted over his second term in office as economic performance faltered, falling to a low of 24 percent in 1998 (Weyland 2002: 184), making his potential candidacy for a third term a threat to the party's interests. As Echegaray and Elordi (2001: 209–211) demonstrate, rising unemployment was especially damaging to the president's popularity. The unemployment rate averaged over 15 percent during Menem's second term, and as the threat of inflation receded after 1991, public perceptions of economic problems experienced an important shift. In 1990, 67.1 percent of individuals listed inflation as a major concern, compared to only 16.2 percent who cited unemployment. By 1995, however, inflation had disappeared from the rankings, while 86.4 percent of individuals listed unemployment and 63.7 percent identified low wages as major concerns (Echegaray and Elordi 2001: 201). In 1996–1997, simmering discontent over unemployment and cuts in social benefits produced a series of local uprisings and road blockades in economically depressed interior provinces (Wolff 2007). Loosely organized by unions, groups of unemployed workers, and popular assemblies, Argentina's *piquetero* (picketers) movement had been born; as Silva (2009: 76) states, "Because disruption of the workplace had lost effectiveness in severely depressed local economies, the unemployed and their allies disrupted vital transportation arteries."

In short, the economy remained highly salient politically, but a major shift had occurred in the relative saliency of different economic problems. As Weyland (2000) argues, public officials may derive political gains from the resolution of an economic crisis, but these political gains are subject to a law of diminishing returns: once a crisis is resolved, its political salience declines, and other issues are likely to rise in prominence. With hyperinflation vanquished, the Peronist government was increasingly held accountable for the social deficits of the neoliberal model. At this juncture, however, the UCR and FREPASO were hard-pressed to articulate an alternative to this model, so they focused their criticisms on the Menem administration's corruption, cronyism, and questionable adherence to the rule of law. These valence issues were tailor-made for parties like FREPASO and the UCR that appealed to middle-class sectors that were not incorporated into the PJ's vast patronage networks, and they provided these parties with relatively safe campaign planks to differentiate themselves from Peronism without offering an alternative economic model.

Indeed, as the UCR and FREPASO prepared to challenge Peronism in the 1999 national elections, they pledged to uphold the convertibility plan, fearing that any uncertainty on this issue would trigger a loss of investor confidence and reignite inflationary pressures. A continuation of convertibility meant relinquishing standard levers of monetary and exchange-rate policy, essentially precluding any significant departure from Menem's economic model other than paying greater attention to social problems like unemployment and education. In short, neoliberal convergence remained intact as Argentina hurtled toward a new financial crisis.

Meanwhile, the PJ increasingly resembled a collection of provincial machines lacking any center of gravity. During Menem's second term, a growing number of Peronist state governors asserted their independence, blocked Menem's efforts to streamline provincial spending, and expressed discontent with the neoliberal model (Levitsky 2003: 177–182; Eaton 2005). These internal opposition currents eventually prevailed to give the PJ's presidential nomination to Duhalde rather than Menem.

The 1999 presidential election thus pitted Duhalde against Fernando de la Rúa of the UCR-FREPASO alliance and Menem's former economy minister, Domingo Cavallo, who formed a pro-neoliberal party known as Action for the Republic (AR) to support his own candidacy. De la Rúa captured the presidency with 48.4 percent of the vote, compared to 38.7 percent for Duhalde and 9.8 percent for Cavallo. The UCR-FREPASO alliance also won a plurality in the lower house of congress, claiming 46.3 percent of the seats versus 38.5 percent for the PJ. Surveys of voting intentions suggest that much of the middle- and upper-class support that Menem attracted in 1995 swung over to de la Rúa and Cavallo in 1999, leaving the PJ heavily dependent on its core working- and lower-class constituencies (*Estudio Mora y Araujo & Asociados* 1999). Even among these groups, support fell off sharply, as de la Rúa's appeal crossed class lines to penetrate deeply into the popular sectors.

Nevertheless, both the UCR's political comeback and FREPASO's rise to prominence proved to be ill-timed and short-lived. De la Rúa inherited an economy in recession that had been battered by a series of international shocks over the latter half of the 1990s, producing serious fiscal and current account deficits and a very high level of dependence on foreign borrowing and capital inflows. With monetary and exchange-rate policies locked into place by convertibility, thus precluding stimulus measures, and with fiscal options sharply limited, de la Rúa took office in December 1999 and immediately adopted austerity measures "to lower the fiscal deficit and reduce Argentina's borrowing needs" (Starr 2003: 69). These measures were followed by a second round of spending cuts in early 2000 – in essence, pro-cyclical policies that deepened the recession (Feldstein 2002). To make matters worse, de la Rúa adopted a controversial labor-reform bill that backfired politically when government intelligence and labor ministry officials were implicated in a bribery scandal to purchase the votes of Peronist senators. The scandal severely damaged the public image of a coalition that had run for office on a platform to clean up government, and it ultimately led to the resignation from the government of FREPASO leader and vice president Chacho Alvarez.

Within a year of taking office, the UCR-FREPASO alliance was in tatters, and the government's credibility was faltering. Desperate for financial relief, the government negotiated several IMF bailouts and a debt-restructuring accord between November 2000 and August 2001, and it brought Cavallo back as the economy minister to secure investor confidence. These steps failed to stem capital flight, however; with the banking system on the verge of collapse, de la Rúa and Cavallo froze bank deposits in November 2001 to prevent further withdrawals and currency movements. The IMF then rejected an Argentine request to waive its fiscal targets and disburse the balance on its loan (Starr 2003: 70).

Simmering unrest exploded in a wave of protests and riots on December 18, when rioters looted stores, neighborhood residents banged pots and pats, and *piqueteros* set up roadblocks to halt transportation and demand jobs and state benefits (Epstein 2003; Auyero 2007). Police repression resulted in dozens of fatalities, fueling the outrage against the government. Rebuffed by the Peronists in a bid to form a government of national unity, de la Rúa resigned from office on December 20, inaugurating a chaotic two-week period in which Argentina had five acting presidents. De la Rúa was replaced by a caretaker until Congress could elect Peronist governor Adolfo Rodríguez Saá as president, who immediately defaulted on $155 billion in foreign debt – the largest government default in history. With protests continuing, Rodríguez Saá failed to elicit the support of other Peronist governors and resigned after one turbulent week in office. Following another caretaker, congress finally elected PJ senator and Buenos Aires machine boss Eduardo Duhalde to the presidency on January 1, 2002 – ironically, turning to the loser of the 1999 presidential race to try to restore order.

Duhalde quickly scrapped the convertibility plan, producing a 200-percent currency devaluation that reignited inflation, bankrupted countless firms with dollar denominated debts, and deepened Argentina's worst recession since the 1930s. The economic and human costs of the recession were staggering. The economy contracted by 16.3 percent from the first quarter of 2001 to the first quarter of 2002, while unemployment soared to 21.5 percent. In October 2002 official studies classified 57.5 percent of the population as living in poverty, up from 35.9 percent in May 2001 and 16.1 percent in 1994. In 2002 the income of the wealthiest decile of Argentines was thirty-two times that of the poorest decile, more than double the 15:1 ratio of 1990 (Economist Intelligence Unit 2002a: 19, 2002b: 29, 2003b: 27–28). Meanwhile, the number of *piquetero* roadblocks swelled from 170 in 1997 to 1,383 in 2001 and 2,336 in 2002 (Wolff 2007: 6).

The re-descent into economic crisis and the explosion of social protests wreaked havoc on Argentina's party system. As with the late 1980s hyperinflationary crisis, however, the political costs of the crisis were over-whelmingly concentrated on the anti-Peronist side of the party system. Prior to de la Rúa's resignation, these costs were apparent in the October 2001 mid-term congressional elections, when the vote for the UCR-FREPASO alliance fell to less than a quarter of the electorate and its congressional representation was slashed from 46.3 to 28 percent of lower house seats. Although the PJ's congressional bloc increased from 38.5 to 47.1 percent of the seats, an unprecedented 24 percent of voters cast blank or spoiled ballots (Nohlen 2005, vol. 2: 94), suggesting widespread disillusionment with the entire party system. The protest chant *que se vayan todos!* – loosely translated as "out with them all" – seemingly pointed to a rejection of Argentina's political class and a receptiveness to new alternatives (Torre 2005).

Nevertheless, this new cycle of economic crisis and social protest did not lead to systemic decomposition, much less an organizational reconstitution of the party system. For all its social mobilization from below, the protest cycle did not spawn a new movement party or the rise of a populist outsider. Indeed, the protest cycle gradually tapered off as the economy stabilized and began a tentative recovery under Duhalde over the second half of 2002. Released from the straightjacket of convertibility and IMF-mandated monetary and fiscal policies, Duhalde and Economy Minister Roberto Lavagna followed a prag-matic strategy to reactivate the economy and cushion the social impact of the depression. The devaluation eventually provided a stimulus to exports and local industry, while the government delivered an employment program, food aid, and social emergency funds for the unemployed and some two million house-holds. These distributive programs – some of which Duhalde allowed *piquetero* organizations to administer – helped to revive the clientelist networks at the core of the PJ's local and provincial machines. In so doing, they brought many working- and lower-class constituencies back into the Peronist fold, largely containing anti-system sentiments to non-Peronist sectors of society.

Indeed, these distributive programs demobilized the protest movement by driving a wedge between politically moderate tendencies – which sought social relief from the government and collaborated with Peronism to obtain it – and radical factions linked to small leftist parties that advocated more far-reaching change (Wolff 2007). As Auyero (2007) demonstrates, grassroots Peronist net-works had been deeply involved in coordinating many protest activities, dem-onstrating once again the PJ's unparalleled ability to influence the political rhythms and timing of social mobilization in the streets as well as the workplace. With the UCR out of office and Peronist control of the presidency restored, the PJ was positioned to use state power and resources to reincorporate popular sectors from above, defusing the protest movement and marginalizing its more intransigent tendencies. This Peronist capacity for governance – the ability to perform the most basic governmental function of maintaining public order – was the reverse side of its capacity to create ungovernability when the party was out of power by vetoing political and economic accords and promoting social mobilization from below. De la Rúa, then, was not simply a victim of unfortunate timing by ascending to power at the onset of a crisis; he was, more fundamentally, the victim of an underlying social and political power imbalance that made him the fourth consecutive UCR president since the rise of Peronism in the 1940s to fail to complete a term in office.

For the second time in thirteen years, then, the PJ had taken over for a UCR president who had resigned in a context of acute crisis, giving Peronism an opportunity to reap the political rewards for restoring economic stability and social peace. When Duhalde moved elections forward to April 2003, the PJ emerged from the crisis with an unprecedented, if internally fractious, stranglehold over the Argentine political system, and with the anti-Peronist bloc in tatters. FREPASO and AR disappeared from the political map, while the UCR bumbled through a contentious primary election that included charges of vote fraud and the resignation of the party president. UCR leaders Elisa Carrió and Ricardo López Murphy eventually abandoned the party to run independent campaigns for the presidency at the head of new electoral fronts. Attempting to fill the void left by FREPASO's collapse, Carrió ran a moderately left of center, anti-corruption campaign and earned 14.1 percent of the presidential vote for her Alternative for a Republic of Equals (ARI), which later formed the Civic Coalition (CC). López Murphy, a University of Chicago-trained economist who had briefly served in de la Rúa's cabinet, ran on a neoliberal platform and won 16.4 percent of the vote. Official UCR candidate Leopoldo Moreau received a mere 2.3 percent of the vote, the worst showing in the party's history.

The top two vote-getters in 2003, however, and three of the top five, were Peronist candidates. The long-standing leadership dispute between Menem and Duhalde prevented the PJ from uniting behind a single candidate, as Menem insisted on making another bid for the presidency, which was adamantly opposed by Duhalde and many of the party's governors. Fearing a victory by Menem, Duhalde and his backers canceled a primary election that was designed to select a unified PJ candidate, then threw their support to Santa Cruz governor Néstor Kirchner, who joined Menem and Adolfo Rodríguez Saá as Peronist candidates in the first round of the election. Although Menem captured a plurality with 24.5 percent of the vote, Kirchner followed closely with 22.2 percent, and Rodríguez Saá added 14.1 percent, giving Peronist candidates over 60 percent of the total vote against a fragmented opposition. The PJ also captured a majority in both houses of congress, including 50.2 percent of the seats in the lower house compared to only 21 percent for the UCR. Menem's polarizing candidacy led most of the PJ and opposition forces to rally behind Kirchner, who was declared the president when Menem read the writing on the wall and withdrew from the second-round run-off.

Kirchner's presidential term left no doubt that the institutional outcome of Argentina's critical juncture – neoliberal convergence – had been thoroughly transformed by the reactive sequences of the aftermath period. This transformation occurred along three primary dimensions: (1) the organizational decomposition of the anti-Peronist side of the party system; (2) the consolidation of Peronist dominance of Argentine politics; and (3) a sharp turn away from the neoliberal model of the 1990s. Peronist dominance went hand-in-hand with the demise of rival parties; not only did Kirchner and his wife, Cristina Fernández de Kirchner, win the presidency in 2003, 2007, and 2011, but they did so against much-weakened and fragmented partisan opposition. For the first time in its history, the UCR declined to field a presidential candidate in 2007, instead lending its support to an independent front that backed the candidacy of Kirchner's former economy minister Roberto Lavagna. Carrió also formed a new front to run for the presidency against Cristina Fernández, whose husband had declined to run for re-election. Fernández won comfortably with 44.9 percent of the vote to 23 percent for Carrio and 16.9 percent for Lavagna. Following Kirchner's death in 2010, Fernández was re-elected in 2011 with 54 percent of the vote – the highest percentage in an Argentine presidential election since Perón in 1973. The distant second- and third-place contenders in the 2011 presidential race were Socialist leader Hermes Binner and Ricardo Luis Alfonsín of the UCR, a son of the former president, with 16.9 and 11.2 percent of the vote, respectively.

The Peronists also remained by far the largest party in both houses of congress, although the dominant party faction led by Kirchner and Fernández, the Front for Victory (FPV), did not incorporate several dissident Peronist factions and lost its legislative majority in 2009. Kirchner and Fernández drew legislative support from non-Peronist sectors of the fragmented congress, however, while the UCR, Carrió's Civic Coalition, and a new conservative front known as Republican Proposal (PRO) formed the leading minority delegations for most of this period. These latter parties, however, won a mere 14.8, 2.3, and 4.3 percent of legislative seats, respectively, in 2011, hardly enough to challenge Peronist dominance of Argentine politics.

Rather than turn the clock back to the Menem era, Kirchner and Fernández broke sharply with the neoliberal model and revived Peronism's statist, nationalist, and redistributive traditions. With roots in the left-leaning Peronist youth movement of the 1970s, Kirchner and Fernández steered public policy along a heterodox course that placed Argentina within the regional "left turn" under Peronist direction (Etchemendy and Garay 2011). A staunch critic of neoliberalism, Kirchner negotiated a rescheduling of Argentina's defaulted debt with foreign bondholders on highly favorable terms, and paid off the country's debt to the IMF. He also imposed higher taxes and quotas on exporters, subsidized domestic producers, nationalized private pension funds along with oil, electricity, water, telephone, postal, and airlines industries, and adopted price controls for public utilities, food, and gasoline. With a new economic expansion generating fiscal and current account surpluses, Kirchner used this financial latitude to increase wages and launch a series of new social programs. These included public works programs and microenterprise subsidies to generate employment, an expansion of the pension system to near universal coverage, new family allowances, and housing subsidies. In the labor sphere, Kirchner encouraged collective bargaining, decreed wage hikes, re-regulated labor markets to enhance job security, and patched up the tattered relationship between the PJ and the Peronist-led national labor confederation, as well as its smaller left-leaning rival (Etchemendy and Collier 2007). Representatives from labor unions and the unemployed workers' association were brought into policymaking arenas, and both types of organizations mobilized pro-government demonstrations when landowners protested against Fernández' attempt to raise export taxes in 2008.

Although this heterodox course stoked inflationary pressures – which the government was accused of masking in official figures – the rise in prices did not sidetrack the economic recovery that occurred after 2003. With export commodity prices soaring and domestic industry expanding, GDP growth averaged a stunning 7.8 percent annual rate from 2003–2011, despite the global recession toward the end of this period (World Bank 2012). The minimum wage increased nearly four-fold between 2002 and 2010, by far the steepest rise in Latin America, while the Gini index of inequality dropped from 53.3 to 44.3, also the steepest decline in the region (Cornia 2012: 3, 26). The u-turn away from market orthodoxy was reflected in Argentina's score on the Heritage Foundation/*Wall Street Journal*'s "Index of Economic Freedom": within Latin America, only Cuba and Venezuela had lower scores on the index than Argentina in 2012, and the 22-point drop in Argentina's score between 2000 and 2012 was the largest in the region.

Consequently, over the first decade of the 21st century, Argentina veered sharply away from the neoliberal convergence that marked the endpoint of the country's critical juncture. Reactive sequences in the aftermath period – namely, a profound economic crisis and explosive social protests – undermined both the competitive equilibrium in the party system and the technocratic consensus for market liberalism that were the hallmarks of neoliberal convergence. The anti-Peronist side of the party system bore the brunt of this new crisis – as it did in the late 1980s – and entered into steep decline, while the PJ once again reaped the political rewards from stabilization and recovery. After leading the market reform process in the 1990s, the PJ channeled much of the social and political backlash against it in the 2000s, making it the only major bait-and-switch reformer in the region not to get outflanked on the Left by new partisan or populist contenders.

The remarkable programmatic flexibility and organizational resiliency of Peronism thus limited decomposition to the anti-Peronist side of the party system. The steep decline of the UCR and the disappearance of FREPASO allowed the PJ to dominate the electoral arena, with intra-Peronist factionalism a driving force behind much of the country's political competition.[1] Indeed,

---

[1] As of the end of 2013, it appeared unlikely that Cristina Fernández would run for a third term in office, and a variety of Peronist leaders were positioning themselves for the looming competition to

through the first decade of the 21st century Argentina did not have a nationally competitive centrist or conservative party to defend market liberalism against an increasingly left-leaning Peronism; the runner-up to Fernández in the 2011 presidential campaign, in fact, was a socialist. As such, the breakdown of neo-liberal convergence did not elicit a transition toward contested liberalism in the aftermath period, as occurred in the Costa Rican case analyzed in the previous section. Instead, Argentina consolidated a form of single-party dominance and veered programmatically toward statist development alternatives – an institutional and policy legacy that was clearly orthogonal to the unstable baseline of neoliberal convergence with which Argentina entered the aftermath period.

Party System Decomposition and New Forms of Populism: Venezuela and Ecuador

The final two countries – Venezuela and Ecuador – experienced programmatically de-aligning critical junctures with variants of neoliberal convergence that culminated in party system decomposition and the election of populist outsiders. Although the timing of these patterns varied, critical junctures produced legacies of deinstitutionalized and highly personalistic political representation. Reactive sequences in the aftermath period reproduced polarized populism in Venezuela while driving Ecuador from serial to more polarized forms of populism. Both countries, then, veered decisively toward the left – Venezuela at the end of the critical juncture, and Ecuador in the aftermath period.

Reproducing Polarized Populism in Venezuela

The Venezuelan case is perhaps the more straightforward. As explained in Chapter 8, Venezuela experienced two different rounds of bait-and-switch market reform, producing powerful reactive sequences during the critical juncture: a cycle of mass protests and riots, several military coup attempts, a presidential impeachment, and a progressive decomposition of the party system. These reactive sequences culminated in the election of a highly polarizing populist outsider, Hugo Chávez, at the end of the critical juncture in 1998. Chávez's election made Venezuela the only country in the region to exit the critical juncture with an institutional outcome of polarized populism. This outcome was subsequently reproduced in the aftermath period, which left Venezuela with high levels of programmatic and ideological contestation, but weakly institutionalized forms of political representation. In short, the legacy of Venezuela's critical juncture was a deep sociopolitical cleavage that aligned electoral competition and defined programmatic alternatives, yet found expression in personalistic terms more than institutionalized partisan representation.

choose her successor. Given the organizational weakness and fragmentation of non-Peronist parties, it seemed highly likely that her successor would be drawn from the ranks of the PJ.

Having made the election of a constituent assembly the centerpiece of his presidential campaign, Chávez moved with lightning speed after taking office in February 1999 to sweep away the old political order and re-found regime institutions. With a charismatic touch and a moralistic, manichean discourse that railed against "savage neoliberalism" and "partyarchy" (Zúquete 2008; Hawkins 2010), Chávez relied heavily on plebistarian appeals to implement his mandate for institutional change. He won a referendum to convoke a constituent assembly and introduced a plurality electoral formula that allowed his coalition to capture 125 of the 131 assembly delegates. Claiming "supra-constitutional" powers, the assembly dissolved both houses of congress (where Chávez' MVR did not have a majority) along with regional legislative bodies, declared a judicial emergency so that judges could be purged, and nominated a commission from its ranks to perform legislative functions (Brewer-Carías 2010: 73–79). The new constitution, ratified in yet another popular referendum with 71.8 percent of the vote, strengthened presidential powers and mandated broad developmental and social welfare roles for the state. It also prescribed a "protagonistic" role for civil society and popular constituencies through a variety of consultative mechanisms and referenda, including recall elections for public officials (Alvarez 2003: 151–155).

By the end of 1999, Chávez had weakened institutional checks and balances on executive authority and set the stage for new elections in 2000 under the terms of his Bolivarian constitution. None of the traditional parties ran a presidential candidate in this election, and Chávez' primary contender was a former ally, Francisco Arias Cárdenas, a co-conspirator in the 1992 military rebellion. Elected governor of the oil-rich state of Zulia under the banner of Chávez' movement, Arias broke with Chávez in early 2000 and quickly emerged as the preferred candidate of diverse opposition groups. Chávez trounced Arias by a vote of 59.8 to 37.5 percent, earning the highest vote percentage ever received by a presidential candidate in post-1958 Venezuelan elections. Chávez's party, the MVR, captured 46.7 percent of the seats in the new National Assembly, while the MAS and other allied leftist parties added another 15.1 percent, giving the president a strong legislative majority. AD was reduced to 18.2 percent of the assembly seats, while COPEI won only 4.9 percent (see Appendix Tables 15 and 16).

Chávez's first year-and-a-half in power was thus dominated by a process of institutional transformation and political consolidation, with the president employing his popular support in a plebiscitary manner to overwhelm the fractious opposition. On the economic front, Chávez was initially more cautious, avoiding sharp departures from the orthodox course he inherited from Caldera. Although much of the business community had opposed Chávez in the 1998 election, he successfully courted some business figures who sought access to state policymaking channels and resources (Gates 2010), and his electoral support clearly crossed class lines, even if it was strongest in lower-class districts (López Maya 2003: 84; Dunning 2008: 173–174).

Consequently, as Corrales and Penfold (2011: 50) state, during his initial period in office Chávez's "political goals were more radical than his economic plans," and the president sought to allay business concerns by maintaining Caldera's finance minister. Inheriting an economy in recession, with oil prices at a rock-bottom low of $8 a barrel, Chávez followed relatively austere fiscal policies, continued Caldera's exchange-rate policies, and declined to control prices and interest rates (Buxton 2003: 124). While harshly critical of neoliberalism, Chávez nevertheless avoided radical redistributive or nationalization policies, and he provided new credits and trade protection to stimulate small- and medium-sized private enterprise. In a controversial move, he also used the armed forces for infrastructure projects and the delivery of social services (Norden 2003: 104–105). Under Chávez' oil minister, Ali Rodríguez, Venezuela asserted a new leadership role in OPEC, advocating an enforcement of production quotas that raised the international price of oil, thus generating new revenues for the state (Mommer 2003). This cautious approach helped Chávez maintain a multi-class base of support during his first year in office; a November 1999 survey, for example, found that over 70 percent of the lower and middle classes and 55 percent of the upper class approved of the president's performance (Alfredo Keller and Associates 1999).

Chávez's new constitution, however, provoked open opposition from the business community. Although the constitution was not explicitly socialist in inspiration, it was avowedly statist, prescribing a broad range of social rights, prohibiting the privatization of social security and the state oil company, strengthening job protection guarantees for workers, incorporating housewives and informal sector workers into the social security system, and allowing private property to be expropriated for social use. Venezuela's peak business association, FEDECAMARAS, criticized the statist character of the constitution and called for Venezuelans to vote against it in the December 1999 referendum. Business opposition hardened as political reforms buttressed Chávez's power and exacerbated uncertainty over the course of economic policy. Private investment fell by 25 percent during Chávez's first year in office, and a survey found that 97 percent of business executives wanted the president to change his economic course (Economist Intelligence Unit 2000: 9).

Consequently, as the July 2000 elections approached, the Chávez/anti-Chávez political cleavage was increasingly undergirded by class distinctions – in effect, deepening the "new politicization of class" that had been underway since the demise of Venezuela's oil-based *rentier* state in the 1980s and the onset of market reforms in 1989 (Dunning 2008: 169). Surveys showed that upper-middle and upper-class Venezuelans favored Arias Cárdenas over Chávez by better than four to one, while the poor supported Chávez by more than two to one (http://archivo.eluniversal.com/2000/04/06). Elite opposition intensified after the elections when the national assembly passed an enabling law that allowed Chávez to rule by decree for one year. Chávez used this authority to issue forty-nine legislative decrees in November 2001, including new laws that allowed for the expropriation of unutilized farm lands and strengthened executive control over financial institutions and the state-owned oil company (Buxton 2003: 128–129).

This exercise of decree powers and the prospect of a policy shift to the Left triggered a new stage of political conflict – in essence, a backlash by business elites and other elements of the traditional establishment. This elite and establishment backlash spawned reactive sequences that were quite different from those experienced by countries where neoliberal convergence provided the institutional baseline for the aftermath period; in Venezuela the conflicts "bolstered the presidency" and sharpened polarization (Corrales and Penfold 2011: 22), thus reinforcing and reproducing the legacy of polarized populism. To be sure, the axis of political conflict was not a conventional class cleavage, as Chávez also faced staunch opposition from the central labor confederation, the CTV, whose leadership remained closely bound to AD. Although Chávez had attempted to wrest control of the CTV from AD labor bosses by requiring union elections and promoting loyal union currents, he met with little success (Ellner 2003). Chávez thus relied heavily on new grassroots "Bolivarian" networks in poor communities, while the CTV joined business elites in supporting a two-day general strike in December 2001 and a wave of protests and demonstrations in early 2002. Managers of the state oil company went out on strike in March 2002 to protest government-imposed changes in its executive board, while Chávez's supporters mobilized counter-demonstrations, leading to violent clashes that culminated in a military coup on April 12, 2002 (Trinkunas 2005: 215–220).

A new, business-dominated government led by FEDECAMARAS president Pedro Carmona was quickly imposed, only to collapse two days later when a counter-mobilization of Chávez supporters in urban slums and the armed forces restored the elected president to office. Public opinion surveys at the time of the coup showed very high levels of social polarization: while 81 percent of upper-middle- and upper-class respondents disapproved of Chávez, and only 15 percent approved, 60 percent of the poor expressed approval, compared to 33 percent who disapproved (Consultores 21, S.A. 2002, question 31). The reversal of the coup did not end the elite political backlash, however. Managers and some workers from the state oil company launched a devastating two-month strike in December 2002, demanding Chávez' resignation, but the government eventually broke the strike by putting the industry under military control and dismissing 18,000 of the firm's 40,000 employees. The oil strike cost Venezuela an estimated $5 billion (Economist Intelligence Unit 2003a: 8) and triggered a severe recession that caused GDP to plunge by 8.9 percent in 2002 and 7.8 percent in 2003 (World Bank 2012).

Although the opposition had failed to dislodge Chávez through a military coup and an oil strike, it was heartened by public opinion surveys that showed the president's approval ratings dropping below the 50-percent mark in 2002 and 2003 (Corrales and Penfold 2011: 25). Hoping to capitalize on this discontent, the opposition changed tactics and employed institutional measures to try to bring about political change: a petition drive for a recall referendum as provided for in the new constitution. By the time the referendum was held in August 2004, however, the economic context had changed dramatically, and political momentum had swung decisively to Chávez's advantage. A sharp rise in oil prices, combined with the government's heightened control over the revenues of the state oil company, stimulated a vigorous economic recovery and gave Chávez command over windfall rents. The economy surged forward to grow at annual rates of 18.3 percent in 2004, 10.3 percent in 2005, and 9.9 percent in 2006, while a rising current account surplus allowed the government to accumulate massive foreign reserves.

Chávez poured much of this revenue – estimated at 3.5 percent of GDP between 2003 and 2005 – into social programs, or *misiones*, that gave new content to his pledge to address the social and economic needs of his core lower-class constituenices. The *misiones* included health clinics (often staffed with Cuban doctors), literacy and education programs, subsidized food markets, housing programs, and vocational training initiatives in low-income communities. These programs had a strong participatory character, as they encouraged the formation of local committees for planning, land and water use, health care provision, and other communal needs. As such, they provided a new stimulus for grassroots organization both inside and out of the partisan networks of Chávez' MVR (Hawkins 2010: 199–203; Ellner 2008: 180–193).

With the economy booming and massive oil rents being redistributed downward, the opposition's prospects faded in the 2004 recall referendum, and Chávez swept to victory when 58.3 percent of voters rejected a recall. A demoralized opposition made little effort to contest local and gubernatorial elections later in 2004, allowing Chávez supporters to capture twenty-one out of twenty-three state governments and over 90 percent of municipalities. The following year the main opposition parties decided to boycott national legislative elections entirely, giving Chávez's MVR and allied leftist parties a complete lock on the national assembly. The opposition managed to form an electoral front to challenge Chávez in the 2006 presidential elections, coalescing behind the candidacy of Manuel Rosales of a new party known as *Un Nuevo Tiempo* (UNT, A New Era), but once again Chávez prevailed with a record 62.8 percent of the vote.

As Chávez defeated the elite political backlash in the middle of the decade, he also turned more aggressively toward statist and redistributive development policies. For the first time, he proclaimed his intention to build "socialism for the 21st century" (Hawkins 2010: 83), and his reformist measures increasingly challenged property rights and market principles. He introduced exchange and price controls, expanded the public provision of social services, launched a program of land redistribution in both urban and rural areas, established worker cooperatives and a new pro-government labor confederation, and nationalized electricity, telephone, steel, and other industries (see Ellner 2008: 121–134). Although these reforms fell short of a full-fledged socialist model of development – and relied heavily on the oil windfall to remain financially viable – they clearly gave Venezuela the most state-directed economy in Latin America outside of Cuba, while placing Chávez at the forefront of anti-neoliberal forces in the region.

Chávez' statist and redistributive policies sharpened the populist/anti-populist cleavage in Venezuela, while grounding it more firmly in class distinctions and programmatic preferences, rather than charismatic authority alone. This cleavage remained poorly institutionalized in the partisan arena, however. Although *Chavismo* was highly resilient as an electoral force, and the president took steps after 2006 to construct a new unified party of the Left (the *Partido Unificado Socialista de Venezuela*, PSUV), charismatic authority kept the party subordinate and under-institutionalized. Grassroots participation in community-based *Chavista* networks dwarfed anything found in countries with more institutionalized Left-party governments, including the PT's highly-touted participatory budgeting initiatives in Brazilian municipalities (see Handlin and Collier 2011), but these popular constituencies often resisted integration into Chávez's party organization. Indeed, both Chávez and his adherents favored direct, unmediated forms of contact over the bureaucratized mediation of a party organization – hardly a surprising development in a country that had so recently rebelled against the AD–COPEI *partidocracia*.

Centrist and conservative opposition forces, meanwhile – like those in Argentina after the 2001 debacle – were even slower to reconstitute the anti-populist side of the party system in the aftermath period. AD and COPEI were marginal players after 1998, while new parties like *Primero Justicia* (Justice First) and *Un Nuevo Tiempo* (A New Era) struggled to gain a foothold. These new parties coalesced with the remnants of AD and other opposition forces in a new electoral front known as *Mesa por la Unidad Democrática* (MUD, or Coalition for Democratic Unity) before the 2010 legislative elections, claiming 47.2 percent of the vote compared to 48.3 percent for Chávez's PSUV. Although the PSUV won a legislative majority with 55.8 percent of the seats, the combined opposition forces made their strongest electoral showing and achieved their highest level of representation since the dissolution of the 1998 congress.

Consequently, as Chávez prepared to run for yet another re-election in October 2012 – in the midst of a personal battle against cancer and new signs of popular discontent over crime, corruption, and governmental inefficiency – his populist leadership faced an increasingly competitive electoral arena. The opposition front held primary elections to nominate a unified presidential candidate, Henrique Capriles, a former COPEI congressional deputy and a founder of *Primero Justicia*. Behind a massive electoral mobilization campaign that drove turnout up to more than 80 percent of the electorate, Chávez defeated Capriles by a vote of 55.1 to 44.3 percent, his fourth consecutive presidential victory. Chávez succumbed to cancer shortly after the start of his new term, however, forcing a new election in April 2013 in which his designated successor, Nicolás Maduro, narrowly defeated Capriles with 50.6 percent of the vote.

The death of Chávez left behind a profound sociopolitical cleavage that is likely to be a durable axis of competition whether or not *Chavismo* holds onto power, much like the cleavages forged by Peronism in Argentina and *Sandinismo* in Nicaragua. It is uncertain whether this central cleavage will attain the levels of political cohesion and organizational development – on both sides of the divide – that are required to institutionalize a reconstituted party system. Whatever its organizational expression, however, political mobilization for and against *Chavismo* reproduced polarized populism and cleaved the political order throughout Venezuela's aftermath period – a most unexpected legacy of the reactive sequences that shattered neoliberal convergence, demolished the party system, and reversed the country's bait-and-switch process of market reform.

Ecuador's Aftermath: From Serial to Polarized Populism

Ecuador also developed an institutional legacy of polarized populism, which crystallized in the aftermath period as the unstable equilibrium of neoliberal convergence gave way to a pattern of serial populism and then eventually to the more polarizing populist leadership of Rafael Correa. As explained in Chapter 7, Ecuador's critical juncture involved successive attempts at market reform by conservative, populist, and center-left leaders, and efforts to deepen the liberalization process continued into the aftermath period, making it difficult to identify a clear-cut end-point to the critical juncture. By 1997, however, when a popular uprising led to Abdalá Bucaram's removal from office, the window of opportunity for comprehensive structural adjustment had effectively been closed by the emergence of a powerful, indigenous-led protest movement that created a social veto against strict market orthodoxy. By that point the country's most important center-left (ID) and populist (PRE) parties had taken a stab at structural adjustment, making Ecuador a case of de-aligning, bait-and-switch reform, virtually ensuring that societal resistance would be channeled outside and against the established party system. Mass protests, then, drove the reactive sequences of the aftermath period, which toppled two more presidents after Bucaram, decomposed Ecuador's fragile party system, and eventually produced a populist left turn that sharply broke with the neoliberal model that every elected president since 1984 had tried to impose.

This turbulence reflected the profound chasm that separated Ecuador's mobilized popular sectors from formal representative and governing institutions. Ecuador's critical juncture arguably generated the most sustained and consistent pattern of social mobilization against the neoliberal model seen in Latin America, but this mobilization did not get channeled into established parties, as occurred (at least partially) in Argentina after 2002. Neither did it spawn a new "movement party" (Kitschelt 2006) that was capable of contesting state power in the electoral arena, as occurred in Bolivia with the rise of the MAS. Ecuador's indigenous movement formed *Pachakutik* as a partisan vehicle, but it never attained the broad, majoritarian electoral appeal of the MAS (Madrid 2012), and both the party and the movement were weakened by divisive choices as to whether or not to support independent populist figures who were more electorally competitive (first Lucio Gutiérrez, then Rafael Correa). Ironically, then, when neoliberal convergence and serial populism finally gave way to a more polarizing populist alternative – Correa – who steered Ecuador sharply toward the Left, this alternative was notably detached from the social movements that had been at the forefront of the struggle against neoliberalism.

As in Argentina, reactive sequences in the aftermath period were conditioned by a new cycle of economic crisis, ultimately the most severe in Ecuador's modern history. The economy slumped in the late 1990s when oil prices declined, causing export revenues to fall at the same time that the Asian crisis tightened global financial markets. In the midst of a financial crisis in Ecuador's newly liberalized banking system, the political establishment and the party system made their last stand when Jamil Mahuad of the centrist DP-UDC alliance was elected president in 1998 with support from the conservative PSC. Unlike Bucaram, Mahuad took office with strong business support and a clear pro-market agenda, and he moved quickly to propose yet another package of orthodox adjustment measures, including cuts in public employment and the elimination of price subsidies for gasoline, electricity, and public transportation. Between August 1998 and October 1999, however, half of Ecuador's private banks failed, leading to a massive, $6 billion bailout of eighteen financial institutions – equivalent to a staggering 23 percent of GDP (Lucero 2001: 62). The bailout caused the fiscal deficit to swell, while monetary emissions led to currency depreciation and a steep rise in inflation (Martinez 2006). Unable to make interest payments on international debt and bond obligations, the Mahuad government turned to the IMF for a new loan in 1999, but the attendant austerity measures provoked widespread unrest, including a wave of labor strikes and road blockages by indigenous communities (Silva 2009: 176–184). Social spending was cut in half in 1999, while the real minimum wage declined by 25 percent. Mahuad tried to achieve stabilization by declaring a state of emergency and freezing bank deposits, while Ecuador sank into its deepest recession in modern history – a contraction of 6.3 percent, accompanied by a record-high inflation rate of 96.1 percent.

Desperate to stem capital flight and avoid a currency collapse, Mahuad began 2000 with a controversial decision to dollarize the economy. In response, the indigenous confederation CONAIE spearheaded a massive uprising in January 2000 that culminated in the occupation of the national congress when sympathetic military troops refused to repress the protestors. Colonel Lucio Gutiérrez and other officers then launched a military coup against Mahuad, forming a short-lived ruling junta that included CONAIE leader Antonio Vargas. Under international pressure, however, the junta relinquished power to Vice President Gustavo Noboa, who filled out the remainder of Mahuad's term and maintained the dollar as the national currency.

Rising oil prices finally helped stabilize the economy after 2000, but the corrosive effect of these reactive sequences on political institutions intensified.

With the exception of Durán Ballén's election to the presidency in 1992, electoral volatility through 1998 in Ecuador was largely an intra-systemic phenomenon, reflecting vote shifts among the PSC, ID, DP-UDC, and CFP/PRE. These parties jointly captured an average of 71.7 percent of congressional seats between 1978 and 1998, along with 69.6 percent of the presidential vote. Even Durán Ballén was a prominent member of the political establishment as a long-time leader of the PSC. In the aftermath of the 2000 mobilization, however, votes shifted *en masse* from these established parties to new parties, movements, and independent personalities. The percentage of congressional seats claimed by the aforementioned major parties slipped to 58.5 percent in 2002 and then 31 percent in 2006, while their presidential vote share plummeted to 38 percent in 2002 and 26.5 percent in 2006 (see Appendix Tables 9 and 10). With established parties no longer defining the leading electoral alternatives, decomposition and serial populism rose to the forefront.

Indeed, elements of serial populism were already present in the 1990s before the party system broke down. Durán Ballén had broken with the PSC to run a maverick independent campaign for the presidency, and Bucaram was a vintage populist figure from a party, the PRE, constructed around his charismatic leadership (de la Torre 2010). As established parties declined after 2000, the personalization of the vote became even more pronounced on both the Right and the Left. On the Right, votes shifted to billionaire banana magnate Álvaro Noboa – Ecuador's wealthiest citizen – who broke with the PRE to found his own political movement known as PRIAN (the Institutional Renewal Party of National Action). Noboa sought to parlay his private wealth into a political foundation for a conservative, market-friendly brand of populism, finishing as the runner-up in the 2002 and 2006 presidential elections.

On the Left, personalized voting also predominated, as the indigenous party *Pachakutik* (MUPP-NP) had limited success in capitalizing on the demise of established parties. Although *Pachakutik* was a significant force in the election of provincial and municipal governments in areas with large indigenous populations (see Van Cott 2005: 127), its national vote stagnated and then declined following its promising debut in 1996. *Pachakutik* often ran in alliance with small leftist parties, allowing it to capture 8 percent of congressional seats in 1996, 4.2 percent in 1998, 7 percent in 2002, and 6 percent in 2006. In presidential elections, however, the party never produced a competitive candidate from within its ranks; it either endorsed an independent personality (as in 1996, 1998, and 2002), or ran a candidate of its own with little success (2006). Initially, the party supported the candidacy of television personality Freddy Ehlers, who earned 20.6 and 14.7 percent of the vote in 1996 and 1998, respectively. *Pachakutik* and CONAIE planned to run one of their own leaders in 2002, but indigenous groups were unable to settle on a consensus candidate (Van Cott 2005: 133–137). Consequently, *Pachakutik* withdrew its proposed candidate and jumped on the bandwagon of Lucio Gutiérrez, the ex-military rebel who had formed a new party vehicle known as the January 21st Patriotic Society Party (PSP).

Campaigning as a left-leaning populist outsider, Gutiérrez won the election in a run-off against Noboa of PRIAN, but his fledgling PSP held only eight of the ninety-nine seats in congress. After pledging to oppose a regional free-trade agreement and the privatization of oil and social security, Gutiérrez induced *Pachakutik* to place four ministers and eight sub-secretaries in his administration. Shortly after taking office, however, Gutiérrez signed a letter of intent with the IMF, came out in support of regional free trade, and proposed a package of economic adjustments that included major privatizations, price hikes, and a wage freeze – in essence, Ecuador's third major case of bait-and-switch reform after Borja in 1988 and Bucaram in 1996. Six months later, with *Pachakutik* opposing his legislative initiatives and the conservative PSC lending support, Gutiérrez broke his alliance with the indigenous party (Madrid 2012: 102).

Following the rupture of their alliance with Gutiérrez, CONAIE and *Pachakutik* reverted back to their customary opposition role, albeit it in a weakened and divided state. As Jonas Wolff argues, participation in government – particularly one that did not live up to its programmatic commitments – "had brought to the fore the serious contradictions inherent in the simultaneous engagement of party and social movement politics." As movement leaders assumed government positions, their "ties to the base of the movement were weakened and with it CONAIE's capacity for mobilisation" (Wolff 2007: 25). Indeed, Gutiérrez manipulated government appointments and resources to divide and demobilize the indigenous movement, offering inducements to Amazonian and evangelical indigenous groups to collaborate with his government, while sidelining the oppositional currents within CONAIE and highlands indigenous communities (Wolff 2007: 25–26; Madrid 2012: 102). Gutiérrez himself would eventually be removed from office by a vote of congress during a new cycle of social protest in April 2005, triggered in part by the president's effort to stack the supreme court and drop corruption charges against former president Bucaram (de la Torre 2010: 110–113). Although CONAIE participated in this new, more urban round of protests and strikes, it did not play a leading role, and evangelical indigenous groups sought to defend Gutiérrez (Becker 2008: 187).

Gutiérrez was the third consecutive elected president to adopt market reforms and be driven from office in a context of mass protest, demonstrating the chasm between a mobilized civil society and unresponsive governing institutions. The failed Gutiérrez experiment made CONAIE and *Pachakutik* wary of alliances with outsiders. Prior to national elections in 2006, *Pachakutik* debated an alliance with Rafael Correa, an independent left-wing economist who had briefly served as economy minister in the interim government that replaced Gutiérrez, where he earned a reputation as a critic of neoliberalism, dollarization, the IMF, and regional free-trade pacts. In the end, however, *Pachakutik* rejected alliances and ran an indigenous candidate, Luis Macas, from its own ranks for the first time (Madrid 2012: 102–104). With *Pachakutik* increasingly isolated from former allies in non-indigenous labor and civic associations, however, Macas obtained a mere 2.2 percent of the first-round vote, while Correa and banana magnate Noboa passed into the second round. Correa won with 56.7 percent of the vote, even though his hastily formed "party," *Alianza PAIS* (Proud and Sovereign Fatherland Alliance), did not even sponsor congressional candidates – an example of personalism taken to the extreme, albeit one that "unequivocally identified Correa with the electorate's antipolitical mood" (Conaghan 2011: 266). Lacking a major party or civic organization to mobilize support, Correa and his small circle of left-leaning intellectuals and activists relied heavily on television, radio, and internet appeals to broadcast his populist message to a mass audience.

Despite this exceptionally weak organizational base, however, Correa represented more than just another cycle in the pattern of serial populism – a pattern that had reproduced market liberalism with only minimal forms of partisan organization and no stable axis of programmatic contestation. Under Correa, populism turned in a more polarizing direction, as the new president set out to re-found the constitutional order and break with the neoliberal model, potentially creating a more durable sociopolitical cleavage at the heart of Ecuador's democratic order.

Following the examples of Chávez in Venezuela and Evo Morales in Bolivia, Correa had campaigned on a pledge to convoke a constituent assembly, write a new constitution, sweep aside the corrupt political establishment, and unleash a "citizens' revolution" with new forms of popular participation (de la Torre 2010: 186–187). Upon taking office, he moved quickly and decisively to implement this pledge, relying heavily on his plebiscitary appeal and verbal attacks on the political establishment to dismantle institutional constraints on his plan. When congress balked at his proposal to hold a referendum on a constituent assembly, Correa pressured the electoral tribunal to dismiss fifty-seven of the 100 deputies and replace them with substitutes; the new, more compliant congress then voted to remove the judges on the constitutional tribunal who had ruled against the original dismissals (Conaghan 2011: 271). The referendum itself produced an 81.7 percent majority in favor of elections for a constituent assembly.

With Correa's novice "party" winning eighty of the 130 seats, the constituent assembly drafted a new constitution that strengthened executive powers, expanded social rights, enhanced the state's role in the economy, and allowed presidents to be re-elected. Public policies also shifted in a more statist and redistributive direction; as Conaghan (2011: 280) argues, Correa's project was "profoundly state-centric in the scope of its aspirations." Although Correa did not engage in widespread nationalizations of private banks or businesses, he subjected them to new taxes and regulatory controls. The government strengthened existing public enterprises, promoted strategic planning, adopted new tariffs and trade restrictions, and joined OPEC and the Venezuela-led regional trade bloc ALBA. Correa also launched or increased spending on a broad range of social programs, including poverty assistance, public health care, housing, education, and micro-enterprise development. Spending on government social programs increased from 5.4 percent of GDP in 2005 to 8.3 percent in 2008, while overall public investment as a share of GDP more than doubled in Correa's first term (Conaghan 2011: 276).

With the economy growing and the government addressing social concerns, Correa was re-elected in 2009 with 52 percent of the first-round vote, defeating former president Gutiérrez with 28.2 percent and Noboa with 11.4 percent. Correa's vote was by far the highest of any Ecuadorean president since the return to democracy in 1979, and it made *Alianza PAÍS* the first incumbent party to achieve re-election. Indeed, Correa was the first president to complete a term in office since Durán Ballén in the mid-1990s, and his party obtained the largest percentage of legislative seats, 47.6 percent, since the return to democracy. None of the four major parties of the 1980s and 1990s – PSC, PRE, DP-UDC, and ID – bothered to run a candidate for president, and they jointly won only 7.2 percent of legislative seats. Correa subsequently won a third term as president in 2013 with over 57 percent of the vote, while his party expanded to win 73 percent of the seats in congress. Conservative opposition forces reorganized in yet another political movement, Creating Opportunities (CREO), which earned 22.7 percent of the presidential vote for businessman Guillermo Lasso, but only 8.1 percent of legislative seats.

The consolidation of a populist bloc behind Correa cannot simply be attributed to fortuitous timing – that is, his good fortune to govern during a commodity export boom that relaxed fiscal and foreign-exchange constraints. Indeed, Ecuador's economy grew nearly twice as fast under Gutiérrez (an average of 5.9 percent from 2003 to 2005) as it did during Correa's first term (an average of 3.2 percent from 2007 to 2009), yet the former was removed from office in the midst of a popular uprising, while the latter was twice re-elected in landslides (World Bank 2012). What differentiated the two populist figures was not their economic performance, but rather their economic policies: those of Gutiérrez violated his electoral mandate and de-aligned political competition, whereas those of Correa followed his electoral mandate and created a central axis of programmatic contestation between orthodox and statist alternatives.

But if Correa's polarized populism created a central political cleavage grounded in programmatic distinctions, it did not necessarily institutionalize that alignment. Even more than in Venezuela, Correa's party was in gestation when he captured executive office, and would inevitably be built from the top down, using state power and resources to construct new organizational networks around its initial technocratic core. The capacity of those networks to incorporate popular constituencies remained in doubt; despite Correa's electoral appeal, his party was relatively detached from organized popular sectors, and his government often clashed with autonomous groups like the teachers' union and CONAIE. The latter no longer wielded the mobilizational capacity that it boasted in the early aftermath period, but its claims for communal autonomy and control over land and water resources spawned conflict with a government that was committed to an extractive mode of state-led development. Meanwhile, on the other side of the political divide, centrist and conservative opposition forces abandoned traditional parties and gravitated toward independent personalities and new political movements. Polarized populism, therefore, created a central cleavage around which new representative institutions could be built and aligned, something that Ecuador's party system has lacked throughout the country's modern political history. The construction of new party organizations, however, was both delayed and asymmetrical, lagging behind the process of cleavage formation, and occurring on the pro-government, populist side of the divide well in advance of the conservative side.

CONCLUSION

The aftermath to neoliberal critical junctures was often as turbulent and transformative for party systems as the critical juncture itself, depending on political alignments during decisive periods of market reform. The re-politicization of socioeconomic inequalities and the strengthening of societal resistance to market liberalization provided new opportunities for leftist alternatives in the post-adjustment era, but these alternatives varied dramatically across different types of critical junctures. Patterns of market reform that aligned party systems programmatically produced institutional legacies of contested liberalism that were electorally stable, allowing institutionalized parties of the Left to strengthen gradually and access power at the head of moderate redistributive coalitions. Conversely, bait-and-switch patterns of market reform that programmatically de-aligned party systems produced highly unstable institutional outcomes, including widespread social protest, the demise of established parties, and their outflanking on the Left by new populist or movement alternatives. The latter often proposed sharp breaks with neoliberal orthodoxy and existing regime institutions.

The recent Latin American experience suggests that critical junctures do not simply generate an institutional equilibrium that locks in over time. They produce outcomes that shape the reactive sequences to which institutions must respond, and these reactive sequences may reinforce, destabilize, or realign the original outcome. The longer-term legacies of critical junctures may thus depart significantly from their initial institutional outcomes, which vary widely in their resiliency – a point that has not been fully appreciated in much of the comparative historical research on critical junctures and institutional development.

10

Conclusion: Political Legacies and the Crisis of Representation

Latin America's crisis-induced transition from state-led development to market liberalism altered the social bases of political representation in fundamental ways. In so doing, it posed fundamental challenges to the ways in which parties had organized and represented popular interests and mediated between states and societies in the ISI era. In most countries, party systems at the beginning of the second decade of the 21st century looked strikingly different from those that were in place at the beginning of the democratic period in the early 1980s.

Party system change over the course of these three decades was indelibly marked by the dual transitions to democracy and market liberalism, but it was far from uniform in its character and effects. Although a handful of party systems were only lightly touched by the politics of crisis management and structural adjustment, most were realigned or partially reconstituted, and some broke down and decomposed along the way. Among the latter set of cases, the reconstruction of party systems proved to be a highly uncertain and asymmetrical process.

Such varied outcomes were not pre-determined by the institutional strength of national party systems at the outset of the period. Surely no one at the beginning of the 1980s would have said that Honduras' party system, the region's most stable over the next three decades, or Brazil's, which progressively consolidated, was stronger than Venezuela's, which suffered the region's most spectacular collapse. Neither was the fate of traditional party systems a simple function of the severity of economic crises or the depth of structural adjustment; relatively stable and unstable party systems could be found at both ends of those continuums.

To explain the divergent fate of party systems in modern Latin America, this book began with an argument about stable partisanship being grounded in strong linkages between parties and voters and deep cleavages between rival partisan camps (and between the constituencies they represent; see Chapter 2).

The book then proposed a critical juncture framework to explain why the transition from state-led development to market liberalism eroded the societal linkages and blurred the political cleavages in some party systems more than others. The framework identifies three principal stages in a comparative historical and institutionalist account of party system change and continuity. First, the antecedent stage refers to party system development during the ISI era in the middle of the 20th century, following the onset of mass politics and labor incorporation in the early stages of industrialization. This stage was important not only because it established the institutional baselines required for a comparative assessment of party system transformation at the end of century, but also because antecedent conditions influenced the gravity of economic crises during the transition from ISI to neoliberalism. Economic crises during this critical juncture – in particular, hyperinflation – were more severe and prolonged in countries that developed LM party systems in the middle of the century and pursued more aggressive strategies of state-led development. They were less severe where elitist party systems held sway and state-led development strategies were less ambitious.

Party system disruption during the critical juncture – the second stage of the comparative historical analysis – was attributable in part to the gravity and duration of these economic crises. As such, it was partially endogenous to antecedent patterns of party system development during the statist era, with LM party systems being especially prone to electoral instability and institutional decay as ISI collapsed in the 1980s. Severe economic crises encouraged widespread anti-incumbent voting behavior and, therefore, high levels of electoral volatility, while prolonged crises tended to generalize these costs across the entire party system. In a country like Peru, party system decomposition was well underway due to the effects of a severe and prolonged economic crisis, even before the disruptive effects of structural adjustment began.

In most of the region, however, the relative stability of party systems was attributable not simply to the varied political costs of economic crises, but also to the impact of market reform on the programmatic alignment of party systems. Programmatic alignments around the process of market reform were not predetermined by antecedent party system attributes; they were, instead, the product of more contingent political dynamics during the critical juncture itself, in particular the strategic policy choices made by parties to adopt, support, or oppose market reforms. These choices, and the political identities or orientations of the actors who made them, largely determined whether parties could forge strong linkages to voters on the basis of programmatic commitments, or deep cleavages that were grounded in programmatic distinctions. It was the contingent character of these reform alignments during the process of structural adjustment that made the juncture truly "critical" for shaping political outcomes (rather than outcomes being determined by antecedent conditions or random occurrences).

Simply put, market reforms that were led by centrist or conservative political actors and consistently opposed by a major party of the Left aligned party systems programmatically, allowing for stronger party–society linkages and deeper sociopolitical cleavages. Aligning critical junctures produced an outcome of "contested liberalism" that was found in the cases of Brazil, Chile, and Uruguay, as shown in Chapters 7–9. Alternatively, "neutral" critical junctures occurred where conservative parties led the process of market reform in the absence of a major party of the Left in opposition, as in the Honduran case. Finally, programmatically de-aligning critical junctures occurred where center-left or labor-based populist parties imposed structural adjustment policies in a bait-and-switch manner that clashed with their historic policy commitments or campaign promises. Such de-aligning patterns of reform occurred in Argentina, Costa Rica, Ecuador, and Venezuela, among the cases analyzed here. Both neutral and de-aligning critical junctures produced party system outcomes of "neoliberal convergence," whereby all the major parties had adopted or supported market reforms, leaving party systems without an institutionalized channel for dissent from market orthodoxy. Under neoliberal convergence, programmatic commitments and policy distinctions provided little basis for party–society linkages or deep partisan cleavages.

The effects of these reform alignments on party system stability were not always apparent during the critical juncture itself, as neoliberal convergence could be a stable competitive equilibrium where inflationary crises and the disarticulation of popular subjects undermined political alternatives. The tenuous character of this competitive equilibrium was more apparent in the aftermath to the critical juncture, however – that is, in the third stage of the comparative historical analysis that corresponds to the post-adjustment era beginning in the latter half of the 1990s. In the aftermath period, societal resistance to market liberalization often intensified, and the renewed capacity of popular sectors to mobilize in social and political arenas helped to revive leftist alternatives and spawn potentially destabilizing reactive sequences.

The character of these reactive sequences and the leftist alternatives they spawned varied dramatically across the different types of critical junctures, producing sharply divergent institutional legacies in the post-adjustment era. The outcome of neoliberal convergence produced by programmatically de-aligning critical junctures typically broke down in aftermath periods (or, in Venezuela, at the end of the critical juncture) when reactive sequences channeled societal dissent into extra-systemic forms of social and/or electoral protest. These reactive sequences were characterized by explosive mass protests, the demise of pro-market centrist and conservative parties, and an outflanking on the Left of established populist and center-left parties that had participated in the market-reform process. Only in Argentina did an established party, the Peronist PJ, succeed in channeling societal resistance to market orthodoxy by veering back toward the Left. Elsewhere, a new left party (Costa Rica) or populist figure (Venezuela and Ecuador) emerged to contest the neoliberal model – in the latter two cases, along with Argentina, in the absence of an institutionalized conservative party to defend market orthodoxy. Although neoliberal convergence was a more durable outcome of Honduras' neutral critical juncture, the reproduction of that institutional legacy was eventually eclipsed by the fracturing of one of the two traditional parties and the emergence of a new electoral movement on the Left.

Conversely, the outcome of contested liberalism produced by programmatically aligning critical junctures proved to be a stable competitive equilibrium in the aftermath period in Chile and Uruguay, and a stabilizing equilibrium that helped to institutionalize Brazil's previously inchoate party system. In these cases, societal resistance to market orthodoxy was channeled toward institutionalized opposition parties on the Left, moderating anti-systemic forms of social and electoral protest. Reactive sequences in the aftermath period progressively strengthened the establishment Left, ultimately bringing them into national executive office, while pro-market centrist and conservative parties remained electorally competitive and placed institutional constraints on new leftist governments. "Left turns" in these countries thus occurred by means of an institutionalized alternation in office that left the constitutional order intact and produced only modest reforms of inherited neoliberal models, in contrast to the patterns in a number of countries that experienced de-aligning critical junctures and destabilizing reactive sequences.

The arguments developed here about the institutional effects of neoliberal critical junctures are generalizable to a broader set of regional cases beyond the eight countries covered in this study. Bolivia, for example, was clearly a case of programmatically de-aligning, bait-and-switch market reform, and like the other cases of de-alignment analyzed here, it experienced a turbulent aftermath period marked by massive social protest, party system decomposition, and the electoral ascendance of a new movement party of the Left, the *Movimiento al Socialismo* (MAS). In a context of acute hyperinflation, neoliberal shock treatment was imposed in 1985 by the historic populist party that had led the 1952 Bolivian Revolution, the *Movimiento Nacionalista Revolucionaria* (MNR). Liberalizing reforms were subsequently deepened and consolidated by presidents from the country's leading leftist (the *Movimiento de la Izquierda Revolucionaria*, or MIR) and conservative (*Acción Democrática Nacionalista*, or ADN) parties, providing an example of neoliberal convergence *par excellence* (see Conaghan and Malloy 1994; Slater and Simmons 2012).

These three parties rotated in office through 2003, but a groundswell of popular resistance among indigenous communities, coca growers, peasant organizations, and labor unions produced a series of mass protests that contested the neoliberal model after 2000 (Silva 2009). Protests against water privatization (the "water wars") and natural gas exports (the "gas wars") culminated in a popular upheaval that forced the resignation of President Gonzalo Sánchez de Lozada of the MNR in 2003 and his successor Carlos Mesa in 2005. The uprising was channeled politically by the new movement party MAS, which swept to a crushing victory over the established parties in 2005 and placed the coca growers union leader Evo Morales in the presidency (Madrid 2012). Like Chávez in Venezuela and Correa in Ecuador, Morales moved quickly to convoke a constituent assembly, re-found the constitutional order, and achieve a landslide re-election in 2009, sharply changing the trajectory of Bolivia's political development in the aftermath period.

Paraguay, like Honduras, experienced a programmatically neutral critical juncture, producing an outcome of neoliberal convergence that was relatively stable in the short term but subject to disequilibrium as the aftermath period unfolded. The longstanding dictatorship of Alfredo Stroessner locked into place an oligarchic party system and blocked the development of labor and popular movements during the ISI era, which only lightly touched Paraguay's political economy (Abente 1995). Following a military coup that toppled Stroessner in 1989, his conservative Colorado party remained electorally dominant, winning presidential elections over its centrist rival, the *Partido Liberal Radical Auténtico* (PLRA), in 1989, 1993, 1998, and 2003. The Colorados thus led a moderate process of market liberalization in the 1990s, presiding over a party system that lacked major populist or leftist competitors.

By 2008, however, with the regional "left turn" in full swing, the two traditional parties were outflanked on the Left by an independent leader, activist Catholic bishop Fernando Lugo, who had become prominent as an advocate for peasant land claims. Lugo was elected president at the head of a twelve-party coalition that included the PLRA, but his presidency was weakened by the absence of a loyal party organization or a secure base of support in organized mass constituencies – a far cry from the Bolivian case noted above. Consequently, in a similar manner to the iconoclastic populist administration of Manuel Zelaya in Honduras, Lugo was undermined by a backlash from the conservative political establishment following a violent clash over a peasant land occupation. Abandoned by the PLRA and staunchly opposed by the Colorados, Lugo was abruptly impeached by congress in 2012 – in essence, a legislative coup against a leftist president who lacked an organized base of social and political support. The conservative backlash thus reversed Paraguay's tentative left turn and allowed the Colorados to regain the presidency in 2013, but as in Honduras, a restoration of the traditional political order is under challenge from heightened popular contestation.

The Mexican case offers interesting variation on the general patterns, as a critical juncture that started with de-aligning characteristics changed course and realigned the party system programmatically, producing a relatively stable institutional legacy of contested liberalism. Market reforms began in 1983 in a bait-and-switch manner under the hegemonic leadership of the historic post-revolutionary populist party, the *Partido Revolucionario Institucional* (PRI), which had won the 1982 presidential election with nearly three-quarters of the vote. The consolidation of a technocratic pro-reform leadership in the mid-1980s, however, led PRI traditionalists to break with the party, coalesce with a number of small leftist groups, and found a major new opposition party of the Left (Bruhn 1997), thus providing an institutional channel for societal resistance to the neoliberal model at a relatively early stage of the reform process. This predecessor to the *Partido de la Revolución Democrática* (PRD) nearly won the 1988 elections – to that point, the most competitive in Mexico's post-revolutionary history – and subsequently anchored the left side of a program-matically realigned party system as structural adjustment advanced under the next two PRI administrations.

During this period, the small traditional conservative party, the *Partido Acción Nacional* (PAN), also strengthened by articulating support for demo-cratic reforms as well as market liberalization. The critical juncture thus pro-duced a more competitive and programmatically aligned tripartite system with institutionalized conservative, centrist, and leftist alternatives – in short, a form of contested liberalism that provided a relatively stable competitive equilibrium in the aftermath period. These three parties continued to dominate the electoral arena, with relatively modest vote shifts across election cycles; the PAN finally broke the PRI's seventy-one-year reign in office in 2000, and narrowly defeated the PRD in the 2006 presidential campaign, making Mexico a major holdout from the regional left turn in the first decade of the 21st century. The PRI defeated the PRD to return to power in 2012, no longer a hegemonic force, but still a major player in Mexico's realigned tripartite system.

The Peruvian case also conforms to the general patterns, albeit with several distinctive features. Peru experienced a de-aligning process of market reform under bait-and-switch populist figure Alberto Fujimori in the early 1990s, but a decomposition of the country's LM party system was already well under way by that point; traditional parties had been pummeled in the 1980s by the combina-tion of acute hyperinflation, multiple economic recessions, and political vio-lence, including a highly repressive state response to the brutal Maoist insurgency of the Shining Path. Traditional parties were thus replaced by a fluid set of populist figures and rival personalities, including (but not limited to) Fujimori and the post-adjustment presidents Alejandro Toledo and Alan García (the latter's historic populist party, APRA, was an electorally negligible political force after 1990 when García was not on the ticket) (see Levitsky and Cameron 2003; Sanchez 2009; Cameron 2011).

Since these rival personalities did not structure electoral competition along a central cleavage between supporters and opponents of the liberalization process, Peru's critical juncture produced an outcome of serial populism, which contin-ued well into the aftermath period. This legacy was challenged by regionally based social protest movements and by the rise of a more polarizing left-populist candidate in 2006, Ollanta Humala. These protests, however, did not reach the scale of those that toppled presidents in neighboring countries, and Humala backed away from his more polarizing stands as he contested and won the presidency in 2011. Peru, then, unlike Ecuador, did not transition from serial to polarized populism in the early aftermath period, but social and political pressures for such a shift were clearly present. More than twenty years after the collapse of the traditional party system, parties remained little more than electoral labels and circles of collaborators formed by rival personalities; although Fujimori's daughter, Keiko Fujimori, began to build a new conservative party organization, a reconstitution of the party system remained an elusive target.

LESSONS FROM THE LATIN AMERICAN EXPERIENCE: CRITICAL JUNCTURES AND INSTITUTIONAL LEGACIES

The comparative analysis of Latin American party systems during the transition from ISI to neoliberalism offers a number of lessons about the relationship between critical junctures and institutional change. Previous work on critical junctures has emphasized the lock-in effects – or the durable, self-reproducing legacies – of institutional choices and configurations established during critical junctures (Pierson 2000). Neoliberal critical junctures had such effects on Latin American party systems, but only where they aligned them programmatically along a competitive axis between pro- and anti-market reform parties. In comparative terms, this outcome of contested liberalism was a stable competitive equilibrium during the first several decades of the post-adjustment era; indeed, it produced institutional legacies that moderated the reactive sequences of the aftermath period and reproduced themselves over time, even when the electoral balance between specific parties shifted (typically to the advantage of the Left).

De-aligning critical junctures, on the other hand, also had identifiable institutional legacies, but these legacies were hardly locked into place. Patterns of neoliberal convergence magnified the reactive sequences of the aftermath period, as party systems provided no meaningful institutional outlets for dissent from neoliberal orthodoxy. So long as such dissent was minimal or disarticulated, neoliberal convergence could be electorally stable. Where this dissent grew or congealed politically, however, it fueled destabilizing, anti-systemic reactive sequences in the form of mass social and/or electoral protest. Such protest cycles were harbingers of major institutional change in party systems in the aftermath period.

A critical juncture approach may be hard-pressed to explain the specific timing and organizational forms of such reactive sequences, but it nevertheless sheds light on their basic political character, their relative intensity, the conditions under which they are more or less likely to occur, and their probable institutional effects. Indeed, the approach can help explain why some institutional equilibria are not only susceptible to certain types of perturbances, but may actually generate them, and thus be predisposed toward specific patterns of institutional change down the road. This can be seen in the patterns of extra-systemic outflanking in our de-aligned cases, as well the intra-systemic electoral shifts in the aligned cases; these different kinds of reactive sequences were conditioned by their respective critical junctures, and they ultimately produced very different types of left turns in the aftermath period.

Critical juncture approaches, therefore, are not only useful for explaining institutional lock-in; they can explain why similar types of crises reconfigure institutions in ways that are highly resilient in some types of cases, and highly fluid or prone to future cycles of institutional change in others. This requires that critical juncture approaches examine how different institutional configurations shape and respond to reactive sequences as social or political conditions change in the aftermath period. It also suggests that they should take seriously the possibility of on-going institutional realignment or even de-institutionalization as a legacy of a critical juncture, especially in a comparative analysis that examines a broad range of cases and outcomes. As the Peruvian case amply demonstrates, de-institutionalized forms of political representation are quite capable of reproducing themselves over time, and should not be seen as a mere prelude to an eventual process of party system reconstitution.

The findings of this study also have important implications for understanding the crisis of political representation in contemporary Latin American democracies. Most fundamentally, perhaps, they suggest that this crisis is not an inevitable byproduct of universalizing trends away from the development of mass party organizations in modern democracies. Neither is the crisis inherent to the constraints on state activities under the pressures of market globalization. To be sure, neoliberal critical junctures and their aftermath periods were less likely to spawn powerful mass organizations in civic or partisan arenas, much less weld them together in interlocking political alliances, than the labor-incorporating, institution-building critical junctures studied by Collier and Collier (1991). The general trends toward personalistic and professional – electoral party organizations and pluralistic civil societies have undoubtedly eroded parties' ability to encapsulate organized mass constituencies. Likewise, the pressures of market globalization have narrowed parties' programmatic space and limited their policy latitude when elected to public office.

Shallower social roots and confined programmatic space may thus pose challenges to political parties, but the Latin American experience suggests that they do not preordain a crisis of representation. Parties may not encapsulate social blocs as they once did (in part of the region), but they are still capable of forging meaningful and stable programmatic linkages to individual voters, as well as sociopolitical cleavages – or competitive alignments – that are grounded in programmatic distinctions and preferences. Global market forces surely narrow the range of viable alternatives, and many voters lack well-defined (or coherent) ideological positions, but neither of these factors prevents parties from differentiating themselves and sorting portions of the electorate into relatively stable blocs with distinct preferences toward the respective roles of states and markets in economic development and social welfare.

This study finds, then, that the crisis of representation in contemporary Latin America is more confined and historically contingent than universalizing explanations might suggest. More specifically, the crisis of representation has largely been concentrated in countries where parties failed to differentiate themselves programmatically and sort the electorate into rival camps with identifiable policy preferences during the process of market liberalization in the 1980s and 1990s – a major turning point in the region's development trajectory. Conservative-led market reforms that were consistently opposed by a major party of the Left were unlikely to produce a crisis of political representation, as they funneled dissent into institutionalized partisan outlets. Party systems that converged on the neoliberal model, on the other hand, were far more likely to be disrupted by anti-systemic social and electoral protest, especially in the post-adjustment era. The Washington Consensus may have been reassuring to technocrats, but it was deeply unsettling for party systems, and the social backlash it triggered often threatened the continuity of the neoliberal model itself.

These findings clearly lend support to other recent work, more micro-analytic in inspiration, that emphasizes the importance of programmatic linkages or partisan "brands" for stable representation (Lupu 2011; Morgan 2011; Seawright 2012). This study suggests, however, that the importance of programmatic alignment for party system stability may well be historically contingent rather than universal; as such, it calls for greater comparative historical analysis of party system linkage and cleavage patterns and the conditions under which they thrive or unravel. The historical record in Latin America provides clear examples of highly stable forms of partisan competition that were not structured along programmatic divides, much less the social cleavages that typically undergird them. Oligarchic party systems grounded electoral competition in rival patronage machines rather than social cleavages or programmatic divides, and in a handful of countries such party systems remained electorally stable throughout the ISI era and even through the neoliberal critical junctures analyzed here. Indeed, during the transition from ISI to neoliberalism they were often less prone than programmatically aligned party systems to the reciprocal destabilizing effects of severe economic crises and acute distributive conflicts.

To be electorally stable, programmatically de-aligned party systems must disarticulate popular sectors and depoliticize socioeconomic exclusion. This often occurred during neoliberal critical junctures, when the weakening and fragmentation of ISI-era labor and popular movements allowed for the construction of a technocratic consensus around market orthodoxy as a response to the crisis of state-led development. Social demobilization and technocratic convergence at least partially insulated new third-wave democracies from the kinds of destabilizing distributive conflicts that led elite groups to abandon the democratic arena in the 1960s and 1970s. The political context changed, however, once the primary tasks of economic stabilization and structural adjustment had been completed by the second half of the 1990s. In post-adjustment Latin America, the technocratic consensus was challenged by the groundswell of social and political resistance to market orthodoxy, which politicized inequalities and strengthened or spawned leftist alternatives in most of the region.

This societal resistance restructured political competition along a more programmatic left–right axis, but it did not have to generate a crisis of political representation, much less destabilize democratic regimes. Where party systems were programmatically aligned by market reforms and a major opposition party of the Left was available to channel discontent, the Polanyian backlash was moderated and largely institutionalized, reinforcing the competitive dynamics of contested liberalism. In most cases,[1] these dynamics were conducive to the consolidation of democratic regimes as a form of institutionalized pluralism, with relatively robust checks and balances on executive authority, secure rights for political minorities, and regular alternation in office between established parties from opposite sides of the ideological spectrum.

A crisis of representation – and its correlate, an unsettling of regime institutions – was far more likely to emerge where neoliberal convergence drove programmatic contestation outside the party system into forms of social or electoral protest. Patterns of non-programmatic partisan competition that were relatively stable beforehand were often plunged into crisis by the post-adjustment shift in the social and political landscape. Although no country reverted back to openly authoritarian governance, democratic regimes, as Dan Slater (2013: 730–731) puts it, often "careened" in an unsettled manner "between populist and oligarchic modes of politics" that involved temporary breakdowns, periodic institutional overhauls, or transgressions of basic democratic norms that fell short of overt authoritarian reversals. Careening toward oligarchic restoration occurred in countries like Honduras and Paraguay, where traditional conservative parties were returned to power by means of a military coup and an ill-disguised legislative coup, respectively, after facing popular challenges to their authority. Conversely, where established party systems decomposed in contexts of mass social protest – in countries like Venezuela, Ecuador, and Bolivia – careening toward new movement or populist modes of politics led to the plebiscitary refounding of regime institutions.

The plebiscitary reordering of democratic institutions created new channels of representation and participation for previously marginalized social groups. In so doing, it restructured political competition along a programmatic axis with roots in deep sociopolitical cleavages (Handlin 2013). It also, however, generated tensions between hegemonic and pluralistic conceptions of popular sovereignty, leaving uncertainty about the scope of opposition political rights, the reach of executive authority, and the vitality of institutional checks and balances on popular democratic majorities. In terms of Dahl's (1971) two-dimensional conceptualization of democracy (or polyarchy), post-adjustment careening toward populist politics created more inclusive and participatory forms of democratic governance, while posing challenges to democratic contestation; careening toward oligarchic restoration, on the other hand, produced low rankings on both participation and contestation. The institutional legacies of neoliberal critical junctures, therefore, were not limited to the partisan sphere, as

---

[1] The Nicaraguan case is less certain.

they also shaped the character and stability of democratic governance in the region.

The different political dynamics of the adjustment and post-adjustment periods attest to the historically contingent processes by which Latin America's social and economic inequalities become politicized. Such contingency is lost in formal models of democratic competition that derive aggregate individual preferences directly from structural or class positions and the objective material interests they create (Acemoglu and Robinson 2006). Such models assume that under conditions of socioeconomic inequality, popular majorities will vote in accordance with their material self-interests and support redistributive politics. The historical record of Latin America demonstrates that the social and political construction of such majorities is hardly a given; indeed, it is quite rare. The bottom seven deciles of the population may, in theory, share an objective material interest in redistributive policies (see Huber and Stephens 2012, Chapter 3), but as this book shows, any number of impediments can block the translation of structural majorities into collective political subjects. In the post-adjustment era, however, at least some of those impediments have been whittled down, allowing leftist alternatives with redistributive agendas to surpass the 60 percent electoral threshold in Venezuela, Bolivia, and Nicaragua, and to approach it in Ecuador. And even where those impediments remain more formidable – in countries like Colombia, Honduras, and Paraguay – traditional oligarchic rivalries are under pressure from new forms of popular contestation. The aftermath to market liberalization has thus witnessed a diminishing capacity on the part of elite actors to organize forms of democratic contestation that do not challenge prevailing inequalities.

The critical juncture approach adopted here grounds the study of democratic representation in underlying patterns of socioeconomic development and their transformation over time – in particular, transformations that alter the organization of societal interests, the political articulation of social inequalities or cleavages, and the partisan mediation of societal demands on the state. Such an approach calls for a tighter theoretical integration of the study of party systems, electoral competition, and social movements – that is, institutionalized and non-institutionalized forms of political representation and participation. As McAdam and Tarrow (2010) argue, the study of social movements or "contentious politics" is all too often isolated from the analysis of parties and elections, and both fields of study would benefit from more systematic exploration of their points of intersection and reciprocal conditioning effects. In the recent Latin American experience, the most explosive forms of social protest have been a response to failed or ineffectual partisan representation (Rice 2012) – in particular, the technocratic narrowing of programmatic space and the attendant exclusion of lower-class interests and preferences from the arena of democratic contestation. This suggests that party systems and their structuring of political representation may well be part of the "political opportunity structure" that fosters or inhibits social movements. The crisis of political representation in

Latin America's post-adjustment era is best understood through a tighter coupling of these different fields of scholarly inquiry.

Indeed, even in the relatively stable and institutionalized cases of contested liberalism, legacies of the critical juncture have recently been challenged by new cycles of social protest in Chile (2011–2012) and Brazil (2013), following extended periods of relative quiescence in both countries. These protests have articulated claims for deeper political and social reforms than those delivered, to date, by their moderate leftist parties and governments; in Chile, a powerful student protest movement has taken direct aim at a highly privatized educational system that is one of the social pillars of a neoliberal model that successive socialist governments left largely intact (Donoso 2013). In both countries, the partisan Left has responded to such protests with proposals for more fundamental reform of democratic institutions – evoking the specter of "Bolivarianism" to their critics – and, in the Chilean case, for higher taxes and universal social citizenship rights in the educational sphere.

Particularly in Chile, these new cycles of social mobilization do not cut against the basic political logic of contested liberalism. Indeed, they pressure it to become more contestatory by forcing increasingly moderate leftist parties to offer more vigorous alternatives to a neoliberal model that they inherited but only lightly touched. It remains to be seen whether institutionalized leftist parties in both countries will succeed in channeling these new social pressures – thus reinforcing or even deepening the partisan configuration of contested liberalism – or be outflanked by anti-establishment forms of electoral protest.

Either way, the trend lines point toward a higher level of programmatic contestation, whatever its institutional configuration (or stability). This programmatic restructuring of political competition may well prove to be the most durable legacy of neoliberal critical junctures, but it neither requires nor presumes that the post-adjustment electoral balances that ushered the left into power in much of the region will continue indefinitely. This book is too heavily influenced by the dialectical understanding of historical social processes found in authors like Marx and Polanyi to be tempted by such static interpretations. Even if the "left turn" recedes in the years ahead, the sociopolitical cleavages that spawned it are very likely to endure, so long as democratic contestation continues on the highly unequal social landscape of contemporary Latin America. Neoliberal critical junctures began with a disarticulation of labor-mobilizing patterns of popular incorporation that had been forged during the ISI era. Their legacies were a re-articulation – under varied institutional forms – of popular representation that once again placed the politics of inequality at the forefront of partisan and electoral competition. The divergent fate of party systems in the region has rested heavily on their capacity to channel this re-articulation of popular subjects in the aftermath to market liberalization – that is, to manage Latin America's second historical phase of lower-class political incorporation. It will continue to rest on this capacity in the years ahead.

APPENDIX

Election Results in Latin America

TABLE 1. *Presidential Election Results in Argentina, 1983–2011 (percentage of the votes)*

Party/Coalition	1983	1989	1995	1999	2003	2007	2011
PJ	39.1	49.3	49.9	38.1	60.4[b]	44.9	54.0
UCR	48.8	32.5	17.0	48.5[a]	2.3	–	11.2
FREPASO	–	–	29.3	–	–	–	–
UceDé	–	7.2	–	–	–	–	–
AR/UCD	–	–	–	10.1	–	–	–
ARI/CC	–	–	–	–	14.1	23.0	1.8
Electoral Fronts	–	–	–	–	16.4[c]	16.9[d]	16.9[e]
Others	12.0	11.1	3.8	3.3	8.0	16.3	16.2

Sources: Nohlen (2005: 112–114, vol. 2) and Georgetown University's *Political Database of the Americas* (http://pdba.georgetown.edu/).

[a] In 1999 the UCR ran in alliance with FREPASO.

[b] Includes 24.3 percent for Carlos Menem, 22 percent for Nestor Kirchner, and 14.1 percent for Adolfo Rodríguez Saá.

[c] Front supporting the candidacy of Ricardo López Murphy.

[d] Front supporting the candidacy of Roberto Lavagna.

[e] Front supporting Socialist candidate Hermes Binner.

TABLE 2. *Legislative Election Results in Argentina, 1983–2011 (percentage of the vote in Chamber of Deputies elections)*

Party	1983	1985	1987	1989	1991	1993	1995	1997	1999	2001	2003	2005	2007	2009	2011
PJ/FPV	39.1	34.6	42.9	44.7	40.2	42.5	51.0	46.3	38.5	47.1	50.2	54.3	50.0[a]	37.4[b]	44.7
UCR	48.8	43.6	38.6	28.8	29.0	30.2	26.5	25.7	31.9	25.3	21.0	15.0	10.7	16.7	14.8
FREPASO	–	–	–	–	–	3.5	8.6	14.8	14.4	2.7	–	–	–	–	–
UceDé	1.6	3.2	6.0	9.6	5.2	2.6	3.2	–	–	–	–	–	–	–	–
ARI/CC	–	–	–	–	–	–	–	–	–	6.2	5.1	6.3	8.4	7.4	2.3
Socialist Party	–	–	–	–	–	–	–	–	–	–	–	3.9	3.8	2.3	2.3
Dissident PJ	–	–	–	–	–	–	–	–	–	–	–	8.7	2.7	6.6	10.5
Others	10.4	18.6	12.5	13.0	25.7	21.3	13.9	13.2	15.2	18.7	23.7	4.7	20.2	19.5	21.1

Sources: Nohlen (2005, vol. 2): 104–107; Georgetown University's *Political Database of the Americas* (http://pdba.georgetown.edu/); and Inter-Parliamentary Union (http://www.ipu.org/english/home.htm).

[a] This figure does not include 11.1 percent of the seats claimed by pro-Kirchner allies of the FPV.
[b] This figure does not include 6.6 percent of the seats claimed by pro-Kirchner allies of the FPV.

TABLE 3. *Presidential Election Results in Brazil, 1989–2010 (percentage of the votes)*

Party	1989	1994	1998	2002	2006	2010
PDS/PPR	8.9	2.7	–	–	–	–
PMDB	4.7	4.4	–	–	–	–
PT	17.2 (47.0)	27.0	31.7	46.4 (61.3)	46.6 (60.8)	46.9 (56.1)
PDT	16.5	3.2	–	–	–	–
PFL	0.9	–	–	–	–	–
PSDB	11.5	54.3	53.1	23.2 (38.7)	41.6 (39.2)	32.6 (44.0)
PRN	30.5 (53.0)	0.6	–	–	–	–
PPS	–	–	11.0	12.0	–	–
PSB	–	–	–	17.9	–	–
Partido Verde	–	–	.3	–	–	19.3
Others	9.8	7.8	15.3	.5	9.8	1.2

Sources: Nohlen (2005: 233–234, vol. 2) and Georgetown University's *Political Database of the Americas* (http://pdba.georgetown.edu/). Second-round run-off election results are in parentheses.

TABLE 4. *Legislative Election Results in Brazil, 1982–2010 (percentage of seats in the Chamber of Deputies)*

Party	1982	1986	1990	1994	1998	2002	2006	2010
PDS/PPR/PPB/PP	49.1	6.8	8.4	10.1	11.7	9.6	8.0	7.9
PMDB	41.7	53.4	21.7	20.9	16.2	14.4	17.3	15.3
PT	1.7	3.3	7.0	9.6	11.3	17.7	16.2	17.2
PDT	4.8	4.9	9.2	6.6	4.9	4.1	4.7	5.4
PFL/DEM	–	24.2	16.5	17.3	20.5	16.4	12.7	8.3
PSDB	–	–	7.4	12.1	19.3	13.6	12.9	10.3
PRN	–	–	8.2	0.2	–	–	–	–
Others	2.7	7.3	21.8	23.1	16.2	24.2	28.2	35.6

Sources: Nohlen (2005: 225–226, vol. 2) and Georgetown University's *Political Database of the Americas* (http://pdba.georgetown.edu/).
Note: The ex-ARENA PDS merged with smaller parties to form the Reformist Progressive Party (PPR) in 1993, then the Brazilian Progressive Party (PPB) in 1995, later known simply as the Progressive Party (PP).

TABLE 5. *Presidential Election Results in Chile, 1989–2009 (percentage of votes)*

Party/Coalition	1989	1993	1999	2005	2009
Concertación	55.2	58.0	48.0 (51.3)	46.0 (53.5)	29.6 (48.4)
Rightist Coalition	29.4	24.4	47.5 (48.7)	–	44.1 (51.6)
RN	–	–	–	25.4 (43.5)	–
UDI	–	–	–	23.2	–
PCCh/Left Coalitions	...	4.7	3.2	5.4	6.2
Others/Independents	15.5	13.0	1.3	...	20.1

Sources: Nohlen (2005: 288, vol. 2) and Georgetown University's *Political Database of the Americas* (http://pdba.georgetown.edu/). Second-round run-off election results are in parentheses.

TABLE 6. *Legislative Election Results in Chile, 1989–2009 (percentage of vote in Chamber of Deputies, seats in parentheses)*

Coalition/Parties	1989	1993	1997	2001	2005	2009
Concertación	51.5 (69)	55.4 (70)	50.5 (69)	47.9 (62)	51.8 (65)	44.4 (54)[b]
PDC	26.0 (38)	27.1 (37)	23.0 (38)	18.9 (23)	20.8 (20)	14.2 (19)
Socialists	–	11.9 (15)	11.1 (11)	10.0 (10)	10.1 (15)	9.9 (11)
PPD	11.5 (16)	11.8 (15)	12.6 (16)	12.7 (20)	15.4 (21)	12.7 (18)
Others	14.1 (15)	4.5 (3)	3.9 (4)	6.2 (9)	5.5 (9)	5.6 (6)
Rightist Coalition	34.2 (48)	36.7 (50)	36.3 (47)	44.3 (57)	38.7 (54)	43.4 (58)
UDI	9.8 (11)	12.1 (15)	14.5 (17)	25.2 (31)	22.4 (33)	23.1 (37)
RN	18.3 (29)	16.3 (29)	16.8 (23)	13.8 (18)	14.1 (19)	17.8 (18)
Others	6.1 (8)	8.3 (6)	5.0 (7)	5.3 (8)	2.2 (2)	2.6 (3)
Communist Party/ Coalitions	5.3 (2)[a]	6.4 (0)	7.5 (0)	5.2 (0)	7.4 (0)	2.0 (3)
Others	8.9 (1)	1.5 (0)	5.8 (4)	2.6 (1)	2.1 (1)	12.2 (5)

Sources: Georgetown University's *Political Database of the Americas* (http://pdba.georgetown.edu/) and *Ministerio del Interior, Gobierno de Chile* (http://www.elecciones.gov.cl/).

[a] In 1989 two members of the then-divided Socialist Party were elected to congress from the coalition list led by the Communist Party. Other Socialists were elected that year under the PPD label within the *Concertación*.

[b] The Communist Party elected three candidates to Congress in 2009, although they ran on the list of the *Concertación*, technically giving the latter coalition fifty-seven seats rather than fifty-four.

TABLE 7. *Presidential Election Results in Costa Rica, 1978–2010 (percentage of the votes)*

Party/Coalition	1978	1982	1986	1990	1994	1998	2002	2006	2010
PLN	43.8	58.8	52.3	47.2	49.6	44.6	31.1 (42.0)	40.9	46.9
PUSC*	50.5	33.6	45.8	51.5	47.7	47.0	38.6 (58.0)	3.6	3.9
PAC	–	–	–	–	–	–	26.2	39.8	25.1
PML	–	–	–	–	–	0.4	1.7	8.5	20.9
Others	5.7	7.6	1.9	1.3	2.7	8.0	2.4	7.1	3.3
Turnout	81.2	78.6	81.8	81.8	81.1	70.0	68.9	65.4	69.1

Sources: Nohlen (2005: 180–183, vol. 1) and Georgetown University's *Political Database of the Americas* (http://pdba.georgetown.edu/). Second-round run-off election results are in parentheses.
* In 1978 and 1982, the conservative parties that eventually coalesced in the PUSC ran under the label of the *Partido Unidad*.

TABLE 8. *Legislative Election Results in Costa Rica, 1978–2010 (percentage of seats)*

Party/Coalition	1978	1982	1986	1990	1994	1998	2002	2006	2010
PLN	43.9	57.9	50.9	43.9	49.1	40.4	29.8	43.9	42.1
PUSC*	47.4	31.6	43.9	50.9	43.9	47.4	33.3	8.8	10.5
PAC	–	–	–	–	–	–	24.6	29.8	19.3
PML	–	–	–	–	–	1.8	10.5	10.5	15.8
Others	8.7	10.5	5.3	5.3	7.0	12.3	1.8	7.0	12.3

Sources: Nohlen (2005: 174–175, vol. 1) and Georgetown University's *Political Database of the Americas* (http://pdba.georgetown.edu/).
* In 1978 and 1982, the conservative parties that eventually coalesced in the PUSC ran under the label of the *Partido Unidad*.

TABLE 9. *Presidential Election Results in Ecuador, 1978–2013 (percentage of votes)*

Party	1978/79	1984	1988	1992	1996	1998	2002	2006	2009	2013
CFP	27.7 (68.5)	13.5	7.9	1.3	–	–	–	–	–	–
PSC	23.9 (31.5)	27.2 (51.5)	14.7	25.0 (42.7)	27.2 (45.5)	–	12.1	9.6	–	–
ID	12.0	28.7 (48.5)	24.5 (54.0)	8.5	–	16.1	14.0	14.8	–	–
PLRE	22.7	–	1.6	1.6	–	–	–	–	–	–
PRE	–	–	17.6 (46.0)	22.0	26.3 (54.5)	26.6 (48.8)	11.9	2.1	–	1.2
DP-UDC	–	4.7	11.6	1.9	13.5	34.9 (51.2)	–	–	–	–
PUR	–	–	–	31.9 (57.3)	–	–	–	–	–	–
MUPP-NP	–	–	–	–	20.6	14.7	–	2.2	–	–
PSP	–	–	–	–	–	–	20.6 (54.8)	17.4	28.2	6.7
PRIAN	–	–	–	–	–	–	17.4 (45.2)	26.8 (43.3)	11.4	3.7
Alianza PAIS	–	–	–	–	–	–	–	22.8 (56.7)	52.0	57.2
CREP	–	–	–	–	–	–	–	–	–	22.7
Others	13.7	25.9	22.1	8.9	12.3	7.6	24.0	4.2	9.3	8.5
Turnout	72.8	70.9	77.7	71.1	68.0	64.2				81.1

Sources: Nohlen (2005: 401–404, vol. 2) and Georgetown University's *Political Database of the Americas* (http://pdba.georgetown.edu/). Second-round run-off election results are in parentheses.

TABLE 10. *Legislative Election Results in Ecuador, 1979–2013 (percentage of seats)*

Party	1979	1984	1986	1988	1990	1992	1994	1996	1998	2002	2006	2009	2013
CFP	42.0	9.9	10.0	7.0	5.0	1.3	1.3	1.0	–	–	–	–	–
PSC	4.3	12.7	20.4	11.3	25.0	27.3	33.8	27.0	21.7	24.2	13.0	3.2	4.4
ID	21.7	33.8	23.9	43.7	18.3	9.1	10.4	4.0	12.5	15.1	7.0	1.6	–
PCE	6.9	2.8	1.7	1.4	3.3	7.8	7.8	1.0	0.8	–	–	–	–
PLRE	5.8	5.6	5.1	1.4	5.0	2.6	1.3	–	–	–	–	–	–
PRE	–	4.2	5.1	11.3	15.0	16.9	14.3	19.0	20.0	15.2	6.0	2.4	0.7
DP-UDC	1.4	7.0	6.8	11.3	11.7	6.5	5.2	11.0	26.7	4.0	5.0	–	–
PUR	–	–	–	–	–	15.6	3.9	2.0	–	–	–	–	–
MUPP-NP	–	–	–	–	–	–	–	8.0	4.2	7.0	6.0	3.2	3.6
PRIAN	–	–	–	–	–	–	–	–	–	10.1	28.0	5.6	–
PSP	–	–	–	–	–	–	–	–	–	8.0	24.0	15.3	3.6
Alianza PAIS	–	–	–	–	–	–	–	–	–	–	–	47.6	73.0
CREO	–	–	–	–	–	–	–	–	–	–	–	–	8.0
Others	8.7	22.5	27.1	7.1	7.1	7.1	22.0	8.2	14.2	16.0	16.0	21.0	2.9

Sources: Nohlen (2005: 395–396, vol. 2) and Georgetown University's *Political Database of the Americas* (http://pdba.georgetown.edu/).

TABLE II. *Presidential Election Results in Honduras, 1981–2013 (percentage of the votes)*

Party	1981	1985	1989	1993	1997	2001	2005	2009	2013
PLH	53.9	51.0	44.3	53.0	52.7	44.3	49.9	38.0	20.3
PNH	41.6	45.5	52.3	43.0	42.8	52.2	46.2	57.0	36.9
PINU-SD	2.5	1.5	1.9	2.8	2.1	1.5	1.0	2.0	.14
PUD	–	–	–	–	1.2	1.1	1.5	2.0	0.1
LIBRE	–	–	–	–	–	–	–	–	28.8
PAC	–	–	–	–	–	–	–	–	13.4
Others	1.9	2.0	1.5	1.2	1.3	1.0	1.0	2.0	.47
Turnout	78.5	84.0	76.1	64.8	66.3	66.3	55.1	49.9	61.2

Sources: Nohlen (2005: 416–417, vol. 1) and Georgetown University's *Political Database of the Americas* (http://pdba.georgetown.edu/).

TABLE I2. *Legislative Election Results in Honduras, 1981–2013 (percentage of seats)*

Party	1981	1985	1989	1993	1997	2001	2005	2009	2013
PLH	53.7	50.0	43.8	55.5	54.1.	43.0	48.4	35.2	21.1
PNH	41.5	47.0	55.5	43.0	41.4	47.7	43.0	55.5	37.5
PINU-SD	3.7	1.5	–	1.6	2.3	2.3	1.6	2.3	0.8
PUD	–	–	–	–	.8	3.9	3.9	3.1	–
LIBRE	–	–	–	–	–	–	–	–	28.9
PAC	–	–	–	–	–	–	–	–	10.2
Others	1.2	1.5	.8	–	1.5	3.1	3.1	3.9	

Sources: Nohlen (2005: 413, vol. 1) and Georgetown University's *Political Database of the Americas* (http://pdba.georgetown.edu/).

TABLE I3. *Presidential Election Results in Uruguay, 1984–2009 (percentage of votes)*

Party/Coalition	1984	1989	1994	1999	2004	2009
PC	41.2	30.3	32.3	22.3 (54.1)	10.6	16.9
PN	35.0	38.9	31.2	32.8	35.1	28.9 (43.5)
FA	21.3	21.2	30.6	40.1 (45.9)	51.7	48.2 (52.4)
Others	2.5	9.5	5.9	4.8	2.6	3.1
Turnout	87.9	88.7	91.4	91.8	90.0	88.0

Sources: Nohlen (2005: 525–527, vol. 2) and Georgetown University's *Political Database of the Americas* (http://pdba.georgetown.edu/. Second-round run-off election results are in parentheses.

TABLE 14. *Legislative Election Results in Uruguay, 1984–2009 (percentage of seats)*

Party/Coalition	1984	1989	1994	1999	2004	2009
PC	41.4	30.3	32.3	33.3	10.1	17.2
PN	35.4	39.4	31.3	22.2	34.3	30.3
FA	21.2	21.2	31.3	40.4	53.5	50.5
Others	2.0	9.1	5.1	4.0	2.0	2.0

Sources: Nohlen (2005: 514–515, vol. 2) and Georgetown University's *Political Database of the Americas* (http://pdba.georgetown.edu/).

TABLE 15. *Presidential Election Results in Venezuela, 1978–2013 (percentage of the votes)*

Party	1978	1983	1988	1993	1998	2000	2006	2012	2013
AD	43.3	58.4	52.9	23.6	0.4	–	–	–	–
COPEI	46.6	33.5	40.4	22.7	–	–	–	–	–
MAS	5.2	3.5	2.7	–	–	–	–	–	–
LA Causa R	–	0.1	0.3	21.9	.1	–	–	–	–
CN	–	–	–	30.5	–	–	–	–	–
MVR/PSUV	–	–	–	–	56.2	59.8	62.8	55.1	50.6
PV	–	–	–	–	40.0	–	–	–	–
Anti-Chávez Coalitions	–	–	–	–	–	37.5	36.9	44.3	49.1
Others	4.8	4.5	3.6	1.3	3.3	2.7	1.9	0.6	0.2
Turnout				60.2	63.8	56.6	74.7	80.5	79.7

Sources: Nohlen (2005: 581–583, vol. 2) and Georgetown University's *Political Database of the Americas* (http://pdba.georgetown.edu/).

TABLE 16. *Legislative Election Results in Venezuela, 1978–2010 (percentage of seats)*

Party	1978	1983	1988	1993	1998	2000	2005	2010
AD	44.2	56.5	48.3	27.1	29.5	18.2	–	13.3
COPEI	42.2	30.0	33.3	26.1	12.5	4.9	–	3.6
MAS	4.5	5.0	9.0	11.8	11.6	12.7	–	–
LA Causa R	–	0.0	1.5	19.7	2.4	1.8	–	1.2
CN	–	–	–	12.8	2.9	2.4	–	0.6
MVR/PSUV	–	–	–	–	16.9	46.7	69.5	55.8
PV	–	–	–	–	9.7	4.3	–	1.8
Primero Justicia	–	–	–	–	–	3.0	–	9.1
Un Nuevo Tiempo	–	–	–	–	–	–	–	7.3
Others	8.0	8.5	9.0	2.5	14.5	10.3	30.5[a]	4.8

Sources: Nohlen (2005: 576–577, vol. 2) and Georgetown University's *Political Database of the Americas* (http://pdba.georgetown.edu/).

[a] These seats were obtained by small leftist parties that generally supported the Chávez government.

References

Abente, Diego. 1995. "A Party System in Transition: The Case of Paraguay," in Scott Mainwaring and Timothy R. Scully, eds. *Building Democratic Institutions: Party Systems in Latin America*. Stanford, CA: Stanford University Press, 298–322.

Acemoglu, Daron and James A. Robinson. 2006. *Economic Origins of Dictatorship and Democracy*. New York: Cambridge University Press.

Acuña, Carlos H. 1994. "Politics and Economics in the Argentina of the Nineties (Or, Why the Future No Longer Is What It Used to Be)," in William C. Smith, Carlos H. Acuna, and Eduardo A. Gamarra, eds. *Democracy, Markets, and Structural Reform in Latin America*. New Brunswick, NJ: University of Miami North-South Center and Transaction Publishers, 31–73.

1995. *La Nueva Matriz Política Argentina*. Buenos Aires: Ediciones Nueva Visión.

Adimark Gfk. 2011. *Encuesta: Evaluación Gestión del Gobierno. Informe Mensual Septiembre 2011*. Santiago, Chile: Adimark Gfk.

Ajenjo Fresno, Natalia. 2003. "Honduras," in Manuel Alcántara and Flavia Freidenberg, eds. *Partidos Políticos de América Latina: Centroamérica, México y República Dominicana*. Mexico City, Mexico: Instituto Federal Electoral and Fondo de Cultura Económica, 179–273.

Aldrich, John A. 2011. *Why Parties? A Second Look*. Chicago, IL: University of Chicago Press.

Aldunate, Adolfo. 1985. "Antecedentes Socioeconómicos y Resultados Electorales," in Adolfo Aldunate, Angel Flisfisch, and Tomás Moulián, eds. *Estudios Sobre el Sistema de Partidos en Chile*. Santiago, Chile: FLACSO, 111–149.

Alesina, Alberto and Allan Drazen. 1991. "Why Are Stabilizations Delayed?" *The American Economic Review* 81, 5 (December): 1170–1188.

Alesina, Alberto and Enrico Spolaore. 2003. *The Size of Nations*. Cambridge, MA: The MIT Press.

Alfaro Salas, Sergio Iván. 2003. "Costa Rica," in Manuel Alcántara and Flavia Freidenberg, eds. *Partidos Políticos de América Latina: Centroamérica, México y Republicana Dominicana*. Mexico City, Mexico: Instituto Federal Electoral and Fondo de Cultura Económica, 31–134.

Alfredo Keller and Associates. 1999. *Estudio de Opinión Pública en las Diez Principales Ciudades de Venezuela*. November.

Altimir, O. 2008. "Distribución del Ingreso e Incidencia de la Pobreza a lo Largo del Ajuste," *Revista de la CEPAL*, 96 (December): 95–119.

Alvarez, Angel E. 1996. "La Crísis de Hegemonía de los Partidos Políticos Venezolanos," in Angel E. Alvarez, ed. *El Sistema Político Venezolano: Crísis y Transformaciones*. Caracas, Venezuela: Universidad Central de Venezuela, 131–154.

2003. "State Reform Before and After Chávez's Election," in Steve Ellner and Daniel Hellinger, eds. *Venezuelan Politics in the Chávez Era: Class, Polarization, and Conflict*. Boulder, CO: Lynne Rienner Press, 147–160.

Ames, Barry. 2001. *The Deadlock of Democracy in Brazil*. Ann Arbor, MI: University of Michigan Press.

Anderson, Charles. 1967. *Politics and Social Change in Latin America*. Princeton, NJ: Van Nostrand.

Ansell, Christopher and M. Steven Fish. 1999. "The Art of Being Indispensable: Non-Charismatic Personalism in Contemporary Political Parties," *Comparative Political Studies* 32, 3 (May): 283–312.

Anuário Estatístico do Brasil. 1993. Vol. 53. Rio de Janeiro: Instituto Brasileiro de Geografia y Estatística.

Arce, Moíses. 2005. *Market Reform in Society: Post-Crisis Politics and Economic Change in Authoritarian Peru*. University Park, PA: Pennsylvania State University Press.

2008. "The Repoliticization of Collective Action after Neoliberalism in Peru," *Latin American Politics and Society* 50, 3 (Fall): 37–62.

2010. "Parties and Social Protest in Latin America's Neoliberal Era," *Party Politics* 16, 5: 669–686.

Arce, Moíses and Paul T. Bellinger, Jr. 2007. "Low-Intensity Democracy Revisited: The Effects of Economic Liberalization on Political Activity in Latin America," *World Politics* 60, 1 (October): 97–121.

Archer, Ronald P. 1995. "Party Strength and Weakness in Colombia's Besieged Democracy," in Scott Mainwaring and Timothy R. Scully, eds. *Building Democratic Institutions: Party Systems in Latin America*. Stanford, CA: Stanford University Press, 164–199.

Armijo, Leslie Elliott and Philippe Faucher. 2002. "'We Have a Consensus': Explaining Political Support for Market Reforms in Latin America," *Latin American Politics and Society* 44, 2 (Summer): 1–40.

Arnold, Jason Ross and David J. Samuels. 2011. "Evidence from Public Opinion," in Steven Levitsky and Kenneth M. Roberts, eds. *The Resurgence of the Latin American Left*. Baltimore, MD: Johns Hopkins University Press, 31–51.

Arthur, Brian W. 1994. *Increasing Returns and Path Dependence in the Economy*. Ann Arbor, MI: University of Michigan Press.

Auyero, Javier. 2000. *Poor People's Politics: Peronist Survival Networks and the Legacy of Evita*. Durham, NC: Duke University Press.

2007. *Routine Politics and Violence in Argentina: The Gray Zone of State Power*. New York: Cambridge University Press.

Baer, Werner. 1989. *The Brazilian Economy: Growth and Development*, 3rd ed. New York: Praeger.

Baiocchi, Gianpaolo, ed. 2003. *Radicals in Power: The Workers' Party and Experiments in Urban Democracy in Brazil.* London: Zed.

Baker, Andy. 2003. "Why Is Trade Reform So Popular in Latin America? A Consumption-Based Theory of Trade Preferences," *World Politics* 55 (April): 423–455.

2009. *The Market and the Masses in Latin America: Policy Reform and Consumption in Liberalizing Economies.* New York: Cambridge University Press.

Baker, Andy and Kenneth F. Greene. 2011. "The Latin American Left's Mandate: Free Market Policies and Issue Voting in New Democracies," *World Politics* 63, 1 (January): 41–77.

Barr, Robert. 2009. "Populists, Outsiders and Anti-Establishment Politics," *Party Politics* 15, 1: 29–48.

Barrera, Manuel and J. Samuel Valenzuela. 1986. "The Development of Labor Movement Opposition to the Military Regime," in J. Samuel Valenzuela and Arturo Valenzuela, eds. *Military Rule in Chile: Dictatorship and Oppositions.* Baltimore, MD: Johns Hopkins University Press, 230–269.

Barros, Robert. 2002. *Constitutionalism and Dictatorship: Pinochet, the Junta, and the 1980 Constitution.* Cambridge: Cambridge University Press.

Bartolini, Stefano. 2000. *The Political Mobilization of the European Left, 1860–1980: The Class Cleavage.* Cambridge: Cambridge University Press.

Bartolini, Stefano and Peter Mair. 1990. *Identity, Competition, and Electoral Availability: The Stabilisation of European Electorates 1885–1985.* Cambridge: Cambridge University Press.

Becker, Marc. 2008. *Indians and Leftists in the Making of Ecuador's Modern Indigenous Movements.* Durham, NC: Duke University Press.

Bergquist, Charles. 1986. *Labor in Latin America: Comparative Essays on Chile, Argentina, Venezuela, and Colombia.* Stanford, CA: Stanford University Press.

Bitar, Sergio and Tulio Mejías. 1995. "Mas Industrialización: ¿Alternativa para Venezuela?" in Moisés Naím and Ramón Piñango, eds. *El Caso Venezuela: Una Ilusión de Armonía.* Caracas, Venezuela: Ediciones IESA, 102–121.

Boix, Carles. 2003. *Democracy and Redistribution.* New York: Cambridge University Press.

Booth, John A. 1987. "Costa Rica," in Gerald Michael Greenfield and Sheldon L. Maram, eds. *Latin American Labor Organizations.* Westport, CT: Greenwood Press, 213–242.

Borón, Atilio A. 2000. "Ruling Without a Party: Argentine Dominant Classes in the Twentieth Century," in Kevin J. Middlebrook, ed. *Conservative Parties, the Right, and Democracy in Latin America.* Baltimore, MD: Johns Hopkins University Press, 139–163.

Bowman, Kirk S. 2002. *Militarization, Democracy, and Development: The Perils of Praetorianism in Latin America.* University Park, PA: Pennsylvania State University Press.

Brewer-Carías, Allan R. 2010. *Dismantling Democracy in Venezuela: The Chávez Authoritarian Experiment.* New York: Cambridge University Press.

Bruhn, Kathleen. 1997. *Taking on Goliath: The Emergence of a New Left Party and the Struggle for Democracy in Mexico.* University Park, PA: Pennsylvania State University Press.

Brusco, Valeria, Marcelo Nazareno, and Susan C. Stokes. 2004. "Vote Buying in Argentina," *Latin American Research Review* 39, 2 (June): 66–88.

Brysk, Alison. 1994. *The Politics of Human Rights in Argentina: Protest, Change, and Democratization.* Stanford, CA: Stanford University Press.

Bulmer-Thomas, Victor. 1996. "Introduction," in Victor Bulmer-Thomas, ed. *The New Economic Model in Latin America and Its Impact on Income Distribution and Poverty.* London: Institute of Latin American Studies, 7–28.

Burgess, Katrina. 1999. "Loyalty Dilemmas and Market Reform: Party-Union Alliances Under Stress in Mexico, Spain, and Venezuela," *World Politics* 52, 1 (October): 105–134.

2004. *Parties and Unions in the New Global Economy.* Pittsburgh, PA: University of Pittsburgh Press.

Burgess, Katrina and Steven Levitsky. 2003. "Explaining Populist Party Adaptation in Latin America: Environmental and Organizational Determinants of Party Change in Argentina, Mexico, Peru, and Venezuela," *Comparative Political Studies* 36, 8 (October): 881–911.

Burnham, Walter Dean. 1970. *Critical Elections and the Mainsprings of American Politics.* New York: W. W. Norton.

Buxton, Julia. 2003. "Economic Policy and the Rise of Hugo Chávez," in Steve Ellner and Daniel Hellinger, eds. *Venezuelan Politics in the Chávez Era: Class, Polarization, and Conflict.* Boulder, CO: Lynne Rienner Press, 113–130.

Calvo, Ernesto and María Victoria Murillo. 2004. "Who Delivers? Partisan Clients in the Argentine Electoral Market," *American Journal of Political Science* 48, 4 (October): 742–757.

Cameron, David R. 1984. "Social Democracy, Corporatism, Labour Quiescence and the Representation of Economic Interests in Advanced Capitalist Society," in J. Goldthorpe, ed. *Order and Conflict in Contemporary Capitalism.* Oxford: Clarendon Press, 143–178.

Cameron, Maxwell A. 2011. "Peru: The Left Turn That Wasn't," in Steven Levitsky and Kenneth M. Roberts, eds. *The Resurgence of the Latin American Left.* Baltimore, MD: Johns Hopkins University Press, 375–398.

Campbell, Angus, Philip E. Converse, Warren E. Miller, and Donald E. Stokes. 1960. *The American Voter.* Chicago, IL: University of Chicago Press.

Campello, Daniela. Forthcoming. *Globalization and Democracy: The Politics of Market Discipline in Latin America.* New York: Cambridge University Press.

Capoccia, Giovanni and R. Daniel Kelemen. 2007. "The Study of Critical Junctures: Theory, Narrative, and Counterfactuals in Historical Institutionalism," *World Politics* 59, 3 (April): 341–369.

Cardoso, Eliana and Ann Helwege. 1995. *Latin America's Economy: Diversity, Trends, and Conflicts.* Cambridge, MA: MIT Press.

Cardoso, Fernando Henrique and Enzo Faletto. 1979. *Dependency and Development in Latin America.* Berkeley, CA: University of California Press.

Carey, John M. 1996. *Term Limits and Legislative Representation.* New York: Cambridge University Press.

Carmines, Edward G., John P. McIver, and James A. Stimson. 1987. "Unrealized Partisanship: A Theory of Dealignment," *Journal of Politics* 49, 2 (May): 376–400.

Carranza, Carlos and José C. Chinchilla. 1994. "Ajuste Estructural en Costa Rica, 1985–1993," in Gerónimo de Sierra, ed. *Los Pequeños Países de América Latina en la Hora Neoliberal*. Caracas, Venezuela: Editorial Nueva Sociedad, 39–68.

Carrasquero, José Vicente and Friedrich Welsch. 2000. "Opinión Pública y Cultura Política en Venezuela: La Consolidación del Chavecismo," in Friedrich Welsch and Frederick C. Turner, eds. *Opinión Pública y Elecciones en América Latina*. Caracas: International Political Science Association and Universidad Simon Bolivar, 173–192.

Castañeda, Jorge G. 1993. *Utopia Unarmed: The Latin American Left after the Cold War*. New York: Vintage Books.

Catterberg, Edgardo. 1991. *Argentina Confronts Politics: Political Culture and Public Opinion in the Argentine Transition to Democracy*. Boulder, CO: Lynne Rienner Publishers.

Cavarozzi, Marcelo. 1994. "Politics: A Key for the Long Term in South America," in William C. Smith, Carlos Acuña, and Eduardo Gamarra, eds. *Latin American Political Economy in the Age of Neoliberal Reform*. New Brunswick, NJ: Transaction Publishers, 127–155.

Centeno, Miguel Angel. 1994. *Democracy Within Reason: Technocratic Revolution in Mexico*. University Park, PA: Pennsylvania State University Press.

Centro Nicaraguense de Derechos Humanos. 1995. *El Derecho a la Libertad Sindical y la Actuación de las Autoridades Administrativas y Judiciales*. Managua, Nicaragua.

Chávez, Daniel, and Benjamin Goldfrank, eds. 2004. *The Left in the City: Participatory Local Governments in Latin America*. London: Latin American Bureau and Transnational Institute.

Chilean National Commission on Truth and Reconcilation. 1991. *Report of the Chilean National Commission on Truth and Reconciliation*. Santiago. http://www.usip.org/files/resources/collections/truth_commissions/Chile90-Report/Chile90-Report.pdf.

Cid, José Rafael del. 1990. "Logros y Perspectivas del Proceso de Democratización en Honduras," in Rafael del Cid, Hugo Noé Pino and Alcides Hernández, *Honduras: Crísis Económica y Proceso de Democratización Política*. Tegulcigapa: Centro de Documentación de Honduras, 1–24.

Clark, Terry Nichols and Seymour Martin Lipset. 1991. "Are Social Classes Dying?" *International Sociology* 6, 4 (December): 397–410.

Cohen, Youssef. 1994. *Radicals, Reformers and Reactionaries: The Prisoner's Dilemma and the Collapse of Democracy in Latin America*. Chicago, IL: University of Chicago Press.

Colburn, Forrest D. 2002. *Latin America at the End of Politics*. Princeton, NJ: Princeton University Press.

Collier, David, ed. 1979. *The New Authoritarianism in Latin America*. Princeton, NJ: Princeton University Press.

Collier, David and James Mahoney. 1996. "Insights and Pitfalls: Selection Bias in Qualitative Research," *World Politics* 49, 1 (October): 56–91.

Collier, Ruth Berins. 1992. *The Contradictory Alliance: State-Labor Relations and Regime Change in Mexico*. Berkeley, CA: University of California International and Area Studies.

Collier, Ruth Berins and Christopher Chambers-Ju. 2012. "Popular Representation in Contemporary Latin American Politics: An Agenda for Research," in Peter Kingstone and Deborah J. Yashar, eds. *Routledge Handbook of Latin American Politics*. New York and London: Routledge, 564–578.

Collier, Ruth Berins and David Collier. 1979. "Inducements versus Constraints: Disaggregating Corporatism," *American Political Science Review* 73, 4 (December): 967–986.

   1991. *Shaping the Political Arena: Critical Junctures, the Labor Movement, and Regime Dynamics in Latin America.* Princeton, NJ: Princeton University Press.

Collier, Ruth Berins and Samuel Handlin, eds. 2009. *Popular Participation and Interest Regimes in Latin America: From Union-Party Hubs to Associational Networks.* University Park, PA: Pennsylvania State University Press.

Conaghan, Catherine M. 1995. "Politicians Against Parties: Discord and Disconnection in Ecuador's Party System," in Scott Mainwaring and Timothy R. Scully, eds. *Building Democratic Institutions: Party Systems in Latin America.* Stanford, CA: Stanford University Press, 434–458.

   2011. "Ecuador: Rafael Correa and the Citizens' Revolution," in Steven Levitsky and Kenneth M. Roberts, eds. *The Resurgence of the Latin American Left.* Baltimore, MD: Johns Hopkins University Press, 260–282.

Conaghan, Catherine M. and James M. Malloy. 1994. *Unsettled Statecraft: Democracy and Neoliberalism in the Central Andes.* Pittsburgh, PA: University of Pittsburgh Press.

Conniff, Michael L., ed. 1999. *Populism in Latin America.* Tuscaloosa, AL: University of Alabama Press.

Consultores 21 S.A. 1996. *Cultura Democrática en Venezuela: Informe Analítico de Resultados.* Caracas.

Consultores 21 S.A. Various editions. *Estudio de Temas Económicos.*

Converse, Philip E. 1969. "Of Time and Partisan Stability," *Comparative Political Studies* 2, 2 (July): 139–171.

Cook, María Lorena. 2007. *The Politics of Labor Reform in Latin America: Between Flexibility and Rights.* University Park, PA: Pennsylvania State University Press.

Coppedge, Michael. 1994. *Strong Parties and Lame Ducks: Presidential Partyarchy and Factionalism in Venezuela.* Stanford, CA: Stanford University Press.

   1997. "A Classification of Latin American Political Parties." Working Paper, Kellogg Institute for International Studies, University of Notre Dame.

   1998a. "The Dynamic Diversity of Latin American Party Systems," *Party Politics* 4, 4: 547–568.

   1998b. "The Evolution of Latin American Party Systems," in Scott Mainwaring and Arturo Valenzuela, eds. *Politics, Society, and Democracy in Latin America.* Boulder, CO: Westview Press, 171–206.

Cornia, Giovanni Andrea. 2012. "Inequality Trends and Their Determinants: Latin America over 1990–2010." Working Paper No. 2012/09. Helsinki: UNU-WIDER.

Corrales, Javier. 2000. "Presidents, Ruling Parties, and Party Rules: A Theory on the Politics of Economic Reform in Latin America," *Comparative Politics* 32, 2 (January): 127–150.

   2002. *Presidents Without Parties: The Politics of Economic Reform in Argentina and Venezuela in the 1990's.* University Park, PA: Pennsylvania State University Press.

Corrales, Javier and Michael Penfold. 2011. *Dragon in the Tropics: Hugo Chávez and the Political Economy of Revolution in Venezuela.* Washington, D.C.: Brookings Institution.

Crewe, Ivor and David Denver. 1985. *Electoral Change in Western Democracies: Patterns and Sources of Electoral Volatility.* New York: St. Martin's Press.

Crisp, Brian F. 2000. *Democratic Institutional Design: The Powers and Incentives of Venezuelan Politicians and Interest Groups.* Stanford, CA: Stanford University Press.

Dahl, Robert A. 1971. *Polyarchy: Participation and Opposition.* New Haven, CT: Yale University Press.

Dalton, Russell. 2006. *Citizen Politics: Public Opinion and Political Parties in Advanced Industrial Democracies,* 4th ed. Washington, D.C.: Congressional Quarterly Press.

Dalton, Russell J., Scott C. Flanagan, and Paul Allen Beck, eds. 1984. *Electoral Change in Advanced Industrial Democracies: Realigment or Dealignment?* Princeton, NJ: Princeton University Press.

Dalton, Russell J. and Martin P. Wattenberg, eds. 2000. *Parties Without Partisans: Political Change in Advanced Industrial Democracies.* Oxford: Oxford University Press.

de Janvry, Alain. 1981. *The Agrarian Question and Reformism in Latin America.* Baltimore: Johns Hopkins University Press.

de la Fuente, Ariel. 2000. *Children of Facundo: Caudillo and Gaucho Insurgency During the Argentine State-Formation Process (La Rioja, 1853–1870).* Durham, NC: Duke University Press.

de la Torre, Carlos. 2000. *Populist Seduction in Latin America: The Ecuadorian Exerience.* Athens, OH: Ohio University Center for International Studies.

2010. *Populist Seduction in Latin America,* 2nd ed. Athens, OH: Ohio University Center for International Studies.

de Sierra, Gerónimo. 1994. "Neoliberalismo, Ajuste y Cambios Sociopolíticos en Uruguay," in Gerónimo de Sierra, ed. *Los Pequeños Países de América Latina en la Hora Neoliberal.* Caracas, Venezuela: Editorial Nueva Sociedad, 191–218.

De Soto, Hernando. 1989. *The Other Path: The Invisible Revolution in the Third World.* New York: Harper and Row.

DeShazo, Peter. 1983. *Urban Workers and Labor Unions in Chile, 1902–1927.* Madison, WI: University of Wisconsin Press.

Dewachter, Sara and Nadia Molenaers. 2011. "Who Takes a Seat at the Pro-Poor Table? Civil Society Participation in the Honduran Poverty Reduction Strategy," *Latin American Research Review* 46, 3: 112–132.

Díaz Alejandro, Carlos F. 2000. "Latin America in the 1930s," in Jeffrey Frieden, Manuel Pastor Jr., and Michael Tomz, eds. *Modern Political Economy and Latin America: Theory and Policy.* Boulder, CO: Westview Press, 140–151.

Di Tella, Torcuato S., ed. 1998. *Crisis de Representatividad y Sistemas de Partidos Políticos.* Buenos Aires, Argentina: Grupo Editor Latinoamericano.

Dix, Robert H. 1989. "Cleavage Structures and Party Systems in Latin America," *Comparative Politics* 22, 1 (October): 23–37.

Dix, Robert. 1992. "Democratization and the Institutionalization of Latin American Political Parties." *Comparative Political Studies* 24, 4 (January): 488–511.

Domínguez, Jorge I. 1992. "On Understanding the Present by Analyzing the Past in Latin America: A Review Essay," *Political Science Quarterly* 107, 2 (Summer): 325–329.

1997a. "Latin America's Crisis of Representation," *Foreign Affairs* 76, 1 (Jan.-Feb.): 100–113.

ed. 1997b. *Technopols: Freeing Politics and Markets in Latin America in the 1990s.* University Park, PA: Pennsylvania State University Press.

Donoso, Sofia. 2013. "Dynamics of Change in Chile: Explaining the Emergence of the 2006 *Pingüino* Movement," *Journal of Latin American Studies* 45, 1 (February): 1–29.

Downs, Anthony. 1957. *An Economic Theory of Democracy.* New York: Harper and Row.

Drake, Paul W. 1978. *Socialism and Populism in Chile, 1932–1952.* Urbana, IL: University of Illinois Press.

    1991. "Comment," in Rudiger Dornbusch and Sebastian Edwards, eds. *The Macroeconomics of Populism in Latin America.* Chicago, IL: University of Chicago Press, 35–40.

    1996. *Labor Movements and Dictatorships: The Southern Cone in Comparative Perspective.* Baltimore, MD: Johns Hopkins University Press.

Dresser, Denise. 1991. *Neopopulist Solutions to Neoliberal Problems: Mexico's National Solidarity Program.* San Diego, CA: Center for U.S.-Mexican Studies.

Dunning, Thad. 2008. *Crude Democracy: Natural Resource Wealth and Political Regimes.* New York: Cambridge University Press.

Duverger, Maurice. 1964. *Political Parties: Their Organization and Activity in the Modern State.* London: Methuen and Company.

Eaton, Kent. 2005. "Menem and the Governors: Intergovernmental Relations in the 1990s," in Steven Levitsky and María Victoria Murillo, eds. *Argentine Democracy: The Politics of Institutional Weakness.* University Park, PA: Pennsylvania State University Press, 88–112.

Echegaray, Fabián and Carlos Elordi. 2001. "Public Opinion, Presidential Popularity, and Economic Reform in Argentina, 1989–1996," in Susan C. Stokes, ed. *Public Support for Market Reform in New Democracies.* New York: Cambridge University Press, 187–214.

Echevarría, Oscar. 1995. *La Economía Venezolana 1944–1994.* Caracas, Venezuela: FEDECAMARAS.

Echeverría, Ruben G. 2000. "Opciones para Reducir la Probreza Rural en América Latina," *CEPAL Review* 70 (April): 147–160.

Eckstein, Susan. 2001. "Where Have All the Movements Gone? Latin American Social Movements at the New Millennium," in Susan Eckstein, ed. *Power and Popular Protest: Latin American Social Movements.* 2nd ed. Berkeley, CA: University of California Press, 351–406.

Eckstein, Susan Eva and Timothy P. Wickham-Crowley, eds. 2003. *What Justice? Whose Justice? Fighting for Fairness in Latin America.* Berkeley, CA: University of California Press.

Economía y Trabajo en Chile: Informe Anual. 1993–1994. Vol.4. Santiago, Chile: Programa de Economía y Trabajo.

Economic Commission for Latin America and the Caribbean. Various editions. *Statistical Yearbook for Latin America and the Caribbean.* Santiago, Chile: United Nations.

Economist Intelligence Unit. 2000. *Country Report: Venezuela.* (March). London.

    2002a. *Country Profile 2002: Argentina.* London.

    2002b. *Country Report: Argentina.* (March). London.

    2003a. *Country Profile: Venezuela 2003.* London.

    2003b. *Country Report: Argentina.* (March). London.

Edelman, Marc. 1999. *Peasants against Globalization: Rural Social Movements in Costa Rica.* Stanford, CA: Stanford University Press.

Edwards, Sebastian. 1995. *Crisis and Reform in Latin America: From Despair to Hope.* Oxford: Oxford University Press.

El Sindicalismo Ante los Proceses de Cambio Económico y Social en América Latina. 1998. Buenos Aires, Argentina: CIEDLA-Fundación Konrad Adenauer.

Ellner, Steve. 1995. *El Sindicalismo en Venezuela en el Contexto Democrático (1958–1994).* Caracas, Venezuela: Tropykos.

2003. "Organized Labor and the Challenge of *Chavismo*," in Steve Ellner and Daniel Hellinger, eds. *Venezuelan Politics in the Chávez Era: Class, Polarization, and Conflict.* Boulder, CO: Lynne Rienner Publishers, 161–178.

2008. *Rethinking Venezuelan Politics: Class, Conflict, and the Chávez Phenomenon.* Boulder, CO: Lynne Rienner.

Ellner, Steve and Daniel Hellinger, eds. 2003. *Venezuelan Politics in the Chávez Era: Class, Polarization, and Conflict.* Boulder, CO: Lynne Rienner Publishers.

Ensalaco, Mark. 2000. *Chile Under Pinochet: Recovering the Truth.* University Park, PA: Pennsylvania State University Press.

Epstein, Edward. 2003. "The Piquetero Movement of Greater Buenos Aires: Working Class Protest During the Current Argentine Crisis," *Canadian Journal of Latin American and Caribbean Studies* 28, 55 & 56: 11–36.

Epstein, Leon D. 1980. *Political Parties in Western Democracies.* New Brunswick, NJ: Transaction.

Escaith, Hubert and Igor Paunovic. 2004. *Reformas Estructurales en América Latina y el Caribe en el Período 1970–2000: Índices y Notas Metodológicas.* Documentos de Proyectos. October. Santiago, Chile: CEPAL.

Esping-Andersen, Gøsta. 1990. *The Three Worlds of Welfare Capitalism,* Princeton, NJ: Princeton University Press.

Estudio Mora y Araujo y Asociados. 1995. (February). Buenos Aires, Argentina: Mora y Araujo y Asociados.

Estudio Mora y Araujo y Asociados. 1999. (September). Buenos Aires, Argentina: Mora y Araujo y Asociados.

Etchemendy, Sebastián and Ruth Berins Collier. 2007. "Down but Not Out: Union Resurgence and Segmented Neocorporatism in Argentina (2003–2007)," *Politics and Society* 35, 3: 362–401.

Etchemendy, Sebastián and Candelaria Garay. 2011. "Argentina: Left Populism in Comparative Perspective, 2003–2009," in Steven Levitsky and Kenneth M. Roberts, eds. *The Resurgence of the Latin American Left.* Baltimore, MD: Johns Hopkins University Press, 283–305.

Evans, Geoffrey, ed. 1999. *The End of Class Politics? Class Voting in Comparative Context.* Oxford: Oxford University Press.

Evans, Peter. 1979. *Dependent Development: The Alliance of Multinational, State, and Local Capital in Brazil.* Princeton, NJ: Princeton University Press.

Evans, Ronald. 1998. *Desnutrición en Venezuela: Período 1990–1996.* Caracas, Venezuela: Instituto Nacional de Nutrición.

Falleti, Tulia G. and Julia Lynch. 2008. "Causation in Time," *Qualitative Methods* 6,1 (Spring): 2–6.

Faúndez, Julio. 1988. *Marxism and Democracy in Chile: From 1932 to the Fall of Allende.* New Haven, CT: Yale University Press.

Feldstein, Martin. 2002. "Argentina's Fall: Lessons from the Latest Financial Crisis." *Foreign Affairs* 81, 2 (March-April): 8–14.

Filgueira, Fernando and Jorge Papadópulos. 1997. "Putting Conservatism to Good Use? Long Crisis and Vetoed Alternatives in Uruguay," in Douglas A. Chalmers, Carlos M. Vilas, Katherine Hite, Scott B. Martin, Kerianne Piester, and Monique Segarra, eds. *The New Politics of Inequality in Latin America: Rethinking Participation and Representation*. Oxford: Oxford University Press.

Fiorina, Morris P. 1981. *Retrospective Voting in American National Elections*. New Haven, CT: Yale University Press.

Fitch, John Samuel. 1977. *The Military Coup d'Etat as a Political Process: Ecuador 1948–1966*. Baltimore, MD: Johns Hopkins University Press.

Foreign Labor Trends. Various editions. Washington, D.C.: U.S. Department of Labor.

Fleet, Michael. 1985. *The Rise and Fall of Chilean Christian Democracy*. Princeton, NJ: Princeton University Press.

Flores-Macías, Gustavo. 2012. *After Neoliberalism: The Left and Economic Reforms in Latin America*. Oxford: Oxford University Press.

Foxley, Alejandro. 1983. *Latin American Experiments in Neoconservative Economics*, Berkeley, CA: University of California Press.

Franklin, Mark N., Thomas T. Mackie, and Henry Valen et al. 1992. *Electoral Change: Responses to Evolving Social and Attitudinal Structures in Western Countries*. Cambridge: Cambridge University Press.

Freidenberg, Flavia. 2003. "Ecuador," in Manuel Alcántara and Flavia Freidenberg, eds. *Partidos Políticos de América Latina: Países Andinos*. Mexico City: Instituto Federal Electoral and Fondo de Cultura Económica, 235–406.

Gallagher, Michael, Michael Laver, and Peter Mair. 2011. *Representative Government in Modern Europe*, 5th ed. New York: McGraw-Hill.

Gargiulo, Martín. 1989. "The Uruguayan Labor Movement in the Post-Authoritarian Period," in Edward Epstein, ed. *Labor Autonomy and the State in Latin America*. Boston: Unwin Hyman, 219–246.

Garrett, Geoffrey. 1998. *Partisan Politics in the Global Economy*. New York: Cambridge University Press.

Garretón, Manuel Antonio. 1987. "En Qué Consistió la Renovación Socialista? Síntesis y Evaluación de Sus Contenidos," in *La Renovación Socialista: Balance y Perspectivas de un Proceso Vigente*. Santiago, Chile: Ediciones Valentín Letelier, 17–43.

  1989a. "La Oposición Política Partidaria en el Régimen Militar Chileno: Un Proceso de Aprendizaje para la Transición," in Marcelo Cavarozzi and Mañuel Antonio Garretón, eds. *Muerte y Resurrección: Los Partidos Políticos en el Autoritarismo y las Transiciones del Cono Sur*. Santiago, Chile: FLACSO, 395–465.

  1989b. "Popular Mobilization and the Military Regime in Chile: The Complexities of the Invisible Transition," in Susan Eckstein, ed. *Power and Popular Protest: Latin American Social Movements*. Berkeley, CA: University of California Press, 259–277.

  2000. "Atavism and Democratic Ambiguity in the Chilean Right," in Kevin J. Middlebrook, ed. *Conservative Parties, the Right, and Democracy in Latin America*. Baltimore, MD: Johns Hopkins University Press, 53–79.

  2003. *Incomplete Democracy: Political Democratization in Chile and Latin America*. Chapel Hill, NC: University of North Carolina Press.

Garretón, Manuel Antonio, Marcelo Cavarozzi, Peter S. Cleaves, Gary Gereffi, and Jonathan Hartlyn. 2003. *Latin America in the 21st Century: Toward a New Sociopolitical Matrix*. Miami, FL: University of Miami North-South Center Press.

Gates, Leslie C. 2010. *Electing Chávez: The Business of Anti-Neoliberal Politics in Venezuela*. Pittsburgh, PA: University of Pittsburgh Press.

Gay, Robert. 1994. *Popular Organization and Democracy in Rio de Janeiro: A Tale of Two Favelas*. Philadelphia, PA: Temple University Press.

Geddes, Barbara. 1994. *Politician's Dilemma: Building State Capacity in Latin America*. Berkeley, CA: University of California Press.

  1995. "The Politics of Economic Liberalization," *Latin American Research Review* 30, 2: 195–214.

Gervasoni, Carlos H. 1995. "El Impacto Electoral de las Políticas de Estabilización y Reforma Estructural en América Latina," *Journal of Latin American Affairs* 3,1: 46–50.

Gibson, Edward L. 1996. *Class and Conservative Parties: Argentina in Comparative Perspective*. Baltimore, MD: Johns Hopkins University Press.

  1997. "The Populist Road to Market Reform: Policy and Electoral Coalitions in Mexico and Argentina," *World Politics* 49 (April): 339–370.

Gibson, Edward L. and Ernesto Calvo. 2000. "Federalism and Low-Maintenance Constituencies: Territorial Dimensions of Economic Reform in Argentina," *Studies in Comparative International Development* 35, 3 (Fall): 32–55.

Gillespie, Charles Guy. 1991. *Negotiating Democracy: Politicians and Generals in Uruguay*. New York: Cambridge University Press.

Godio, Julio, Héctor Palomino, and Achim Wachendorfer. 1988. *El Movimiento Sindical Argentino (1880–1987)*. Buenos Aires, Argentina: Puntosur Editores.

Golden, Miriam. 1993. "The Dynamics of Trade Unionism and National Economic Performance," *American Political Science Review* 87, 2 (June): 439–454.

Goldfrank, Benjamin. 2011. *Deepening Local Democracy in Latin America: Participation, Decentralization, and the Left*. University Park, PA: Pennsylvania State University Press.

Gómez, Sergio and Emilio Klein, eds. 1993. *Los Pobres del Campo: El Trabajador Eventual*. Santiago, Chile: FLACSO/PREALC.

González, Luís E. 1995. "Continuity and Change in the Uruguayan Party System," in Scott Mainwaring and Timothy R. Scully, eds. *Building Democratic Institutions: Party Systems in Latin America*. Stanford, CA: Stanford University Press, 138–163.

Graham, Carol and Cheikh Kane. 1998. "Opportunistic Government or Sustaining Reform? Electoral Trends and Public-Expenditure Patterns in Peru, 1990–1995," *Latin American Research Review*, 33, 1: 67–104.

Graham, Richard. 1990. *Patronage and Politics in Nineteenth Century Brazil*. Stanford, CA: Stanford University Press.

Green, Donald, Bradley Palmquist, and Eric Schickler. 2002. *Partisan Hearts and Minds: Political Parties and the Social Identities of Voters*. New Haven, CT: Yale University Press.

Greenfield, Gerald Michael and Sheldon L. Maram, eds. 1987. *Latin American Labor Organizations*. New York: Greenwood Press.

Grief, Avner and David D. Laitin. 2004. "A Theory of Endogenous Institutional Change," *American Political Science Review* 98, 4 (November): 633–652.

Gwartney, James, Robert Lawson, and Walter Block. 1996. *Economic Freedom of the World, 1975–1995*. Vancouver, B.C.: Fraser Institute.

Hacker, Jacob S. and Paul Pierson. 2005. *Off-Center: The Republican Revolution and the Erosion of American Democracy*. New Haven, CT: Yale University Press.

Haggard, Stephan and Robert R. Kaufman, eds. 1992. *The Politics of Economic Adjustment*. Princeton, NJ: Princeton University Press.

 1995. *The Political Economy of Democratic Transitions*. Princeton, NJ: Princeton University Press.

Hagopian, Frances. 1996. *Traditional Politics and Regime Change in Brazil*. New York: Cambridge University Press.

 1998. "Democracy and Political Representation in Latin America in the 1990s: Pause, Reorganization, or Decline?" in Felipe Aguero and Jeffrey Stark, eds. *Fault Lines of Democracy in Post-Transition Latin America*. Miami, FL: University of Miami North-South Center Press, 99–144.

Hagopian, Frances, Carlos Gervasoni, and Juan Andrés Moraes. 2009. "From Patronage to Program: The Emergence of Party-Oriented Legislators in Brazil," *Comparative Political Studies* 42, 3 (March): 360–391.

Hale, Henry E. 2006. *Why Not Parties in Russia? Democracy, Federalism, and the State*. New York: Cambridge University Press.

Hall, Peter A. and David Soskice, eds. 2001. *Varieties of Capitalism: Institutional Foundations of Comparative Advantage*. Oxford: Oxford University Press.

Handlin, Samuel. 2013. "Social Protection and the Politicization of Class Cleavages during Latin America's Left Turn," *Comparative Political Studies* 46, 12: 1582–1609.

Handlin, Samuel and Ruth Berins Collier. 2011. "The Diversity of Left Party Linkages and Competitive Advantages," in Steven Levitsky and Kenneth M. Roberts, eds. *The Resurgence of the Latin American Left*. Baltimore, MD: Johns Hopkins University Press, 139–161.

Harper, F. John, ed. 1987. *Trade Unions of the World*. Essex, UK: Longman.

Hartlyn, Jonathan. 1988. *The Politics of Coalition Rule in Colombia*. New York: Cambridge University Press.

 1998. *The Struggle for Democratic Politics in the Dominican Republic*. Chapel Hill, NC: University of North Carolina Press.

Hawkins, Kirk. 2010. *Venezuela's Chavismo and Populism in Comparative Perspective*. New York: Cambridge University Press.

Hellinger, Daniel. 2003. "Political Overview: The Breakdown of *Puntofijismo* and the Rise of *Chavismo*," in Steve Ellner and Daniel Hellinger, eds. *Venezuelan Politics in the Chávez Era: Class, Polarization, and Conflict*. Boulder, CO: Lynne Rienner Publishers, 27–53.

Hellman, Joel S. 1998. "Winners Take All: The Politics of Partial Reform in Postcommunist Transitions," *World Politics* 50, 2: 203–234.

Hetherington, Marc J. 2011. "Resurgent Mass Partisanship: The Role of Elite Polarization," in Richard G. Niemi, Herbert F. Weisberg, and David C. Kimball, eds. *Controversies in Voting Behavior*. Washington, D.C.: CQ Press, 242–265.

Higley, John and Richard Gunther, eds. 1992. *Elites and Democratic Consolidation in Latin America and Southern Europe*. New York: Cambridge University Press.

Hirschman, Albert O. 1970. *Exit, Voice, and Loyalty*. Cambridge, MA: University of Harvard Press.

Huber Stephens, Evelyne. 1983. "The Peruvian Military Government, Labor Mobilization, and the Political Strength of the Left," *Latin American Research Review* 43: 57–93.

Huber, Evelyne and Frank Safford, eds. 1995. *Agrarian Structure and Political Power: Landlord and Peasant in the Making of Latin America*. Pittsburgh, PA: University of Pittsburgh Press.

Huber, Evelyne and Fred Solt. 2004. "Successes and Failures of Neoliberalism," *Latin American Research Review* 39, 3 (October): 150–164.

Huber, Evelyne and John D. Stephens. 2010. "Successful Social Policy Regimes? Political Economy, Politics, and Social Policy in Argentina, Chile, Uruguay, and Costa Rica," in Scott Mainwaring and Timothy R. Scully, eds. *Democratic Governance in Latin America*. Stanford, CA: Stanford University Press, 155–209.

2012. *Democracy and the Left: Social Policy and Redistribution in Latin America*. Chicago, IL: University Press of Chicago.

Hug, Simon. 2001. *Altering Party Systems: Strategic Behavior and the Emergence of New Political Parties in Western Democracies*. Ann Arbor, MI: University of Michigan Press.

Huneeus, Carlos. 2003. "A Highly Institutionalized Political Party: Christian Democracy in Chile," in Scott Mainwaring and Timothy R. Scully, eds. *Christian Democracy in Latin America*. Stanford, CA: Stanford University Press, 121–161.

Hunter, Wendy. 2010. *The Transformation of the Workers' Party in Brazil, 1989–2009*. New York: Cambridge University Press.

Hunter, Wendy and Timothy Power. 2007. "Rewarding Lula: Executive Power, Social Policy, and the Brazilian Elections of 2006," *Journal of Latin American Politics and Society*. 49, 1 (Spring): 1–30.

Huntington, Samuel P. 1968. *Political Order in Changing Societies*. New Haven, CT: Yale University Press.

1991. *The Third Wave: Democratization in the Late Twentieth Century*. Norman, OK: University of Oklahoma Press.

Inglehart, Ronald. 1984. "The Changing Structure of Political Cleavages in Western Society," in Russell J. Dalton, Scott C. Flanagan, and Paul Alan Beck, eds. *Electoral Change in Advanced Industrial Democracies: Realignment or Dealignment*. Princeton, NJ: Princeton University Press, 25–69.

Inter-American Development Bank. Various editions. *Economic and Social Progress in Latin America*. Washington, D.C.: IDB.

Inter-American Development Bank. 1997. *Latin America After a Decade of Reforms*. Washington, D.C.: IDB.

Inter-American Development Bank. 2004. *Good Jobs Wanted: Labor Markets in Latin America*. Washington, D.C.: IDB.

International Labour Organization. 1997a. *Latin America and the Caribbean: 1997 Labour Overview*. Lima: ILO.

1997b. *World Labour Report 1997–98: Industrial Relations, Democracy, and Social Stability*. Geneva: ILO.

1998. *Latin America and the Caribbean 1998 Labour Overview*. Lima: ILO.

2005. *Latin America and the Caribbean 2005 Labour Overview*. Lima: ILO.

Jones, Mark P. 1995. *Electoral Laws and the Survival of Presidential Democracy*. Notre Dame, IN: University of Notre Dame Press.

Karl, Terry Lynn. 1987. "Petroleum and Political Pacts: The Transition to Democracy in Venezuela," *Latin American Research Review* 22: 63–94.

1997. *The Paradox of Plenty: Oil Booms and Petro-States*. Berkeley, CA: University of California Press.

2000. "Economic Inequality and Democratic Instability," *Journal of Democracy* 11, 1 (January): 149–156.

Katz, Richard S. and Peter Mair. 1995. "Changing Models of Party Organization and Party Democracy: The Emergence of the Cartel Party," *Party Politics* 1, 1: 5–31.

Katzenstein, Peter J. 1985. *Small States in World Markets: Industrial Policy in Europe.* Ithaca, NY: Cornell University Press.

2005. *A World of Regions: Asia and Europe in the American Empirium.* Ithaca, NY: Cornell University Press.

Kaufman, Robert and Barbara Stallings, eds. 1989. *Debt and Democracy in Latin America.* Boulder, CO: Westview Press.

Kay, Cristóbal. 1999. "Rural Development: From Agrarian Reform to Neoliberalism and Beyond," in Robert N. Gwynne and Cristóbal Kay, eds. *Latin America Transformed: Globalization and Modernity.* London and New York: Arnold Publishers and Oxford University Press, 272–304.

Keck, Margaret. 1992. *The Workers' Party and Democratization in Brazil.* New Haven, CT: Yale University Press.

Keck, Margaret E. and Kathryn Sikkink. 1998. *Activists Beyond Borders: Advocacy Networks in International Politics.* Ithaca, NY: Cornell University Press.

Key, Jr., V. O. 1955. "A Theory of Critical Elections," *Journal of Politics* 17: 3–18.

Kiewiet, D. Roderick. 1983. *Macroeconomics and Micropolitics: The Electoral Effects of Economic Issues.* Chicago, IL: University of Chicago Press.

Kinder, Donald R. and D. Roderick Kiewiet. 1979. "Economic Discontent and Political Behavior: The Role of Personal Grievances and Collective Economic Judgments in Congressional Voting." *American Journal of Political Science* 23, 3 (August): 495–327.

Kingstone, Peter J. 1999. *Crafting Coalitions for Reform: Business Preferences, Political Institutions, and Neoliberal Reform in Brazil.* University Park, PA: Pennsylvania State University Press.

Kirchheimer, Otto. 1966. "The Transformation of the Western European Party Systems," in Joseph LaPalombara and Myron Weiner, eds. *Political Parties and Political Development.* Princeton, NJ: Princeton University Press, 177–200.

Kitschelt, Herbert. 1994. *The Transformation of European Social Democracy.* New York: Cambridge University Press.

2000. "Linkages Between Citizens and Politicians in Democratic Politics," *Comparative Political Studies* 33, 6/7 (August–September): 845–879.

2006. "Movement Parties," in Richard S. Katz and William Crotty, eds. *Handbook of Party Politics.* Thousand Oak, CA: Sage, 278–290.

Kitschelt, Herbert, Kirk A. Hawkins, Juan Pablo Luna, Guillermo Rosas, and Elizabeth J. Zechmeister. 2009. *Latin American Party Systems.* New York: Cambridge University Press.

Kitschelt, Herbert, Zdenka Mansfeldova, Radoslaw Markowski, and Gabor Toka. 1999. *Post-Communist Party Systems: Competition, Representation, and Inter-Party Cooperation.* New York: Cambridge University Press.

Kornblith, Miriam and Daniel H. Levine. 1995. "Venezuela: The Life and Times of the Party System," in Scott Mainwaring and Timothy R. Scully, eds. *Building Democratic Institutions: Party Systems in Latin America.* Stanford, CA: Stanford University Press, 37–71.

Krueger, Anne O. 1990. "Government Failures in Development," *Journal of Economic Perspectives* 4, 3 (Summer): 9–23.

Kurian, George T. 1982. *The Encyclopedia of the Third World*. New York: Facts on File.

Kurtz, Marcus. 2004a. "The Dilemmas of Democracy in the Open Economy: Lessons from Latin America," *World Politics* 56, 2 (January): 262–302.

2004b. *Free Market Democracy and the Chilean and Mexican Countryside*. New York: Cambridge University Press.

La Democracia en América Latina: Hacia una Democracia de Ciudadanas y Ciudadanos. 2004. New York: Programa de las Naciones Unidas para el Desarrollo.

La Economía Argentina. Various issues. Buenos Aires, Argentina: Consejo Técnico de Inversiones S. A.

La Nación. Buenos Aires, Argentina. Feb. 11, 1992.

Laclau, Ernesto. 1977. *Politics and Ideology in Marxist Theory*. London: NLB.

Lanzaro, Jorge. 2004a. "La Izquierda se Acerca a los Uruguayos y los Uruguayos se Acercan a la Izquierda. Claves de Desarrollo del Frente Amplio," in Jorge Lanzaro, ed. *La Izquierda Uruguaya: Entre la Oposición y el Gobierno*. Montevideo, Uruguay: Editorial Fin de Siglo, 13–107.

ed. 2004b. *La Izquierda Uruguaya: Entre la Oposición y el Gobierno*. Montevideo, Uruguay: Editorial Fin de Siglo.

2011. "Uruguay: A Social Democratic Government in Latin America," in Steven Levitsky and Kenneth M. Roberts, eds. *The Resurgence of the Latin American Left*. Baltimore, MD: Johns Hopkins University Press, 348–374.

LatinNews Daily Report, July 12, 2012.

Latinobarómetro. Various editions. *Informe Latinobarómetro*. Santiago, Chile: Latinobarómetro.

Lawson, Kay. 1980. *Political Parties and Linkage: A Comparative Perspective*, New Haven, CT: Yale University Press.

Lehoucq, Fabrice. 2005. "Costa Rica: Paradise in Doubt," *Journal of Democracy* 16, 3 (July): 140–154.

Levitsky, Steven. 1998a. "Crisis, Party Adaptation and Regime Stability in Argentina: The Case of Peronism, 1989–1995," *Party Politics* 4, 4: 445–470.

1998b. "Institutionalization and Peronism: The Concept, the Case, and the Case for Unpacking the Concept," *Party Politics* 4, 1: 77–92.

2003. *Transforming Labor-Based Parties in Latin America: Argentine Peronism in Comparative Perspective*. New York: Cambridge University Press.

Levitsky, Steven and Maxwell A. Cameron. 2003. "Democracy Without Parties? Political Parties and Regime Change in Fujimori's Peru," *Latin American Politics and Society* 45, 3 (Fall): 1–33.

Levitsky, Steven and María Victoria Murillo. Forthcoming. "Building Institutions on Weak Foundations: Lessons from Latin America," in Scott Mainwaring, Daniel Brinks, and Marcelo Leiras, eds. *Reflections on Uneven Democracies: The Legacy of Guillermo O'Donnell*. Baltimore, MD: Johns Hopkins University Press.

Levitsky, Steven and Kenneth M. Roberts. 2011a. "Latin America's 'Left Turn': A Framework for Analysis," in Steven Levitsky and Kenneth M. Roberts, eds. *The Resurgence of the Latin American Left*. Baltimore, MD: Johns Hopkins University Press, 1–28.

eds. 2011b. *The Resurgence of the Latin American Left*. Baltimore, MD: Johns Hopkins University Press.

Lewis-Beck, Michael S. 1988. *Economics and Elections: The Major Western Democracies*. Ann Arbor, MI: University of Michigan Press.

Lindert, Kathy, Anja Linder, Jason Hobbs, and Bénédicte de la Briéreèè. 2007. *The Nuts and Bolts of Brazil's Bolsa Familia Program: Implementing Conditional Cash Transfers in a Decentralized Context*. SP Discussion Paper No. 7079. Washington, D.C.: World Bank.

Linz, Juan J. and Alfred Stepan. 1996. *Problems of Democratic Transition and Consolidation: Southern Europe, South America, and Post-Communist Europe*. Baltimore, MD: Johns Hopkins University Press.

Lipset, Seymour Martin. 1959. "Some Social Requisites of Democracy: Economic Development and Political Legitimacy," *American Political Science Review* 53, 1 (March): 69–105.

Lipset, Seymour Martin and Stein Rokkan. 1967. "Cleavage Structures, Party Systems, and Voter Alignments: An Introduction," in Seymour Martin Lipset and Stein Rokkan, eds. *Party Systems and Voter Alignments: Cross-National Perspectives*. New York: Free Press, 1–64.

Loayza, Norman, Pablo Fajnzylber and César Calderón. 2004. *Economic Growth in Latin America and the Caribbean: Stylized Facts, Explanations, and Forecasts*. Central Bank of Chile Working Papers No. 265. Santiago, Chile: Banco Central de Chile.

Londoño, Juan Luis and Miguel Székely. 2000. "Persistent Poverty and Excess Inequality: Latin America, 1970–1995." *Journal of Applied Economics*, 3(1): 93–134.

López Maya, Margarita. 1997. "The Rise of Causa R in Venezuela," in Douglas A. Chalmers, Carlos M. Vilas, Katherine Hite, Scott B. Martin, Kerianne Piester, and Monique Segarra, eds. *The New Politics of Inequality in Latin America: Rethinking Participation and Representation*. Oxford: Oxford University Press, 117–143.

2003. "Hugo Chávez Frías: His Movement and His Presidency," in Steve Ellner and Daniel Hellinger, eds. *Venezuelan Politics in the Chávez Era: Class, Polarization, and Conflict*. Boulder, CO: Lynne Rienner Press, 73–92.

2005. *Del Viernes Negro al Referendo Revocatorio*. Caracas, Venezuela: Alfadil Ediciones.

Lora, Eduardo. 2001. "Structural Reforms in Latin America: What Has Been Reformed and How to Measure It," Working Paper 348. Washington, D.C.: Inter-American Development Bank.

Lora, Eduardo and Ugo Panizza. 2003. "The Future of Structural Reform." *Journal of Democracy* 14, 2 (April): 123–137.

Lucero, José Antonio. 2001. "Crisis and Contention in Ecuador," *Journal of Democracy* 12, 2 (April): 59–73.

2008. *Struggles of Voice in Latin America: The Politics of Indigenous Representation in the Andes*. Pittsburgh, PA: University of Pittsburgh Press.

Luebbert, Gregory M. 1991. *Liberalism, Fascism, and Social Democracy: Social Classes and the Political Origins of Regimes in Interwar Europe*. Oxford: Oxford University Press.

Luengo D., Nestor Luis and Maria Gabriela Ponce Z. 1996. "Lectura Oblicua del Proceso Electoral de 1995," *Politeia* 19: 63–80.

Luna, Juan Pablo. 2006. *Programmatic and Non-Programmatic Party-Voter Linkages in Two Institionalized Party Systems: Chile and Uruguay in Comparative Perspective*. Ph.D. Dissertation, University of North Carolina at Chapel Hill.

Luna, Juan Pablo and Fernando Filgueira. 2009. "The Left Turns as Multiple Paradigmatic Crises," *Third World Quarterly* 30, 2 (March): 371–395.

Lupu, Noam. 2011. *Party Brands in Crisis: Partisanship, Brand Dilution, and the Breakdown of Political Parties in Latin America*. Ph.D. dissertation, Princeton University.

Lupu, Noam and Susan Stokes. 2010. "Democracy, Interrupted: Regime Change and Partisanship in Twentieth-Century Argentina," *Electoral Studies* 29, 1: 91–104.

Madrid, Raúl. 2003. *Retiring the State: The Politics of Pension Privatization in Latin America and Beyond*. Stanford, CA: Stanford University Press.

2005. "Ethnic Cleavages and Electoral Volatility in Latin America," *Comparative Political Studies* 38, 1 (October): 1–20.

2008. "The Rise of Ethno-Populism in Latin America," *World Politics* 60, 3 (April): 475–508.

2009. "The Origins of the Two Lefts in Latin America," *Political Science Quarterly* 125, 4 (Winter): 1–23.

2012. *The Rise of Ethnic Politics in Latin America*. New York: Cambridge University Press.

Madsen, Douglas and Peter G. Snow. 1991. *The Charismatic Bond: Political Behavior in Time of Crisis*. Cambridge, MA: Harvard University Press.

Maguire, Maria. 1983. "Is There Still Persistence? Electoral Change in Western Europe, 1948–1979," in Hans Daalder and Peter Mair, eds. *Western European Party Systems: Continuity and Change*. Beverly Hills, CA: Sage, 67–94.

Mahon, James. 1996. *Mobile Capital and Latin American Development*. University Park, PA: Pennsylvania State University Press.

Mahoney, James. 2001a. *The Legacies of Liberalism: Path Dependence and Political Regimes in Central America*. Baltimore, MD: Johns Hopkins University Press.

2001b. "Path Dependent Explanations of Regime Change: Central America in Comparative Perspective," *Studies in Comparative International Development* 36, 1 (Spring): 111–141.

Mahoney, James and Kathleen Thelen, eds. 2010. *Explaining Institutional Change: Ambiguity, Agency, and Power*. New York: Cambridge University Press.

Mainwaring, Scott P. 1999a. *Rethinking Party Systems in the Third Wave of Democratization: The Case of Brazil*. Stanford, CA: Stanford University Press.

1999b. "The Surprising Resilience of Elected Governments," *Journal of Democracy* 10, 3 (July): 101–114.

Mainwaring, Scott, Ana María Bejarano, and Eduardo Pizarro, eds. 2006. *The Crisis of Democratic Representation in the Andes*. Stanford, CA: Stanford University Press.

Mainwaring, Scott and Aníbal Pérez-Liñán. 2005. "Latin American Democratization since 1978: Democratic Transitions, Breakdowns, and Erosions," in Frances Hagopian and Scott P. Mainwaring, eds. *The Third Wave of Democratization in Latin America*. New York: Cambridge University Press, 14–59.

Mainwaring, Scott and Timothy R. Scully, eds. 1995a. *Building Democratic Institutions: Party Systems in Latin America*. Stanford, CA: Stanford University Press.

1995b. "Introduction: Party Systems in Latin America," in Scott Mainwaring and Timothy R. Scully, eds. *Building Democratic Institutions: Party Systems in Latin America*. Stanford, CA: Stanford University Press, 1–34.

Mainwaring, Scott and Edurne Zoco. 2007. "Political Sequences and the Stabilization of Interparty Competition: Electoral Volatility in Old and New Democracies," *Party Politics* 13, 2 (March): 155–178.

Malloy, James M., ed. 1977. *Authoritarianism and Corporatism in Latin America.* Pittsburgh, PA: University of Pittsburgh Press.

March, James G. and Johan P Olsen. 1989. *Rediscovering Institutions: The Organizational Basis of Politics.* New York: Free Press.

Martinez, Gabriel X. 2006. "The Political Economy of the Ecuadorian Financial Crisis," *Cambridge Journal of Economics* 30: 567–585.

Martz, John D. 1980. "The Regionalist Expression of Populism: Guayaquil and the CFP, 1948–1960," *Journal of Interamerican Studies and World Affairs* 22, 3 (August): 289–314.

McAdam, Doug and Sidney Tarrow. 2010. "Ballots and Barricades: On the Reciprocal Relationship Between Elections and Social Movements," *Perspectives on Politics* 8, 2 (June): 529–542.

McClintock, Cynthia. 1981. *Peasant Cooperatives and Political Change in Peru.* Princeton, NJ: Princeton University Press.

McGuire, James W. 1995. "Political Parties and Democracy in Argentina," in Scott Mainwaring and Timothy R. Scully, eds. *Building Democratic Institutions: Party Systems in Latin America.* Stanford, CA: Stanford University Press, 200–246.
    1997. *Peronism Without Perón: Unions, Parties, and Democracy in Argentina.* Stanford, CA: Stanford University Press.

Meltzer, Allan H. and Scott F. Richard. 1981. "A Rational Theory of the Size of Government," *Journal of Political Economy* 89, 5 (October): 914–927.

Mesa-Lago, Carmelo with Alberto Arenas de Mesa, Ivan Brenes, Verónica Montecinos, and Mark Samara. 2000. *Market, Socialist, and Mixed Economies: Comparative Policy and Performance in Chile, Cuba and Costa Rica.* Baltimore, MD: Johns Hopkins University Press.

Middlebrook, Kevin J. 1995. *The Paradox of Revolution: Labor, the State, and Authoritarianism in Mexico.* Baltimore, MD: Johns Hopkins University Press.

Mitchell, Neil J. 1996. "Theoretical and Empirical Issues in the Comparative Measurement of Union Power and Corporatism," *British Journal of Political Science* 26 (July): 419–428.

Molina Vega, José E. and Carmen Pérez Baralt. 1996. "Elecciones Regionales de 1995: La Consolidación de la Abstención, el Personalismo, y la Desalineación," *Cuestiones Políticas* 16: 73–90.

Mommer, Bernard. 2003. "Subversive Oil," in Steve Ellner and Daniel Hellinger, eds. *Venezuelan Politics in the Chávez Era: Class, Polarization, and Conflict.* Boulder, CO: Lynne Rienner Publishers, 131–146.

Mora y Araujo, Manuel and Ignacio Llorente, eds. 1980. *El Voto Peronista: Ensayos de Sociología Electoral Argentina.* Buenos Aires, Argentina: Editorial Sudamericana.

Morales Quiroga, Mauricio. 2012. "The Concertación's Defeat in Chile's 2009–2010 Presidential Elections," *Latin American Politics and Society* 54, 2 (Summer): 79–107.

Morgan, Jana. 2011. *Bankrupt Representation and Party System Collapse.* University Park, PA: Pennsylvania State University Press.

Morgan, Jana, Jonathan Hartlyn, and Rosario Espinal. 2011. "Dominican Party System Continuity amid Regional Transformations: Economic Policy, Clientelism, and Migration Flows," *Latin American Politics and Society* 53, 1: 1–32.

Morgenstern, Scott. 2004. *Patterns of Legislative Politics: Roll-Call Voting in Latin America and the United States.* New York: Cambridge University Press.

Morley, Samuel A., Roberto Machado, and Stefano Pettinato. 1999. "Index of Structural Reform in Latin America," *Serie Reformas Económicas* 12. Santiago, Chile: Comisión Económica Para América Latina y el Caribe.

Munck, Gerardo. 1998. *Authoritarianism and Democratization: Soldiers and Workers in Argentina, 1976–1983*. University Park, PA: Pennsylvania State University Press.

Murillo, María Victoria. 2000. "From Populism to Neoliberalism: Labor Unions and Market Reforms in Latin America," *World Politics* 52, 2 (January): 135–174.

2001. *Labor Unions, Partisan Coalitions, and Market Reforms in Latin America*. New York: Cambridge University Press.

2009. *Political Competition, Partisanship, and Policymaking in Latin American Public Utilities*. New York: Cambridge University Press.

Murillo, María Victoria, Virginia Oliveros, and Milan Vaishnav. 2011. "Economic Constraints and Presidential Agency," in Steven Levitsky and Kenneth M. Roberts, eds. *The Resurgence of the Latin American Left*. Baltimore, MD: Johns Hopkins University Press, 52–70.

Myers, David J. 1998. "Venezuela's Political Party System: Defining Events, Reactions, and the Diluting of Structural Cleavages," *Party Politics* 4, 4 (October): 495–521.

Naím, Moisés. 1993. *Paper Tigers and Minotaurs: The Politics of Venezuela's Economic Reforms*. Washington, D.C.: Carnegie Endowment for International Peace.

Nash, June. 1993. *We Eat the Mines and the Mines Eat Us*. New York: Columbia University Press.

Nelson, Joan, ed. 1990. *Economic Crisis and Policy Choice: The Politics of Adjustment in the Third World*. Princeton, NJ: Princeton University Press.

ed. 1994. *A Precarious Balance: Democracy and Economic Reform in Latin America*. San Francisco, CA: Institute for Contemporary Studies.

Nie, Norman H., Sidney Verba, and John R. Petrocik. 1976. *The Changing American Voter*. Cambridge, MA: Harvard University Press.

Nohlen, Dieter, ed. 2005. *Elections in the Americas: A Data Handbook*, Vols. 1 and 2. Oxford: Oxford University Press.

Norden, Deborah L. 2003. "Democracy in Uniform: Chávez and the Venezuelan Armed Forces," in Steve Ellner and Daniel Hellinger, eds. *Venezuelan Politics in the Chávez Era: Class, Polarization, and Conflict*. Boulder, CO: Lynne Rienner Publishers, 93–112.

Novaro, Marcos and Vicente Palermo. 1998. *Los Caminos de la Centroizquierda: Dilemas y Desafíos del Frepaso y de la Alianza*. Buenos Aires, Argentina: Editorial Losada.

O'Donnell, Guillermo. 1973. *Modernization and Bureaucratic-Authoritarianism: Studies in South American Politics*. Berkeley, CA: Institute of International Studies.

1994a. "Delegative Democracy," *Journal of Democracy* 5,1 (January): 55–69.

1994b. "The State, Democratization, and Some Conceptual Problems," in William Smith, Carlos Acuña, and Eduardo Gamarra, eds. *Latin American Political Economy in the Age of Neoliberal Reform: Theoretical and Comparative Perspectives for the 1990s*. New Brunswick, NJ: Transaction Books, 157–180.

O'Donnell, Guillermo and Philippe C. Schmitter. 1986. *Transitions from Authoritarian Rule: Tentative Conclusions about Uncertain Democracies*. Baltimore, MD: Johns Hopkins University Press.

Ossowski, Stanislaw. 1963. *Class Structure in the Social Consciousness*. New York: Free Press of Glencoe.

Ostiguy, Pierre. 1998. *Peronism and Anti-Peronism: Class-Cultural Cleavages and Political Identity in Argentina*. Ph.D. dissertation, University of California, Berkeley.

Oxhorn, Philip. 1995. *Organizing Civil Society: The Popular Sectors and the Struggle for Democracy in Chile*. University Park, PA: Pennsylvania State University Press.

1998. "Is the Century of Corporatism Over? Neoliberalism and the Rise of Neopluralism," in P. Oxhorn and G. Ducatenzeiler, eds. *What Kind of Democracy? What Kind of Market? Latin America in the Age of Neoliberalism*. University Park, PA: Pennsylvania State University Press, 195–217.

2011. *Sustaining Civil Society: Economic Change, Democracy, and the Social Construction of Citizenship in Latin America*. University Park, PA: Pennsylvania State University Press.

Paige, Jeffery M. 1975. *Agrarian Revolution: Social Movements and Export Agriculture in the Underdeveloped World*. New York: Free Press.

Pakulsi, Jan and Malcolm Waters. 1996. *The Death of Class*. London: Sage Publications.

Palermo, Vicente and Marcos Novaro. 1996. *Política y Poder en el Gobierno de Menem*. Buenos Aires, Argentina: Grupo Editorial Norma.

Panebianco, Angelo. 1988. *Political Parties: Organization and Power*. Cambridge: Cambridge University Press.

Pastor Fasquelle, Rodolfo. 2011. "The 2009 Coup and the Struggle for Democracy in Honduras," *NACLA Report on the Americas* 44, 1 (January–February): 16–21.

Payne, James L. 1968. *Patterns of Conflict in Colombia*. New Haven, CT: Yale University Press.

Paz Aguilar, Ernesto. 1992. "The Origin and Development of Political Parties in Honduras," in Louis W. Goodman, William M. LeoGrande, and Johanna Mendelson Forman, eds. *Political Parties and Democracy in Central America*. Boulder, CO: Westview Press, 161–174.

Pearson, Neale J. 1987. "Honduras," in Gerald Michael Greenfield and Sheldon L. Maram, eds. *Latin American Labor Organizations*. Westport, CT: Greenwood Press, 463–494.

Pedersen, Mogens N. 1983. "Changing Patterns of Electoral Volatility in European Party Systems, 1948–1977: Explorations in Explanation," in Hans Daalder and Peter Mair, eds. *Western European Party Systems: Continuity and Change*. London: Sage Publications, 29–66.

Peeler, John A. 1998. *Building Democracy in Latin America*. Boulder, CO: Lynne Rienner Publishers.

Pereira, Anthony W. 1997. *The End of the Peasantry: The Rural Labor Movement in Northeast Brazil, 1961–1988*. Pittsburgh, PA: University of Pittsburgh Press.

Pierson, Paul. 2000. "Increasing Returns, Path Dependence, and the Study of Politics," *American Political Science Review* 94, 2 (June): 251–267.

2004. *Politics in Time: History, Institutions, and Social Analysis*. New York: Cambridge University Press.

Pino, Hugo Noé and Alcides Hernández. 1990. "La Economía Hondureño en los Ochenta y Perspectivas para los Noventas," in Rafael del Cid, Hugo Noé Pino and Alcides Hernández, *Honduras: Crisis Económica y Proceso de Democratización Política*. Tegulcigalpa, Honduras: Centro de Documentación de Honduras.

Pizarro Leongómez, Eduardo. 2006. "Giants with Feet of Clay: Political Parties in Colombia," in Scott Mainwaring, Ana María Bejarano, and Eduardo Pizarro, eds.

The Crisis of Democratic Representation in the Andes. Stanford, CA: Stanford University Press, 78–99.

Polanyi, Karl. 1944. *The Great Transformation*. New York: Farrar and Rinehart.

Portes, Alejandro and Kelly Hoffman. 2003. "Latin American Class Structures: Their Composition and Change During the Neoliberal Era," *Latin American Research Review* 38, 1 (February): 41–82.

Posas, Mario. 1992. "Los Sindicatos y la Construcción de la Democracia en Honduras," in *Puntos de Vista: Temas Políticos*. Tegulcigalpa, Honduras: Centro de Documentación de Honduras.

2004. *Breve Historia de las Organizaciones Sindicales de Honduras*. Tegulcigalpa, Honduras: Universidad Pedagógica Nacional Francisco Morazán.

Powell, Eleanor Neff and Joshua A. Tucker. 2009. "New Approaches to Electoral Volatility: Evidence from Postcommunist Countries," paper presented at the 2009 Annual Meeting of the American Political Science Association, Toronto, September 3–6.

Powell, John Duncan. 1971. *Political Mobilization of the Venezuelan Peasant*. Cambridge, MA: Harvard University Press.

Power, Timothy J. 2000. *The Political Right in Postauthoritarian Brazil: Elites, Institutions, and Democratization*. University Park, PA: Pennsylvania State University Press.

Pribble, Jennifer. 2013. *Welfare and Party Politics in Latin America*. New York: Cambridge University Press.

Pribble, Jennifer and Evelyne Huber. 2011. "Social Policy and Redistribution: Chile and Uruguay," in Steven Levitsky and Kenneth M. Roberts, eds. *The Resurgence of the Latin American Left*. Baltimore, MD: Johns Hopkins University Press, 117–138.

Queirolo, Rosario. 2013. *The Success of the Left in Latin America*. Notre Dame, IN: Notre Dame University Press.

Ragin, Charles. 1987. *The Comparative Method: Moving Beyond Qualitative and Quantitative Strategies*. Berkeley, CA: University of California Press.

Ramos, Joseph. 1986. *Neoconservative Economics in the Southern Cone of Latin America, 1973–1983*. Baltimore, MD: Johns Hopkins University Press.

Ranis, Peter. 1995. *Class, Democracy, and Labor in Contemporary Argentina*. New Brunswick, NJ: Transaction Publishers.

Remmer, Karen L. 1980. "Political Demobilization in Chile, 1973–1978," *Comparative Politics* 12, 3 (April): 275–301.

1984. *Party Competition in Argentina and Chile: Political Recruitment and Public Policy, 1890–1930*. Lincoln, NE: University of Nebraska Press.

1990. "Democracy and Economic Crisis: The Latin American Experience," *World Politics* 42, 3 (April): 315–335.

1991. "The Political Impact of Economic Crisis in Latin America in the 1980s," *American Political Science Review* 85, 3 (September): 777–800.

1992–1993. "The Process of Democratization in Latin America." *Studies in Comparative International Development* 27, 4 (Winter): 3–24.

2003. "Elections and Economics in Contemporary Latin America," in Carol Wise and Riordan Roett, eds. *Post-Stabilization Politics in Latin America: Competition, Transition, Collapse*. Washington, D.C.: Brookings Institution Press, 31–55.

2012. "The Rise of Leftist-Populist Governance in Latin America: The Roots of Electoral Change," *Comparative Political Studies* 45, 8: 947–972.

República de Venezuela. 1995. *Venezuela Ante la Cumbre Mundial sobre Desarrollo Social*. Caracas.

Rice, Roberta. 2012. *The New Politics of Protest: Indigenous Mobilization in Latin America's Neoliberal Era*. Tucson, AZ: University of Arizona Press.

Roberts, Kenneth M. 1995. "Neoliberalism and the Transformation of Populism in Latin America: The Peruvian Case," *World Politics* 48, 1 (October): 82–116.

  1998. *Deepening Democracy? The Modern Left and Social Movements in Chile and Peru*. Stanford, CA: Stanford University Press.

  2002. "Social Inequalities Without Class Cleavages in Latin America's Neoliberal Era," *Studies in Comparative International Development*, 36, 4: 3–34.

  2008. "The Mobilization of Opposition to Economic Liberalization," in Margaret Levi, Simon Jackman, and Nancy Rosenblum, eds. *Annual Review of Political Science*, Vol. 11. Palo Alto, CA: Annual Reviews, 327–349.

Roberts, Kenneth M. and Moises Arce. 1998. "Neoliberalism and Lower-Class Voting Behavior in Peru," *Comparative Political Studies* 31, 2 (April): 217–246.

Roberts, Kenneth M. and Erik Wibbels. 1999. "Party Systems and Electoral Volatility in Latin America: A Test of Economic, Institutional, and Structural Explanations," *American Political Science Review* 93, 3 (September): 575–590.

Rodríguez, Francisco. 2010. "Does One Size Fit All in Policy Reform? Cross-National Evidence and Its Implications for Latin America," in Scott Mainwaring and Timothy R. Scully, eds. *Democratic Governance in Latin America*. Stanford, CA: Stanford University Press, 88–128.

Rodríguez, Miguel. 1994. "Comment," in John Williamson, ed. *The Political Economy of Policy Reform*. Washington, D.C.: Institute for International Economics, 376–381.

Rogowski, Ronald. 1993. "Comparative Politics," in Ada Finifter, ed. *Political Science: The State of the Discipline*. Washington, D.C.: American Political Science Association, 431–450.

Romero, Aníbal. 1997. "Rearranging the Deck Chairs on the Titanic: The Agony of Democracy in Venezuela," *Latin American Research Review* 32, 1: 3–36.

Rosenblum, Nancy. 2008. *On the Side of Angels: An Appreciation of Parties and Partisanship*. Princeton, NJ: Princeton University Press.

Ruiz, Carlos. 2012. "New Social Conflicts under Bachelet," *Latin American Perspectives* 39, 4 (July): 71–84.

Salamanca, Luis. 1995. "La Incorporación de la Confederación de Trabajadores de Venezuela al Sistema Político Venezolano: 1958–1980," *Revista de la Facultad de Ciencias Jurídicas y Políticas* 95: 189–399.

  1998. *Obreros, Movimiento Social y Democracia en Venezuela*. Caracas, Venezuela: Facultad de Ciencias Jurídicas y Políticas, Universidad Central de Venezuela.

Samuels, David. 2004. "From Socialism to Social Democracy: Party Organization and the Transformation of the Workers' Party in Brazil," *Comparative Political Studies* 37, 9: 999–1024.

Samuels, David and Matthew Shugart. 2010. *Presidents, Parties and Prime Ministers*. New York: Cambridge University Press.

Sanchez, Omar. 2009. "Party Non-Systems: A Conceptual Innovation," *Party Politics* 15, 4: 487–520.

Sandbrook, Richard, Marc Edelman, Patrick Heller, and Judith Teichman. 2007. *Social Democracy in the Global Periphery: Origins, Challenges, Prospects*. New York: Cambridge University Press.

Sandoval, Salvador A. M. 2001. "The Crisis of the Brazilian Labor Movement and the Emergence of Alternative Forms of Working-Class Contention in the 1990s," *Revista Psicologia Política* 1, 1 (January–June): 173–193.

Sartori, Giovanni. 1976. *Parties and Party Systems: A Framework for Analysis.* Cambridge: Cambridge University Press.

Sawyer, Suzana. 2004. *Crude Chronicles: Indigenous Politics, Multinational Oil, and Neoliberalism in Ecuador.* Durham, NC: Duke University Press.

Schady, Norbert R. 2000. "The Political Economy of Expenditures by the Peruvian Social Fund (FONCODES), 1991–95," *American Political Science Review* 94, 2 (June): 289–304.

Schamis, Hector. 1991. "Reconceptualizing Latin American Authoritarianism in the 1970s: From Bureaucratic-Authoritarianism to Neoconservatism," *Comparative Politics* 23, 2 (January): 201–220.

1999. "Distributional Coalitions and the Politics of Economic Reform in Latin America," *World Politics* 51, 2: 236–68.

Schattschneider, E. E. 1975. *The Semi-Sovereign People: A Realist's View of Democracy in America.* Hinsdale, IL: Dryden Press.

Schelotto, Salvador. 2004. "Por el Ojo de una Cerradura. Una Mirada sobre la Experiencia de Gobierno Municipal de la Izquierda en Montevideo (1990–2004)," in Jorge Lanzaro, ed. *La Izquierda Uruguaya: Entre la Oposición y el Gobierno.* Montevideo, Uruguay: Editorial Fin de Siglo, 381–434.

Schmitter, Philippe C. 1971. *Interest Conflict and Political Change in Brazil.* Stanford, CA: Stanford University Press.

2001. "Parties Are Not What They Once Were," in Larry Diamond and Richard Gunther, eds. *Political Parties and Democracy.* Baltimore, MA: Johns Hopkins University Press, 67–89.

Schuldt, Jurgen. 1994. "Crísis, Ajuste y Cambio Sociopolítico en Ecuador, 1982–1992: Algunos Impactos del Neoliberalismo," in Gerónimo de Sierra, ed. *Los Pequeños Países de América Latina en la Hora Neoliberal.* Caracas, Venezuela: Editorial Nueva Sociedad, 121–152.

Schumpeter, Joseph A. 1950. *Capitalism, Socialism and Democracy,* 3rd ed. New York: Harper and Row.

Scully, Timothy R. 1992. *Rethinking the Center: Party Politics in Nineteenth and Twentieth Century Chile.* Stanford, CA: Stanford University Press.

1995. "Reconstituting Party Politics in Chile," in Scott Mainwaring and Timothy R. Scully, eds. *Building Democratic Institutions: Party Systems in Latin America.* Stanford, CA: Stanford University Press, 100–137.

Seawright, Jason. 2012. *Party System Collapse: The Roots of Crisis in Peru and Venezuela.* Stanford, CA: Stanford University Press.

Seligson, Mitchell A. 2002. "Trouble in Paradise? The Erosion of System Support in Costa Rica, 1978–1999," *Latin American Research Review* 37, 1: 160–186.

Seligson, Mitchell A. and John A. Booth. 2009. *Predicting Coups? Democratic Vulnerabilities, the AmericasBarometer, and the 2009 Honduran Crisis.* AmericasBarometer Insights Series. Vanderbilt University, Latin American Public Opinion Project (http://www.vanderbilt.edu/lapop/insights/I0821en.pdf).

Seligson, Mitchell A. and Juliana Martínez Franzoni. 2010. "Limits to Costa Rican Heterodoxy: What Has Changed in 'Paradise'?" in Scott Mainwaring and

Timothy R. Scully, eds. *Democratic Governance in Latin America*. Stanford, CA: Stanford University Press, 307–337.

Shefter, Martin. 1994. *Political Parties and the State: The American Historical Experience*. Princeton, NJ: Princeton University Press.

Short, R. P. 1984. "The Role of Public Enterprises: An International Statistical Comparison," in R. Floyd, C. Gray, and R. P. Short, eds. *Public Enterprise in Mixed Economies: Some Macroeconomic Aspects*. Washington, D.C.: International Monetary Fund, 110–181.

Shugart, Matthew Soberg and John M. Carey. 1992. *Presidents and Assemblies: Constitutional Design and Electoral Dynamics*. New York: Cambridge University Press.

Siavelis, Peter M. 2000. *The President and Congress in Postauthoritarian Chile: Institutional Constraints to Democratic Consolidation*. University Park, PA: Pennsylvania State University Press.

Silva, Eduardo. 1996. *The State and Capital in Chile: Business Elites, Technocrats, and Market Economics*. Boulder, CO: Westview Press.

2009. *Challenging Neoliberalism in Latin America*. New York: Cambridge University Press.

Skidmore, Thomas E. 1967. *Politics in Brazil, 1930–1964: An Experiment in Democracy*. New York: Oxford University Press.

1977. "The Politics of Economic Stabilization in Postwar Latin America," in James M. Malloy, ed. *Authoritarianism and Corporatism in Latin America*. Pittsburgh, PA: University of Pittsburgh Press, 149–190.

Slater, Dan. 2013. "Democratic Careening," *World Politics* 65, 4 (October): 729–763.

Slater, Dan and Erica Simmons. 2008. "Critical Antecedents and Informative Regress," *Qualitative Methods* 6, 1: 6–13.

2012. "Coping by Colluding: Political Uncertainty and Promiscuous Powersharing in Indonesia and Bolivia," *Comparative Political Studies* 30: 1–28.

Smith, Peter H. 2005. *Democracy in Latin America: Political Change in Comparative Perspective*. Oxford: Oxford University Press.

Smith, William C. 1989. *Authoritarianism and the Crisis of the Argentine Political Economy*. Stanford, CA: Stanford University Press.

Smith, William C., Carlos H. Acuña, and Eduardo A. Gamarra, eds. 1994. *Latin American Political Economy in the Age of Neoliberal Reform: Theoretical and Comparative Perspectives for the 1990s*. Miami, FL: North-South Center.

Smith, William C. and Roberto P. Korzeniewicz. 1997. "Latin America and the Second Great Transformation," in William C. Smith and Roberto P. Korzeniewicz, eds. *Politics, Social Changes, and Economic Structuring in Latin America*. Boulder, CO: Lynne Rienner, 1–20.

Sniderman, Paul M. and Edward Stiglitz. 2012. *The Reputational Premium: A Theory of Party Identification and Policy Reasoning*. Princeton, NJ: Princeton University Press.

Snyder, Richard. 2001. *Politics after Neoliberalism: Reregulation in Mexico*. New York: Cambridge University Press.

Snyder, Richard and Gabriel Torres. 1998. *The Future Role of the Ejido in Rural Mexico*. La Jolla, CA: Center for U.S.-Mexican Studies, University of California, San Diego.

Sosa-Buccholz, Ximena. 1999. "The Strange Career of Populism in Ecuador," in Michael L. Conniff, ed. *Populism in Latin America*. Tuscaloosa, AL: University of Alabama Press, 138–156.

Stallings, Barbara. 1978. *Class Conflict and Economic Development in Chile, 1958–1973*. Stanford, CA: Stanford University Press.

1992. "International Influence on Economic Policy: Debt, Stabilization, and Structural Reform," in Stephan Haggard and Robert R. Kaufman, eds. *The Politics of Economic Adjustment*. Princeton, NJ: Princeton University Press, 41–88.

ed. 1995. *Global Change, Regional Response: The New International Context of Development*. New York: Cambridge University Press.

Stallings, Barbara and Wilson Peres. 2000. *Growth, Employment, and Equity: The Impact of the Economic Reforms in Latin America and the Caribbean*. Washington, D.C.: CEPAL and Brookings Institution Press.

Starr, Pamela K. 2003. "Argentina: Anatomy of a Crisis Foretold," *Current History* (February): 65–71.

Stepan, Alfred. 1971. *The Military in Politics: Changing Patterns in Brazil*. Princeton, NJ: Princeton University Press.

Stokes, Susan Carol. 1995. *Cultures in Conflict: Social Movements and the State in Peru*. Berkeley, CA: University of California Press.

2001a. *Mandates and Democracy: Neoliberalism by Surprise in Latin America*. New York: Cambridge University Press.

ed. 2001b. *Public Support for Market Reforms in New Democracies*. New York: Cambridge University Press.

2005. "Perverse Accountability: A Formal Model of Machine Politics with Evidence from Argentina," *American Political Science Review* 99, 3 (August): 315–325.

Swanson, David L. and Paolo Mancini, eds. 1996. *Politics, Media, and Modern Democracy: An International Study of Innovations in Electoral Campaigning and Their Consequences*. Westport, CT: Praeger.

Tanaka, Martin. 1998. *Los Espejismos de la Democracia: El Colapso del Sistema de Partidos en el Peru*. Lima, Peru: Instituto de Estudios Peruanos.

Tarrow, Sidney G. 1994. *Power in Movement: Social Movements, Collective Action, and Politics*. New York: Cambridge University Press.

Taylor, Michelle M. 1996. "When Electoral and Party Institutions Interact to Produce Caudillo Politics: The Case of Honduras," *Electoral Studies* 15, 3: 327–337.

Taylor-Robinson, Michelle M. 2006. "The Difficult Road from *Caudillismo* to Democracy: The Impact of Clientelism in Honduras," in Gretchen Helmke and Steven Levitsky, eds. *Informal Institutions and Democracy: Lessons from Latin America*. Baltimore, MD: Johns Hopkins University Press, 106–124.

Teichman, Judith A. 2001. *The Politics of Freeing Markets in Latin America: Chile, Argentina, and Mexico*. Chapel Hill, NC: University of North Carolina Press.

Thelen, Kathleen. 2004. *How Institutions Evolve: The Political Economy of Skills in Germany, Britain, the United States, and Japan*. New York: Cambridge University Press.

Thiesenhusen, William C. 1995. *Broken Promises: Agrarian Reform and the Latin American Campesino*. Boulder, CO: Westview Press.

Thorp, Rosemary. 1998. *Progress, Poverty, and Exclusion: An Economic History of Latin America in the 20th Century*. Baltimore, MD: Johns Hopkins University Press.

Torcal, Mariano and Scott Mainwaring. 2003. "The Political Recrafting of Social Bases of Party Competition: Chile, 1973–95," *British Journal of Political Science* 33: 55–84.

Torre, Juan Carlos. 2005. "Citizens Versus Political Class: The Crisis of Partisan Representation," in Steven Levitsky and María Victoria Murillo, eds. *Argentine*

Democracy: The Politics of Institutional Weakness. University Park, PA: Pennsylvania State University Press, 165–180.

Trinkunas, Harold A. 2005. *Crafting Civilian Control of the Military in Venezuela: A Comparative Perspective.* Chapel Hill, NC: University of North Carolina Press.

Tsebelis, George. 2002. *Veto Players: How Political Institutions Work.* New York and Princeton: Russell Sage Foundation and Princeton University Press.

Tuesta Soldevilla, Fernando. 1989. *Pobreza Urbana y Cambios Electorales en Lima.* Lima, Peru: DESCO.

United Nations Development Programme. 2004. *Democracy in Latin America: Towards a Citizens' Democracy.* New York: United Nations.

Upham, Martin, ed. 1996. *Trade Unions of the World,* 4th ed. London: Catermill International.

Valenzuela, Arturo. 1977. *Political Brokers in Chile: Local Government in a Centralized Polity.* Durham, NC: Duke University Press.

  1978. *The Breakdown of Democratic Regimes: Chile.* Baltimore, MD: Johns Hopkins University Press.

Valenzuela, Arturo and J. Samuel Valenzuela. 1986. "Party Oppositions under the Chilean Authoritarian Regime," in J. Samuel Valenzuela and Arturo Valenzuela, eds. *Military Rule in Chile: Dictatorship and Oppositions.* Baltimore, MD: Johns Hopkins University Press, 184–229.

Valenzuela, J. Samuel. 1992. "Democratic Consolidation in Post-Transitional Settings: Notion, Process, and Facilitating Conditions," in Scott Mainwaring, Guillermo O'Donnell, and J. Samuel Valenzuela, eds. *Issues in Democratic Consolidation: The New South American Democracies in Comparative Perspective.* Notre Dame, IN: University of Notre Dame Press, 57–104.

Van Cott, Donna Lee. 2005. *From Movements to Parties in Latin America: The Evolution of Ethnic Politics.* New York: Cambridge University Press.

van de Walle, Nicolas. 2001. *African Economies and the Politics of Permanent Crisis, 1979–1999.* New York: Cambridge University Press.

Vega Carballo, José Luis. 1992. "Political Parties, Party Systems, and Democracy in Costa Rica," in Louis W. Goodman, William M. LeoGrande, and Johanna Mandelson Forman, eds. *Political Parties in Central America.* Boulder, CO: Westview Press, 203–212.

Vellinga, Menno, ed. 1999. *The Changing Role of the State in Latin America.* Boulder, CO: Westview Press.

Walker, Ignacio. 1990. *Socialismo y Democracia: Chile y Europa en Perspectiva Comparada.* Santiago, Chile: CIEPLAN-Hachette.

Walton, John and David Seddon, eds. 1994. *Free Markets and Food Riots: The Politics of Global Adjustment.* Oxford: Blackwell.

Weinstein, Barbara. 1996. *For Social Peace in Brazil: Industrialists and the Remaking of the Working Class in São Paulo, 1920–1964.* Chapel Hill, NC: University of North Carolina Press.

Weyland, Kurt. 1996. "Neoliberalism and Neopopulism in Latin America: Unexpected Affinities," *Studies in Comparative International Development* 31, 3 (Fall): 3–31.

  1997. "'Growth with Equity' in Chile's New Democracy," *Latin American Research Review* 32: 37–67.

  1998. "Swallowing the Bitter Pill: Sources of Popular Support for Neoliberal Reform in Latin America," *Comparative Political Studies.* 31, 5 (October): 539–568.

2000. "A Paradox of Success? Determinants of Political Support for President Fujimori," *International Studies Quarterly* 44, 3 (September): 481–502.

2001. "Clarifying a Contested Concept: Populism in the Study of Latin American Politics," *Comparative Politics* 34(1): 1–22.

2002. *The Politics of Market Reform in Fragile Democracies: Argentina, Brazil, Peru, and Venezuela.* Princeton, NJ: Princeton University Press.

2006. *Bounded Rationality and Policy Diffusion: Social Sector Reform in Latin America.* Princeton: Princeton University Press.

Weyland, Kurt, Raúl L. Madrid, and Wendy Hunter, eds. 2010. *Leftist Governments in Latin America: Successes and Shortcomings.* New York: Cambridge University Press.

Wilkie, James W., Eduardo Aleman, and José Guadalupe Ortega, eds. Various editions. *Statistical Abstract of Latin America.* Los Angeles, CA: UCLA Latin America Center Press.

Williamson, John. 1990. "What Washington Means by Policy Reform," in John Williamson, ed. *Latin American Adjustment: How Much Has Happened?* Washington, D.C.: Institute for International Economics, 7–20.

ed. 1994. *The Political Economy of Policy Reform.* Washington, D.C.: Institute for International Economics.

Wilson, Bruce M. 1994. "When Social Democrats Choose Neoliberal Economic Policies: The Case of Costa Rica," *Comparative Politics* 26, 2 (January): 149–168.

1999. "Leftist Parties, Neoliberal Policies, and Reelection Strategies: The Case of the PLN in Costa Rica," *Comparative Political Studies* 32, 6 (September): 752–779.

Winn, Peter. 1986. *Weavers of Revolution: The Yarur Workers and the Chilean Road to Socialism.* Oxford: Oxford University Press.

Winn, Peter and Lilia Ferro-Clérico. 1997. "Can a Leftist Government Make a Difference? The Frente Amplio Administration of Montevideo, 1990–1994," in Douglas A. Chalmers, Carlos M. Vilas, Katherine Hite, Scott B. Martin, Kerianne Piester, and Monique Segarra, eds. *The New Politics of Inequality in Latin America: Rethinking Participation and Representation.* Oxford: Oxford University Press, 447–468.

Wise, Carol and Riordan Roett, eds. 2003. *Post-Stabilization Politics in Latin America: Competition, Transition, Collapse.* Washington, D.C.: Brookings Institution Press.

Wolff, Jonas. 2007. "(De-)Mobilising the Marginalised: A Comparison of the Argentine *Piqueteros* and Ecuador's Indigenous Movement," *Journal of Latin American Studies* 39, 1 (February): 1–29.

Wolford, Wendy. 2010. *This Land Is Ours Now: Social Mobilization and the Meanings of Land in Brazil.* Durham, NC: Duke University Press.

World Bank. Various years. *World Development Indicators.* Washington, D.C.: http://web.worldbank.org.

Wright, Erik Olin. 2000. "Working-Class Power, Capitalist-Class Interests, and Class Compromise," *American Journal of Sociology* 105, 4 (January): 957–1002.

Yashar, Deborah. 1995. "Civil War and Social Welfare: The Origins of Costa Rica's Competitive Party System," in Scott Mainwaring and Timothy Scully, eds. *Building Democratic Institutions: Party Systems in Latin America.* Stanford, CA: Stanford University Press, 72–99.

1997. *Demanding Democracy: Reform and Reaction in Costa Rica and Guatemala, 1870s–1950s.* Stanford, CA: Stanford University Press.

1999. "Democracy, Indigenous Movements, and the Postliberal Challenge in Latin America," *World Politics* 52, 1 (October): 76–104.

2005. *Contesting Citizenship in Latin America: The Rise of Indigenous Movements and the Postliberal Challenge.* New York: Cambridge University Press.

Zamosc, Leon. 1994. "Agrarian Protest and the Indian Movement in the Ecuadorian Highlands," *Latin American Research Review* 29, 3: 37–68.

Zeitlin, Maurice and Richard Earl Ratcliff. 1988. *Landlords and Capitalists: The Dominant Class of Chile.* Princeton: Princeton University Press.

Zoco, Edurne. 2006. "Legislators' Positions and Party System Competition in Central America," *Party Politics* 12, 2: 257–280.

Zuckerman, Alan S. Josip Dasović, and Jennifer Fitzgerald. 2007. *Partisan Families: The Social Logic of Bounded Partisanship in Germany and Britain.* New York: Cambridge University Press.

Zúquete, José Pedro. 2008. "The Missionary Politics of Hugo Chávez," *Latin American Politics and Society* 50, 1 (Spring): 91–121.

Index

Others Books in the Series (*continued from page iii*)

Anthony W. Marx, *Making Race, Making Nations: A Comparison of South Africa, the United States, and Brazil*

Doug McAdam, John McCarthy, and Mayer Zald, eds., *Comparative Perspectives on Social Movements*

Bonnie M. Meguid, *Party Competition between Unequals: Strategies and Electoral Fortunes in Western Europe*

Joel S. Migdal, *State in Society: Studying How States and Societies Constitute One Another*

Joel S. Migdal, Atul Kohli, and Vivienne Shue, eds., *State Power and Social Forces: Domination and Transformation in the Third World*

Scott Morgenstern and Benito Nacif, eds., *Legislative Politics in Latin America*

Kevin M. Morrison, *Nontaxation and Representation: The Fiscal Foundations of Political Stability*

Layna Mosley, *Global Capital and National Governments*

Layna Mosley, *Labor Rights and Multinational Production*

Wolfgang C. Müller and Kaare Strøm, *Policy, Office, or Votes?*

Maria Victoria Murillo, *Labor Unions, Partisan Coalitions, and Market Reforms in Latin America*

Maria Victoria Murillo, *Political Competition, Partisanship, and Policy Making in Latin American Public Utilities*

Monika Nalepa, *Skeletons in the Closet: Transitional Justice in Post-Communist Europe*

Ton Notermans, *Money, Markets, and the State: Social Democratic Economic Policies since 1918*

Eleonora Pasotti, *Political Branding in Cities: The Decline of Machine Politics in Bogotá, Naples, and Chicago*

Aníbal Pérez-Liñán, *Presidential Impeachment and the New Political Instability in Latin America*

Roger D. Petersen, *Understanding Ethnic Violence: Fear, Hatred, and Resentment in Twentieth-Century Eastern Europe*

Roger D. Petersen, *Western Intervention in the Balkans: The Strategic Use of Emotion in Conflict*

Simona Piattoni, ed., *Clientelism, Interests, and Democratic Representation*

Paul Pierson, *Dismantling the Welfare State? Reagan, Thatcher, and the Politics of Retrenchment*

Marino Regini, *Uncertain Boundaries: The Social and Political Construction of European Economies*

Kenneth M. Roberts, *Party Systems in Latin America's Neoliberal Era: Changing Course*

Marc Howard Ross, *Cultural Contestation in Ethnic Conflict*

Ben Ross Schneider, *Hierarchical Capitalism in Latin America: Business, Labor, and the Challenges of Equitable Development*

Lyle Scruggs, *Sustaining Abundance: Environmental Performance in Industrial Democracies*